managed, while being consistently controversial, also
responsibly to avoid endangering lives or operations."
REAR ADMIRAL NICHOLAS WILKINSON, D-NOTICE SECRETARY
1999–2004 AND AUTHOR OF *SECRECY AND THE MEDIA*
– *THE OFFICIAL HISTORY OF THE UNITED KINGDOM'S D-NOTICE SYSTEM*

"Chapman Pincher's penetrating investigations of intelligence
enigmas informed without endangering our security
in the lucid style that is his trademark."
HAYDEN PEAKE, RETIRED CIA OFFICER AND
INTELLIGENCE BIBLIOGRAPHER

"For half a century Chapman Pincher was a thorn in the side
of successive governments. No investigative journalist, before
or since, has managed to reveal quite so many things that the
government wanted kept secret. British Cold-War politics would
not have been the same without him."
DR MICHAEL GOODMAN, DEPARTMENT OF WAR STUDIES,
KING'S COLLEGE, LONDON

"Chapman Pincher will go down in history as one of this
country's greatest investigative journalists. Blessed with a natural
talent for research and writing, and armed with an extraordinary
range of contacts, he has spent a lifetime outwitting the censors
that operate at the heart of the British secret state. As a person,
there is more to him than most people know: the fisherman, the
family man, the friend. For anyone interested in modern British
history – the power, the politics and the personalities – this book is
essential reading."
DR CHRISTOPHER MORAN, ASSISTANT PROFESSOR OF NATIONAL
SECURITY AT WARWICK UNIVERSITY

CHAPMAN PINCHER

DANGEROUS TO KNOW

A LIFE

Biteback Publishing

To all my informants, who, often at risk to themselves, have given my life such purpose and satisfaction in breaching the barriers of excessive official secrecy.

First published in Great Britain in 2014 by
Biteback Publishing Ltd
Westminster Tower
3 Albert Embankment
London SE1 7SP
Copyright © Chapman Pincher 2014

ISBN 978-1-84954-651-5

10 9 8 7 6 5 4 3 2 1

A CIP catalogue record for this book is available from the British Library.

Set in Baskerville

Printed and bound in Great Britain by
CPI Group (UK) Ltd, Croydon CR0 4YY

CONTENTS

ACKNOWLEDGEMENTS

In preparing these memoirs in my hundredth year I have been greatly assisted in essential ways, particularly in overcoming physical deficiencies, by family and friends in this delightful village which has proved to be a marvellous place in which to grow old. I am deeply indebted to the Voluntary Service, a group of men and women who, at short notice, provide chauffeured transport for medical purposes. Of those who have been especially helpful to me and my wife, Chris Doyle, a retired airline pilot, has been outstanding.

I must also record my gratitude to my neighbour, David Litten, for essential services and friendship over many years.

As with previous books, John Maher, a professional computer wizard and also a neighbour, has repeatedly sorted out my technical difficulties, usually at short notice.

I am especially indebted to Michael Smith of Biteback Publishing, for his enthusiasm and advice and his confidence in the book, and to Hollie Teague, my managing editor, for her patient and efficient care.

INTRODUCTION

As a Fleet Street journalist specialising in defence issues, I had encountered Lord Mountbatten when he was First Sea Lord and, later, Chief of the Defence Staff at conferences and interviews but he had always been formal, aloof and visibly conscious of his near-royal status. Then came a day when, after standing next to him in the line of eight guns, on the splendid pheasant shoot owned by Sir Thomas Sopwith, the aircraft pioneer, we assembled for the shoot lunch. Lady Sopwith, who was placing us at table, commanded in a loud voice, 'Dickie, sit next to Harry and don't mumble!'

From then on, as I was the Harry referred to, the great man was just another human being. I shot with him on his Broadlands estate and many times more at the Sopwiths', which was close by, and he was always keen to tell me his own views about defence so that they would colour my reporting. He would ensure that I travelled alone with him in his Land Rover as he wanted to know what might be going on in Whitehall behind his back and I was always happy to repay his confidences. On one occasion, he dictated a naval scoop to me as he drove.

This chance encounter was only one of so many super-lucky breaks which enhanced my professional status, that I feel that they are worthy of public record, especially as some of my consequent reporting became historic, as released Cabinet papers and official volumes, such as *Secrecy and the Media*, testify.

In offering this book in my 100th year I have three main purposes. My first is to present an informative and, hopefully, entertaining account of the many extraordinary issues and events with which

I have been closely involved through a long era of unparalleled change. In the process, I will put on record intriguing secrets which can no longer harm those involved.

My second, which derives from the exceptionally high number of distinguished people I have encountered in nearly seventy unbroken years of investigative writing, is to demonstrate the extent to which our lives are moulded by our friends and opponents, even those of brief acquaintance leaving some impression on our characters and, often, our careers.

My third purpose is to record a life which has been, perhaps outrageously, exceptional in the extent to which it has been so regularly punctuated by strokes of good fortune, many of them arising out of the fluke chance of being somewhere at a particular time.

The narrative will not always be chronological but often discursive when advantageous. Nor will it tell much about my private life, which is of sparse general interest, though I will pay tribute to my family and the support they have given me. Instead, I will concentrate on conveying some of the excitement of being privy to so many events of national, and sometimes international, importance which, at the time, were shrouded in secrecy and might have remained so for much longer but for my exposures. I will also take the opportunity to reveal how, and why, so many distinguished people facilitated my exploits, often at risk to themselves. It is only because so many of those who assisted me have died that I can name them.

When I entered Fleet Street as a defence and science specialist in July 1946, on demobilisation from the army, I was aware that the daily challenge I faced was to secure classified information and to find a way of exposing it without undue risk of prosecution. From my wartime involvement with secret weapons, I knew that the only way to succeed was to find ways of inducing those high-level officials who knew the secrets to pass them to me, usually surreptitiously. In doing so, I was pioneering a new kind of investigative journalism which would become the norm, though I was not aware of that at the time. Previously, because of their seniority, the sources I nurtured seem to have been regarded as unapproachable.

The severe official reactions to my successes, with details of the many attempts to discover my sources, are now on open record in a series of Cabinet papers which have recently been released and which I will describe in detail. They show that while I have not been mad and do not think I have been bad, for many people I have, certainly, been dangerous to know.

Fortunately, my recall of events remains detailed and I have retained a strong sense of continuity with the past whereas some people tell me that they recall their early life objectively, almost seeing themselves as someone different. In addition, I have thirty-eight large volumes containing all my newspaper and magazine cuttings recording the events in which I have been involved, along with their, often rowdy, repercussions which I thoroughly enjoyed. This, possibly unique, collection has enabled me to make immediate checks with the printed record concerning the accuracy of my recall.

Also, there are many box-files containing the official documents and notes on which many of my disclosures about the strange world of secret intelligence – both in newspapers and in my published books – were based. All these records have been passed or are willed to the War Studies Department at King's College London, where they will be available for examination.

I apologise if my CV, with the many distinguished names which I must drop in describing my activities, sounds immodest but this cannot be avoided and my account is truly how it was.

CHAPTER 1

IN THE BEGINNING

Perhaps as an indicator of an unusual future, my entry into the external world was odd because my first glimpse of it was within the confines of a large tent which served as the maternity ward of the field hospital of the Second Battalion of the Northumberland Fusiliers – the famed 'Fighting Fifth'. The date was 29 March 1914. The place was the then small town of Ambala, in India's Punjab. My father, Richard Chapman Pincher, was the Drum Major and my mother, Helen, née Foster, and then aged twenty, was with him because he expected to be stationed there for at least two years.

'You felt like a ton of bricks coming', was how my forthright, Yorkshire mother recalled my arrival. She also told me many times how, shortly after my birth, a lizard fell from the top of the tent on to her bed and shed its tail, which continued to writhe. Whether it was that experience, the 'ton of bricks' or the sight of me, my mother, though a devout Roman Catholic and therefore supposedly banned from birth control, decided she would never have another child. I have never regretted having no siblings and, however that may have affected my character, I revelled in all the advantages I did not have to share.

A child born into a British regiment on foreign soil was simply registered with the Orderly Room, almost as part of the baggage. So, I was not issued with a birth certificate and have never been able to acquire one. Fortunately, I possess a certificate of baptism, as Henry Chapman Pincher, signed by Father O'Brien at the Church of the Holy Redeemer in Ambala, which has always been accepted as evidence of my birth. (An event which would establish Ambala's place in the history of villainy had already occurred two years earlier – the birth of Kim Philby, the traitor who would eventually occupy a fair slice of my time.)

My strange name derives from two ancient words connected with the British countryside, with which I have always been enamoured. A chapman (my paternal grandmother's surname) was a peddler who walked from village to village, selling pins and other small goods, while a pincher was the man who looked after the village pound, where stray animals were held until reclaimed. Hardly an intellectual background! My first name has never applied to me as I have always been known as Harry.

Shortly after the outbreak of the First World War, in August 1914, my father was recalled to the UK to serve in France. I have been domiciled in Britain ever since. My father was quickly commissioned in the field into the East Surrey Regiment. He survived the war and I was then dragged around from one posting to another, during which I experienced thirteen different schools, one of them a famous Catholic convent near the major army base of Aldershot. Called Hillside, in Farnborough, it was also a school for girls but there was a small preparatory school for boys. I vividly recall being told by a nun that our souls, at the age of eight, looked as though she had put up a white sheet and spattered it with ink!

My mother and I made many visits to the historic town of Pontefract, in West Yorkshire, where she had been born and where her mother still lived. I learned that she had been reared in destitution. Her father had been a coal-miner in one of the many pits near Pontefract and had been killed in an underground accident. His young wife, my grandmother, was heavily pregnant with another child but, apart from an occasional free load of coal, received no compensation. I never fathomed how they had managed to survive.

Oddly, my father had endured similar circumstances, when nine, in the North Yorkshire town of Richmond, where his father, a sergeant in the Green Howards, was killed in a rifle-shooting incident. So, I have never known a grandfather. My widowed grandmother, née Mary Chapman, was a seamstress and, with what my father earned from a newspaper round, they managed to survive until he relieved the situation at the age of fourteen by joining the Northumberland Fusiliers as a drummer boy.

Stability entered my life after 1922 when my father was forced to leave the army in a round of economy cuts and my parents settled in Darlington, then a 49,000-population market-town in Durham, where my paternal grandmother was living. With his gratuity, my father opened a sweet shop close to a cinema and bought a modest house (for £500) where we lived in great contentment for eight years.

I was installed in a nearby elementary school which gave me a fine start and, when I was only ten, I won a scholarship to the Darlington Grammar School. I had always found learning easy because I was endowed with such a good memory; one of the masters said I absorbed facts like blotting paper. Stacking my memory with facts continues to appeal to me in my 100th year, if only on the time-worn principle: you never know when they might come in useful. 'Who knows wins' has been a life-long slogan.

I also had the advantage of a strong speaking voice which enabled me to win the Elocution Prize regularly and channelled me into acting in school plays. I recall being Falstaff (stuffed with cushions) in some scene from *Henry IV* and I was also prominent in the Debating Society, learning to speak at length without notes. So far, my loud voice has also survived.

The biology master, W. W. Allen, aroused my interest in natural history, which would condition my life. He fired my imagination by opening the ripe, green bud of a wild poppy and smoothing out the large, crinkled, red petals. He then explained how the petals had formed tightly folded inside the confined space of the bud in a most intricate and pre-determined manner so that they could eventually unfold into flat surfaces. I was so impressed by the way this had all been programmed by the plant's genes that I decided then to concentrate on botany, and genetics in particular, if I could.

One of the joys of Darlington was its proximity to the magnificent countryside of Teesdale, Swaledale and Wensleydale, which were all reachable on the bicycle which my father had bought me for winning the scholarship. It was those visits which made me into a countryman who has always been rather allergic to concrete.

My mother, Helen, an amateur actress with a fine singing voice, was prominent in the local dramatic society with such success that she was invited to turn professional by the repertory company which performed for six months each year at Darlington's delightful Theatre Royal. Through her friendship with the female partner of the theatre's owner, my father was invited to become the manager – an event which conditioned my life in many ways.

Firstly, it meant that every night, except Sunday, for six months each year, I was alone. From the age of thirteen, I returned from school around 5 p.m. to an empty house to which my parents did not return until 11 p.m., when I would be in bed but reading some book. I did not in any way feel neglected but revelled in my freedom, learning to enjoy solitude through reading and listening to music on a gramophone.

Peculiarly, ever since my boyhood, I have disliked 'pop' music and jazz but am greatly in debt to classical music not just for the pleasure it gives me but for helping me endure the pressures of working long hours, often against the clock, to meet a writing deadline.

Sometimes, in the evening, I would have pals into the house to fry chips, listen to the radio or play billiards, the cushions being lines of books on the living-room table with gaps serving as pockets, the balls being large marbles, and the cue a broomstick. One of these friends, called Douglas Warth, was the son of the vicar, whose vicarage was located at the top of my street, and I mention him now because, by a series of extraordinary flukes, he would prove to be a key figure in my life-history.

Occasionally, the sixteen-year-old maid, hired by my mother to light a coal fire and prepare my tea, would remain for a couple of hours and, on one occasion, answered the door to a boy who was due to see me. To my surprise, she told the boy I was out and rushed upstairs to my bedroom where I found her in an inviting posture. Never one to waste an opportunity, I lost my virginity with all the masculinity I could muster, repeating the encounter over many months. We were not at risk because desire and its climax are quite separate from potency and I knew that I was not yet capable of producing sperm. (I did not tell my pals of my good fortune because they would have wanted to share it and, no doubt, talk about it. Even at thirteen, I appreciated the value of keeping a secret, a trait that was to prove so important in my professional life.)

Not long afterwards, the repertory company staged a play in which a young boy needed to make an appearance. My mother suggested me for the role, which became the first of several including Sherlock Holmes's assistant. Never short of confidence, and with my Falstaff experience behind me, I played the roles to praise from the local press. I was paid seven shillings and sixpence per play (which lasted three nights, twice nightly) and my stage money was the first I had earned. My parents insisted that I should not spend it, urging me to save and never to borrow money, 'out of debt, out of danger' being their slogan. As a result, I have never bought anything without immediate payment and have never had a mortgage.

Visiting the backstage, as the manager's son, soon became a regular habit which continued during the six months of each year when the theatre staged a different revue or variety show each week. During those visits I met many famous performers and asked them for signed photographs. They included Gracie Fields, Bud Flanagan (whose recorded voice I still hear on TV singing the introduction to *Dad's Army*), Tommy Trinder and even veterans like Florrie Forde. So, quite early in life, I became used to meeting celebrities.

During the revues and variety shows some of the chorus girls were only too happy to extend the education of the manager's son in handy places behind scenery. By that time I had learned the need for what are now called condoms, which could be bought in a shop where they were displayed in the window as 'mystery tins', each screw-top tin containing three for tenpence.

When I was twelve, I had been introduced to the joys of river fishing (mainly with maggots and worms in those days) by a school friend with whom I made regular Saturday visits to one of the two local rivers, the Tees and the Swale. To encourage me, my father bought me hip-high waders and, though both rivers were fast-flowing and subject to rapid flooding, it never occurred to my parents to worry about my safety out there, often alone. No doubt, today, their attitude would be considered reprehensible but it taught me self-reliance, which was worth all the risk.

Occasionally, I would visit a stretch of the Tees, near the village of Gainford, with two or three friends, on our bicycles. There, when I was fifteen, I experienced a frightening event in the form of a full-blooded visual hallucination – seeing something that looked as real as reality but was not there. I was preparing a fire on the river bank while a friend climbed a big, ivy-covered elm on which we hid our cooking utensils. He had just reached the main crotch, about twenty feet up, when there was a tremendous crack as a huge limb of the tree crashed down. I saw the boy fall, clinging desperately to the limb as he was smashed between it and the hard cobbled ground. I suppose I blinked with horror, believing that the boy must be dead or gravely injured. Then I heard him shout from the still-standing trunk. The limb had fallen but not the boy.

Later, I realised that under extreme emotional stress the brain has the capacity to project an imagined scene on to a real scene so that it is, momentarily, impossible for it to distinguish what is real from what is not. Had I imagined the entire episode it would have been no more remarkable than a dream. Instead, the image of the falling boy had been inserted, inside my brain, into the image of the real circumstances with extraordinary speed and accuracy. I can still see the boy's jacket caught in the wind as he crashed down, so vivid is my memory of that false experience.

When I reflected on it, there was an obvious similarity to most alleged visions of a ghost. The sentry on duty at the Tower of London may convince himself that he has seen the headless ghost of Anne Boleyn but he sees her walking across the real Tower Green with all the real ancient buildings in the background. Later, as a scientific journalist, I was to investigate several alleged ghosts and hauntings, as I will describe in another chapter.

Looking back, I thoroughly enjoyed the magic of childhood which is not a nostalgic myth but a reality compounded of curiosity, novelty, a sense of wonder and the feeling of time stretching endlessly ahead. As will be increasingly apparent, the child was father of this man in so many ways.

In 1930, when I was sixteen and had just become a prefect at school, my life changed again. My father decided to take over a country pub, called the Comet, in the village of Croft, plumb on the Durham–North Yorkshire border three miles outside Darlington. It was named after a locally bred bull, called Comet, which was the progenitor of the Shorthorn breed and had sold in 1810 for the then colossal sum of 1,000 guineas.

The pub was so close to the River Tees that I woke each morning to the sound of it. There was a regular half-hour bus service to Darlington, for sixpence return, so attending school was no problem.

In the evenings, and at weekends, I earned my keep by serving in the bar and learned the art of easy conversation with men of all ages and all ranks, which would prove to be of huge advantage in my future career in journalism.

To be convivial, I had to join in the beer-drinking but, sometimes witnessing the results of excess, I rationed myself carefully and in the whole of my life I have never been sufficiently under the influence of alcohol to be described as drunk. Nor have I ever felt that I 'needed' a drink, being able to dance my way through life fairly merrily without need of that crutch. I attribute my longevity partly to remaining on good terms with my liver.

The art of drinking the minimum while encouraging others to drink more would serve me well in my journalistic life, where my successes would be largely based on inducing lunch guests to loosen their tongues. I needed to have all my wits about me at such meetings because I never made a written note, being aware that nothing would be more likely to cause an informant to clam up than seeing his comments noted down.

In the pub, with so much practice easily available, I became a dab hand at dominoes and darts and, through such activities, developed a strong feeling of kinship with farmers, agricultural labourers, gamekeepers and river-keepers which has remained with me.

Angling remained my preferred sport for the rest of my life

– when ninety-seven, I caught an eleven-pound rainbow trout – and, as I will explain later, fishing has played a crucial role in my professional career.

While running a pub was exacting for the landlord and his wife, for their son it was one long round of pleasure with a continuous flow of invitations: 'Come on ferreting!', 'Come on rook-shooting!', 'Cub-hunting tomorrow!' However, being in the sixth form with exams pending and a university career in prospect, I also needed to work scholastically. With my subjects – botany, zoology, chemistry and physics – being descriptive, I needed to study the relevant books and had a room upstairs where I also had a microscope.

My necessary study of evolution inevitably cast doubts on my religious beliefs, because it seemed self-evident that Primitive Man had invented God, rather than the reverse, and that the concept of an afterlife had been spawned to allay the fear of death, Man being the only creature to be aware that eventually his own life must surely end. So, I was driven to tell my mother that I was no longer prepared to attend Mass or take communion at the Catholic church in Darlington. My mother was upset but, surprisingly, accepted my position. In fact, I had less trouble with her than I had with my headmaster when it was reported to him that, in an essay on photosynthesis – the process whereby plants use the energy of light to build sugars from carbon dioxide and water – I had written, bumptiously but with truth, 'A great preacher once expressed the popular fallacy that the lilies of the field toil not neither do they spin but he was a carpenter and had never studied botany.'

Sadly, my mother, having been strikingly beautiful, developed a disorder of the thyroid gland which, though not incapacitating, caused a disfiguring protrusion of the eyes. When 'storming Heaven with prayer', as she put it, proved negative she concluded that she was being punished by God for allowing her son to lose his faith. I could see the crunch coming and it did – she asked me to go with her to confession and communion in the belief that the Almighty might then be appeased.

Unable to decline, I accompanied her on the 6 a.m. bus on our route to Darlington's St Augustine's Church and I entered the darkness of the confessional box where, through the square of gauze in the wall separating us, I could see the Irish priest intoning to himself in Latin until he asked me, 'How long since your last confession?' Unable to lie to him, I replied, 'Three years, Father.'

There followed a robust argument which ended in his refusal to give me absolution and I left the box to be followed there by my mother. By the time she emerged I had decided to say nothing to her and to join her in the queue to the altar, where I would commit the mortal sin of swallowing the communion wafer while, knowingly, not in a state of grace. I suppose that my rather searing experience made me 'a died-again Christian'.

My mother seemed relieved and I never told her what had happened. Her illness eventually burned itself out, as it normally did in those days before there was adequate treatment.

In 1932, my dear father decided that he could and would afford to send me to university and I elected to go to King's College London for two reasons. It was where my inspiring mentor, W. W. Allen, had read botany and the professor there, Ruggles Gates, was a pioneer in genetics, in which I wanted to make my mark.

So, in early October, I left my beloved Croft to go by night bus (the cheapest way) down the Great North Road to the 'Big Smoke', as the capital was known. My destination was a boarding house for students in Bloomsbury run by a Mrs Moffat, who provided a bed-sitter, breakfast and a good evening meal every day for 35 shillings – less than £2 – a week. It was only a ten-minute walk down Southampton Row to King's College so there were no fares. A cheap lunch was to be had in the college refectory.

After evening dinner on most week-days I shut myself in my room with my books 'swotting away' and my efforts were rewarded by winning the Hare Prize for Zoology and the Carter Gold Medal for Botany, which helped to convince my parents that their money was not being wasted. There were, however, evenings when I took some time off with other students to walk to the Brasserie of the Café Royal, in Regent Street, which, in its former name of the Domino Room, had been the haunt of Oscar Wilde and his cronies, the painter James McNeill Whistler, Aubrey Beardsley, D. H. Lawrence,

Bernard Shaw and so many other memorable personalities and was still patronised by recognisable Bohemians like Augustus John. With one lager and a couple of sandwiches, we could sit at one of the historic, marble-topped tables for hours, scanning the scene and wondering which of its famous customers had sat there in the past. I little thought that through my eventual friendship with the Café Royal's future owner, Lord Forte, who would also become my publisher, I would write its history in the form of a novel, as, later, I will relate.

On the occasional evenings when, perhaps being broke, I stayed in the general sitting room of the several 'digs' which I occupied in my three years at King's College, I would, almost invariably, be verbally assailed by those other residents peddling the Communist creed. My morning walks to college, when Welsh miners would be singing in the gutter to raise a few pennies, had made me aware of the shortcomings of capitalism. So I was induced to go and listen to Communist leaders, like the unimpressive Harry Pollitt, and, occasionally, to read the *Daily Worker*.

I tried putting these views to my father during the long vacations when, with minimum delay, I returned to the Comet, renewing my barman duties and taking full advantage of the fishing and other pastoral facilities. He assured me that the British were far too realistic ever to subject themselves to the whims of a dictator like Stalin. That also seemed to be the view of all our customers.

My interest in Communism was finally extinguished when one of my mentors admitted that, in the event of a successful revolution, my country would first have to be governed from Moscow. 'Well bugger that!' was my robust, Yorkshire response. I wonder how many of my old Communist friends lived to see the final collapse of Soviet Communism under the weight of its deficiencies and how they felt about it.

Meanwhile, I had staggered Professor Ruggles Gates by producing two such original research papers on botanical genetics that he secured their rapid publication, which was a most unusual achievement for a 21-year-old undergraduate. (Oddly, these papers can both be seen by Googling H. C. Pincher, as the whole of the journal in which they appeared, the *New Phytologist*, is now on the internet.)

Gates assured me that, once I had secured my honours degree, he wanted me to join his department in the junior rank of demonstrator, which would start me on an academic career. Sadly, when the time came, he could not secure a grant to pay my modest salary, because of the worsening of the depression, so, as lecturing was an essential aspect of academic life, he suggested that I should find a job in a good school where I could teach sixth-form botany and zoology until he could call me back. I took his advice. (Though, sadly, I was never to achieve my ambition of being on the King's College staff, I was honoured in 1979 with a life fellowship – FKC – in appreciation of my contributions to investigative journalism.)

CHAPTER 2

TEACHER MAN

In the summer of 1936 I secured a post as the biology master at the Liverpool Institute, a large school for boys located near Liverpool's Anglican cathedral, and which, long after my time there, would become famous for producing two of the Beatles – McCartney and Harrison. I thoroughly enjoyed teaching botany and zoology to the sixth-formers who had elected to specialise in those subjects, and later I would see, with satisfaction, some of them achieving success.

I was also required to teach some chemistry and physics to younger pupils and, of course, to take my share of overseeing some of the sports, soon being put in charge of cricket, which involved working on Saturdays. For all that, and more, my starting salary under a fixed national scale was £249 per annum rising by annual increments of £15 to a maximum of £480. So, by staying in teaching until my retirement at sixty-five, the most I could hope to earn, unless I secured a headship, which was unlikely with a science degree in those days, was less than £10 per week.

I became friendly with the excellent headmaster, J. R. Edwards, a Welshman who was a keen fisherman, and he arranged for me to earn an extra seven shillings and sixpence a week by teaching gymnastics and boxing to boys at an evening club called the Florence Institute. So, to my CV I could add 'Boxing Instructor'.

I lived modestly within walking distance of the school in a bed-sitter with a tiny kitchen in which I cooked for myself. Fortunately, my life there was enlivened by the tenant of the larger flat next to mine – Eric ('Bill') Williams, a charmer who would achieve fame after the Second World War, in which he served in the RAF and was shot down and imprisoned in Germany. He and two of his fellow prisoners escaped by, most ingeniously, building a vaulting horse which was carried out into the exercise area. Concealed inside was a fellow prisoner with a digging tool who, each day, excavated a little further down a tunnel until it eventually reached beyond the wire boundary. How they managed to cover up the entrance to their tunnel each day before the vaulting horse was taken back was as astonishing as it was bold. Eventually, the three diggers escaped and found their way back to Britain, as Williams revealed in 1949 in his bestselling book, *The Wooden Horse*, which was made into a successful film for which he wrote the screen play.

Most of my evenings in Liverpool were spent making charts, diagrams and paintings large enough to adorn the laboratory walls and which I could use in my lectures, as I had always found such visual aids so helpful in implanting facts into the memory. They were not popular, however, with other masters who used the laboratory to teach other subjects and found their pupils more interested in my charts than in their blackboards.

Among the advice my father gave me, on leaving home for my first job, was 'Keep clear of slow horses and fast women'. I have always managed to evade the slow horses but, regarding the women, I had the misfortune – at a party given by Bill Williams – to meet a Liverpool girl who was so strikingly beautiful that she, literally, turned heads in the street and, because so many men were attracted to her, I decided that I had better marry her quickly before she was snapped up. We were totally unsuited and I soon discovered that she had married me to get out of her father's house where she was unhappy. Though, at twenty-one, she was two years younger than I was, I was far too immature for her. She was used to being taken out by older men in ways we could not afford so I needed to find some way of earning more money, especially as we had moved into a larger flat which needed furnishing.

My only solution was to write freelance articles for magazines and my first was for the *Farmer and Stockbreeder*, which had been shown to me by one of the many farmers at Croft. The article's purpose was to show farmers how to tell when their soil was acid and needed lime by recognising certain weeds which grow only on acid soil. I illustrated it by drawing pictures of the weeds and described myself by the deliberately exalted title 'Head of the Biology Department at the Liverpool Institute'. (I reckoned that my headmaster was never likely to see it.) It earned me two guineas and was the first of many I wrote for that magazine. I expanded into the *Farmers' Weekly*, the *Dairy Farmer*, *Poultry World* and other agricultural magazines, making maximum use of the libraries at Liverpool University, which had a fine veterinary department near enough to visit during my school lunch-break. Spurred on by success, I was soon responsible for titles like 'How to take care of your dairy herd', 'Foaling down a mare', 'Making the most of ducks', 'Potatoes in stock-feeding', though I had never kept a cow, a horse or a duck or grown a potato.

I moved on to scientific magazines and then popular magazines, always illustrating the articles myself, and learned about what did, or did not, make news and how to present it succinctly. Soon, I was earning more from writing than from teaching but, so far as my young wife was concerned, the whole exercise was a failure because it meant that I had to work most nights while she sat bored stiff, sipping cheap sherry and chain-smoking her lungs away.

Enraptured by the writing trade, and the satisfaction of seeing my name in print, my output soared and I also wrote my first book, a simple guide to genetics for farmers, which I eventually called *The Breeding of Farm Animals*, illustrated with my own line drawings. Many years later, as will be seen, it would play an unusual and quite unforeseeable part in furthering my journalistic investigations into secret affairs of state.

When the Second World War began, in September 1939, the teaching profession was declared to be a reserved occupation so I was temporarily exempt from call-up. There were occasional night bombings of Liverpool which meant getting out of bed when the sirens sounded to go down to a cellar, which served as an air-raid shelter, or lying in bed listening to the whine of falling bombs, hoping they would not fall on us and sighing with relief when the explosion, some distance away, meant that others were dead or trapped under rubble.

Then, in the autumn of 1940, my life was abruptly changed

forever by the arrival of my call-up papers – but my luck returned: I was to report for training at the 56th Training Regiment of the Royal Armoured Corps in Cambrai Lines at Catterick Camp, two miles from Richmond and only eight miles from Croft!

Regrettably, the facilities of the Comet would no longer be available to me. On the outbreak of war, my father had been recalled for duty and, being too old to fight, was posted to army records in York, where he was promoted to major. For some months he commuted to and from York daily by rail but eventually found the strain too much, as did my mother. So, he ended his days as a landlord to live in York and my beloved Comet days were over in what was definitely another mutation moment of my life. I severed my last physical link with them in 1990 when I donated a drinking cup made from one of Comet's horns (which had been given to me long before by a customer) to Reading University's Museum of English Rural Life. Scratched on its base, in an ancient script, is the single word 'Comet'.

On reporting for duty at Catterick Camp, I found myself in a squad of about thirty men, many of whom were schoolmasters or university graduates in other professions, so I soon made friends. To ease the transition to barrack room life, we were housed for the first week in a large room with small iron bedsteads and sheets. After that we all slept on the floor in rough blankets. Being cooped up in a barrack room quickly widened one's knowledge of human nature.

Our mentors were mainly corporals and sergeants who had left the army but had been recalled on the outbreak of war. They concentrated first on getting us fit for duty by physical exercise and drill, claiming that in the first six weeks they would break us down and in the second six weeks build us up. In the process, we did much 'square-bashing' – the collective name for drill and marching on the large concrete training ground where we were warned that, in the army, the only thing to which we were entitled was eighteen inches in the ranks. We were also encouraged to spend much of our off-duty time on 'bullshit', a major aspect of which was 'spit and polish' – the art of making one's boots and any brass buttons as shiny as possible.

Appreciating that I was trapped in the army for a long time, I decided to learn as much there as I could on the off-chance that some of it might be of use later. As a result, I became fascinated by weapons and how they worked. It saved me from becoming 'browned off' – the army term for boredom and near-despair which afflicted many of my comrades at intervals.

It was surprising how quickly we were coarsened by army life, especially regarding our language. One of our squad, called Gabbitas, was a rather gentle and refined man yet, within a fortnight, he was 'Rabbitarse' among the instructors and eventually we too began using it to his face.

Padres, both Protestant and Catholic, visited us, especially to warn those of us who were married about the dangers of infidelity. Their advice, if we were ever tempted, was to think about our wives and any children and tell ourselves that it was not sensible to break our lifetime vows for ten minutes' illicit pleasure. It was alleged to have elicited only one audible response – 'How do you make it last ten minutes?'

After the initial training we were instructed in tank gunnery, tank-driving and radio operation. I was detailed to be a tank gunner and my deep fascination with weapons dates from the moment I found myself sitting in a tank behind a machine gun called the Besa. To fire a burst from that beautifully constructed instrument of death gave Trooper Pincher a sense of power he had not experienced before. My enthusiasm, coupled with my professional teaching skills, led to quick promotion to the dizzy rank of full corporal. As a gunnery instructor, Corporal Pincher passed on his fascination to many others. (Later in life, a series of lucky strokes was to extend my experience to almost every kind of weapon, from hand-held grenades to the H-bomb, involving distant travel in many vehicles, including V-bombers and an atomic submarine.)

Along with most of my original squad, I had been selected for quick dispatch to the Royal Armoured Corps (RAC) Cadet School for training as an officer but, because the regiment was short of instructors, my departure was delayed, which did not upset me because I was enjoying life in the countryside I loved.

Eventually, I and several of my original squad were told that applications for the Royal Armoured Corps Cadet School had been suspended for several months as the RAC had become over-loaded with officers and we were advised to switch to the Cadet School of the Royal Army Service Corps, which was short of them. We did so and found ourselves at Clifton College in Bristol, a public school which had been commandeered by the army and, later, would figure in my investigative researches.

After six months' tough training, involving much travel in beautiful Somerset, I was commissioned and posted to a unit in the Sixth Armoured Division based first in Bedford then in Scotland, where, in various lochs, I much enjoyed practising landing operations for the coming invasion of France.

Then, after a minor motorcycle accident, my medical status was downgraded from A1, which was a requirement for service in any armoured division, and I was posted to a small unit based in Winthorpe Hall, near Newark (Notts). The commanding officer, a major, set great store by the military requirement of 'liaising' with the locals. Newark was then a brewing town and some of the brewers lived in Winthorpe. They all appeared to have attractive daughters who, because of petrol-rationing, were village bound. So, the CO made them all honorary members of our mess so that they could drift in any evening and enliven the scene.

Winthorpe was also in the heart of that part of Bomber Command which was equipped with the Lancaster, generally agreed to have been the outstanding night bomber of the war. So our dashing CO also 'liaised' with the commanders of several local airfields, inviting their aircrews to our mess where, having encountered the lively ladies, they became regular visitors. That way, as the officer in charge of the mess, I was able to meet many much-decorated pilots and other aircrew who were making regular bombing raids over Germany. Several of them were to take part in the rightly famed 'Dambusters' raid, as I will detail later.

Still in my twenties, I had never flown, which was not unusual in those days, and, on hearing that deficiency, one of the pilots, who I only ever knew as 'Goldie', invited me to a practice flight in a

Lancaster at his airfield, Swinderby. He was waiting when I arrived and, without any ceremony, took me to one of the giant four-engine machines which was being used to train new pilots. Without a parachute or other equipment, I just stood in the vast belly of the airplane looking out of a window, besotted by the experience, while Goldie watched the trainee pilot who was flying the machine. It was my first view of the countryside from the air as the pilot practised landings and immediate take-offs – called 'circuits and bumps'.

Many wartime soldiers, far from home on regimental duty, cheered up their routine lives with extra-marital romances but the one that I recall with most enjoyment, thrill and deep affection was not with a nubile woman but with the superb Lancaster. How I, as a young army officer (then dubbed 'a brown job' by blue-uniformed RAF men), was able to pursue this strange relationship still fills me with wonder when I recall the extraordinary circumstances which had made it possible.

Such was my exhilaration and awe of the Lancaster that I managed to make about twenty more flights, with several different pilots, the most exciting being all-night 'searchlight operations', in which the plane simulated a German bomber to give the searchlight-operators practice at illuminating it while we tried to dodge them. I dreamed of going on a raid but found that to be an ambition too far.

On my last expedition – a searchlight op – I returned for breakfast in the RAF mess and asked where Goldie was. The response was a curt 'He's gone'. My efforts to find out where were quickly stifled as it was quietly explained to me that he had been shot down on a mission. The rule was that the dead were never mentioned in the mess again. It seemed insensitive but was necessary for morale when so many crews were not returning and you might be among the next to 'go'.

As part of my plan to learn as much as possible, I volunteered to attend almost all of the specialised instructional 'courses', usually lasting a week, offered at intervals by various army departments. On one of them I encountered two sergeants from Bulford, a Royal Armoured Corps camp where I knew that my boyhood friend from

Darlington, Douglas Warth, the vicar's son, had been based for training. I had already heard that Douglas, whose right arm had been slightly malformed by polio, had gained entry to the army by lifting his medical examiner on to his shoulder with it. I had also heard that, in spite of any disability, he was the best rifle-shot in his squad. Nevertheless, the sergeants told me that Douglas had been invalided from the army because he could not salute properly!

In 1943, as the army needed some scientifically qualified officers to liaise with the scientists developing new weapons, Lieutenant Pincher was selected to attempt the tough, six-month Advanced Class Ammunition and Explosives course at the Military College of Science. Now with the prefix 'Royal' and based at Shrivenham, the wartime section of the college which I attended was located at Stoke-on-Trent and the experience acquainted me with 'the Potteries'.

The course involved visits to factories concerned with the production of weapons and explosives and greatly widened my knowledge. On the other hand, the mathematics of gun ballistics were horrendous, involving differential calculus, which I had never studied and never properly understood. Fortunately, my photographic memory came to my rescue and in the final examinations I recalled the mathematical solutions to questions. Of eighteen who started the course only nine of us qualified.

I was then posted, as captain, to the Rocket Division of the Supply Ministry to help develop rocket weapons for the RAF and navy as well as the army – all of which was greatly to enhance my fascination with weapons and set me on the road to a career which I could never have foreseen. My guiding principle – who knows wins – had served me well.

CHAPTER 3

ROCKET MAN

To start my rocket work as a technical staff officer I was required to report to an office in the Royal Arsenal at Woolwich and, on the way there, I spent a couple of hours revisiting some old student haunts. While walking down Charing Cross Road, I came face to face with my old friend, Douglas Warth. He told me that he was working as a reporter for the *Daily Express,* then an influential broadsheet with the world's largest circulation. He offered me a room in a large house he was renting in Lincoln Street, near Sloane Square in Chelsea, and I noted his phone number. Later, having discovered that I could live where I wished and that the Sloane Square Underground made the journey to Woolwich easy, I accepted and moved into the room with my camp bed and other equipment.

From then until 1946, I was involved in the development and field-testing of rocket weapons and other devices, which familiarised me with all three services. The devices included small rockets for clearing paths through minefields, such as the Conger, which was, essentially, a fireman's hose which could be laid across a minefield by means of a rocket and was then pumped full of nitroglycerine which was then exploded. There were assault rockets being readied for the D-Day landings, the largest codenamed the Sea Mattress, which was a cubical metal box containing a large array of tubes each containing a five-inch diameter rocket carrying a 29-pound shell. It was designed to be carried in a landing craft and, when a salvo of all the rockets was fired, it was equivalent to the broadside of a cruiser. I was also involved with a rocket which enabled the RAF's Typhoon fighter planes to attack small specialised targets with a new degree of precision, as eventually happened with important effect. Excitingly, my contribution involved some flying with the RAF as an observer and some brief trips on naval ships.

Such weapons also involved me with special committees which introduced me to the secrets world. In the process, I became friendly with several officers and civil servants who would, later, become very senior in the defence establishment, such as Solly Zuckerman (later Lord) and William Cook (later Sir).

My office was in an out-station of the Arsenal but my work required many visits to that sprawling establishment, which had been founded in 1671 as a gun storage depot and then became a gun foundry and gunpowder factory stretching over 100 acres surrounded by a high wall. (By 1886 there had been enough workers there to found and support the professional football club which still bears its name.) When I began to go there in 1944, it covered 1,300 acres and employed 30,000 workers. To visit it was like entering a walled town. Because so much research on new explosives and weapons was in progress there, security at the gates was tight and to reach most of my destinations I needed a car and a driver who knew the terrain. Otherwise, one could get lost, as was exemplified by the fable of a servicewoman (a Wren) who, when admonished for being found lost in the Arsenal in an advanced stage of pregnancy, had explained 'I wasn't like this when I came in'.

There were some large buildings, like the barracks and head-quarters of the Royal Artillery, which had been located there for more than 200 years. (Whether that was the reason for the Arsenal footballers being called 'the Gunners' or whether that was due to the cannon on the team's crest seems to be in doubt.) Most of the buildings, including those of interest to me, were very small to limit the effect of any accidental explosions inside them.

Over the years, a tradition arose that sons would follow their fathers into working in the Arsenal, beginning as apprentices, and I encountered a number who could boast membership for several generations. The workers had their own slang and it was said that an Arsenal worker could be recognised from behind by his 'Arsenal waddle'. They also had their own brand of humour which they expressed by putting up large printed notices in their various offices such as: 'The possible we do immediately. The impossible takes a little longer.' My favourite, which expressed the Arsenal workers' bolshie attitude, as well as their humour, was in bold capitals in dog Latin – NOLI ILLEGITIMI CARBORUNDUM! – translated as 'Don't let the bastards grind you down!'

Back in my out-station, I soon became friendly with my commanding officer, Lieutenant Colonel Hastings Read, who was a countryman intent on retiring to farming as soon as the war was over. So, we had much in common. I quickly introduced him to Douglas Warth for a special reason. Douglas had become a member of the Players' Theatre Club, located in a large basement in Albemarle Street, and evenings spent there were so delightfully escapist from the grim atmosphere of war that I knew the colonel would enjoy them. A show regenerating the Victorian music hall through songs and comedy was rendered, nightly, by a succession of people, several of whom would become household names such as Peter Ustinov, Hattie Jacques, Bill Owen and Alec Clunes. It was brilliantly compèred by its founder, Leonard Sachs, with the bearded eventual film star James Robertson Justice, in his naval uniform, occasionally replacing him.

My colonel and I both became members and spent many happy evenings there. One night, Douglas arranged for the colonel and me to see the *Daily Express* being printed, a memorable first experience of the Fleet Street world for both of us. My friendship with my commanding officer would prove to be of enormous assistance to those of my activities which did not conform with army regulations and often dangerously transgressed them.

I was grateful to my colonel for lore about the appointment of staff, whom he classed into four groups – the clever and idle, the clever and industrious, the stupid and idle and the stupid and industrious. The top jobs should be awarded to the clever and idle because, having the ability and the time to think, they were the likeliest to generate new ideas. The clever and industrious should be in the action jobs with the stupid and idle doing the routine work. The stupid and industrious were to be avoided at all costs.

My rocket work required many visits to factories and army, naval and RAF stations, often in the company of my colonel, who seized any opportunity to be out of his office, and, the more I saw and learned, the stronger was my realisation that I needed to find a post-war profession in which I could use all the knowledge and skills I was acquiring in the army with what I had known before. (Further, my marriage had collapsed and the prospect of returning to Liverpool, teaching boys and sitting in the masters' common room marking their essays, filled me with gloom.)

Rockets, botany and zoology! What possible profession was there? Then out of the blue – and with my usual luck – came what would prove to be the break I needed.

Early one evening in 1944, shortly after I had returned to my room in Chelsea, I received a telephone call from Douglas Warth speaking from his office in the *Daily Express*. He explained that, with the war situation so grim, Churchill had become desperate for some good news to impart to the people. He had been told about a new, more highly powered explosive called RDX, which had been developed at Woolwich. The military authorities would have preferred it to remain secret but Churchill insisted on an announcement to the media though without giving any of the details required to make the news into a prominent 'story'. Douglas asked me if I could give him any help or advice.

I gave him several leads which enabled his paper to produce a more detailed story than any other, especially as one of the scientists involved with RDX was a Dr Rotter, whose address I knew. Douglas received warm praise and told me that his news editor had been listening to our conversation on an extension and had been so impressed that he noted my name for future use. Used for its purpose, RDX would blow thousands to eternity but it propelled me towards prosperity.

I told my colonel about the episode and he approved of it though warned me that, should there ever be a row about my relations with the press, he had known nothing about them. I agreed.

A major technical problem for Fleet Street was posed in June 1944 by the sudden arrival of the flying bombs, known to the

Germans as V1s, which were to inflict enormous damage over the ensuing four months, with 9,500 of them causing 22,000 casualties. As the weapons were clearly visible as they came in at low altitude, making a distinctive buzzing noise, the media could not be forbidden to report and speculate about them. Again, luck was with me as a result of visits I had made to the Royal Aircraft Establishment at Farnborough where I had seen flying bombs assembled from recovered parts. So, the *Daily Express* speculated with remarkable accuracy. To guide the artist responsible for the sketch which the paper printed I needed to visit the newspaper's office, where I also met the news editor.

I provided the same service after September 1944 when the rocket weapon, the V2, began to bombard London. Being the first large-scale ballistic missile, from which all modern long-range rockets are derived, it was of special interest to me and, again, I had had the luck to see a complete mock-up made from recovered parts at Farnborough. So, once again, I visited the *Daily Express* office where I was introduced to the impressive editor, Arthur Christiansen, who was most grateful and encouraging. He had a further problem for me in that his chief, the proprietor Lord Beaverbrook, had been chiding him for the failure of the paper's foreign correspondents to discover the purpose of some massive, near bomb-proof, concrete structures which the Germans had hurriedly built in the Calais area. Within a few days I found, from RAF sources, that they were ancillary to the V2 housing plant for making liquid oxygen, which fuelled the rockets, and other associated purposes.

Christiansen insisted on giving me a generous payment which I accepted, knowing that to do so was a serious offence in my army capacity. I accepted mainly because I had seen the glimmer of a possible post-war career that would enable me to employ both my scientific and military knowledge – in national journalism, specialising in defence and science. I confided in my colonel, who approved with the remark, 'You can be sure that, when you are demobbed, the army won't do anything to help you.'

When the *Daily Express* news editor, Cyril Morton, suggested that I should spend my Sundays in the newspaper office learning the basics of the trade, being paid two guineas for doing so, I accepted, always attending in civilian clothes, which probably compounded my army offence. I usually had some information that would make an exclusive story.

I also learned a great deal from the old hands. Morton, who had been a successful pre-war reporter, stressed how important it was to assess the personalities of likely sources and exploit any weaknesses. As an example, he told me of his pre-war experience with the Dame of Sark, who was then the autocratic owner of that tiny Channel Island. The Dame had caused a commotion by her treatment of her staff and reporters from all the Fleet Street newspapers, including Morton, had arrived on Sark by the boat service from the mainland. On knocking on her door, they were all informed, emphatically, that the Dame never gave interviews. So they all decided to leave, except Morton, who told his colleagues that, as he would never visit Sark again, he intended to have a look round the island and catch a later boat. He then returned to the Dame's home and requested 'an audience', which she immediately granted, giving Morton a much-envied scoop.

As the Fleet Street newspapers have always operated in fierce competition in the fight for circulation, 'scoops' – stories which all the competitors have missed – have always been specially valued in the belief that readers will buy the paper that is most successful in producing them, With Sunday usually being a bad day for news, particularly exclusive news, a scoop had special value then and, from my inside knowledge, especially about the V2, I was sometimes able to provide one.

The other reporters with whom I came in contact frequently stressed the difficulties of entering Fleet Street journalism, which was usually done only after first learning the trade on local papers. They also reminded me that, when the war ended, the many established members of the staff who were in the forces or serving as war correspondents would be returning.

When, in August 1945, news of the destruction of Hiroshima by one atomic bomb astonished the world, Christiansen was told by Lord Beaverbrook that the event was so historic that he must keep the story going on the front page for a fortnight. (Foreseeing the vast political implications, Beaverbrook himself had dictated the front-page headline: 'The Bomb that Has Changed the World'.)

Bound by a secrecy deal with the US, the government issued no newsworthy information. So the editor turned to me in some desperation. I knew that Professor Marcus Oliphant, of Birmingham University, had been involved in the British atomic effort so I telephoned him. Oliphant told me that the US government had released a thick report describing the whole project and that the UK atomic HQ in London had an advance copy. With the agreement of my colonel, who was fascinated to know what was in it, I went there in civilian clothes, gave Oliphant's name and was allowed to see the now-historic Smyth Report, as it was called, and make notes. The colonel gave me a week's leave, provided that I reported my findings to him each evening, and I went daily to take notes and then write my story which, of course, did not mention the report.

The result was a succession of world scoops because there had been a hold-up on the release of the Smyth Report in Washington! The editor was so impressed and relieved that he offered me the post of defence and scientific reporter on my release from the army, meanwhile expecting me to continue with my clandestine contributions. The salary he offered was many times greater than anything I had earned before and was not restricted by fixed annual increments but would be entirely performance based. I accepted immediately with delight, having entered the one profession in which I could utilise all my acquired knowledge. It also meant that I would be out of the teaching profession and not returning to Liverpool.

My name had never appeared on any of my newspaper reports because of the obvious danger but, after Hiroshima, Christiansen insisted that some name must appear on items I wrote about the atomic bomb, especially those expressing an opinion. He gave me the choice of using my own name or a pseudonym with which I would be saddled when I formally joined the staff on my demobilisation. Rashly, perhaps, having the bit between my teeth, I chose my own name. He then declared that 'Harry' or 'Henry' would not do as he liked 'pompous names', like those of two established staff reporters whose by-lines were Sefton Delmer and Selkirk Panton. He then decided that Chapman Pincher sounded 'very pompous' and I have been saddled with it ever since. Fortunately, being so unusual, it is a name which people tended to remember.

Shortly afterwards, I was summoned by my brigadier, with whom I had become socially friendly through the Players Theatre, to be given the shock news that I was to be posted abroad. Though the Americans had seized all the captured V2 rockets and shipped them to the US – along with the chief German rocket scientists – the British had collected enough spare parts to build three, which were to be test-fired into the sea at Cuxhaven, in Germany. The three services would each have an officer in the team and I was to be the army's – with the rank of lieutenant colonel! While affecting to be thrilled and grateful, I realised that the project would take so long that I would lose touch with the *Express* so, after a few days' thought, I decided to reject the post if I could, tempting though the promotion was. I wrote to the brigadier pointing out that the Cuxhaven experience should belong to a soldier who would be staying in the army, which I was determined to leave. Happily, he agreed.

After the defeat of Germany, I had been switched to developing rocket weapons for the continuing war against Japan. The Japanese troops were expected to fight to the end and we had been developing weapons to burn them in their bunkers. That work ceased with the end of the war and I was posted away from Woolwich to await my demobilisation. I dreaded a posting out of London but when it came it was to a military office in the Mansion House, just up the road from Fleet Street. My colonel was also sent to a new post – at the Supply Ministry in the Strand where he had access to secret documents and became a useful source whom I could meet easily for lunch.

Each morning when I entered my Mansion House office there was nothing to do but examine the few documents in my in-tray, which yielded scoop after scoop. With so many civilians and service men and women about to lose their wartime jobs, the huge Ministry of Supply, which employed most of them, had decided that they should be given first chance of the posts in the new defence research stations being established to deal with developments like atomic weapons, guided missiles and biological warfare. The job offers required some description of the new research stations and their locations, which had not yet been publicly announced. So, scoops on these places fell into my lap for lunchtime transfer to my newspaper, a brief bus-ride down the road. So far as I know, no official ever connected Chapman Pincher with Captain Pincher.

I had a further stroke of luck when I encountered a colleague, a Captain Ismay, whom I had not seen for several months and who had just returned from Germany. He had been in an Anglo-American military team rounding up German scientists for interrogation about their war work. He told me that the whole V2 rocket team from Peenemunde had been found in Bavaria and were being held in a schoolhouse in Garmisch-Partenkirchen. The inventor of the V2, called Wernher von Braun, was among them.

I raced to the *Daily Express* to see the editor, who immediately dispatched a reporter to the scene, where he secured a much-envied story. (Years later, I was to meet von Braun in the US where he was, happily, developing rockets for his former enemy.)

My demobilisation eventually arrived in June 1946, when, aged thirty-two, my medical examiner kindly restored my medical status to A1. I was at my desk in the *Daily Express* office the next day. I had, formally, entered Fleet Street journalism in a specialist role at the start of the atomic age, the missile age, the space age and the electronic age and was qualified to deal with all of them. Further, it was at a time – before the current impact of television, radio and the internet – when the printed word was paramount in the dissemination of news.

CHAPTER 4

DEFENCE MAN

In the past, when a major war ended, public interest in defence affairs quickly subsided, with the government's production` and development of weapons rapidly reduced in the drive to restore the economy. In September 1945, however, only a month after the Japanese surrender, an event which would trigger a massive rearmament with new weapons by Britain and the USA occurred in Canada. A young Russian cipher clerk called Igor Gouzenko, working in the Soviet embassy in Ottawa, defected with a mass of documentary evidence revealing that the Soviet government, headed by Josef Stalin while posing as an ally, was really planning to undermine its democratic allies to impose a Moscow-controlled, Communist regime on them, however long it might take.

For that purpose, the Soviet Union had been conducting extensive espionage operations, which included the penetration of the ultra-secret projects that had produced the atomic bomb. The Canadian Prime Minister, Mackenzie King, who was severely shocked, informed the British Prime Minister, Clement Attlee, and the US President, Harry Truman, who were deeply dismayed. Their realisation of the Soviet perfidy was the beginning of the Cold War and the East–West 'arms race', which were to last until the collapse of Soviet Communism forty-five years later.

British interest in defence issues, particularly in the atomic and rocket spheres, was immediately intensified and offered limitless opportunities to a journalistic sleuth like myself, provided I could secure the necessary information. The question was: 'How do I find it?' I was not inclined to sit around, boringly waiting for hand-outs, press conferences or statements by ministers to Parliament.

Whenever possible, I wanted to be the source whereby MPs first heard of contentious developments, the ensuing parliamentary turmoil being good both for my reputation and my newspaper's.

Further, any secret quickly became a challenge to me as I knew so much of the official secrecy to be unnecessary and, often, just a convenience for politicians and civil servants. My derision of unnecessary secrecy probably dates back to a stormy night in 1943, when I was the duty officer of my small army unit and a dispatch rider, dripping rainwater, was shown into my office with a message marked 'Secret'. When I opened the envelope the message read 'Tinned sausages are now available'. In those days 'sausages' was redolent of Germany. (The KGB codename for Germans was 'sausage-makers'.) So, I imagined that the message might be a code, alerting my unit of some German activity requiring action by us. My telephone inquiries quickly showed that it meant no more than it said.

So, I faced a daily challenge to discover classified information which could come only from those who knew it – government ministers, the civil servants serving them and other members of the government, senior forces officers and, possibly, members of firms producing secret weapons. In the process of using such information I was determined to develop a reputation for reliability with my employers, the public and my informants in the sense that I could be relied on to deliver, that my statements would be accurate and that my secret sources would not be revealed.

The civil servants, who were mainly located in the Whitehall area, seemed the most promising targets, especially as the government in office in 1946 was Labour, which, officially, would not be inclined to assist a Tory-supporting newspaper. I decided first to concentrate on the press and public relations chiefs of the three services – the navy, army and RAF, who, before the creation of a full-blown Ministry of Defence in 1964, were in separate buildings, each with a Secretary of State in political command.

The three services quickly appreciated that anyone with such access to mass-circulation publicity could be helpful in the defence revolution occasioned by the arrival of the atomic bomb and the ballistic missile. The chiefs of staff knew that, with Britain financially exhausted by the war, they would have to compete hard for the money and facilities to construct atomic weapons and new bombers and missiles to carry them. So they and their political masters needed regular press support for their expansion by explaining that necessity in simple terms to the mass of voters.

Obviously, a journalist who was a trusted, former insider, keen to support them and their projects, could be helpful in the coming political struggles. In the process, I made good friends of a succession of directors of public relations of all three services and did not neglect their deputies and junior staff. I operated, mainly, by inviting my targets to convivial lunches at restaurants within walking distance of their offices. (One of the directors, Brigadier Gilbert Monckton, would later express his friendly respect by ensuring that, when individual passes into the Defence Ministry were issued to accredited defence reporters, number 007 was reserved for me. I still treasure it.)

I soon learned that each public relations department had a log book containing official answers to sensitive questions about issues which it was hoped would not be raised by journalists but could be used if they were. Being regularly informed of what was sitting in the log book provided me with many exclusives. Further, when I had secured something new about a subject on which I needed more information, I could approach these public relations friends confident that they would not tip off any of my Fleet Street rivals who were beset by the same daily problem. Daily success in such a competitive field, which is what demanding editors expected, was very much a matter of 'who knows wins'. On any daily paper, a victory was short lived because however dazzling a scoop might be, it was, quickly, the next one that mattered. Happily, I enjoyed the challenge, as witnessed by my *Who's Who* entry, which, for the last sixty years, has listed one of my hobbies as 'ferreting in Whitehall and bolting politicians'.

At the various press conferences, which I always attended, I never asked a question but studiously listened to the responses to those who did. If I detected something to ask which might lead to a news story I would wait until the conference had ended and was back in my office, when I would ask the question privately over the telephone. Such behaviour did not endear me to competing journalists but that caused me no grief. Many journalists consorted, during and out of working hours, in bars such as El Vino in Fleet Street, but my time was precious. Having remarried – to a girl called Mona who I had met at the Players Theatre and with whom I had a daughter, Pat, and a son, Michael – I was commuting from Farnham, in Surrey, and needed to get away as early as I could in the evening. It also seemed obvious that the person from whom one was least likely to glean information was a competing journalist. (Years later, on arrival at a remote Scottish hotel for salmon fishing, the landlady declared, 'I've heard about you. You are the Lone Wolf of Fleet Street.' It was an apt description.)

From the start, I had the great advantage of serving a newspaper with a proprietor (Lord Beaverbrook) and an editor who were strongly in favour of Britain's becoming a nuclear power with sufficient military, air and naval strength to merit 'a seat at the top table' and, especially, to continue its special defence relationship with the USA.

How to get access to the most senior civil servants, who were personally involved in the decision-making processes through their advice to ministers, was my major problem. It seemed that top civil servants, such as the Permanent Secretaries of departments of state, had been regarded by Fleet Street as unapproachable, as were Cabinet ministers, except through the public relations channels. Then, out of the blue, circumstances were to provide me with a stroke of luck which would solve my problem.

While awaiting my release from the army, I had completed my simple guide to genetics for farmers, *The Breeding of Farm Animals*, and published it in 1946 as a Penguin Handbook. Priced one shilling and sixpence, it did not make me much money but was to prove to be worth many times its weight in gold. Soon after its appearance, at the end of a press facility visit to the aeronautical research station at Farnborough, I boarded a bus to take me and the other journalists to the main gate and sat opposite a man of medium height wearing a black jacket, pin-stripe trousers and bowler hat. He introduced himself as Fred Brundrett, saying that his hobby was farming and that he had enjoyed my book. He invited me to see his herd of Redpoll cattle on his farm near Emsworth, where I found that, during the week, he was deputy to the Chief Defence Scientist, Sir Henry Tizard, whom he soon succeeded whereupon he became Sir Frederick.

Fred, who was involved with every major defence development, attending Cabinet committee meetings as an adviser, became a firm friend, meeting me regularly for long lunches at my favourite restaurant, the Ecu de France in Jermyn Street, near Piccadilly, which was equidistant between Whitehall and Fleet Street.

Ignoring the general Whitehall view that any official information was 'an official secret covered by the Official Secrets Acts until it was officially released', Fred believed that the taxpayers, who would be funding the unusually heavy peacetime defence costs occasioned by the atomic and missile age, were entitled to be kept informed about their investments and the reasons for them. He also suspected that mutual reliance by the West and Russia on the nuclear deterrent to keep the peace would be difficult for many people to accept without repeated explanation and assurance. Further, as Britain's policy was to deter Stalin and his associates from any attack by assuring them that the UK could retaliate with nuclear weapons, Fred was keen to support a newspaper which would repeatedly deliver this message in the form of front-page news. He chose me as his medium for imparting that information, probably influenced by my being a former insider who understood the technology and knew how the Whitehall machinery worked.

From then on, until his retirement in 1960, Fred gave me scoop after scoop, confident that I would never reveal their source during his lifetime. I recall the inner glow I felt so many times when returning to my office from lunch with a scoop certain to trigger a commotion.

Fred also introduced me to his chief assistants, who were specialists on various aspects of defence, and assured them that I could be trusted. The atomic specialist Victor Macklen became a major source. I developed the regular habit of visiting the specialists in their offices when I had urgent issues on which I needed advice. Through them I met others, like John Drew, the Defence Ministry's specialist in deception operations. Once in a charmed circle, it inevitably widens.

My many meetings with Fred gradually enhanced my interrogation techniques which, unlike the aggressive approach adopted by so many television reporters today, concentrated on allowing my guest to do the talking, prompting him only when necessary, always avoiding pumping him too obviously and never taking a written note. With good intelligence from other sources it was often possible to predict events and then check out a hunch by asking searching questions.

Brundrett's relationship with me was much resented in the higher Whitehall echelons and in the Security Service, MI5. So, I was certainly dangerous for Fred to know but he was his own man and had the backing of ministers such as Duncan Sandys, the Defence Minister in the late 1950s, with whom I forged a long-lasting relationship profitable to us both. I also made a close friend of Kenneth Post, an unofficial adviser in whom Sandys confided in his efforts to ensure that he was not being bamboozled by his civil servants.

As long as such people remained in office, Fred was safe in continuing his friendship with me but there were several senior civil servants who regarded his behaviour as unprofessional and in serious breach of the Official Secrets Acts. (These 'mandarins' took childish revenge on Fred on his retirement by withholding the award of the GCB (Grand Cross of the Order of the Bath), which was ritual for a public official of such rank and distinction.)

On the atomic front, I paid close attention to the new Atomic Energy Research Station, opened on a disused airfield at Harwell, Berkshire, as several of my existing contacts had secured jobs there. They kept me informed about progress there, especially when it was lagging, providing me with scoops resulting in a statement in the station's magazine, 'We may not have made an atom bomb but we have certainly made Chapman Pincher.'

I applied an equally critical eye to the new Rocket Research

Station at Westcott, Buckinghamshire, and I recall with particular joy a front-page story following a call from one of the scientists there alerting me to a farcical security situation. The Bicester Hunt, in full regalia and in full cry, had penetrated the guarded wire fence and killed a fox near a secret workshop, the scientists there being startled at 2.30 p.m. by the sound of the horn and cries of the hounds.

Without question, the greatest of the many advantages offered by high-level journalism is the repeated opportunity for meeting people of distinction. Among these is Sebastian de Ferranti, the retired chairman of the electricity and electronics pioneering company Ferranti, who provides a good example of the journalistic advantage of being known and trusted by 'captains of industry'.

In 1964, the now-historic 'Ferranti affair' caused an ongoing parliamentary furore which I was able to stoke up daily to the fury of Harold Wilson, then in opposition. The firm had been involved in making an advanced anti-aircraft missile called Bloodhound and for a total outlay of £7 million had made a profit of £5,772,000, a large sum in those days. When this became known, there were two parliamentary debates about the 'scandal' and the Aviation Minister, Julian Amery, was called on to resign for allowing the deal.

As I fuelled the row with new disclosures day after day, Amery, who was known to be a friend of mine, was accused of leaking to me when in fact I was being briefed by Sebastian, then only thirty-six, who insisted that his firm was being pilloried for a success. After an independent inquiry, to which Sebastian agreed and which lasted six months, the firm paid back £4 million. I secured a scoop on the findings of the inquiry but Wilson reignited the row by demanding another inquiry into my sources.

It all ended in a censure debate, the whole episode being, for me, a milestone in my war on unnecessary secrecy. (Thank you, Sebastian! We had a lot of fun together, shooting grouse.)

When Air Marshal Sir Geoffrey Tuttle retired from the RAF he joined what became the British Aircraft Corporation (later British Aerospace Corporation) and continued to be a valuable source. Through him I met the extraordinary Yorkshireman Geoffrey Edwards, through whose stubborn patience Britain secured massive arms deals with Saudi Arabia of enormous value especially as they created thousands of jobs.

In the early 1960s, the Saudi royal family had decided to establish a modern defence force, the task put in the hands of Prince Sultan, who was the Defence Minister. So the British Aircraft Corporation was keen to sell him its Lightning fighter plane and representatives were sent out to Jeddah to negotiate a deal. Sultan proved to be so inaccessible that, after waiting several days without an 'audience', they had all returned empty handed. Geoffrey Edwards, a freelance, then secured the agency and sat outside Sultan's office, day after day, for a whole month and, finally, secured a meeting at which a deal, codenamed Operation Magic Carpet, was struck in 1967. It involved not only Lightnings but much ancillary equipment. Edwards's commission was huge.

The deal also included a secret arrangement whereby Sultan received personal kick-backs which, over the years, amounted to many millions. This has led to frequent claims that the British Aircraft Corporation was using bribes to secure and keep the Saudi contract but these have always been, quite correctly, denied. As Edwards confirmed to me, any money which ended up in the private hands of Sultan (who died in 2011) was Saudi money specially paid into the scheme by the Saudi Defence Ministry for that purpose.

Geoffrey Edwards and I became close friends and met regularly in London and at a house he built in Barbados with his delightful partner, Aimi MacDonald. My wife and I were present when he rented a London theatre and launched Aimi on a successful stage and TV career.

Among the 'captains of industry' who were helpful to me were Sir Arnold Weinstock (later Lord), known for the General Electric Company, one of Britain's largest businesses, and the brothers Sir John and Michael Clark, who ran Plessey, an electronics and telecommunications company with many defence contracts. Weinstock's office was close to Fleet Street and he encouraged me to visit him regularly. A dynamic Jew, he kept me informed of technological developments in many fields. Everything he touched turned to success, including his interest in horse-racing, in which he won the Derby in 1979. Later, Arnold visited my house in Kintbury, delighting me by saying 'You have a beautiful home and lots of nice things in it'. He lived to be seventy-seven, departing in 2002.

I became close to both the Clark brothers through pheasant-shooting as they each owned splendid estates which I often visited: John's at Redenham Park in Hampshire and Michael's at Braxted Park in Essex. They both visited my home and Michael, a keen angler, was my guest on the Kennet, where I ensured that the conversation was not just about trout, especially during the long lunches my wife staged in the fishing hut. John died in 2001 and Michael in 2010.

Over the years, from many sources I received – and usually published – such a steady stream of classified information that it led to my most cherished professional compliment, made by the historian E. P. Thompson, that I was 'a public urinal where ministers and officials queued up to leak'! Some journalistic critics claimed that I was allowing myself to be 'used' but if the information was true and especially if it was exclusive, I was open for 'use' at any time – as I still am. I confess to having been obsessed with unnecessary secrecy and to having derived personal pleasure from revealing what most of the senior civil servants seemed to regard as their property. (The extent of my penetration and the fierce reaction of officialdom to it were independently put on public record in 2013 by Dr Christopher Moran of Warwick University in his book *Classified*.)

The danger of being prosecuted for breaching the Official Secrets Acts posed a recurring problem, especially as the Fleet Street lawyers and most editors were seriously scared of it, not wanting, as my editor put it, 'to end up in the Tower'. With my wartime experience of secret matters, I was aware that my efforts would entail some personal risk of prosecution which I decided to reduce by a private decision vowing never to see or handle a classified document if offered the opportunity.

Fortunately, I found a solution in the shape of Rear Admiral George Thomson, the wartime censor who had been appointed to operate the peacetime D-notice system. This involved the issue of advisory notices to editors about areas of defence and intelligence which it would be not only patriotic but wise to avoid. I cultivated the delightful admiral through regular lunches at the Arts Theatre Club and we quickly devised a *modus vivendi*. In those days, the D-notice secretary was truly independent with an office outside Whitehall and Thomson believed it his duty to secure publication if possible without real damage to the national interest. In return, editors trusted him to be telling the truth when he assured them or their reporters that publication would really damage security, which no responsible journalist wished to do.

So, whatever I was writing about defence or intelligence, I read it over to the admiral by telephone. Sometimes he needed to take Whitehall advice before responding but, almost invariably, we were able to devise a form of words which permitted publication and allowed me to assure the editor that the copy had been 'passed by Admiral Thomson'. The advantage to the admiral was substantial because as soon as copies of the first edition of the *Daily Express* reached the offices of rival newspapers – around 10.30 p.m. – their reporters would telephone him at home to ask if it was safe for them to copy the story. Thanks to our close collaboration, he was always able to answer without disturbing senior Whitehall officials for information at ungodly hours.

In 1946, while in the Players Theatre Club, I had encountered a *Daily Express* foreign correspondent who had been on the island of Tinian, where the American bombers which delivered the atomic bombs on Hiroshima and Nagasaki had been based. Before the take-off of the first one, he and other journalists had been called out by the commanding US general to be shown the uranium bomb, 'Little Boy', before it was loaded. They had been told its all-up weight – four tons. That was a major secret which I was keen to divulge because I had figured out, from the Smyth Report, that the Hiroshima bomb had been essentially a gun in which a bullet of uranium-235 had been fired through a hollow cylinder of U-235 to form a critical mass and I wanted to publish a cut-away picture of it. I felt sure that Admiral Thomson would veto the all-up weight but, instead, he assured me that, since it was an American weapon, I could publish what I liked. The news, with a huge diagram, filled my newspaper's front page. (Recently, while a guest at the nuclear weapons research establishment at Aldermaston, Berkshire, I was gratified to see that the official sketch showing the gun-bomb principle was almost identical to mine which had graced the front page half a century earlier.)

Shortly afterwards, I had a further front-page headline – also based on the US general's information to my colleague – announcing that the US had a stockpile of ninety-six atomic bombs. That proved to be so accurate that the senior MI5 officer Guy Liddell recorded in his diary that MI5 was likely to be involved in an inquiry into my source.

My publicity was not well received in the US where General Leslie Groves, who had headed the 'Manhattan Project', which produced the bomb, formally complained that my efforts were 'an unfriendly act'. I refrained from telling him that all my information had originated from another American general who had simply told my informant that the rate of output of their atomic bomb facilities was eight a month. As I knew that they had been in production for a year, I simply multiplied eight by twelve to give a total, ninety-six, which proved to be almost spot on.

There followed occasions on which, after consulting Whitehall 'mandarins', as very senior civil servants were known, the admiral informed me that if I attributed a leak to an unnamed American source all would be well. It was regarded as even more satisfactory if I could delay an embarrassing revelation until one of my regular visits to the US, when I could give it a Washington date-line.

Another source-protecting ploy was to make use of the many international conferences which I attended, those on astronautics, for example, being ideal for releasing secret information about new rocket weapons which I had surreptitiously acquired. One instance was my revelation that, pending the time when the US had developed nuclear missiles with inter-continental range, American forces were to deploy intermediate-range Thor missiles at Feltwell in Norfolk. The fact was sensitive because there was widespread political resentment against such a move as it could increase the risk of a pre-emptive Soviet strike on Britain. Few in Whitehall were fooled by my Amsterdam date-line, giving the impression that I had acquired the intelligence from some scientist at the conference there, but all were relieved that there would be no parliamentary claims that some minister had leaked it to me. (It had, in fact, been leaked to me by Lieutenant Colonel Sammy Lohan, of whom more later.)

My long experience has enabled me to understand some of the reasons why distinguished men risked damaging their careers by leaking information which they knew was likely to cause a commotion. Sometimes, it was to inflict professional damage on an opponent in a competing political party or government department. Frequently, it was to take the sting out of something unpleasant which was due to be announced in Parliament a few days later. Occasionally, it was to publicise something to the leaker's advantage which he had been forbidden to announce for some diplomatic reason.

Usually, there was a sensible purpose behind a loose tongue, an example being a memorable leak from Harold Watkinson, then Defence Minister, whose department had pulled off a huge arms deal with Saudi Arabia that ensured thousands of British jobs. Fearful that the Saudis might wish the deal be kept secret, the Foreign Office had banned any publicity. I published the news, to the satisfaction of all those who had worked so hard to secure the deal, with no bleats from Saudi Arabia.

Sometimes a government would contrive a leak of something that would be embarrassing to announce. One such, in 1964, was a much-envied scoop that the British MI6 agent Greville Wynne, who was in a Russian jail under tough conditions, was to be exchanged in Berlin for a KGB officer operating under the name Gordon Lonsdale and held in Britain. The Russians had released photographs of Wynne, showing him so emaciated that the British authorities had felt forced to offer the much more significant Lonsdale in exchange. The Foreign Office decided to leak the dramatic event in such a way that it would become public shortly after the two spies had each reached Berlin when, it was believed, the Russians would be unable to retract from their exchange (dramatically at dawn on a bridge over a river). In choosing me as the medium, the Foreign Office reckoned that, as I had a reputation for accurate leaks, the other media would follow up the story – as they did.

Many leaks were given to me to smite opponents in the various struggles invariably in progress within the government machinery. Others, especially from politicians, were designed to inflate their public reputations or deflate those of parliamentary opponents. Many more, it seemed, were an aspect of male vanity as some informants, clearly, derived pleasure from letting someone who they knew would never reveal their names in their lifetime that they had access to secrets denied to ordinary mortals. The pleasure may have intensified when they witnessed the subsequent commotion. I call it the 'peacock factor' because it seems to be peculiar to men. The few women I met who knew secrets were absolute clams.

Never having been a member of any trade union, I had little truck with any of them with one most rewarding exception. I discovered that a body called the Institution of Professional Civil Servants (IPCS) was, effectively, a trade union for Whitehall mandarins and their staffs and I quickly made a friend of its general secretary, Stanley Mayne, taking him out to lunch regularly and inviting him to my home. Mayne was big, handsome and highly intelligent with a good sense of humour. Because nearly all the scientists working in secret government research stations were members of his outfit, Mayne had access to all those establishments when visiting his representatives there. He learned a great deal on these visits about internal problems and became a steady source of leaks to me which made good newspaper reports.

The main ones concerned IPCS members who were 'purged' from secret establishments, like the Harwell Atomic Energy Research Establishment, when it was discovered that they were Communists. Under new government rules, nobody who had Communist connections or had relatives behind the Iron Curtain was allowed access to secret information and had to be removed because of the danger that it might end up in Moscow. So, when anyone was subjected to what some, including Mayne, regarded as 'victimisation', I was the first newsman to know and gave the story full publicity. What I did not know for many years (as neither did the Professional Civil Servants) was that Mayne himself was a committed Communist. I learned this from another trade union leader who had been a Communist but had genuinely abandoned that creed in view of the 'Cold War' between Britain and the Soviet Union. He told me that he had served on Communist committees with Mayne, who had also been closely involved with the Communist newspaper, the *Daily Worker*, for many years. I made some discreet inquiries and found that the Whitehall civil service authorities had no knowledge of Mayne's true allegiance. While reluctant to betray my friend, I was in no doubt where my duty lay, especially in view of my personal antipathy to Communism and the threat which the Soviet Union was posing through espionage and subversion. Clearly, I needed to alert the security authorities to the fact that a committed Communist had regular access to their most secret establishments. Nevertheless, I felt uneasy about betraying a friend and, to be honest, about losing such a fruitful source. Fortunately my problem was resolved for me by two unexpected events. First, Mayne told me that he would be retiring in 1961 and, in due course, introduced me to the successor he had handpicked and who, I quickly discovered, was another Communist. Then, shortly afterwards, the government set up a high-level inquiry into security headed by the distinguished judge Lord Radcliffe and I was invited to give evidence, in private, about various exposures I had reported revealing defects in MI5 and MI6. So, I seized the opportunity to reveal the facts about Mayne and, especially, about his would-be successor. Lord Radcliffe and his distinguished colleagues in the inquiry were clearly astonished by the situation which had lasted so many years.

In the result, the government took quick action, making it clear that, in future, it would not negotiate with the IPCS or any similar body if its leader was a Communist. The successor chosen by Mayne was ruled out and replaced by a political moderate who proved to be an excellent choice. I became friends with him and, one day, was able to tell him of my part in securing him his appointment. It is surprising what goes on behind the scenes in dull-looking Whitehall!

I had long known that when one of my defence or intelligence scoops had caused a serious Whitehall commotion, an inquiry called 'The Leak Procedure' was put into effect by the Cabinet Secretary or some other very senior civil servant. The precise nature of this procedure has now become known as the secret Cabinet papers recording them have been declassified. The details, so typical of Whitehall, would have made a marvellous instalment of *Yes Minister*.

Here is a typical instance of what happened following a report of mine about nuclear missiles published in the *Daily Express* in July 1973, Three months later, the chairman of the Official Committee on Security reported to the Head of the Civil Service that 171 people who might have leaked the secret information to me had been interrogated in various Whitehall departments! They ranged from chiefs of staff and government ministers to middle-level officials selected for inquisition because they knew the secrets concerned and might also have known me. They were asked: 'Do you know Chapman Pincher?' 'When did you last see him?' 'What did you talk about?' followed by many more questions. After all that effort, in which they never questioned me because – as the report states – I would have made a story out of it, the security interrogators concluded that 'though one cannot rule out the possibility of a deliberate leak, we do not believe there was one'. (They were wrong.)

The amount of time wasted interrogating senior officials and forces personnel about my reports was so intrusive that as far back as 27 November 1958, Sir Richard Powell, the Defence Ministry's Permanent Secretary, had advised his minister against any more time-wasting 'witch hunts' of me (which were to include having me watched), stating: 'I believe that we must live with the man and make the best of it. We can console ourselves that his writings, though embarrassing at times to Whitehall, disclose nothing that Russian intelligence does not already know.'

However, that did not deter Prime Minister Harold Macmillan from asking the Defence Minister on 4 May 1959, in a written message marked 'Secret' of which a copy has adorned a wall of our downstairs lavatory for many years, 'Can nothing be done to suppress or even get rid of Mr Chapman Pincher? I am getting very concerned about how well informed he always seems to be on defence matters. It really is very serious if a Cabinet secret cannot be kept for more than two days.' (I wonder what Macmillan meant by 'get rid of'.)

The released documents reveal scores of other instances concerning reports of mine ranging from newspaper articles about MI6, weapons sales to Kenya, aircraft purchases from America, foreign defence bases etc. In not a single instance over all those years did they ever detect any of the many culprits who were my sources. In my case, 'The Leak Procedure' can only be described as a monumental, time-wasting farce. So why did the civil servants continue to apply it? The July 1973 report I mentioned above ends with this statement from the chairman of the Official Committee on Security – 'though the exercise has produced no positive result it has, at least, once again impressed upon all those concerned the importance of being discreet' – the inference being 'So, let's continue it'. You couldn't make it up!

CHAPTER 5

SCIENCE MAN

To fulfil my commitments as the science reporter, I knew that I needed to make friends with the editor of the dullest-looking weekly magazine on the market. Called *Nature*, its letters column had become the prime place for scientists to make public mention of a new discovery. That way they could quickly establish first claim. Obviously, if I could induce the editor of *Nature* to show me advance proofs of the letters column, I could not only scoop my Fleet Street rivals but have more time to do justice to any new discovery there.

My logic worked and the editor, a botanist called Jack Brimble, became a close friend. He favoured me not only because I regularly asked him to lunch but because we were both biologists and had much in common. He even allowed me to challenge Darwin in his letters column, an event resented by several old professors who felt that their sacred ground was being sullied by a hack.

According to Darwin, the giraffe's long neck is the result of natural selection acting through the animal's tree-feeding habit. He wrote, 'The individuals which were the highest browsers and were able, during dearths, to reach even an inch or two above the others will often have been preserved.' My letter objected to that theory, pointing out that giraffes eat grass if leaves are not available and thrive on hay in zoos. So, it seemed reasonable to suppose that the ancestors of the giraffe were grass-eaters and that, with the lengthening of the neck, a new source of food happened to have become available.

But why had the neck grown so long? I suggested that the answer lay in the extreme length of the forelegs, which gives the animal such a huge stride that, in escaping from lions and other predators, it can reach 32 mph – a major survival advantage. Like other ruminants, the giraffe needs a plentiful supply of water and the increase in shoulder-height necessitated the development of a long neck to get the head down to water level. So, I suggested that, as with the evolution of so many animals, it was the ever-present predator–prey relationship which had been responsible, not occasional food dearths. That now seems to be the accepted view.

Early in our friendship, Brimble introduced me, over lunch, to a handsome well-built man of about thirty who was of Czech origin but spoke perfect English, having served in the British Army. On learning that during the war the numerous scientific institutes in the Soviet Union had continued to operate and had published hundreds of research papers in Russian, he managed to secure copies, had them translated and sold them through a publishing company called Pergamon Press. The demand from western universities was so great that Pergamon flourished, producing a great number of scientific and technical books.

'You are not reviewing many of the books I send you,' his guest complained to Brimble, who replied: 'You get your fair share but *Nature* receives so many books that we can review only a fraction of them.'

'What do you do with the rest?' the guest asked.

'At the end of each year we donate them to various libraries,' Brimble replied.

The guest's response shocked both me and Brimble – 'Send them to me and I will, personally, give you folding money for them because I could sell them on'. I realised that, whatever his other qualities, to have made such an appalling offer to a senior man of such integrity, the guest was seriously deficient in his judgement. His name? Robert Maxwell.

Soon after my official installation in the *Daily Express* I induced the management to stage the world's first public exhibition designed to explain how the advent of the atomic bomb had changed the world. Staged in a hall in London's Lower Regent Street in January and February 1947, it explained the science behind the bomb and its structure. With blown-up photographs and staged panoramas, it showed the bomb's effects on Hiroshima and Nagasaki. It ended with a section describing the constructive possibilities of atomic power.

Through a friend in the Supply Ministry, I secured the loan of several cylindrical bars of uranium-238 – the first time they had ever been seen in public. I also ensured the attendance, as visitors, of several VIPs, including Sir John Cockcroft, the atomic pioneer and head of the Harwell atomic research station, and General Sir 'Bill' Slim, victor of the Burmese campaign against the Japanese, who came together. I wrote and designed the illustrations for the guide booklet, which, a little later, I expanded into the first explanatory book called *Into the Atomic Age*.

Sadly, my usual good fortune deserted me when January and February 1947 turned out to be the bitterest winter months I can recall. Most of the time the exhibition was deserted. It was a disheartening experience and a financial flop but, in return for my efforts, the understanding *Express* management awarded me a fine bonus. Having resolved to be permanently based in the countryside, which would also be better than a London life for my young daughter Pat and son Michael, I bought a cottage in the pretty village of Ewhurst, near Cranleigh in Surrey, and from that, as my career prospered, I acquired a nearby Tudor house called Lowerhouse Farm. With all-round vistas of fields and woods, it was an ideal place for entertaining contacts in complete privacy. It even had a swimming pool – a feature not so common in those days.

Meanwhile, an immediate way of utilising my accumulated biological knowledge to the newspaper's advantage had been devised by a colleague called Bernard Wicksteed. Being a fellow of the Zoological Society, I had taken Bernard to the London Zoo, where he was so impressed by comments I was making about the animals that he summoned a secretary, who took notes of them all. From the notes he produced a full-page feature that appeared in the following Saturday's issue under the title 'It's Fun Finding Out'.

Due to such a positive reader response it became the first of scores of features to appear under that title. Occasionally, Bernard produced an article based solely on his initiative but most of them were accounts of my comments when visiting various places like a puffin colony, a grouse moor or a river bank. Eventually, they all reappeared in a couple of *It's Fun Finding Out* books.

Tragically, Bernard developed a quickly fatal brain tumour. I am forever in his debt for his brilliant idea and his professionalism in converting it as it helped to establish my reputation both in and outside Fleet Street. (Once, when driving down from the north, I picked up a hitchhiker who, when I told him that I was with the *Daily Express*, remarked: 'You must know that fellow who's a walking *Whitaker's Almanack*.' Fame indeed!)

The *Daily Express* also employed an exceptionally talented artist called Bernard Venables, with whom I shared a love of angling and who would eventually make a lasting name by producing bestselling books of strip cartoons about that sport. Jointly, we produced a series of strip cartoons featuring me explaining various scientific developments, which also helped to spread my name.

To keep my academic interests in trim, in 1947 I published *A Study of Fishes*, a book intended mainly for anglers and heavily illustrated with my own line drawings. I followed that in 1950 with *Evolution*, an easy-to-understand account of the process, also illustrated by myself. My next effort, *Spotlight on Animals*, was more professionally illustrated by the excellent Eric Tansley.

In Fleet Street, 'science' embraced many subjects and one result of that which continues to give me pleasure, in spite of its triviality, concerns an occasion not long after the end of the Second World War when victorious, but near bankrupt, Britain was still inflicted with shortages of food, clothes and petrol, generating a general feeling of frustration. The government had called on the British Colour Council to suggest ways in which organisations and individuals could use colour to make the austerity less dreary and cheer up the scene and, hopefully, people's attitudes. After meditation, the council decided to stage a small exhibition in a room at the Royal Academy, off Piccadilly, to present their recommendations. Entrance was to be free and, to swell the publicity, the exhibition was to be opened by Her Majesty the Queen (later the Queen Mum).

I decided to attend the opening ceremony, which was blessed with a glorious, sunny day. The Queen, who had set a friendly, down-to-earth tone by appearing hatless and so informal that she looked as though she had just stepped out of her Buckingham Palace sitting room, made a suitably short speech and declared the exhibition open. I took a quick look round the exhibits and wall posters and left to return to my office, passing through the turnstile which had been set up to record the number of future visitors. Feeling good, I decided to walk back to Fleet Street in the sunshine and overtook a couple of American soldiers in battle dress strolling slowly, as they clearly had time to kill on a day off in London. In what, I suppose, was a spontaneous gesture of friendship towards our greatest ally, I turned round and, when the soldiers reached me, I said, 'Would you like to see the Queen of England?'

'Sure would!' one of them replied.

'Follow me,' I said, 'but we'll have to run.'

So, the many people in Piccadilly suddenly saw a suited civilian racing into the Academy pursued by two soldiers. 'She's still here,' I shouted as we passed the royal limousine. 'There she is!' I cried, as we entered the room, where Her Majesty was being shown round the exhibits. With a look of sublime amazement on their faces, which I have never forgotten, they automatically snatched off their cloth hats and stood, rooted to the spot, gazing silently. 'Go on in,' I urged, pointing to the turnstile, which they duly did. I left them lost in wonder as they stood within a couple of yards of the Queen. I have often pondered on what they told their comrades when they returned to barracks and what they wrote home.

'Science' was such an elastic term that it included such newsworthy aspects of the occult as ghosts and telepathy. The best-known ghost-hunter of his day was Harry Price, who spent much of his inherited fortune on 'psychical research'. I contacted him concerning what he believed was a truly haunted house – the old rectory at Borley near Long Melford in Suffolk. He told me how the grounds were haunted by the ghost of a nun who, allegedly, had been violated and murdered by some aristocrat. He had published his findings in a book, *The Most Haunted House in England*, which sold well.

Sadly, the rectory had been burned down by the time I visited it but the nun was still supposed to be haunting the ruins. The nightly hours I spent there looking for her were fruitless and former servants of the rectory assured me that the weird noises recorded by Price had been caused by jackdaws in the chimneys. In fact, there was no worthwhile evidence that the nun had ever existed in real life.

What I was most keen to find was a case where two or more observers claimed to have seen the same ghost at the same time. Sadly, I have never done so, supporting my theory that sightings of ghosts are tricks of the individual brain. There was a widely reported tale that two British women visiting the Palace of Versailles had both witnessed a scene involving scores of French aristocratic ghosts enacting some pre-revolutionary event there. The women stuck to their unlikely tale until, in old age, one of them – by that time a distinguished academic – admitted that they had invented the whole story for a lark.

The same negative results accrued from my investigations of telepathy – the concept that human brains could transmit and receive mental messages over long distances. Still, it all made good copy for the newspaper. So much so that a competing newspaper, where my old friend Douglas Warth happened to be working, carried out a mass experiment involving as many of its readers as cared to take part.

The readers were told that at a precise time on a certain day, a reporter would be staring for a minute at a drawing of an object. They were invited to concentrate their minds at exactly that time and try to imagine what the object was and then contact the newspaper with the result. While the reporter was staring at the object, which was a drawing of a small yacht, Warth happened to enter the room and ruined the experiment by declaring: 'I know what it is! It's a cat.' When told to shut up, he repeated his certainty that it was a drawing of a cat. None of the thousands who replied identified the drawing as a ship but a large number identified it as a cat.

Soon after I became science reporter I was approached by two left-wing journalists – one of them an avowed Communist – who invited me to join them in setting up an Association of Science Writers. I declined because, not being a natural 'joiner', I knew that I would never attend any of their meetings, which could be held only in the evening or at weekends. My lack of interest in their problems did not endear me to the other science writers who all joined.

That reluctance is, probably, the origin of my reputation of being 'right-wing' when, in fact, I have never belonged to any political party. I regarded myself as a 'flier', for which I needed two wings – a right and a left. Journalistically, I always felt it essential to be free to attack politicians of any party if I thought they deserved it and the record of my newspaper cuttings shows that, though the *Daily Express*, in general, supported the Conservative Party, I frequently attacked its policies and its ministers. Harold Macmillan's 'secret' memo urging my suppression is potent evidence. So, too, are the many Cabinet papers now released about ministerial responses to my efforts showing that I angered the Tory leadership on many occasions. Other papers also show that I was correct in stating that many of the Labour MPs were really Communists, as was the case with some trade union leaders such as the esteemed Jack Jones. Such remarks had led to jibes that I was an extremist seeing 'Reds under the beds'. In fact, they were 'in the beds'. Several former Labour MPs have been officially exposed as paid Soviet agents.

I made the acquaintance of other science writers when attending conferences, such as the annual meetings of the British Association for the Advancement of Science and international conferences held abroad. The latter tended to be in delightful locations such as Paris, Geneva, Vienna, Rome, Stockholm and Venice. Occasionally they enabled me to get behind the Iron Curtain to places like Warsaw, where I had a most unusual experience.

Being a Yorkshireman, I have never been a soft touch for my hard-earned money but there was one extraordinary occasion when, fully in control of my faculties, I encountered two complete strangers and, without even asking who they were or telling them who I was, gave each of them £250 (when that was a lot of cash) knowing that I would never see either of them again. A brainstorm? Judge what you would have done in the circumstances.

In the late 1960s, I visited Warsaw to take part in a five-day international scientific conference and to report on it to my newspaper.
It was during the reign of the Communist dictator Władysław
Gomułka, a stooge of the Soviet Union, and conditions for the
ordinary people were grim. It was my first visit to Poland, which
had been laid waste first by the Germans and then by the Russians,
and I was shocked by the conditions and how little there was in the
shops. There were still plenty of signs of war damage but I was
amazed how the whole of the old section of the city, which had
been destroyed, had been rebuilt brick by brick by the proud Poles.
Expecting to stay a week, I had been to a Warsaw bank and had
changed a substantial number of sterling travellers' cheques into
the Polish currency, złotys, in banknotes.

The conference quickly proved to be disappointing from the news
viewpoint. So, having secured copies of all the scientific papers which
were still to be delivered, I decided to return to London after only four
days. I, therefore, went back to the bank to rechange my unwanted
złoty banknotes back into pounds but was told that, under the
Communist Polish law, that was impossible. Once the Communists
had any foreign currency in their fists they hung on to it.

I was also warned that it was illegal to take złotys out of Poland
and that they would be impounded at the airport. When I asked
what would happen to them I was assured that they would be held
there for me indefinitely, pending my possible return to Poland.
The only alternative suggested by the bank was that I could spend
the money at the airport shop on presents, which I decided to do.

The airport shop proved to be pathetic with nothing whatever on
sale but crude wooden toys and, seeing the uniformed Communist
guards eyeing my złotys, I could imagine what would happen to
them once I had handed them over. So, I went outside and found
two poorly clad, middle-aged workmen repairing a roof. I waved my
złotys at them and gestured to them to come down their ladders.
They did so, probably at record speed. Motioning them to put their
hands out, I shared the £500 of złoty banknotes between them –
'One for you. One for you' – until they had all disappeared into their
eager fists. I will never forget their astounded smiles as the wads of

notes in their hands expanded. Nor will I forget the jealous scowls on the faces of the uniformed guards who were watching me.

The international conferences provided opportunities to meet and talk with leading scientists of many nations and to learn about new fields of research. Always with an eye on what would interest our readers, I was quick to capitalise on the exciting research of Professor Nathaniel Kleitman, who, while recording the electrical brain activity of sleeping people in his laboratory in Chicago, noticed that, at certain stages of the night, the eyes oscillate rapidly under the closed lids. Further, whenever sleepers were awakened during that rapid eye movement (called 'REM sleep'), they could always remember that they had been dreaming but not if they were roused at other times when deeply asleep.

This led to the discoveries that everybody dreams, whether they can remember doing so or not, and that dreaming is an essential part of sleep's recuperative processes. Sleep deprivation, which also means dream deprivation, can be so damaging so quickly that it is used as a form of torture by interrogators trying to abstract confessions.

With most people, there are two main periods of REM dreaming, the first about three hours after falling asleep and the second a couple of hours later. Each lasts about twenty minutes and the brain can dream lightly at other times such as when falling asleep or awakening. Surgeons permitted by patients to probe their exposed brains have established the temporal lobes – two patches of grey cells located just above the ears – as the areas responsible for dreams. Electrical stimulation of those areas can induce dreaming.

As dreams have been of universal interest down the ages, the discoveries made such popular copy for my paper that in 1954 I put it all together in a book, which the *Daily Express* published, called *Sleep – and How to Get More of It*. I sent a signed copy to Lord Beaverbrook whose crisp response (which I should have foreseen) was 'You should write a book called *Sleep and How to Do with Less of It*'.

Sadly, the vogue for sleep research soon petered out, which is a pity as there is so much more to be discovered, especially about dreaming. As a writer, it would be of enormous benefit to me if my imagination could function during consciousness with the clarity

and virtuosity it displays when dreaming! While I have no architec-
tural skills, my dreams often feature splendid buildings which I have
never seen in real life. It is the same with landscapes. Sometimes I
am fishing rivers which I have never seen yet they are there in all
colourful details – the banks, the trees, the rocks, the currents. It is
the same with my game-shooting dreams. The whole landscape
is invariably fictitious. So, too, are the other people in it. My sleeping
brain invents them, too, for I rarely dream about anyone I know. I
have tried to invent people and places visually while awake but with
little success whereas in dreams they seem as real as in conscious
reality. Surely, to understand exactly how the brain does this might
increase our inventive capacity, on which the whole progress of
civilisation has depended.

Down the ages, in most civilisations, dreams have commonly
been regarded as foretelling something about the future. So much
so that, when I was young, it was common for households to possess
a 'dream book' – a cheap paperback purporting to give the meaning of many of the events imagined by the brain during sleep. I am
convinced that dreams are not prophetic, except by coincidental
accident, but I did experience one vivid dream which was to cause a
much-publicised political sensation and deep trouble for the newly
elected Prime Minister. It even had international repercussions in
France and the USA and, no doubt, in the Soviet Union.

In May 1974, I was salmon fishing on the River Dee in Scotland
with a fellow journalist, staying at a hotel in the small town of
Banchory. I used to fish hard and long, wading in the fast water,
and always ended the day very tired, taking to my bed immediately
after dinner. During one night I dreamed that the government
had, secretly, carried out a test of an H-bomb and was determined
not to reveal it. The dream was so vivid that I told my companion
about it at breakfast, saying that I would check out the possibility
with the Defence Ministry on my return to Fleet Street. As I had
written about nuclear weapons regularly since the first atom bomb
destroyed Hiroshima in 1945, and had witnessed several nuclear
blasts, I did not regard the content of my dream as particularly
unusual, especially as I always had the next nuclear 'scoop' in mind.

While I waded the glorious Dee, casting my line in every likely place, I realised that, if there had been a bomb test, it must have taken place in Nevada in the USA because, after the Christmas Island H-bomb blasts in 1957, Britain had signed an agreement not to stage any more tests in the atmosphere to eliminate radioactive fallout. In return, the US government had permitted the UK to use underground testing facilities it had built in Nevada. I also realised that any test must have been in connection with a much-improved nuclear warhead for the navy's Polaris submarine missiles.

On my return to London I consulted the chief of press relations at the Defence Ministry, who was a personal friend, and I realised, from his evasive answers, that he was disturbed to a degree which convinced me that my dream was true. I was aware that the situation was politically fraught for the Prime Minister, Harold Wilson, because Michael Foot, who had led the Aldermaston marches and thundered against nuclear weapons in Trafalgar Square, was a member of his Cabinet along with other nuclear disarmers. Having secured more information, I produced a front-page splash headlined 'Britain's Super H-Bomb Test' which prompted so much interest in Parliament that Wilson was forced to admit that a test to upgrade the H-bomb warhead of the navy's Polaris missiles had already taken place in Nevada.

He had told only three Cabinet colleagues about the test, binding them to secrecy, and had induced the US government to keep it secret, which, after my revelation, stimulated the American newspapers. The French media also had a field day because Labour MPs had, recently, been loudly objecting to nuclear tests by the French!

In 2007, secret papers about the event were released into the National Archives and publicised in newspapers. They revealed that a senior Foreign Office man, called Crispin Tickell (later Sir), had been instructed to discover the source of my information. Someone told him about my dream and in a final memo to Downing Street he had written, 'Against extra-sensory perception and the best contacts in Whitehall we are powerless.'

The 4 October 1957 was a historic day for all mankind when Russian scientists initiated the space age by launching the first

earth-orbiting satellite, Sputnik 1. Lord Beaverbrook, who had
a soft spot for the Russians having met Stalin during the Second
World War, was so keen for me to visit the Soviet rocket-launching
site that he wrote to a friend in the Kremlin requesting facilities.
The Soviet ambassador in London then visited my newspaper and
promised to do his best but with no success. My anti-Soviet attitude
over so many years could not have helped. Then, in April 1961,
Russia notched up another historic first by putting a man into orbit
round the earth – Yuri Gagarin.

The unveiling in 2011 of a London monument in memory of
Gagarin was nostalgic for me as I was among those who met and
talked with this historic pioneer on his celebratory visit to Britain
fifty years before. It was an unforgettable privilege to have shaken
the hand of this five feet two inch, unassuming 27-year-old who,
on 12 April 1961, had broken the space barrier and viewed the
whole earth from 140 miles up as nobody had ever done before.
For 108 minutes, cooped up in a helmeted space suit inside a
capsule called Vostok ('The East'), he had been literally out of
this world and had survived the extremely hazardous processes
of re-entering the atmosphere and finally landing back in his
native Russia.

Gagarin had been chosen for the flight because of his aeronautical skills, his enthusiasm and because he was small enough
to fit in the Vostok capsule, which was blasted off the earth by a
rocket. The choice had been brilliant, psychologically, because he
was loaded with natural charm enhanced by his ready smile. His
visits to foreign countries proved to be of the greatest propaganda
value to the Soviet Union and to its people.

Wearing his khaki Soviet Air Force uniform, he visited London
on 11 July 1961 and the welcome from the London crowds at the
airport and in the streets, as he stood in an open car, the personifi-
cation of courage, was rapturous. At the evening reception at the
Soviet embassy, which I was privileged to attend, he shook hands
smilingly and signed many autographs. All Cold War animosities
were forgotten in a mutual celebration of human achievement. He
also proved to be a natural at a press conference, which I attended,

answering all questions whether technical or personal through an interpreter. He ended his visit by lunching with the Queen.

Back home in Moscow he was awarded all relevant honours and, though barred from further space flights because he had established himself as such a historic figure in human history, he continued to fly aircraft and train others. Such is the all too common unfairness of life that, seven years later in 1968, when he was only thirty-four, he was killed in an air-crash. I possess a signed colour photograph of the smiling Yuri Gagarin and confess to being saddened whenever I see it.

Two years after meeting the first man into space I encountered the first woman – again a Russian, Valentina Tereshkova, a lively, good-looking and gutsy lady who had started her air career as a weekend parachutist for the kicks. Alone inside Vostok 6, and aged just twenty-six, she had endured a three-day mission, orbiting the earth forty-eight times on 16 June 1963. I shook her hand at another Soviet embassy party and am happy to report that, as I write, she is still alive. Though she had done more than Gagarin, the air of excitement at her reception was not nearly as intense. In any field of endeavour there is something very special about being first. Much later, during one of my many visits to American space stations, I was to meet Neil Armstrong, who would become the first man to walk on the moon.

It has always been magical to convert a famous name in science into a real person, even if the encounter is short, and during my long investigative career I have met and conversed with so many. They include Sir Edward Appleton, who has a layer of the atmosphere named after him; Sir John Cockcroft, famed for 'splitting' the atom; Sir James Chadwick, discoverer of the neutron; Otto Frisch, one of the founders of the atomic bomb; Sir William Penney, chief of the UK atomic bomb project; Glenn Seaborg, discoverer of plutonium; and Edward Teller, dubbed 'father of the H-bomb'. Many others will appear in my narrative.

For most journalists foreign travel means visiting foreign towns but my venues as a science reporter were often deep in foreign countryside. One such, in Austria, had all the hallmarks of a Franz

Lehar operetta. The location was on the edge of the picture-postcard village of Brunnwinkl, on Lake Wolfgang near Salzburg. I was visiting the home of Professor Karl von Frisch of Graz University, which proved to be a large, wooden chalet decorated with stag horns. The white-haired professor, in deerskin breeches and grey-edged green jacket with metal buttons and with a twinkle behind his metal-rimmed glasses, looked the part. Yet, what he was about to show me had staggered the scientific world.

He had spent six years studying exactly what goes on within the darkness of a busy beehive and had discovered that a foraging honey bee which has found a good source of nectar can inform its hive-mates exactly where it is by dancing in a particular way.

The professor began his demonstration by taking me to his ingenious glass-sided hive located under a black tent fitted with a dark-room light. He explained that, like a photographic plate, the bee's eye is insensitive to dim red rays so the insects were not disturbed as we watched their honeycomb antics. He showed me how, with extreme patience and skill, he had numbered the few hundred bees in the hive by dabbing them with a fine paint brush. Then, one morning before the bees were out, he had placed a bowl of lavender-scented synthetic nectar in front of the hive and crept into his observation tent.

The first bee to find the nectar and fly back to convert it to honey – No. 56 – broke into a lively jig on the hanging honeycomb. The professor then saw three other bees join in the dance and within a few minutes his assistant reported the trio drinking at the bowl. They too homed back to the hive and danced more workers into seeking a drink.

The professor had repeated the experiment hundreds of times, moving the nectar bowl a few yards further away each day, with the same result until the distance increased beyond 100 yards. Then the pioneer bee would dance differently on the honeycomb, capering along a wide figure of eight course and wagging its tail every time it did the straight steps across the waist of the eight. Using a stopwatch, von Frisch noted that the nearer the nectar was to the hive the faster the bee danced. When it was 100 yards away it performed forty tail-wagging runs every minute. When it was a mile away it did eighteen.

Having received the information, the other bees consistently flew to the bowl located at the exact distance tapped out by the dancer, ignoring nearer bowls they had to fly over to get there. The system was so accurate that, without knowing where his assistant had put the bowl, von Frisch could pinpoint it by timing the rhythm of the bees. For drinks located up to three miles away he was accurate to within 100 yards.

He also discovered that, from a quick glance at a patch of blue sky, a bee can tell the exact position of the sun and get its bearings on a cloudy day. If a bee danced its straight tail-wagging steps up the comb it was saying that the feeding place lay in the same direction as the sun. Dancing downwards meant that it was in the opposite direction. It could communicate the precise angle of the flight path to the sun's direction. It could even allow for the wind when dancing out its instructions.

The professor had successfully repeated all his experiment using bowls filled with wild flowers instead of synthetic nectar. I was humbled by the knowledge – since fully confirmed by others – that the mind of a creature smaller than my thumbnail is intricate to a degree which my brain finds hard to comprehend. It all made fascinating copy for my readers.

Journalists with access to the pages of mass-circulation newspapers are natural prey for conmen needing publicity for dubious inventions and I experienced my share of inventors of perpetual-motion machines and suchlike. In 1957, a story appeared in the *Daily Express* under the name of the motoring reporter, about a man who had invented a low-cost way of powering a motor car with candles. The reporter described how the inventor, with whom he had been sitting in a car, had started off on petrol, of which only a small tank was required, and had then pressed a push–pull tap in a cylinder mounted on the dashboard, announcing: 'And now we are running on candles!'

Clouds of steam were then seen belching from the exhaust but, otherwise, progress seemed normal to the astonished reporter. After driving a few miles, the driver stopped, opened the dashboard cylinder and pulled out two candle-ends which, he said, were only half consumed. 'That's all we've used,' he announced triumphantly. The reporter accepted his story and so did the editor and this revolutionary mode of transport was given prominence in the newspaper. Inevitably, the editor was bombarded with phone calls from readers who did not believe the story and, as the science reporter, I was called in for a conference. I said that the whole concept was impossible, to which the motoring reporter replied rather testily, 'This man is way ahead of the scientists!'

The editor required me to investigate and I telephoned the inventor, who lived outside London, and asked him to bring the car to our London office in Fleet Street so I could examine it. I was confident that he would decline and I would, therefore, be spared the unpleasantness of shaming the motoring reporter, who was a salmon-fishing friend. To my great surprise, the inventor agreed but explained that he could not get down until after work, which meant arriving in the dark as it was winter.

It was bitterly cold as the motoring reporter and I waited in front of the *Express* building and Fleet Street was almost deserted when the inventor appeared at about 9.30 p.m. in a cloud of steam. A quick look under the car revealed that the steam was being generated by water dripping from a tube soldered into the exhaust pipe. I traced the tube to a water tank which had no function other than the inventor's claim that it contributed through a 'jet-effect'. He then showed me the candles in the cylinder, assuring me that he had driven the whole way on them. I looked at the push–pull switch and traced its pipe to another tank under the bonnet. The tank was filled with petrol – the real source of power. The petrol was just an adjunct, the inventor claimed: it was the candles that generated the main motive force.

During our conversation the inventor volunteered that his relatives had been putting up money for the development work and that the publicity had helped to reassure them that a handsome return would be forthcoming if only the purblind scientists and entrepreneurs had the sense to latch on to his great discovery. I patted him on the back for his exceptional innovative skill and did what I could to calm down the editor, suggesting that the only sensible action was to do nothing. Reader interest quickly died away.

CHAPTER 6

SPY MAN

On entering Fleet Street as a specialist writer on defence and scientific issues I quickly discovered that the other specialists, such as the political, diplomatic and crime reporters, guarded their turf most jealously, fiercely resting any intrusion. Spies – an obvious defence issue – had always been classed as criminals and were dealt with by the crime reporter. So, when the first atomic spy, Alan May, was exposed in 1946, my contribution was restricted to a few comments. In 1950, however, when Klaus Fuchs, the ex-German scientist who had worked on the atomic bomb, was also arrested as a Russian spy, the crime reporter, Percy Hoskins, asked me to cover the Old Bailey trial because he thought it beyond his expertise, as much of the evidence would be technical. I leapt at the chance, especially as I knew that the editor already had a special interest in the case. On the day that Fuchs had been arrested I had put my head round his door to tell him that the night's big story was likely to be the discovery of an atomic spy.

'What's his name?' he asked.

'Fuchs,' I replied.

'Marvellous! I've always wanted to get that word into a headline.'

Attending the Old Bailey itself was exciting and, using information supplied by friends in the Harwell atomic research station, I produced a front-page account headlined 'Fuchs Gave Bomb to Russia', which turned out to be entirely true. I had discovered that some of Fuchs's calculations had been declassified and had obtained copies which illustrated my report. The editor was so pleased that, from then on, I was also the newspaper's spy man, which kept me busy for there was soon a succession of Russian 'Cold War' spy cases from Maclean, Burgess, Philby, Cairncross, Blunt, Houghton, Lonsdale, Vassall and Blake, to the GCHQ traitor Geoffrey Prime and others, the extent of treachery in Britain being appalling. Eventually, I became the only journalist to have covered all the spy cases as they occurred. There were also espionage aspects to what became known as the Profumo affair and the Hollis affair, about which I acquired inside knowledge from prime sources, including retired officers from MI5 such as Peter 'Spycatcher' Wright, who was to influence my later life so decisively.

A spy can be defined as a person who, surreptitiously, secures information which is secret for reasons of state security to benefit another power. All major nations use spies because, in order to have a realistic foreign policy, they need to know the true intentions of other countries which might be plotting against them. These intentions can often be learned only by securing secret documents.

A major fascination for me has been to discover why highly intelligent men, often from privileged backgrounds, could have been induced to risk everything in support of a faraway foreign country so obviously run by a vicious dictator. Piecing together the evidence, most of which has been held tightly secret, has been like constructing a giant jigsaw puzzle with most of the pieces hidden in officially inaccessible places. At ninety-nine, I continue to receive evidence from various sources, some Russian, and any day that produces a real 'nugget' (as my friends and I call a significant find) increases my determination.

The treachery of Klaus Fuchs was understandable because he had become a committed Communist in reaction to the foul Nazi philosophy from which he had fled, but the joint defection of Donald Maclean and Guy Burgess in 1951 was a watershed event in the life of the nation. Most people found it difficult to understand how, and why, two trusted Foreign Office officials with impeccably patriotic backgrounds should deliberately prejudice their careers and, consequently, have to quit their homeland for the Soviet Union, about which they knew very little.

Thanks to a journalist with French police contacts in Paris, the *Daily Express* was first with the news of the double defection as the Foreign Office had alerted the French authorities to look for the missing diplomats. I was in the Fleet Street office when the tip-off reached us, so I was on the case from the start and, in the course of inquiries over many years, was as angered by governmental attempts to cover up the catastrophe as by the details of the two traitors, as these unfolded. The ongoing attempts by government departments of so many kinds to cover up their disasters stoked my fervour to expose them and still do.

To run spies operating abroad, the nation needs a large organisation usually called the Secret Intelligence Service, which in this country is best known as MI6 because it was originally the sixth branch of Military Intelligence. MI6, which has its headquarters in London, is staffed by career *officers* who operate abroad usually under the guise of being diplomats attached to our foreign embassies. MI6 officers are very rarely able to spy themselves because they do not have access to foreign secrets. They work by recruiting people in the country to which they have been sent who do have access and are prepared to betray their homeland either for money or some other reason. Such people are known as *agents*. It would have been impossible for an MI6 officer to penetrate the Kremlin or a Russian arms factory. A dissident Russian might.

The fictional James Bond is both an MI6 officer and an agent, which rarely happens in real life. It is the agents who are the real spies and, as traitors to their own countries, take the rap if caught. The officers, who often act as couriers for their agents, picking up their information, are covered by diplomatic immunity agreements if they are caught and are simply expelled. All that is part of what has been called 'The Game of Nations', and a dirty game it is.

Dealing with MI6 in my early days in Fleet Street was especially difficult because, as part of the silly game of make-believe, it officially did not exist. (Later, I recall Harold Macmillan stating that the most regrettable event in his political life was having to admit, publicly, that MI6 was controlled by the Foreign Office!) So, my main problem in securing information about MI6's activities was the innate difficulty of securing contacts. However, I soon learned that although the career officers of MI6 have a retiring age, they tend to remain in touch with 'the office', as they call it, usually through younger colleagues who are still in business. I therefore cultivated a retired former deputy chief of MI6 called George Young, who I first met socially, and we regularly lunched together. He was most useful, as he enjoyed airing his expertise and introduced me to Maurice Oldfield, an active MI6 officer who would eventually become its chief.

The UK also has the Security Service, usually called MI5 because, originally, it was the fifth branch of Military Intelligence. Also based in London, it has officers whose duty is to protect the nation from espionage, sabotage and, now, terrorism. It tries to recruit agents working inside foreign embassies and consulates or in other organisations and posts where they have access to useful information. MI5 has a large service of watchers who keep suspects under surveillance and also uses technical devices for eavesdropping, of which phone-tapping is the simplest.

I quickly sensed that there was rivalry between MI6 and MI5 which I could exploit. Oldfield, in particular, distrusted MI5. He gave me his office phone number so that I could alert him to any developments which might affect him and I would often take the opportunity to question him. Through Maurice, I became acquainted with other officers, including his deputy Arthur 'Dickie' Franks, who succeeded him as chief and would play a major role in moulding my career after I had retired from Fleet Street.

Maurice had an unusual sense of humour. Once, when I was giving lunch to a shooting friend in Rules restaurant in London, where Maurice also happened to be lunching, he approached my table and announced: 'The time is 2.30. I am now returning to my office. I thought you would like to know.' He then departed and when I told my friend that he was the chief of the British secret service he found it hard to believe.

While lunching with Julian Amery, he introduced me to a recently retired MI6 officer, Nicholas Elliott, who was the son of a famed headmaster of Eton, where Amery had been Nicholas's fag. Nicholas proved to have been involved in several MI6 operations which would, eventually, become notorious. These included the defection of Philby to the Soviet Union and the disaster in which a frogman called Lionel Crabb, hired by Elliott to inspect, surreptitiously, the underside of a Russian cruiser paying a courtesy visit to Portsmouth, lost his life.

I lunched regularly with Elliott in London and when, after retiring from Fleet Street in 1979, I moved to the village of Kintbury in Berkshire I found that he lived close by and we regularly visited each other's homes. He was a fount of information and hilarious with it.

My contact with MI5 was limited to a few retired officers until the first public emergence in Moscow of the defector-spies Maclean and Burgess in February 1956, when my friend Admiral Thomson, secretary of the D-notice Committee, informed me that the Security Service urgently needed my help. The D- (for defence) notice Committee is a small group of government and media representatives which issues agreed advice to media chiefs intended to preserve secrecy about certain issues in the national interest. I attended his office where I met the head of MI5's legal department, Bernard Hill, who said that intelligence analysis had convinced MI5 that the two renegades had been produced so that they could be used to make further damaging allegations about the Foreign Office, and MI5 itself, whenever it suited the Kremlin to sow distrust between the US and Britain. He wanted me to publish a prominent article warning the public that whatever the defectors might say in future would be KGB lies.

He admitted that MI5 had acquired evidence of Maclean's treachery over many years and claimed that, though there was nothing legal to prevent the return of Burgess to Britain, they knew that 'he was a bloody spy'. I detected almost a sense of panic in the urgency with which Hill required the publicity – without, of course, any mention of MI5. When he had left, Thomson told me that he and the MI5 man were acting on the instructions of Roger Hollis, then MI5's deputy director general.

The *Daily Express* obliged with a front-page news story, headlined 'Beware the Diplomats!', and the admiral telephoned me to say that MI5 was delighted. In the result, the defectors were never used to make derogatory statements of any kind. (I did not, then, know that Burgess had been employed by MI5, which was clearly embarrassed by that situation.)

Sometimes, it was possible to secure intelligence information from senior politicians who acquired it in the line of duty and were prepared to leak it to me for political advantage. The most extreme example I can recall occurred in 1961 after a Briton of Dutch origin named George Blake, who confessed to spying for Russia, was tried *in camera* in London and sentenced to an unprecedented forty-two years in jail. Harold Macmillan was desperate to hide the fact that Blake had been an officer in MI6, to protect not only MI6's reputation but his own, as most of Blake's appalling crimes had been committed under his government's watch. So, when asked in Parliament to explain the 42-year sentence, Macmillan declined on 'national security' grounds. Sensing a scandal, the Labour opposition, then led by Hugh Gaitskell, persisted in demanding the facts.

To shut them up Macmillan played the 'Privy Counsellors ploy'. He told Parliament that, while he could never reveal the ultra-secret facts where they would become public, he was prepared to reveal them privately to Gaitskell and any two other Labour Privy Counsellors he might choose. While committed to total secrecy under the solemn oath taken by every Privy Counsellor, they could then assure their MPs that nothing was being withheld for party political motives but only for genuine security reasons. The totally honourable Gaitskell agreed and nominated his deputy, George Brown, and former Defence Minister Emanuel Shinwell. The three were then fully briefed about Blake's crimes which shocked them deeply.

A few days later I gave lunch to Brown at the Ecu de France and no sooner were we seated than he began to tell me the whole story, making it clear that he wanted it published without, of course, reference to himself. Blake, who had been based in West Berlin, had given the KGB the names of more than forty agents working for Britain abroad and many had been rounded up and shot. He had passed on copies of hundreds of top secret documents.

He had betrayed details of a 350-foot long tunnel which the Americans had driven under the Russian sector of Berlin to plug into Soviet telephone cables.

All the details duly appeared on the *Daily Express* front page on 20 June 1961, with forty little men in black coats drawn over the headline to ram home the enormity of Blake's treachery.

MI5 quickly named Brown to Macmillan as the culprit responsible for what the Prime Minister regarded as an unforgivable breach of confidence. Later, when I asked Brown how he felt about having betrayed his own oath of secrecy, he was unrepentant, arguing that loyalty to his party, which had stood to gain by discrediting the Macmillan administration, over-rode the loyalty required by his oath.

He took the same stance concerning his betrayal of my chief contact, Sir Frederick Brundrett. After a series of allegations by Brown, in public and in Parliament, that Britain's independent nuclear deterrent was so insignificant that it was a waste of money, Brundrett asked me to tell Brown that he was prepared to give him the 'true facts of atomic life'. Brown agreed and I brought them together over lunch where he learned the impressive size and power of the bomb stockpile. However, the gratitude which he then expressed did not stop him from making political capital in Parliament when he asked Macmillan if he was aware that a senior Whitehall figure was leaking the nation's most vital atomic secrets! Fortunately, the wily Fred had cleared his action with Macmillan, who had agreed to it in the hope of silencing Brown and his senior colleagues. I was so angry by his betrayal of Fred that I went to Parliament, where Brown duly appeared in the Lobby. When I told him he was a shit his response was: 'We are no bigger shits here than you lot in Fleet Street. We eccentrics should stick together, not fall out!'

All power corrupts – meaning that it corrupts judgement – and nowhere is this more true than in the field of politics, especially among those who have reached the pinnacle of power or are hotly in pursuit of it. Brown eventually became Foreign Secretary, one of the greatest offices of state, and we remained in touch.

As an investigative journalist I used every legitimate device to secure exclusive news but I steered clear of any behaviour that could be construed as illegal. There was a strict office rule that we must never pay for news, if only because it would attract peddlers of false information. Nor did I ever attempt to bribe any official unless an expensive meal could be interpreted as a bribe. There were no mobile telephones, which have now made hacking into private calls so easy. However, I have had personal experience in that unpleasant field because, for most of the last sixty years, my own phones have been tapped by the security authorities and may still be.

Many people suspect that their telephone is tapped when they hear clicks and other anomalous sounds. I *know* my phones have been tapped because some of those senior civil servants responsible for arranging it have warned me so after they retired. Further, some of my contacts have paid, heavily, for giving me confidential information on the phone. One who paid a savage price, in the early 1950s, was Air Commodore Finlay Crerar, a distinguished retired RAF officer who had been given the honorary post of inspector general of the RAF and performed his duty faultlessly, save for one mistake. Over the telephone, he told me that two RAF volunteer organisations were to be merged – a harmless item so dull that I did not publish it. When he retired from the unpaid post he was called to the presence of the chief of the RAF, who had just received instructions from the Prime Minister, then Clement Attlee, that my friend was not to be awarded the knighthood, which was usually bestowed, because he had leaked to me.

I called in a contact who had previously worked for the security branch of the Post Office, which organised the taps, to examine my phone. He showed me an extra wire which had been installed after I had reported my phone out of order. The engineers who had deliberately put the phone out of order came to repair it and had surreptitiously installed the wire. Today everything is much more high-tech. To tap a telephone all that MI5, the Cabinet Office or any other major department has to do is to apply for a Home Office Warrant (HOW) to do so and these are rarely refused. The security branch then puts the required telephone out of order and its special engineers come and fix it. These days they can really 'fix' it by inserting a 'combined bug and tap' so that the mouthpiece, which is a sensitive microphone, remains alive when the telephone is hung up. This allows all conversations in the room to be recorded at a special exchange. All the extension phones – even those at the bedside – are similarly fixed so the eavesdroppers hear some fruity stuff, as the renegade MI5 officer Peter Wright told me when he first exposed his secrets to me at his retirement home in Tasmania in 1980.

While my wife and I were away on that trip, Post Office engineers visited my house and told the housekeeper that my phone was out of order and that they had come to fix it. Unwittingly, she let them in and they spent a lot of time crawling about in the loft. Whatever they installed is still there. It has not prevented me from extracting embarrassing official secrets and publishing them.

To reduce the hacking opportunities of the 'authorities', I have never possessed a mobile phone. (When I am fishing with my daughter Pat, who has many business interests, her pocket phone demands attention several times in any morning session. I could never entertain such sacrilege.)

I suppose it was inevitable that, once it became clear from my newspaper reports that I had access to classified information, Soviet intelligence might try to recruit me. That happened in 1961 as a result of my friendship with a Tory MP called Henry Kerby, who held the seat of Arundel with a huge majority. A big man with a bald, cannonball head and rubbery features, he had been born in Russia and was fluent in the language, visiting Moscow frequently in the interests of East–West trade. More than any MP I ever met, he was afflicted by the delusion that when he had said something he had done something and he was forever submitting written parliamentary questions which were rarely answered and tabling motions which were never debated so that, at election time, he could show his constituents how busy he had been.

After Gagarin's amazing performance in space, Lord Beaverbrook agitated for me to go to Russia to visit a space research station, but no visa was forthcoming from the Soviet authorities even though the Russian ambassador visited the *Express* office and assured me that I would receive one. So I raised the issue when lunching with Kerby. Shortly afterwards, I was telephoned by a man who introduced himself as Anatoli Strelnikov, the press attaché at the Soviet embassy. He asked me to lunch and I joined him at a Greek restaurant in Soho. Strelnikov was an impressive man, tall and well built with a pleasant Slavic face and large ears. He dressed well, even carrying a rolled umbrella. His questions quickly made it clear that he was interested in my Whitehall sources of defence and intelligence information so I reported my situation to MI5, which urged me to continue to see the Russian and report everything he asked me. I was introduced to a senior MI5 officer, Michael McCaul, whom I then met regularly. McCaul said that Strelnikov was a senior KGB officer posing as a 'diplomat' and MI5 wanted him expelled from Britain if reason could be found.

I continued to meet the Russian for lunches in London and he visited my home in Surrey but nothing untoward occurred until, later in 1961, I was approached by McCaul with an exclusive newspaper story which, he explained, would do MI5 and the nation a valuable service. He had a series of cards which were case-records of men and women who, while visiting Moscow, had been suborned by KGB agents into giving them secret information. He then explained that Britain was shortly to stage a big electronics exhibition in Moscow and many of those taking part in it worked for firms involved with secret defence contracts and, so, could be prime targets for recruitment, by bribes or blackmail by the KGB, having been induced into blackmailable situations, mainly sexual, which had been surreptitiously photographed. He, therefore, wanted me to issue a warning on MI5's behalf by printing a few of the case-records, allegedly from MI5's files, to publicise what the KGB might try to do. They were so interesting that I did so in a large feature given much prominence. I was quickly asked to lunch by Strelnikov, who complained about my disclosures, which he said, rather menacingly, were 'terrible for peace'. When he asked me why I wrote such things I explained that it was what Beaverbrook Newspapers paid me to do.

'Whatever they pay you we will pay you more,' he replied.

'To do what?' I asked.

'Write for us. Work for us,' he responded.

Then, when he came to pay the bill, he took a bundle of bank-notes out of his wallet and flicked them at me saying: 'Don't forget! Work for us.'

I quickly reported this invitation to treachery to McCaul. 'Marvellous!' he declared. 'We've been waiting for this dangerous bastard to make a mistake. Get your editor to complain to the Foreign Office in writing and we will get Strelnikov expelled.' Sadly, the editor declined, reminding me that it had taken him years to open an office in Moscow and that the Kremlin would respond by shutting it down.

I had been dangerous for Strelnikov to know but not quite dangerous enough. He remained in post and even did a further tour of duty here. I saw him once again, in 1963, at the Soviet embassy reception for Valentina Tereshkova. He avoided me in the crowd. I never made Moscow.

I remained in touch with Kerby and we visited each other's homes. I was aware that he had no respect for his Prime Minister, Harold Macmillan, but was astonished, later, to discover that he hated his own party so much that he was functioning as a spy for the Labour Party, sending damaging written reports to Harold Wilson and George Wigg when they were in opposition. Years later, when Wilson's political secretary Marcia Williams (now Lady Falkender) and I were planning to write a book together, she sent me a thick wad of Kerby's letters which usually began 'Dear Guv'.

It became clear that what motivated Kerby's treachery was the Tory governments' failure to give him any kind of honour. He was desperate to be dignified by a title and in one of his letters, sent shortly before a general election, he told Harold Wilson that he was prepared to pass on 'all the Conservative Party's election secrets' for the promise of a life peerage. When that failed, he reduced his requirement to a knighthood. He died, still plain Mr, in 1971.

Later, when making a speech at a function in Arundel Castle, I revealed these facts but Kerby's faithful former constituents refused to believe them.

CHAPTER 7

MEDICAL MAN

When I joined Fleet Street, the popular newspapers restricted their medical reporting to what could be found in two weekly magazines, *The Lancet* and the *British Medical Journal*, which both became available on Thursday evenings. The *Daily Express* employed what was described as a 'tame doctor', who for a small fee came in and marked the possible 'stories' in the journals which were then given to any handy reporter to write.

Always a glutton for work, I volunteered to replace the tame doctor at no extra charge to the paper. As a biologist who had studied human physiology and anatomy, I had no problem understanding the medical articles or in writing about them. In those days doctors were forbidden to speak to newspapers as that could be interpreted as advertising themselves, which was a professional offence for which they might have to answer to the General Medical Council. However, they always welcomed publicity about their discoveries and experiences when these were openly published in the medical literature.

I knew that there were many other journals specialising in different medical branches and, realising that the Royal College of Surgeons, with its famous museum which I had visited as a student, was just round the corner from Fleet Street, in Lincoln's Inn Fields, I made friends with the secretary there. He gave me permission to use the fine reference library where all the specialist medical journals were on display. I also found there the *Medical Bulletin*, a Health Ministry publication intended for doctors only, which often contained an important announcement. So, if ever I was hard up for a story, or as a matter of routine, I simply went to the college and found one.

To save time, I induced the *Express* management to take out subscriptions for the most productive magazines, such as the *Journal of the American Medical Association* and the *British Heart Journal*, gradually expanding the list to more than 100. So, often, there were journals on my desk when I reached the office. When, as was usual, I read them on the evening train home, I would tear out the articles I needed and throw the magazines on the luggage rack. I was told, more than once, that when I had alighted other passengers would scramble for them.

I also sought review copies of medical books (mentioned in the journals) and, through my reports in the newspaper, made friends with several famous surgeons, physicians and medical researchers who, privately, enjoyed the publicity. Among the first of these was a man whose chance discovery changed the world.

Great men do not obey the laws of optics – the closer you get to them the *smaller* they become and among the many truly great men I have been privileged to meet through my journalistic career, nobody displayed this feature more than the quietly spoken Scotsman to whom everyone, everywhere, owes an ever-continuing debt – Alexander (Alec) Fleming, who discovered penicillin. Not only did his discovery lead to the conquest of previously untreatable diseases like pneumonia, bronchitis, scarlet fever and septicaemia, but it opened up the whole field of antibiotics, which are basic to modern medicine and have spawned a massive pharmaceutical industry.

I first interviewed Fleming in the small green-tiled room which had been the bacteriological laboratory in St Mary's Hospital, Paddington, where his good fortune – and ours – resulted from what had, probably, been a clumsy mistake. While serving as an Army Medical Corps captain in the First World War, Fleming had seen the horrors of wounds infected by the *Staphylococcus* bacterium (known as 'the staph of death') and was hoping to find some way of countering it. He cultured the bacteria in round glass dishes containing a nutrient jelly on which they could feed, producing a spreading colony. Each dish was fitted with a glass cover to prevent contamination by any other bacteria in the air.

Noted for his untidiness, Fleming had pushed several culture dishes into a corner before leaving for a break in September 1928 and, either then or earlier, the glass lid on one of them had flipped open. Then, through the open laboratory window, a spore of a mould had drifted in and settled on the jelly. Recovering his dishes on his return, Fleming had been annoyed to see that one of them was visibly infected by a mould which was spreading rapidly. Then he also noticed that wherever the mould colony touched the edges of the bacterial colony there was only clear space. Something in the mould was killing the bacteria!

He identified the mould as a common species called *Penicillium notatum* and called the substance penicillin. In 1929 he dutifully reported his findings in a scientific journal where it generated little interest. As he lacked the facilities to extract penicillin in quantity and to carry out tests on animals and then humans, his discovery remained unused until the Second World War, when others developed its colossal potential.

After being knighted, awarded the Nobel Prize and lauded everywhere, he remained unpretentious and unspoiled. When, years later, I suggested to him that he had changed the world he simply smiled, fiddled with his red bow-tie and said softly, 'I suppose I did.'

In 1953, a widower, he married a Greek lady microscopist, with whom I became friendly, and when he died of a heart attack in 1955 aged seventy-three, she invited me to write his official biography. The publisher wanted it so quickly that I would have needed six months' leave of absence from my paper, to which Lord Beaverbrook would not agree as so much was happening in the Cold War. The honour went to a famous French author, André Maurois, who made a disappointing job of it. Still, it was an honour in itself to have been asked. Every time I am treated with an antibiotic for my recurrent chest infection I thank that wonderful Scot.

Expanding my medical reporting steadily increased my scope for meeting unusually interesting people, which, in retrospect, was the greatest reward for my efforts. The most pleasant surgeon I met was Russell Brock, who pioneered operations inside the heart and was one of the first to use a heart-lung machine. He had a delightful wife, Germaine, and I was as pleased for her as for him when, in 1965, he was awarded a peerage.

The most unpleasant was a surgeon called Dickson Wright, also of St Mary's Hospital, and whose daughter, Clarissa, is well known on television as a celebrity chef and personality. My first association with him was indirect through one of the fattest men I have ever seen, whom I met salmon fishing on the Scottish Dee. Eventually he became so enormous that his abdominal fat had to be removed by surgery. As the operation was, then, so unusual, Dickson Wright, who performed it, had it recorded on film which I watched as he explained it in a lecture at the Royal College of Surgeons. My interest was, of course, increased by my knowing the patient.

Commenting as he did it, Dickson Wright cut away the fat in one enormous slab which was gradually hoisted aloft by a butcher's meat hook attached to a rope. Eventually, the slab was taken out of the operating theatre on a large stretcher. Dickson Wright, who because of his caustic wit was in demand as an after-dinner speaker, commented hilariously as he cut away and the audience for the film could not help laughing in spite of the patient's dangerous predicament. The following salmon season I met the patient, who was hale and hearty but extraordinary to look at, as one could not help noticing the enormous, now shallow, area left by the missing fat.

Dickson Wright's most unpleasant feature was a sadistic streak. If he came into the operating theatre and found that the very long line of scalpels, probes and other surgical instruments were not in the exact order he demanded, he would deposit the lot on the floor so that they all had to be resterilised.

A surgeon I recall with especial admiration was Ian Aird, a smiling Scot who was Professor of Surgery at the Postgraduate Medical School at Hammersmith, which I often visited. He drove himself relentlessly on behalf of his patients, as he continued to do in the Second World War when he served in the Royal Army Medical Corps in the Libyan desert. In one night, he operated twenty-two times in his tented operating theatre. As he was unwilling to retreat he was once overrun by a German tank column. His captors asked him to operate on a senior German officer who had been badly wounded in the chest. The wound was so severe that the operation did not succeed but the German commander, Rommel, thanked Aird personally.

Aird had a burning zeal to raise the prestige of British medicine and, in 1953, when he heard that 'Siamese' (conjoined) twin girls had been born in Nigeria he had them flown to Britain for possible separation. He found that they shared just one liver but thought they could be separated and be spared an otherwise ghastly life. One twin, Boko, survived to live a normal life but the other, Tomu, collapsed and died because she was found to have no adrenal glands. The operation attracted enormous publicity, with some people accusing Aird of having killed Tomu.

In 1962, I took him out to lunch and he seemed smilingly composed, as usual. Shortly afterwards, however, after a four-week work marathon he committed suicide by taking a drug overdose in a fit of severe depression. He was fifty-seven.

I am grateful for my memory of having met the 'father of plastic surgery', Sir Harold Gillies, known to his colleagues as 'Giles'. Our meeting arose out of a big newspaper review I did of his book *The Principles and Art of Plastic Surgery*, published in 1957 when he was seventy-four. He had specialised in repairing facial injuries in both World Wars and had invited his cousin Archibald McIndoe (later Sir) to join his practice where he was to earn the title 'chief skinner'.

Gillies's book was highly technical but was also the story of men and women who did not relax their grip on life though they were so disfigured that it seemed to hold nothing for them. Above all, it was the account of how Sir Harold and a few disciples learned, by trial and error, to make new noses, ears, eyelids and, in many cases, whole faces. Unwittingly, he destroyed the legend that the surgeon can function well only by being aloof to suffering for he was, clearly, as sensitive as the men and women on whom he carried out his near-miracles. As I recall stating at the time, it was hard for the reader to know what to admire most in his graphic account – the courage of the patients, the skill of the surgeons or the sheer durability of the human spirit.

Through such contacts, some of which developed into friendships, I was able to extend my medical experience by watching a few surgical operations and a childbirth. The most famous physician I encountered was Lord Horder, who, commenting on the media's obsession with 'saving lives', advised me that 'a doctor's prime function is not the saving of life. It is the relief of suffering.' After witnessing so much of it, he told me, 'We live by accident.' He also practised his belief that one should 'never deprive a patient of hope'.

In 1955, aged eighty-four, he suffered himself with a severe coronary thrombosis and, true to form, calmly delivered a running commentary to the doctors who had been called to his bedside. They were astounded by his professional detachment as, with a weakening voice, he described his symptoms in his usual consulting-room manner. All his accumulated art was brought to bear to produce his opinion that his chances of surviving the day were negligible. As usual, his diagnosis proved accurate.

One of the most distinguished gynaecologists of his day, Roger de Vere, was a regular fishing and shooting friend of mine and we often met socially. I sometimes witnessed the slight embarrassment of ladies to whom I introduced him, only to find that he was already acquainted with them rather intimately.

Grey Walter of the Burden Neurological Institute in Bristol was involved in many aspects of brain research. I visited him regularly and watched and reported on his pioneer experiments on patients with epilepsy and other neurological disorders. I vividly remember their sharp, jerking reaction to stroboscopic light and am reminded of Grey every time I hear the, now regular, warning that a TV programme contains flash photography.

As an offshoot of his brain research, the ingenious Grey built two tortoise-like robots (called Elmer and Elsie) which seemed to have some capacity to think. Powered by electric batteries, they would roam around a room and when they felt that they were becoming short of energy would, without further instruction, find their way to a power point, plug into it and disconnect themselves when recharged. It was uncanny to watch.

Tragically, Grey suffered a serious injury to his own brain in a motorcycle accident and never fully recovered before his premature death in 1977.

On the political front of medicine I established regular contact with leaders of the British Medical Association (BMA), which was, effectively, the doctors' trade union. When I entered Fleet Street in 1946, the battle between the Labour Health Minister, Aneurin Bevan, the son of a Welsh miner, who was determined to establish a National Health Service, and most doctors, who bitterly opposed him, was in full flood. Having met him, I could see why the Welshman won – he was a man of great determination, sincerity and charm. At a lunch I attended he was asked about an unusual political situation – with the rapid expansion of the economy after the war there was a general shortage of labour. I will never forget his answer – 'Too few men chasing too many jobs is a headache but too many men chasing too few jobs is a heartache. I'd rather have the headache than the heartache.'

Lord Beaverbrook had taken a liking to my medical reporting and we often talked about it over the lunches to which he, regularly, invited me at his country home. One day he asked me in his peremptory way, 'Do you know what Addison's Disease is?'

'Yes,' I replied. 'It is a disease of the adrenal glands and one of its symptoms is that it darkens the skin and makes it look permanently sun-tanned.'

'Well, President John Kennedy has got it!' he said. Then seeing my immediate interest, because it was soon after Kennedy had been elected, he added, 'But you are not to write anything about it.' I knew that he liked Kennedy and suspected that he had been told about his ailment in confidence.

In pursuit of news, my editor encouraged me to attend medical conferences worldwide and particularly in the United States where, over the years, I visited many cities and made many friends. My medical travelling was extended in the 1950s when there was a rapid growth of interest in the universal process of ageing, the study of which was called gerontology and led to the founding of a British Society of Gerontology by an Oxford University scientist called Vladimir Korenchevsky – a journalist's dream of a name for a headline.

Korenchevsky, a delightful old man with whom I quickly made friends, was soon holding international conferences where I listened to all manner of ideas being discussed, the most interesting being the age-old riddle – why women have an average life-span about five years longer than men. Many reasons were put forward to explain the female advantage. First, it was argued that, childbirth excepted, males faced far more life-threatening hazards. In many work sectors, such as mining, the construction industries, the chemical industry and oil exploration, not only were some fatalities inevitable but many men acquired illnesses, especially to the lungs, which shortened their life-span. Men did far more driving and suffered far more fatalities and injuries on the roads. There was also the hazard of war, which, as two World Wars had shown, took terrible toll of men. The lifetime responsibility of being the bread-winner – again, the standard situation then – might be a factor. Excessive drinking and smoking were then much commoner in men. It was even argued that sexual activity took more out of men; all these facts affecting the average life-span statistics. Indeed, it seemed that if a woman wanted to avoid becoming a little old lady living on her own her only solution was to marry a man five years younger than herself, when the common practice in those days was to marry an older man.

Then a young American scientist had a brilliant idea. He managed to secure the life-span statistics from several monasteries and nunneries and compared them. Clearly, the monks were immune to almost all the hazards facing men in the outside world while the nuns were free from the childbirth risk. So the life expectancy of monks and nuns should be about the same? Not so. The figures clearly showed that the female advantage was still there and nobody has yet explained it. (Damned unfair, chaps, but there it is! I can hear the female response – 'There has to be some reward!')

With little progress to report and Korenchevsky's demise in 1959, interest in gerontology faded but I managed to glean some advantage from my experience. I decided to examine the social and political consequences of the discovery of a simple pill which would stave off ageing and to project them in a novel – my first. With everyone demanding the pill, the consequences were so catastrophic (witness the recent angry response here and in France to just a two-year postponement of retirement) that I called the book, published in 1965, *Not with a Bang*. The title was taken from a poem by T. S. Eliot (who kindly gave me written permission to use it): 'This is the way the world ends / Not with a bang but a whimper.'

My medical reports caught the eye of Bill Hinks, the managing director of the best-known advertising agency in London at that time, J. Walter Thompson, which had its headquarters in Berkeley Square. Hinks had also been at the Darlington Grammar School and, sensing that I might be a source of ideas for advertisements, offered me a consultancy at an attractive fee. I doubted that my editor would agree but, as J. Walter Thompson placed many of their advertisements in the *Express* papers, he welcomed the idea. For two or three years I paid for my keep with ideas and copy but, as with later consultancies I acquired, the deal lapsed because the firms failed to consult me.

Every working day on a national morning newspaper, the staff face a mass of blank pages which have to be filled within about nine hours. So, as a rule, the most popular journalist of the day is the one who breezes in early with a hot scoop that will dominate the front page and provide a commanding headline. There was one day in 1954, however, when I did exactly that and was detested for it – not just by the editor and most of the reporters but by the whole of management and, especially, the advertising department.

One of my highly placed contacts had given me advance information about some awesome news which was about to be published by the Medical Research Council. An epidemiologist called Richard Doll, then unknown to the general public, had secured the cooperation of 40,000 doctors who had been providing him with details of their personal habits and medical statistics. His study had already shown – beyond question – that regular cigarette-smoking caused lung cancer and also increased the risk of heart disease. With a large proportion of British adults then smoking cigarettes, this was news of national and, indeed, international importance because the habit was worldwide.

As the editor and almost all his night staff who worked against the clock to 'put the paper to bed' each evening were chain-smokers, my news was personally disastrous. The idea of giving our eleven million-plus readers, most of whom were likely to be smokers, such news at the breakfast table was preposterous. And what about the revenue from the paper's cigarette advertisements? The immediate response was to reject Doll's finding as utter rubbish. There was a saying that there were 'lies, damn lies and statistics' and all Doll had was statistics. The decision was taken to 'spike' my story, which was the saying for dismissing it as nonsense. (My 'holier-than-thou' position was not helped by the fact that I had never smoked a cigarette in my life.)

All I could do was to warn my editor that the story would break anyway and that the government would have to respond if only because the taxes levied on tobacco almost exactly paid for the health service in those days. I urged them, at least, to start planning for the days when advertising cigarettes would be banned by law – a suggestion that produced guffaws. It was a classic example of the adage that, if the message is bad, shoot the messenger.

The tobacco and advertising industries mounted massive campaigns of resistance which, of course, were supported by most of the smokers but, as the medical evidence mounted, successive governments felt forced to intervene with actions which, progressively, banned tobacco advertisements from the media, which eventually had to accept the facts. Currently only about 26 per cent of the adult population smokes and the places where it is lawful for them to do so have been progressively reduced.

In the process, Richard Doll was knighted and honoured in many other ways and when he died in 2005, aged ninety-two, was rightly credited with having preserved countless millions of lives world-wide. His finding has been one of the key factors in the remarkable rise in longevity. (In Russia, where smoking remains rampant, the average male expectation is fifty-seven, though vodka plays its part.)

With the effects now undeniable and widely publicised, I find it extraordinary that anybody smokes but, as a Yorkshire saying has it, 'there's nowt so queer as folk'. While in our village corner shop recently, I watched an intelligent-looking young lady part with more than £6 for a small carton bearing the warning, in large black letters, SMOKING KILLS!

Having survived my army wartime service and taken a few personal risks in remote places to secure my news, it is ironic that my most dangerous moment should have arisen while on a life-saving mission in line of my duty as a medical reporter.

The *Daily Express* had staged the first post-war air show, the star exhibit being the flying car, an American four-wheeled vehicle carrying, on its roof, wings and a propeller which could all be quickly screwed on. My editor hired it as a promotion stunt to assist reporters in carrying out assignments but, as the machine could take off and land only at an airport, there were few that could not be accomplished more quickly by road or rail. After I had published an article about the new antibiotic streptomycin, I told the editor that a doctor in Stafford Infirmary had telephoned to ask me if I could possibly secure some for a child who was critically ill with tubercular meningitis and that, by chance, a benevolent American had offered me a small supply. I was, immediately, detailed to deliver it by flying car. The date was 14 July 1948.

The journey from Fleet Street to Croydon airport was uneventful, though the little squat vehicle with its four wheels on struts caught many eyes. After the wings and propeller had been fitted, the flight to Wolverhampton airport was also without incident as the driver-pilot, Bob Fulton, an American who was also the inventor and owner, followed the roads and railway lines from low altitude, using a map. While travelling the fifteen miles to the hospital, with the wings and propeller left at the airport, a heater caught fire and had to be doused with an extinguisher.

I delivered the medicine, phoned my report to London and we returned to Wolverhampton airport. As it was a lovely summer's evening, Fulton decided to fly back though members of the Wolverhampton Flying Club strongly advised against it, pointing out that, as his radio did not work on British frequencies, night flight was not legally permissible. Fulton telephoned Croydon airport, which promised to put up a searchlight when they heard us circling overhead.

We had not been airborne long when night began to fall and I realised that Fulton was unsure of the route, especially as he kept tapping his compass, which was misbehaving. 'You can't see the roads here,' he complained. 'In the States there are so many cars on the roads at night that you can navigate as easily as by day.' I pointed out that petrol rationing was still in force. When he told me we had fuel for only three hours' flying I suggested that we should get down while we could still see. 'Yeah, yeah, let's do that! Pick a flat landing field,' he urged, while he watched for electric cables and telephone wires.

In the gloom I spotted a field which looked flat as a billiard table. Bob throttled back and switched off the ignition as we both realised it was a field of standing wheat! After ploughing through fifty yards of it the whole machine turned on its back and slithered to a standstill with all four wheels pointing skywards.

Fulton had the only access to the seat belt encompassing us both and took time undoing it because of the weight of our upside-down bodies. Meanwhile, the fuel tank was leaking and I could feel petrol draining down my neck while wondering about that defective heater. Oddly, considering the danger, I felt no fear – just curiosity about what might happen. I recall having felt the same when, through a window in my wartime office near the Arsenal, I saw a diving flying bomb which looked poised to hit our building but, in the result, demolished a house in the next street. It would seem to have been sensible to be afraid but, perhaps because in both cases I was powerless, fear would have served no purpose.

(Those memories remind me of an occasion when I witnessed the reaction of another person facing a likely violent end. It was at an air show at Farnborough in 1970 and I was on a balcony with my binoculars trained on the pilot of a tiny auto-gyro, which was doing twists and turns at a height of only about 200 feet and about that same distance away. The pilot was a well-known auto-gyro expert called 'Pee Wee' Judge, then forty-eight years old. While his clever antics were drawing loud applause, a sudden gust of wind drove the single rotor against the central support column. The twisted rotor ceased to turn, making a crash inevitable, and I remember crying, 'My God, he's gone!' I watched the pilot as he realised what had happened and what must occur with a few seconds. He seemed composed, accepting the situation as totally beyond his control as he began his fatal vertical fall.)

Fulton and I had crashed the flying car near Leamington and the kindly farmer put us up for the night. Next morning Fulton made arrangements for the machine to be salvaged and returned to the US. No local newspaper got wind of the accident and the *Daily Express* never revealed it. Not a single reader inquired why the much-vaunted flying car had disappeared.

Fulton blamed me, totally, for the calamity. Particularly, he bemoaned my lack of confidence in that searchlight which he was sure he would have found. I still believe that I saved both our lives.

CHAPTER 8

UNFORGETTABLE ENCOUNTERS

While my attention would remain focused on Whitehall and Westminster until my retirement from Fleet Street in 1979, my life was regularly enlivened by exciting experiences in foreign countries. The first, in 1947, was in conquered Germany where two captured scientists held the answer to two riddles which still bugged me and everyone else I knew in the atomic and rocket spheres.

The effective founder of the atomic age was a German scientist called Otto Hahn, who in January 1939 publicly reported that certain atoms of the metal uranium spontaneously explode, releasing large amounts of energy. His discovery spawned immediate speculation that, if enough of these special atoms could be collected and concentrated in one lump, it would explode with enormous force – an atomic bomb.

After the Second World War broke out eight months later, the British and American authorities feared that the Nazis would try to build such a bomb and, by obliterating London, not only win the war but dominate much of the world through threat of its further use. Their fears were exacerbated by the fact that one of the finest brains working in the atomic field, Werner Heisenberg, was German and would, surely, do all he could to help his country to victory. It was fear of a Nazi atomic bomb built by such brilliant pioneers that drove the UK and the US to devote all available resources to develop the weapon before the Germans did.

So, after victory in Europe, the first riddle that needed answering was: why had Germany failed to produce the bomb? The second was: had the V2 rocket been intended to carry an atomic bomb warhead? Research among old friends told me that both Hahn and

Heisenberg were being held in an institute in Göttingen, mainly to ensure that they were not snatched by the Russians. No journalist had interviewed them so, in September 1947, I visited them accompanied by an officer of the Allied Control Commission who urged me to ensure that I, a non-smoker, was equipped with cigarettes, which were then scarce in Germany.

The four of us were provided with lunch and there I sat with two Nobel Prize winners prepared to tell me the story of the bomb-that-never-was.

Both were friendly and unassuming as they explained that Hitler had been keen to develop an atomic bomb and they had been prepared to assist him but, with so many resources already involved in building V1 flying bombs and giant V2 rockets, which the Führer believed would devastate London anyway, he decided that no atomic weapon could be produced in time to affect the outcome of the war. So Heisenberg and his team concentrated on building 'atomic engines' which could produce badly needed power to drive machinery.

On a page torn from an old exercise book, Heisenberg drew the prototype 'engine' for me. It was an aluminium tub about six feet wide and six feet high, surrounded by graphite. Laid on top of the tub were five rods from which hung wires, each bearing two-inch cubes of ordinary uranium like beads on a string. The plan was to pour in the scarce substance 'heavy water' and, as the level rose, the cubes would give off heat which could produce steam. Controlling the level of the heavy water would control the engine. It was a great idea but the scientists never got the tub more than four-fifths full because Allied agents sabotaged a huge hydro-electric plant in Norway which was Germany's only source of the precious liquid.

As Heisenberg finished his sketch (which later adorned the front page of my newspaper) the officer reminded me of the cigarettes, which I hurriedly produced. 'Thank you,' Hahn said, after lighting his fag and inhaling deeply, 'for a cigarette I talk much better.' Then, waving his hand grandiosely, he added, 'For a cigar I talk magnificent!'

Sadly, for history, I had no cigar.

Winston Churchill counselled 'magnanimity in victory' but I have to confess that I felt little sorrow or sympathy when I extended my visit to several other German cities, including Berlin. Having witnessed what the Luftwaffe, the V1 flying bombs and the V2 rockets had done to London and around it, I could not feel sorrow when I saw members of the self-styled 'Master Race' picking their way among acres of rubble, some of them wearing trousers made of old sacks. 'Serve them right!' was my automatic reaction. When my German driver moaned '*Alles kaput!*' as we drove down one shattered Berlin thoroughfare after another, I could feel no sympathy. (He had served in Hitler's Wehrmacht.)

To visit Hitler's bunker where he had, allegedly, shot himself gave me quite a thrill as did collecting a memento – a thick piece of glass from his shattered Chancellery, where he had so often threatened and raved. But, perhaps, my most unalloyed pleasure was to secure some personal reparations by fishing in a private lake belonging to Krupp, the German steel and armaments dynasty, whose guns, tanks and ammunition factories had made Hitler's attacks possible.

The Krupp family had made an angler's paradise in a picturesque hilly area by damming a stream to form a long lake. Accompanied by an army friend, then serving in the Allied Control Commission, and using borrowed tackle, I relieved the lake of some of its large rainbow trout. Krupp's keeper, who soon spotted us, did not like it but simply shrugged resignedly when I told him that I was a British officer (without declaring that I was, by then, a civilian).

Atomic weapons have never ceased to fascinate me. In 1953, I witnessed the test of an all-British atomic bomb, codenamed Operation Totem, in an area of South Australian desert called Emu Field. We had been flown there from our base near Adelaide arriving at 4 a.m., when we were conducted to a tent and offered a breakfast of curry and tea, with whisky for those who wanted it!

Overly concerned about our safety, the scientists had located us so far from the bomb that all we saw was the very distant flash and the mushroom cloud, making the exercise rather disappointing. However, it did give me my first opportunity to meet the extraordinary brain behind the British bomb, William Penney. I had written much about him, provided by others, and he criticised me, good-naturedly, for leaking information about his work.

What I did not know then – as Penney probably did – was that the highest security authority in the land, the Joint Intelligence Committee, had tried to prevent my presence at the test. A recently released JIC document has revealed that the JIC concluded that 'Mr Chapman Pincher's presence at the test would, undoubtedly, be viewed with grave concern by the Americans'. An approach was then made to the *Daily Express* requesting that someone else should be sent instead. It was rejected.

I did not see any emus on Emu Field but was astonished by the number of wild parrots, the most numerous of the large species being a beautifully plumaged white bird with a rose-pink head called the galah. I had first encountered it when visiting the Woomera rocket range in the 'outback' desert area of South Australia to witness the firing of an early long-range missile. It was there I learned that, unlike most parrots which are high in intelligence, it was widely regarded in Australia as being so short in that respect that it was common to call another person 'You stupid galah!'

As Emu Field was too remote, the UK and Australian governments built a testing site in a more accessible area called Maralinga, also in South Australia, and in 1956 I flew again to Adelaide, where observers were to be based and briefed for what was called Operation Buffalo – the test of a more advanced British A-bomb. When all was ready at Maralinga, we would be flown there at short notice to our observation post. We were also warned that there might be delays because many Australians were objecting to the contamination of their land by British-made radioactive fallout. The winds, therefore, had to be such that no fallout could reach populated parts of the country.

Having received an 'All ready!' signal, we flew into Maralinga and moved to the observation post from which, through binoculars, we could see a tall steel tower on which the bomb was mounted. I was surprised to see a cloud of large birds circling the tower and landing on it. We were told that they were galahs, which, being an agricultural pest, were dispensable. Inevitably, there were ribald remarks about atomically fried galah.

Shortly after we were installed, we were told that the test was cancelled for that day due to a sudden adverse wind-change and we returned to Adelaide. This happened several times and always the galahs were hugging the tower in their hundreds. Eventually, all seemed well enough for the bomb to be detonated and at 5 p.m. it caused an enormous fireball which vaporised the tower and every-thing on it. However, on that oh-so-welcome day, there had not been a galah in sight! So, maybe not so stupid.

As I was friendly with the RAF director of the operation, Air Vice Marshal 'Ginger' Weir, I was given information and facili-ties denied to my rival journalists. These included a flight at 500 feet over the bomb-crater only a few minutes after the blast, while scores of fires still raged, to see the effects on vehicles, tanks, old fighter planes and various test structures which had been erected.

I filed an exclusive account of this exciting experience to the London office but, while I had been airborne, Ginger had called a press briefing and told the other journalists, including those work-ing for international agencies, that he was calling the explosion 'The Five-o-Clock Rock', an allusion to rock 'n' roll, which was all the rage then. The night editor in London was so taken by this utterance, which reached him from one of the agency reports, that he decided to lead the front page with it, with my exclusive contri-bution being much reduced and relegated to the bottom.

I had travelled halfway round the world, successfully pulled all possible strings and pulled off a coup yet I had been scooped by an agency! Whenever I see that page while riffling through my cuttings books it still rankles.

In sixty-five years of investigative journalism there have been occasions when a decision to publish or withhold secret information which I had acquired surreptitiously has been difficult. None was so tough as the one I faced on Sunday 28 April 1957. On the previous day I had received a telephone call from the chief scientist at the Defence Ministry, Sir Fred Brundrett, who had long been my most productive secret source. He asked me to visit him at his country home near Emsworth (Hants) as he was in urgent need of my help.

I was particularly in debt to Fred for two scoops, the first that tests of the first all-British H-bomb were to be carried out off Christmas

Island in the Pacific in May, and the second details of the operation, which was codenamed Grapple, so I was only too happy to assist him.

He told me that reliable intelligence had revealed that the Japanese, after their experience at Hiroshima and Nagasaki, were understandably agitated by the dangers of radioactive fallout from the Grapple tests. There had also been an incident in which a Japanese ship had been deluged with fallout from an American H-bomb test. So, the Japanese were planning to make the tests impossible by sailing a thousand small ships into the area. If they forced the tests to be abandoned, Britain's entire defence policy would be ruined.

Because of the radioactive fallout danger, the government had agreed to sign a treaty in October banning any further atomic tests in the atmosphere. So, as Britain had no facilities for underground-testing, the billions spent on developing an independent nuclear deterrent would have been wasted if the Japanese forced abandon-ment of the planned tests off Christmas Island. This would also mean that Britain would lose its seat 'at the top table' if it ceased to be a viable nuclear power.

There was also terrific political pressure for successful H-bomb tests without delay. The wartime atomic partnership with the USA had been shattered by the revelation that British atomic scientists had betrayed vital secrets to Russia. Renewing it was rated as so important by Prime Minister Harold Macmillan that he called it 'The Great Prize'. Once Britain had proved it had an operational H-bomb, renewal would be more likely. So, all round, the stakes could not have been higher.

Fred then explained that the government had decided to fool the Japanese with a deception operation. The object was to delude them, by planted false intelligence, into believing that the tests scheduled for May had been postponed for several weeks. He said that the effort would be greatly enhanced if I could print a front-page article under my name implying that there had been a delay due to technical problems with the bomb.

Fred told me that various senior atomic scientists, including Sir William Penney, had already gone through the misleading motions of cancelling their bookings to reach Christmas Island in time for a May test and had rebooked for late June. His request was that I should 'discover' that to be the case by telephoning the airline next day and then suggest in the newspaper that this indicated that the tests had been delayed, following that by speculation as to the possible reasons.

In all walks of life 'pay-day' eventually arrives. So I told Fred that I would do my best but could not deceive my editor, to whom I owed so much, and would have to carry him with me.

After telephoning the airline and confirming the cancellation of the bookings, I explained the political stakes for the nation to the editor, who asked for time to think, during which he may have contacted Lord Beaverbrook. Eventually he called me to give me the go-ahead so long as we could not be accused of printing outright lies. A front-page disclosure headlined 'Penney – Surprise flight – he goes out to H-island in June', followed by speculation that the tests had, perhaps, been delayed by technical problems, appeared next day and was picked up by other media worldwide.

No Japanese ships appeared and the tests went ahead in May. I attended the second blast, watching from a boat, and received some special facilities from the chief scientist there – my old wartime friend Sir William Cook – in gratitude for my assistance. My contribution was also acknowledged by the Task Force commander, Air Vice Marshal Wilfrid Oulton, who eventually put it on record in his book, *Christmas Island Cracker*, and became another lunch companion. Whether or not there was ever a real danger that the ships would be sent in to foil the tests seems never to have been established but the UK defence chiefs certainly believed it to be a genuine threat.

Through his friendship with President Eisenhower, Macmillan – and the nation – eventually secured 'The Great Prize' and Britain still remains a nuclear power and I have no regrets at having misled my readers.

Like many of my generation, my boyhood fantasy was to drive the *Flying Scotsman* or some other giant steam-driven locomotive because, I suppose, of the sense of power it would give me. I was perhaps excessively smitten by this desire because I grew up in Darlington, which had played a major role in the birth of railways in 1825 and where *Locomotion No. 1*, the first engine to haul passengers, built by George Stephenson – from which all others are derived – then stood proudly in the railway station.

I never achieved my 'puffer-train' ambition but had better fortune with my mid-life fantasy – to drive an atomic-driven nuclear deterrent submarine armed with sixteen missiles, all with their H-bomb warheads at the ready. For that unforgettable experience, I am indebted not to the Royal Navy, where I had many influential friends, but to the navy of the United States of America.

In 1961, the British government allowed the US Navy to station some of its deterrent submarines in Holy Loch – a sea-loch on Scotland's west coast which opened to the Atlantic via the Firth of Clyde. The US continued its use until the collapse of the Soviet Union in 1991.

Because of noisy objections from the nuclear-disarmers, the US Navy needed some good publicity from a defence writer supportive of the nuclear deterrent, as I have always been. So in March 1963 I found myself on the deck of a small launch in the green water of the Firth of Clyde alongside a 6,900-ton submarine named the *Ethan Allen*, after an American Revolutionary War hero.

I managed to jump on to the shark-grey, 410-feet-long vessel and walked over the sixteen separate hatches covering the missiles which, I learned, were known to the crew as 'the doors of doom' – a fitting description should they ever have to be opened for action. Having reached the conning tower entrance I was admitted as a temporary crew member and was soon being debriefed in the officers' mess over a good lunch cooked by heat derived from the uranium furnace which supplied the boat's propulsion and all its other energy needs. By that time, the boat had submerged and we were 'on patrol' operating at a speed of only three knots, which was fast enough as the boat's purpose was simply to remain concealed while staying within range of its sixteen targets, all Soviet cities.

After the briefing by the affable skipper, Captain Paul Lacy, I was shown the missile tubes and how their contents would be armed and launched by pressing the red fire button should the presidential order to do so ever be received.

Though the 113 crew had only eighteen inches of headroom in their bunks, their accommodation elsewhere was surprisingly spacious. Their green-floored mess was enlivened with plastic plants in pots. On the table there were machines to make instant coffee, ice-cream and even popcorn, alcohol being forbidden.

Then came my moment – to drive the £50 million monster. The dive officer sat himself at a small desk where there was a short joystick connected electronically to two large flat fins, called planes, one on each side of the submarine. It was so simple. He sat me in his place and as I pushed the joystick forwards I could sense the vessel diving – to 1,000 feet if necessary – while pulling it back reversed the action. I had rapturous fun for several minutes to the occasional cry of 'Watch those planes!' from the dive officer. At ninety-nine, a thrill to remember – for one day when I get really old.

Nor, hopefully, as a former rocket scientist, will I ever forget the thrill of witnessing the launch of giant rockets, first at White Sands in New Mexico where I encountered Wernher von Braun and other ex-German missile pioneers who had invented the wartime V2, and then at Cape Canaveral in Florida. At 'the Cape', as we called it, enormous three-stage rockets were built and erected in one part of the vast area and then carried on 'the crawler' – a tracked vehicle like a colossal tank – to the launch pad. A night test-launching of such a rocket with the darkness revealing the true dimensions of the flames was unforgettably enthralling.

Further first-hand experiences with weapons of mass destruction seemed to have ended with my retirement from Fleet Street in 1979. Then, in 2002, the directors of the super-secret Atomic Weapons Research Establishment at Aldermaston, Berkshire, decided to celebrate the fiftieth anniversary of the first all-British atomic blast, inviting all the scientists and other witnesses who were still alive. No outsider had observed that first test but, as a witness to the second, I too was invited.

I enjoyed the proceedings, especially when the official sketch of the Hiroshima bomb shown during a lecture was almost identical to my sketch which had appeared in my newspaper half a century earlier. But infinitely more exciting satisfaction was to come. I was invited to see the museum and there, mounted on four long walls, was a full-size replica of every British atomic weapon starting with the primitive four-tonner to the unbelievably small H-bomb warhead for the current Trident submarine missile. Further, each weapon was cut away so the whole internal mechanism could be seen. For an old weapons buff like me – sheer ecstasy!

I have a few other reminiscences which still make the adrenalin flow. One, which is still occasionally strong enough to intrude in my dreams, concerns an unusual flight I made with the RAF in April 1964.

In the 1950s and 1960s the RAF had total Cold War responsibility for Britain's capacity to deter a nuclear attack by the Soviet Union and possibly for mounting a revenge or even a pre-emptive strike on Soviet cities. To that end, it built up a strategic force of about 160 V-bombers – Valiants, Vulcans and Victors – with the capacity to carry nuclear weapons at heights beyond the range of Soviet anti-aircraft missiles and drop them on Moscow and other designated cities. Though it was not generally known, in the event of a joint British and American attack it was the RAF which would have delivered most of the first strike because the UK airfields were so much nearer Russia than those in America.

All went well, with the situation called Mutually Assured Destruction (so aptly abbreviated to MAD) ensuring that the Cold War remained that way, until some worrying intelligence generated a sobering situation. The Russians had developed anti-aircraft missiles capable of shooting down V-bombers above the height at which the planes could fly – about 50,000 feet. In short, the whole strategic nuclear air strike force – both British and American – had become obsolete!

Readers may recall the first event which publicly exposed that situation. In 1960 a CIA spy plane, called the U2 and capable of flying at 70,000 feet, and which had long been taking photographs of Russian bases and defences, was shot down by a Soviet guided missile. The pilot, Gary Powers, bailed out and was captured, tried and imprisoned, causing a political uproar which was exploited by the Soviet leader, Khrushchev.

So, the RAF faced a problem – how could the V-bombers be kept in service when it was obvious to all that they were technically incapable of the task for which they had been designed? There was only one quick answer, should it prove to be practicable: to, somehow, adapt the bombers so that they could fly *under* the Soviet radar and missile screen i.e. at 200 feet. That was cleverly achieved by the development of a navigational device which directed a radar beam from the plane to the ground and then received the echo as it bounced back. Whatever the contours below – low or high ground – the plane responded automatically by adjusting its height from the ground, a process which became known as 'hedge-hopping'.

By 1964 many of the V-bomber crews had been trained in the new system and, as the RAF chiefs wanted some publicity for the change, which, they hoped, would impress the Russians and deter them from attacking the UK, I was invited to spend a day hedge-hopping. Never one to turn down an exclusive story for my newspaper I agreed and, on a nice fine day, arrived at a Victor bomber base for my adventure.

First, I was required to sign the usual statement agreeing that if we 'went in', as my instructor put it, I had been informed of the risks and had accepted them, thereby freeing the RAF from any compensation claims by my dependants. I was told that, as a passenger, I would not have an ejector-parachute escape system as only the pilot and the co-pilot had that life-saving facility. The three men sitting at the all-important navigation desk, watching screens on the look-out for pylons, had ordinary parachutes but the chance of using them at 200 feet was zero, as several accidents had already proved, leading to the quip – allegedly by a pilot as he ejected – 'See you later, Navigator'.

I was offered a parachute 'in case we go in' but knew now that I would never be able to use it. Not a pleasant start! However, the dark side quickly disappeared as we set off hedge-hopping in an area of countryside which had been selected for training because of its varying contours. I had been on a few switchback rides at pleasure centres but this one covered 200 miles, during which the huge plane hugged the ground so closely that I could have seen a rabbit.

As the mission culminated in a mock attack with an H-bomb on a strategic target I have to confess that there were anxious moments when I asked myself 'What the hell am I doing here?'

CHAPTER 9

KENYAN INTERLUDES

In the 1950s, having moved to the Surrey village of Ewhurst, my usual luck in meeting newsworthy people continued when I encountered Lord Russell of Liverpool, a distinguished lawyer, who lived there. With a fine record for bravery – he had won the Military Cross three times in the First World War – he was then, at fifty-nine, a judicial adviser to the army and RAF.

Having been involved in the trials of Nazi war criminals, he was so appalled by the concentration camps, like Belsen, Auschwitz and Buchenwald, that he wanted a record of the German atrocities to be available in every public library because, otherwise, most people would quickly forget them. So, in 1952, he had been given official permission to write a book which he called *The Scourge of the Swastika*. One afternoon in August 1954, he showed me a copy of the newly printed book in advance of publication with the suggestion that my paper, the *Daily Express*, might like to serialise it. My editor declined because he thought that photographs of piles of bodies at the breakfast table were not good for sales.

Russell had also sent a copy to his judicial chief, the Lord Chancellor (Lord Simmonds), who showed it to Cabinet colleagues who were in turn appalled. The imminent publication of the 259-page book, with its yellow cover showing emaciated prisoners standing in the shadow of a huge pair of jackboots and horrific photographs inside, happened to coincide with Anglo-American moves to rearm West Germany. NATO needed all the man-power it could muster to offset the threat posed by the Soviet Union and the book reminded voters of what the Germans had done when armed in the recent past.

Foreign Office chiefs ruled that publication of the book at that time would intensify public anger against the rearmament of Germany, especially in France. So, Russell was warned that if he allowed publication he would have to resign or be sacked. To his credit he resigned and on 11 August our front page was almost filled with that news and its likely repercussions.

There was uproar in Parliament, which always gave me pleasure, and this was reported the following day along with a front-page column by Russell entitled 'Why I Chose Freedom'. The book was duly published but not before my editor decided that, in view of the continuing rumpus, serialising it was not a bad idea after all!

I liked the Ewhurst area so much that when a Tudor farmhouse close to the village came up for sale I bought it. The beautiful, heavily beamed Lowerhouse Farm, totally surrounded by woods and fields, remained my treasured home for twenty-two years and at weekends I entertained many of my contacts there. To enhance the bucolic aspects, I started building walls in the grounds in brick and stone, greatly enjoying it, perhaps because their permanence contrasted with the evanescence of my journalistic words.

As the much larger village of Cranleigh was only a couple of miles away I made many new friends there. On the edge of Cranleigh was a small estate called Knowle, owned by Gordon Harvey, who had inherited an engineering business. Gordon, who looked and was pugnacious, invited me to his shoot there and our wives became friendly. He told me that he had a rich aunt who had a fine collection of Old Master paintings, which he would inherit.

One day, when visiting him, I saw dozens of oil paintings on and propped up against his very large dining table. The aunt had died but, already, a visiting expert had assured him that the paintings were all copies. Gordon was so disappointingly furious that he said to me, and others who visited him, 'They are all fakes. I want rid of them. Take whatever you want.' Having some large rooms myself, I relieved him of six beautiful paintings including one in a carved and gilded wooden frame which I recognised as a copy of an Italian painting of the Muse of Poetry prepared for the rich young Englishmen doing the Grand Tour of Europe. It, and the others,

have graced my walls for more than half a century. During another
visit he showed me a large suitcase filled with miniatures which the
aunt had also left and had proved disappointing. 'Take what you
like,' Gordon said. 'They are no use to me.' I insisted on paying him
£100 a go for a dozen or so of the miniatures and duly acquired an
enviable collection.

When Gordon's wife died young, he quit the area and sold
Knowle to Bruce McKenzie, who proved to be, perhaps, the most
extraordinary man I have ever met. South African born and big
in every way, his main base was Nairobi where, as a settler after
gallant war service, he had entered Kenyan politics, accepting the
fact that Kenyan independence from Britain under black African
rule, established in 1963 after the Mau Mau uprising, had come to
stay. Welcomed by the new President, Jomo Kenyatta, he became a
minister (agriculture) and eventually chief confidant of Kenyatta,
who trusted him because he realised that a white man could never
usurp him, as some of his black colleagues were keen to do.

For several years Bruce was Kenyatta's roving representative
and had become friendly with many of the world's political leaders, including Harold Wilson, to whom he had regular access. He
had also developed close personal relations with British, American,
Canadian, Iranian and Israeli intelligence and at lunches which he
frequently staged at Knowle, I talked with many intelligence officials who would not have wished to be seen with me in London. I
also met David Stirling, the founder of the SAS, who had his own
rules for snooker, at which I played him at Knowle. They included
the privilege of kneeling on the table for certain shots. While doing
that at White's Club in London, his six-foot six-inch frame had
brought down all the lamps, plunging the building into darkness
with a loud bang and causing its evacuation in the belief that the
IRA had struck.

Bruce's lovely wife Christina, who derived from a distinguished
landed family in Northumberland, became very friendly with my
third wife Billee, whom I had met in 1965 a year after Mona, who
was bored with country life as well as with me, had taken off with
a London lawyer. (Pursuing my dictum that any man who makes

merry with the lower half of my wife can also have the half that eats, I quickly divorced Mona and secured custody of the two children, who lived with me and later Billee at Lowerhouse Farm.) Bruce and Christina invited Billee and me to their home in Nairobi where, on and off, they spent about half the year. Neither of us had ever been to Kenya and we were enraptured by it and by those whom we met there. We revisited it several times. In particular, we treasured the introduction to Jack Block, a white Kenyan who owned a string of hotels, including the Stanley and the Norfolk in Nairobi, at both of which we enjoyed great hospitality. He also had a house in one of the world's most stunning locations – on the shore of Lake Naivasha where, on one of our Kenyan trips, we stayed with him and his delightful wife Doria.

The house next door belonged to another white Kenyan called Alan Root, who was rightly acclaimed as a major pioneer in wildlife photography, having produced now-historic films which have won many awards. Such was his zeal and courage that, while filming underwater, he had been bitten by a hippopotamus and had a permanent hole in his thigh to show for it. He had also been bitten by a leopard and picked up by a gorilla, which bit him and threw him down a slope.

Perhaps to commemorate his escape from the enraged hippo, he had acquired a tame baby hippo, Sally, who spent most of her day submerged in shallow water at the edge of Alan's garden and emerged in the evening to graze the lawn.

Alan also had a tame aardvark, which occasionally appeared on the lawn and had generated an ingenious pun. He called it 'Million' after a then-popular song 'Mammy', made famous by the American movie and TV singing star Al Jolson. The song had a line rendered by Root as 'Aardvark a million miles for one of your smiles, Mammy!'

Jack and I fished the lake for bass from his motor boat, which offered good sport, not only for us but for the magnificent white-headed fish-eagles which abstracted them with ease in front of our noses. On the way back from a sortie he took me to see a small group of hippos which had established itself in a corner of the lake and turned off the engine so that we could get a closer look. The top bull hippo immediately objected to the intrusion and came snorting to attack the small boat, which it could have easily upset, in defence of his harem and his territory. My heart sank more than a little as Jack's first two attempts to start the outboard engine with a coil of rope failed but it was third time lucky. By that time, we were closer to an enraged hippo and its open mouth than I ever wanted to be again.

Jack also owned several lodges in game reserves, including Tree Tops, the elevated and illuminated lodge for viewing game at night, made historic as the place where Princess Elizabeth was visiting when she heard the news that her father had died and that she was Queen. At his invitation, Bruce, who piloted his own small airplane, took us to Tree Tops where we spent a night watching the nocturnal behaviour of buffaloes, warthogs, rhinos and antelopes.

From there, Bruce flew us to the Samburu Game Lodge, where the barman suddenly switched off the light so that we could watch, at very close quarters, a leopard climbing a nearby tree to attend to the carcass of a goat put there to attract it. During an early morning safari we saw elephants, rhinos, lions and the rare reticulated giraffes. Later we were taken to Jack's Keekorok Lodge in the Masai Mara where we saw huge herds of antelopes and other plains game, and to a place in the south where, at a salt-lick, we watched more than a hundred elephants.

The best I could do to return Jack's wonderful hospitality was a couple of days' fishing on the hippo-free Test river in Hampshire. It was the last time we would meet. Not long afterwards, Jack was drowned while fishing a torrential river in South America.

The McKenzies also owned a seaside house on Diani Beach, near Mombasa, and kindly took us there, where we encountered a very small creature which, through our interference in its life, had what must have been a unique experience – a world first, never to be repeated.

Billee had collected a few small shells as souvenirs and took them back to our Surrey farmhouse where she put them on our bedroom dressing table. One of them fell on the floor so persistently that she examined it and could just see the pink claws of a tiny hermit crab. As a one-time professional zoologist, I was astonished that it had managed to live so long out of water. So I quickly prepared some artificial brine and tried feeding it with small bits of fish, which it appeared to consume. We called the tough little survivor 'Claws'.

My wife sometimes took Claws with her to lunch with friends, whom he entertained by scurrying on the table. One evening we took him to dinner in London at the famed Ecu de France restaurant, where Billee fazed the waiters as our tiny friend moved round the table dragging his home with him, so much so that they brought him a cooked shrimp.

Inevitably, when Bruce McKenzie paid one of his quick visits from Kenya to his Surrey home, we took Claws there to do his act. Looking very serious, Bruce pointed out that it was a crime in Kenya to take any living creature out of the country without a licence. So, to preserve international relations, Bruce insisted that Claws, complete with his beloved shell, should be returned to his place of origin. We agreed and handed him over for passage to Nairobi with Bruce.

A few days later we received a cable from Mombasa stating 'Operation Hermit Crab completed successfully – as witnessed by Bruce McKenzie and Charles Njonjo, the Kenyan Attorney General'.

As the security authorities were in the regular habit of reading private international cables which might be of interest to them, we all wondered what GCHQ had made of 'Operation Hermit Crab'. It seemed like a typical 'cloak and dagger' codename, especially as Bruce was well known to be involved in Kenyan intelligence affairs.

In helping to develop Kenya, Bruce had decided to set up a small intelligence service for which he had sought help from the foreign intelligence service he admired most – Israel's Mossad. The Mossad chiefs needed some faraway area where they could train their officers and practise operations in complete privacy. In return for such facilities in Kenya, Mossad provided expert knowledge and advice through Bruce, who introduced me to the chief Israeli representative there. I already had a working relationship with Mossad which provided me with some much envied exclusives. With David

Stirling's help, Bruce also set up a small SAS-type unit called the Kenyan General Service Unit, to deal with possible emergencies.

All the lakes in the Rift Valley offer exciting wildlife, especially flamingos in great numbers, but the Kenyan lake that thrilled me most was Lake Turkana, formerly called Lake Rudolf. It contained enormous Nile perch and, easing my sorrows away after losing one in the 200-pound class, I was sitting in a hot spring outside the hut where we were to spend the night when I was joined by Bruce, who had just flown from Nairobi. Joining me in the hot spring, he could not wait to tell me, in confidence, a story which I knew would make world headlines. A few days previously, three Palestinians equipped with Russian anti-aircraft missiles had arrived by car at the perimeter fence of Nairobi airport shortly before an Israeli El Al plane, with many Jews aboard, was scheduled to land on its way to Tel Aviv. Their mission was to shoot the plane down as it came in to land.

Fortunately, Mossad had alerted Bruce and the terrorists had been captured by his General Service Unit within minutes of their arrival. It was a major coup for the new unit, especially when the car was found to contain grenades, sub-machine guns and other weapons smuggled in from neighbouring Uganda.

A couple of days later two West Germans, a man and a woman, arrived – as Mossad had predicted – to find out what had gone wrong, as there had been no publicity. They were seized and, when the woman was examined, she had instructions about other Israeli airliner targets written on her abdomen. Bruce told me that the Kenyan government had been loath to prosecute the five terrorists because that would bring reprisals. So, Mossad had taken them secretly to Israel to stand trial there.

Bruce swore me to secrecy but, five months later, I was able to publish the story – with serious political consequences.

Bruce's many business interests included the sale of motor cars and Land Rovers and he had a sales branch in Kampala, the capital of neighbouring Uganda where the dictator Idi Amin reigned supreme. Bruce, who sometimes dealt directly with Amin, took my wife and me there by flying his little plane into the airport at

Entebbe, where we saw MiG jet fighters provided by Russia lined up there.

Entebbe was to become a focus of world attention on 27 June 1976 when a mixed force of six Arab and German terrorists had hijacked a French airliner and forced it to land there. They then demanded the release of more than fifty Palestinian terrorists held by the Israelis – otherwise the hostage passengers would be shot. By Friday 2 July, they had agreed to free the 165 non-Jewish hostages, who were flown to Paris, with Idi Amin quickly claiming credit for the releases. The freed hostages had agreed to say nothing in public that might inflame the terrorists against the 110 remaining Jews and they kept their word. So the world knew little about what was really happening at Entebbe.

Then, on that Friday morning, one of my contacts in Mossad telephoned me at my home from Paris, where he was based. He provided me with an exclusive account of what had been learned by French intelligence officers who had questioned some of the returned hostages and urged me to give it maximum publicity. I could tell, from his tone, that he regarded publication as being of utmost importance.

Having written and telephoned my story to my newspaper, my wife and I went to Knowle to have dinner with Bruce and his wife. I told them what had happened and learned that he had hardly been off the telephone all day. He was in a mysterious mood, refusing to say much about the Entebbe situation.

Next morning, my front-page lead story, headed 'Amin's Deadly Hijack Game', stated that Idi Amin, a convert to the Muslim faith, had been involved in the hijack from the start, having given the terrorists sub-machine guns, allowing two more Arabs to join them and providing Ugandan troops as guards so that the hijackers could sleep.

It was copied worldwide and I quickly received another call from Paris expressing Mossad's gratitude so fulsomely that I realised that the Israelis had urgently needed me to publish the information – I could not figure out why.

Later that evening we visited the McKenzies again and I found Bruce more mysterious than ever and somewhat exhausted by another day of international telephone calls. On our way home my wife suggested that the Israelis would attempt to rescue the hostages but I thought that unlikely as I knew that they did not have planes capable of making the double journey from Israel and back home.

The following morning, Sunday, we awoke to the news of the brilliant rescue of the hostages by an airborne Israeli squad of 100 commandos who had landed in the night after a flight of 2,500 miles in Hercules transport planes. They had killed all the terrorists and, as a diversion, had destroyed Amin's MiGs.

So why had my Mossad source been so pleased with my Amin story? The Israeli government had realised that, if the raid failed and Ugandans were killed, Israel could be condemned for infringement of sovereign territory. It had been essential for the world to know, in advance from a neutral source, that Amin had been deeply involved. Not all secret service activity is about spies!

It was clear to me that someone in neighbouring Kenya must have played a part. The Hercules planes had been allowed to land at Nairobi, the Kenyan capital, to refuel there for the flight back to Israel and, without that facility, the rescue would have been impossible. They also needed medical assistance for any wounded casualties. As I then assumed, the prime mover had been Bruce McKenzie, who, in his mysterious telephone calls, had organised the arrangements and transmitted them to Mossad. For good measure, I secured Bruce's agreement to print the story he had told me of the attempted pro-Palestinian attack on the Kenyan airliner which helped to explain why the Kenyan authorities had agreed to allow the Israelis to land at Nairobi after the operation.

When the Israelis struck a medal to commemorate the raid (which had been codenamed Operation Thunderbolt and then Jonathan in honour of its commander, Yonatan Netanyahu, who had been killed in it) Bruce was the only non-Jew to receive it – an event immediately noticed by the unpredictable Ugandan dictator, Idi Amin.

Two years later, while visiting Bruce again at his Surrey home, I was astonished to hear that he had visited Amin in Uganda and would be doing so again to sell him some military vehicles. When I suggested that Amin might take revenge for his part in the Entebbe raid Bruce replied that I did not understand the African mind as he did. He was sure that Amin wanted to repair his reputation with the West and urged me to go with him to interview Amin and report the evidence of his good intentions. I reminded him that I, too, was on Amin's hit-list because, with Mossad's help, I had been the journalist who had exposed his monstrous role in the hijack.

Bruce assured me that I was in no danger and, stupidly, I agreed to accompany him and his white Kenyan business partner Keith Savage to Uganda. By chance, however, a Briton called Gavin Whitelaw (who I knew because he had employed my son Michael when working for Lonrho Export) visited Bruce and, also wanting to do business with Amin, asked to be taken with him. My trip was, therefore, postponed.

After friendly talks with Amin, the three passengers and the pilot returned to their plane where a man was waiting with a parcel for delivery in Nairobi. It was taken in and, when the plane was over the Ngong hills, the parcel exploded, resulting in the assassination of all on board.

It fell to me to telephone the news of Bruce's death to our mutual friend, Maurice Oldfield, the MI6 chief. His unemotional response was: 'Did he leave any papers?' I also contacted 'Tiny' Rowland, the Lonrho chief, to inform him of the death of Gavin Whitelaw. His only comment was 'Make it clear that he was not there on our behalf'.

Both my wife and I were deeply saddened by Bruce's death. Such was the force of his character that we regularly reminisce about him after so many years, recalling, in particular, the many big-game safaris he arranged for us.

CHAPTER 10

FISHERMAN

For as long as I can remember, the British countryside has held joys for me which have never been approached by any city, including those with which I have fallen in love, like Venice and Rome. I have always been conscious of its beauty in all seasons, the sheer awareness of being in it generating pleasure. I have been especially enamoured of fast-moving rivers, the sea being too vast and too impersonal for the particular memories one can develop with a river's banks, streams and pools, which often have age-old names. I cannot get to grips with the sea. It gets to grips with me. As for canals, the alimentary is the only one that has ever interested me.

A slightly older boy had first taken me to watch him fish and the sport grabbed me so intensely that it became something of an obsession which has never left me. By the age of twelve I was off on my bicycle whenever I could to fish the nearby Tees or Swale with my rod and landing net strapped to the crossbar. Both rivers contained coarse fish like dace and chub, as well as trout and grayling, and the most successful way of catching them was by trotting downstream a small cork float from which was suspended a short length of so-called cat-gut ending in a tiny hook, on which two or three maggots were impaled. The maggots were carried in a linen bag suspended from the neck, making it easy to rebait and to throw in a few maggots from time to time to bring the fish 'on the feed'.

My attachment to maggots – their smell is still delightfully nostalgic – frequently caused trouble, my mother's reaction being fierce when hordes of bluebottles suddenly emerged out of a maggot tin hidden in a spare room. I recall sitting in a train to Catterick Bridge where, for the sum of sixpence per month, I could fish miles of the lovely Swale, when maggots from my wickerwork creel, which was on the rack, began to fall into the brim of a black straw hat worn by a lady sitting beneath. Fortunately she alighted without noticing.

A creel, which always had a hole in the lid wide enough to slide a fish through, had an additional advantage for the proud young angler. I remember catching a three-quarter-pound trout in a little stream called Cockerbeck and then taking a long detour through Darlington town on the way back so that everybody could spot the trout, which I had arranged so that it was easily visible through the hole.

Most of the coarse fish I caught were inedible but it was the custom to kill them and take them home as evidence of prowess. In fact, anyone seen catching fish and then returning them would have been regarded as peculiar. Now, within the vast angling brotherhood, it is a crime to kill a fish not wanted for the pot.

With encouragement from older anglers I also learned the art of wet-fly fishing – the propulsion downstream of a long length of catgut (now nylon) bearing three 'flies', each consisting of a small hook 'dressed' with silk thread and bits of bird's feather to simulate the small natural insects on which fish feed. I learned how to make the flies, the pleasure being intensified when landing a nice trout caught on a home-tied fly. I recall the names of two of the most successful flies as woodcock and orange and snipe and purple.

As I have described, our family move to the Comet Hotel, when I was sixteen, put me within fifty yards of the Tees and, through the generosity of one customer (Frank Greenway, bless his memory), I had access to about three miles of private fishing, where I honed my skills so persistently that my father prophesied that I would end up growing fins. I was so aware of the privileges I enjoyed that I recall saying to a fishing friend, Bobby Dodds, shortly before the Second World War, which then looked inevitable, that if we were killed in the war we had enjoyed a great life. He agreed. Happily, we both survived to continue our country interests, his as a doctor in the Wensleydale town of Masham, where I fished with him over many years.

Many people believe that fishing is called 'the contemplative man's recreation' because, with so little happening for most of the time, it enables the angler to contemplate. The truth is that it is difficult to think about anything else. Concentration must be absolute and that makes it a fine recreation for the contemplative man in the sense that it enables him to secure relief from contemplation.

On moving permanently south in 1946, with access to slower rivers, I graduated to upstream dry-fly fishing, which has enthralled me ever since. There were no good rivers near Ewhurst so I fished in lakes, which were artificially stocked and usually involved casting from a boat. The most exciting was the pike-fishing in Milford Lake on the Highclere estate of the 7th Earl of Carnarvon, near Newbury in Berkshire. The lake (so full of carp, roach and pike that it needed no restocking) had been rented for only £40 a year by a delightful man called Jack Malden, who had been the games master at Cheam, the nearby preparatory boarding school. As a child, the Duke of Edinburgh was taught there and remembered Jack with affection when I had the opportunity of jogging his memory a few years ago.

Jack invited me to fish the lake, which was such a marvellous weekend retreat from Fleet Street that I eventually shared the rent with him and took many of my friends there. Fishing with spinners and plugs, it yielded a thirty-pound pike every season, but never to my rod, though I hooked and lost one in the reeds which was even bigger. I was saddened when we were eventually no longer able to rent the lake because Henry, the then Lord Porchester, as the heir to the earldom is known, was moving into the small but beautiful eighteenth-century Milford Lake House and did not want his privacy disturbed. Privately cursing his Lordship, I little thought that we were destined to become such close friends that I would be given the fishing free, often catching large pike while standing in front of Milford Lake House after lunching there.

My fishing life changed forever in 1960 when I met Tommy Sopwith, the only son of Sir Thomas Sopwith, the aircraft pioneer and yachtsman. Tommy was a keen game-shot but did not like fishing, apparently because he had been required to do too much of it when he was young. So, when I told him of my fanaticism for rivers and everything in them, he introduced me to his father, who owned eight miles of the River Test, the angler's chalk stream Mecca. Sir Thomas and I took a liking to each other and meeting him proved to be another mutation moment in my professional, as well as my social, life. I found Sir Thomas's wife Phyl to be as charmingly and amusingly friendly as her famous husband, who had contributed to victory in both World Wars by building outstanding aircraft. He had flown himself into history as one of the earliest aviation pioneers then designed, built and test-flew the Sopwith Pups, Camels and other fighters in the First World War. He also founded the Hawker Siddeley company, which built the Hurricane fighter, the backbone of Fighter Command during the Second World War.

Eventually they both treated me almost like a son and when I arrived at their country house, Compton, in Hampshire, I would be greeted with 'Welcome home!'

Soon, Sir Thomas gave me free run of the river and I enjoyed marvellous sport, catching brown and rainbow trout up to eight pounds – far bigger than anything I had ever encountered before. On those hallowed banks I also encountered several distinguished men who would otherwise have escaped my social landing net like Lord Portal of Hungerford, who had headed the wartime RAF with such success, and Lord Dilhorne, the Lord Chancellor. Charles Portal, known to his friends as 'Peter', remained rather aloof but Reggie Dilhorne (formerly Manningham-Buller) became an intimate friend with whom I would spend whole weeks fishing in Scotland. I met Reggie's daughter, Eliza, while staying at their home in the small village of Horninghold in Leicestershire, but he never told me that she was in MI5, of which she would eventually become director general.

I never thought that I would fish a trout stream more productive than the Test but, shortly after I retired from Fleet Street in 1979, my wife Billee and I decided that Lowerhouse Farm was too big and too remote for our future needs and that we needed to move into a village. We were very familiar with the delightful village of Kintbury on the West Berkshire–Wiltshire border, which had a good train service to London and was close to the River Kennet. Billee found an ideally suited residence for sale close to the entrance to the 1,000-year-old churchyard in what, to me, is a lovely corner of Old England. She took me to see it and we bought it, cash on the nail, and moved in. I paid an emotional farewell to my beloved Lowerhouse Farm by kissing the studded oak front door. After over thirty years in Church House, as our Kintbury abode is called, we remain delighted with it and with its surroundings. With so many caring friends, Kintbury is a marvellous village in which to grow old.

Installed in Kintbury, I found some trout fishing only a quarter of a mile away but soon hankered after a rod on a beat three miles upstream on the large Littlecote estate, then owned by Sir Seton Wills of the tobacco family. Seton was keen for me to join his club, which ran the fishing, but the waiting list was already lengthy and, with anglers tending to be long lived, my prospects looked bleak. Then, once again, my lucky streak came to my aid.

On a sunny July afternoon, I walked into the shop in Hungerford where I bought my tackle and the man behind the desk asked me: 'Would you be interested in buying a rod on the Littlecote beat?' He then explained that, a few minutes previously, one of the Littlecote Club members had told him that he was leaving the UK to retire in France and, so, had no further use for his membership. In return for compensating him for the three months' fishing he would lose that season I could take over his membership.

I immediately telephoned Seton, who assured me that he would honour the deal, and thus I began my 32-year membership of, probably, the finest trout stretch in Britain. Set in memorable scenery, the stretch was almost four miles long with a succession of streams and pools each holding many fish. I quickly made friends with the keeper, Peter Woolnough, who not only kept the water and its banks in fine order but reared the brown and rainbow trout with which the river was restocked each season as, at the time of writing, he still does. I am grateful to Peter for his long friendship and many kindnesses.

In some fishing clubs, each member is restricted to a certain day, or days, of the week but the joy of Littlecote for me, living close to it, was that members could fish any time they wished. I could be on the water by 9.15 a.m., usually alone, fish for a couple of hours, then be back at my desk at 11.30. The only restriction was on the total that each rod could catch in the season – then 100. That was more than enough for me and for the neighbours whom I supplied with fish – often in return for vegetables, a delightful village barter. Some of the fish were often so big – up to ten pounds – that a brace at one visit was plenty.

Due to another stroke of luck, I was able to double our limit. One of the new members was the wayward son of a famous noble-man and declined to pay his subscription, regularly assuring Seton that his cheque was in the post, which it never was. By mid-season, July, he was sacked and I heard that the club's committee members were bemoaning the loss of a whole year's subscription. I immedi-ately offered to pay it provided my wife, Billee, a keen fisher, could have the membership. My offer was accepted and we were to enjoy much time together there with our dogs.

We held the Littlecote record for a brown trout – twelve pounds – which has since been broken, but I eventually set a new record for a rainbow trout which is unlikely to be beaten for many years, if ever. On a lovely July morning in 2004, aged ninety and alone, save for my chocolate Labrador Tom, I was fishing a stretch immediately upstream of an old pump house which bestrides the river. I was using a small sinking object called a 'nymph' and representing a small freshwater shrimp which I cast upstream where I had, previ-ously, seen a large fish.

After the third cast I spotted a bow wave moving towards the nymph about ten yards upstream. The line jerked, so I tightened and the fish was hooked, immediately taking out yards of line. It was about 10.35 a.m. and the trout began to race upstream with the reel screeching as it tore out so much line that I had to run along the bank to keep pace with it. The fish continued to swim upstream, darting into every patch of water-weed growing up from the riverbed and doing its best to entangle itself and break the nine feet of thin nylon connecting the hook with the main line. On each knife-edge occasion, I reeled in as much line as I could, while manipulating the rod to induce the fish to extricate itself, and being very conscious that the breaking strain of the nylon was just four pounds. In the process, I saw that the fish was a rainbow trout which, pound for pound, is a doughtier fighter than the native brown. I also realised that it was substantially bigger than the largest previously caught on the water, which had weighed twelve and a half pounds.

That there was nobody around to assist me caused me no concern because, for trout fishing, I have always insisted on one-to-one combat, believing that allowing someone else to operate the landing net is unfair.

Around 11 a.m., and about 120 yards upstream of the hooking point, I managed to bring the fish close and realised that it was much bigger than I had thought – too big to steer into my sixteen-inch-wide landing net in the usual manner. My only hope was to hold the metal rim of the net vertically in the water with my right hand and induce the fish to swim into it. My usual luck held out and the trout went in at the first attempt.

I will never know whether Tom or I was the more astonished at the depth and width of the fish as I hauled it on to the grass. He looked at me and seemed to echo my blasphemous exclamation.

The Littlecote Club rules required the dispatch of all rainbows. So, having administered the last rites with a small truncheon, aptly called a priest, I hauled the fish to the weighing scales in a nearby hut. By that time, two other anglers had arrived and, even with their help, we could not balance the fish on the scales so I rushed it to the fishmonger in Kintbury village. With two lady customers serving as independent witnesses, we watched while, using his modern high-tech scales, he certified the trout as weighing twenty pounds six ounces. From nose to the fork of the tail it measured thirty-four inches. Its girth at the shoulder was twenty-one and half inches and it was proportionately broad.

Though it was immediately listed in the club records alongside a photograph of the fish, I kept unusually quiet about my catch, mainly to avoid encouraging poachers, but a local journalist eventually heard about it and, at the request of the *Daily Mail*, I wrote a big feature about it which appeared in that paper on 21 October 2005.

Meanwhile I had reported the facts to the records authority, who indicated that it was, probably, the heaviest trout ever caught in any British river, though heavier ones had been taken in lakes. Had I been younger, I would probably have taken the fish to a taxidermist. Instead, we had it smoked and it duly fed a large gathering in our house.

When I first joined the Littlecote fishery, the massive Littlecote House, an Elizabethan mansion much involved in the Civil War with strong Cromwellian connections, was lived in by Sir Seton Wills and his wife Gillian, who invited my wife and me there many times. We witnessed the discovery of a splendid Roman mosaic in the grounds after wild rabbits there had chanced to dig out some of the highly coloured tesserae. Later, we holidayed with the Willses in Venice and Rome where I served as guide.

In 1985, Seton sold the house and grounds to the entrepreneur Peter de Savary, whose mother and step-father were neighbours of ours in Kintbury. In 1996 it became a hotel. (While I had been in close touch with Seton I met another titled member of the Wills family in a London club. I asked him if he ever saw Seton, to which he replied, 'No. You see where there's a Wills I'm away.')

In 1950 I had been introduced to salmon fishing in Scotland – on a famous beat of the Dee (Lower Blackhall) – thanks to the kindness of Joe Little, an Aberdeen fish merchant who rented it. It was February and bitterly cold, especially when wading, but I caught my first salmon and several more. After that, thanks to further invitations from Joe and others I will mention, I never missed at least one week's salmon fishing a year until, at eighty-five, old age forced me to desist. During that time on some of Scotland's finest salmon beats on the Dee, Spey, Tay, South Esk and Grimersta I concluded that the take of a salmon, either on a fly or on a bait, is probably the most exciting moment life has to offer.

For much of that delight I was further in debt to Sir Thomas Sopwith, who rented expensive beats on the Spey and South Esk. The Spey is a glorious river and the pools on the Delfur beat, with names like The Otter, Beaufort and Two Stones, hold special memories for me.

The names of salmon pools sometimes date back centuries and remain in the angler's mind, conjuring up, in later life, vivid memories of triumphs and defeats. The oddest I can recall, which was on a beat of the Wye in Herefordshire, was called The Lavatory and tended to be productive. So, more than once, on a fishless morning, I heard the ghillie calling out to my wife, 'I think that Mr Chapman Pincher wants to go to The Lavatory.'

The South Esk, which enters the sea near Montrose, is a tiny river but was the most productive I have ever fished. The main beat, which the Sopwiths, with me and Lord Dilhorne as their guests, fished in April, had a weir, below which was a pool called the Goyle. There was a salmon ladder but the fish would not use it until the water reached a certain temperature, so they all collected in the various pools below it. Standing on a metal bridge, I have seen the salmon stacked like sardines.

As a result, many of the fish we caught were foul-hooked by the baits or flies directed at them, which enabled them to fight all the more. On one day I caught twenty-two salmon and, sadly in retrospect, knocked them all on the head because, as with all others who rented Scottish beats in those days, Sir Thomas wanted them to help pay the rent. Each evening, on most of the Scottish rivers I fished, a van called at all the beats, picked up the salmon left in the fish-trays in the main fishing huts and delivered them to the nearest fish market. Eventually, the person renting the beat received a substantial cheque. Whenever possible, when fishing as a guest, I tried as hard as I could to 'pay for my keep'.

When fishing the Grimersta – a short, small river and a chain of lochs on the island of Lewis – the rather snooty other fishers in the party and the ghillies were convinced that it was essential to fish with very small flies less than half an inch long. I did not have any and, as nobody offered me one, I fished with the flies I would have used on the Dee. I caught ten salmon while nobody else had more than three and some had only one. As I left, the others who were staying on were begging for large flies.

My most enduring memories of salmon fishing are of the Kinnaird beat of the Tay where, for many years, Billee and I were guests of the owner, Reggie Ward, a scion of the Ward family of the Wiltshire village Chilton Foliat, where we had first met him and his

American wife, Connie. Not only was the beat superb but Kinnaird House, where we stayed, was beautiful and most of the other guests were old friends. After Reggie's premature death, Connie continued to invite us both in the spring and the autumn. I came to appreciate the splendour of the Tay and all the other Scottish salmon rivers I fished so much that on the many days when the salmon refused to oblige I would look up the river and look down the river and tell myself what a privilege it was just to be there.

Fate gifts few husbands the sudden and safe choice of deciding whether a hale and healthy wife should continue to live or die but that moment of opportunity was suddenly presented to me on a beautiful spring morning while fishing at Kinnaird. Billee was a skilled and irritatingly successful salmon fisher who had become hooked on the sport after I had taken her salmon fishing in Ireland and she had caught a thirteen-pounder on her first morning. Since then, she had become notorious for her ability to catch a salmon when nobody else could. An explanation of why women catch so many big salmon – the British record, sixty-four pounds, was set by a woman – prompted the theory that female sexual scents, called pheromones, are wafted into the water and stimulate the fish to take. How that happens when a woman is wearing thick rubber waders up to her shoulders has never been explained but has generated some ribald laughs. When a group of us were fishing and Billee hooked a salmon almost immediately, there were anguished downstream cries of 'Waft some down here!'

As the Kinnaird ghillie, a splendid chap called Bob Grant, was rarely with us, having other duties, it was my practice to put Billee into the pool below that in which I was fishing so that I could keep an eye on her at all times, being aware that the big Scottish rivers usually claim at least one fatality each year, and I had done so on that memorable morning, when we had been allotted our favourite pool on the river. To fish the pool effectively one needed to wade in a couple of yards or so to make it easier to cast the bait or fly into the deeper water downstream where the salmon lay. All was going well until I glanced down and all I could see of Billee was her head, the rest of her being totally submerged. At once putting my rod down, I used my long wading staff to help me to run the forty yards or so over the big cobbles on the bank. By the time I reached her she was slowly drifting towards the main stream, which would have carried her away, but I was just able to reach her with my wading stick which, at the top, held a large sharp hook for gaffing salmon. I managed to get the hook into one of the shoulder straps of her chest waders and dragged her in. Inevitably, her first concern was to ensure that her hair was still dry, which, miraculously, it was.

As I was stowing away the tackle in the car to return to Connie's to get Billee dry, Bob Grant suddenly appeared. When Billee told him what had happened he commented blandly, 'You must have fallen into Dick's Hole.' Who Dick was and why Bob had not warned us about his hole was never explained.

Scottish ghillies are a breed unto themselves and I have made a study of them and their ways. They are, usually, expert anglers, the most successful in my experience being Sandy Wilkie, who ran the splendid beat on the Dee called Inchmarlo. He had succeeded his father, 'Old Wilkie', who nevertheless always accompanied his son. I often saw them while fishing on the opposite beat, called Lower Blackhall, and have a vivid memory of an occasion when my ghillie shouted across the river to ask Old Wilkie why the owner of the beat and his guest were not fishing that day. The old man's yell, 'They're awa ty Edinburgh on a drinking and whoooor-ing expedition', reverberated over the water.

My findings included the explanation of why so many Scots are called Sandy. An Aberdeen professor told me that, way back in time, there had been three Scottish kings called Alexander (after Alexander the Great) who had been exceptionally good. It, there-fore, became a fashion to name children after them, Alexander being abbreviated to Sandy.

The Tay beat below Kinnaird was owned by Michael Smith, who sometimes invited us to fish it but to whom I am more indebted for the opportunity to meet his remarkable father, Sir Alan Smith. Sir Alan had founded a highly successful textile business but was of greater interest to me because of his war record. An outstanding fighter pilot, he had made his name history by being 'wingman'

to the legless legend, Douglas Bader. In battle, it was Alan's prime
duty to protect Bader's Spitfire from attack by flying his plane close
behind him and remaining there whatever Bader might do, even
in a 'dogfight' battle. As Bader had visited my Kintbury home, Sir
Alan and I had much to talk about.

On the walls of the billiards room of the grand house where
Connie and Reggie Ward lived, were seven salmon in glass cases
all weighing over forty pounds caught by previous members of the
Ward family or their guests. I was quick to notice that there was just
enough space for one more glass case and, privately, I vowed to fill it.

One fine day, fishing a flashing metal bait called a Toby in the
Green Bank pool, I hooked a salmon which quickly came close to
the bank and flashed its side in the deep water. It was, easily, the
biggest salmon I had ever hooked and I looked at Bob Grant and
declared, 'It could be forty pounds!' He did not disagree.

After a long and tough fight Bob managed to gaff the fish because
the bank was too high for it to be beached. My hopes remained
high as it was slung on to the grass but were quickly dashed by
Bob's cry of 'Oh hell! It's a razor-back!' What he meant was that
the salmon, which had certainly weighed more than forty pounds
when it had come in from the sea, had been so long in the river that
it had lived on its muscles as well as its fat, losing so much weight
that its sharp backbone could be felt by Bob's finger. It weighed
only twenty-eight pounds.

To catch my first (and only) 30-pounder I had to visit Norway,
where a friend owned a beat on the turbulent River Driva in the
Sundalsfjord. On my first day there, fishing from a boat, I caught a
fresh-run salmon weighing thirty-one and a half pounds.

Later, thanks to Sir Charles Forte, the catering entrepreneur,
Billee and I also experienced the wonderful salmon fishing available
in Iceland. For many years, he had hired an expensive beat on the
Haffjardara river and, one season, being unable to go for business
reasons, he offered it to my wife and me.

With the cones of miniature extinct volcanoes, some with their
tops blown off in prehistoric blasts and with the lava they had
produced weathered into grotesque shapes, the landscape was

unusually memorable. So was the wind which made casting difficult but did some good as it grounded the midges which can make fishing there unbearable.

Using a recommended 'prawn fly' – a concoction of red wool and fur, with stiff cockerel whiskers making the tail – I caught four salmon in my first allotted pool. In the next pool downstream my wife had also caught four. They each weighed about nine pounds but, being so fresh from the nearby sea, they fought hard. In eight days, we took ninety-one fish, the biggest being a seventeen-pounder caught by Billee. Except for the few we were allowed to take home on the last day, all the fish went to the Icelandic owner, who supplied them, by air, to French restaurants.

Later, I was to meet a remarkable Icelander called Orri Vigfússon, who, among other business interests, exported vodka to the US and, surprisingly, Russia. As a keen salmon fisher, he became so deeply concerned by the collapse of the Atlantic salmon population that he was dedicated to trying to restore it. The collapse had resulted from the discovery of the salmon's main feeding area in the Atlantic by an American submarine operating under the ice off Greenland. The crew noticed thousands of salmon feeding on plankton adhering to the underside of the ice and the news was published. The Greenlanders then began to fish for them, using invisible nylon drift-nets. They were followed by the Faroese, who found salmon feeding grounds off their islands and caught great numbers on long baited lines.

Anglers soon noticed a massive slump in the numbers of salmon returning to British, Irish, Canadian and European rivers to spawn. There were further savage inroads by the drift-netters licensed to catch them off the north-east coast of Britain and Ireland. As a result, the wild Atlantic salmon population fell by 80 per cent.

The only solution was to offer the fishermen compensation. As Orri put it to me, 'It's no use taking a high moral stance with people trying to earn their living. The original offer would have to be money but, in the long term, more lucrative and more attractive employment would have to be found for the fishermen.' So, in 1989, he founded the North Atlantic Salmon Fund to raise money to buy off the commercial fishing. He has raised over $35 million and in 2007 was awarded the Goldman Environmental Prize. Though there is much more to do, his endeavours have improved salmon populations in several countries including Iceland, where the government banned salmon-netting.

I gave up salmon fishing when I was eighty-five. A slight, silly accident on the drive back from Scotland was enough to convince us that we were too old for such an exacting sport so far away. It was a doubly sad decision because it cut us off, physically, from Connie and our other friends in Scotland and their magnanimous hospitality. We still miss the splendour of Bonnie Scotland, where both of us always felt so fit. Nevertheless, I had not caught my last salmon. My friend Raleigh Place, who has an estate near Overton in Hampshire, had created a lake in which he circulated the water by an electric pump. Well stocked with rainbow trout, it was giving us good sport. Then Raleigh heard of a fish farm in Wales which had a stock of a variety of land-locked salmons secured from the US and I accompanied him there to see it. Excited by the sight of one huge fish in a tank, Raleigh ordered a substantial number, which were duly delivered and gave us great sport over several years.

The year 2012 was to be the eighty-sixth that I had held a fishing licence. Sadly, having become too wobbly to be safe by a deep river, my fishing days are now over.

CHAPTER II

GUN MAN

I began serious game-shooting in a modest way in the 1950s by joining a syndicate shoot near Midhurst in Sussex, where fifty pheasants for nine guns was a good day. Even there, my journalistic luck continued because one of the members was an admiral – Hugh 'Rufus' Mackenzie. When he was put in charge of the navy's Polaris submarine project he quickly left the syndicate to avoid public association with me, a journalist, but we remained in contact.

Then, in 1963, meeting a stranger projected me into a situation which, eventually, would elevate me to what might be called the premier division of the British shooting world. While dining with my friend Hugh Fraser, who was then Air Minister, and his wife Antonia, the historian author, I was introduced to a German-Jewish immigrant called Peter Adam, who had founded a successful business and ran a syndicate pheasant shoot on an estate at Brimpton in West Berkshire, which was mainly owned by Israel Sieff, one of the forces behind Marks and Spencer. He invited me to a day's shooting which I enjoyed so much that I joined the syndicate. It was also my introduction to the Jewish community, the Adam and Sieff families in particular, which has greatly enriched my life experience, as will become apparent.

Later, shooting at Brimpton, I met Charles Forte, founder of the massive chain of hotels, motorway restaurants, Travelodges, Little Chef cafés and other interests, who not only had his own shoot at Ripley in Surrey but rented the major part of the Ickworth shoot near Bury St Edmunds. Charles, who proved to be the most outstanding and most admirable personality I have ever met, invited

me to shoot at both splendid venues. I have many vivid memories of
the Ripley shoot and can visualise all the drives but have only one
of Ickworth. Charles had hired a retired admiral to run the shoot
there for him and his methods had been such that very few pheasants had come my way while at a normally productive stand. When
I asked my loader why there were so few birds he replied, 'Would
you have hired a gamekeeper to fight the Battle of Trafalgar?'

Born in Italy in 1908, Charles had emigrated with his parents to
Scotland aged four and, later, worked for various relatives in their
small cafés. Aged twenty-six, he had started his own business career
by opening a milk and sandwich bar in London's Regent Street and
everything had grown from that.

Charles made me a regular guest at the many lunches he staged
at his London hotels – mainly Grosvenor House and the Hyde Park
– where I made new journalistic contacts among the politicians,
ambassadors, businessmen and even intelligence officers whom I
encountered there. Before each lunch, we all had to watch a short
TV account of the latest state of his vast business. He would stand
by the TV set, smiling, and I always watched him rather than the
TV, as I was forever lost in wide-eyed wonder by the fact that this
physically small man had built up the enormous set-up from one
milk bar. In the process, he had created many thousands of steady
jobs, for which he was rewarded by a knighthood and then a peerage. (The longer I live the more it becomes apparent that a steady
source of income is central to human happiness and those who
create jobs are the pillars of society, richly deserving any honours.)

Further, Charles was entirely unspoiled by his wealth and
honours and revelled in making fun of his lack of height by claim-
ing that he had once held the Scottish record for the long jump.
'Actually,' he would explain, 'I was not competing in that event. I
was throwing the hammer and forgot to let go.' (When his friend
Margaret Thatcher wanted to make a speech about Charles, her
Downing Street aide telephoned me for assistance and the Prime
Minister told the long-jump story with glee.)

Over the years, my wife and I came to be treated almost as
members of the Forte family, an experience we still cherish. Charles

Forte's inherent goodness of heart was demonstrated by his behaviour when I presented him with a damaging discovery I had made about a business opponent. During the 1970s and 1980s I was a paid consultant to the Forte company, and on one occasion I was researching the situation at London's Savoy Hotel, in which the company had a 69 per cent shareholding but little influence because of the way that the shareholders' voting arrangements had been organised by the Savoy chairman, Sir Hugh Wontner. Sir Hugh was a highly successful but arrogant individual who lost no opportunity to claim that his Wontner ancestors were so special that he spent time studying them. When it suited him, in his battle to retain full control of the Savoy, he courted comparison by hinting, publicly, at the ordinary ancestry of Charles Forte, an Italian immigrant.

With great difficulty, I tracked down his birth certificate and discovered that his surname at birth had not been Wontner but Smith and that he was descended from a long line of Smiths who had pursued prosaic careers in and around London. To find a record of a Wontner I had to track back to the mid-1800s, when a woman had brought that name into the family. Sir Hugh's father had been a successful film actor who called himself Arthur Wontner, which sounded more distinctive than Arthur Smith. So he changed his name to Wontner by deed poll but not before his son, Hugh, had been born.

When, eventually, I gave these facts to Giles Shepard, who had been Wontner's right-hand man, he was deeply shocked, feeling that he too had been misled.

Understandably, Charles Forte was amused as well as astonished by my find but he never made any use of it and discouraged me from doing so. When Charles reached old age, my wife and I chatted about how well deserved it was that, taking more time off, he and his Venetian wife Irene could choose, at short notice, whether to take a break in Barbados, Madrid, Rome, Paris or many other places where they owned or managed top-flight hotels. Then, suddenly and without warning, disaster struck and Charles and his family lost the whole company in 1996 after a hostile takeover. He and his children were left with a large sum of money from the unwanted deal but every one of his hotels and everything else in the vast business he had nurtured and loved had been snatched from him.

Charles died in 2007, aged ninety-eight, and Irene has also since left us but our family relationship still continues. Their son Rocco and daughter Olga, both now distinguished in the catering world, brought down a special lunch from London to celebrate my ninety-eighth birthday.

Near to the Forte shoot was Dunsborough Park, the seventeenth-century home of Charles Hughesdon and his wife Dessie, formerly famous as Florence Desmond, a hilarious cabaret star. As Billee had known the brilliant ballerina Margot Fonteyn when both were young, Hughesdon confessed to us that Margot, who was then dead, had been his mistress for many years. At the time when the newspapers were raving about her romantic love-affair with the celebrated young Russian ballet-dancer, Rudolf Nureyev, her real lover had been Charles Hughesdon, Nureyev being totally homosexual. Charles was, eventually, to publicise his affair with Margot, and others, in a book, *Flying Made it Happen*.

Hughesdon ran a partridge and pheasant shoot close by his home where, among other new contacts, I met the extraordinary John Cowdray, the Sussex landowner who had lost the whole of his left arm in the battle at Dunkirk. Using his heavy gun like a pistol, he shot his share of the difficult birds. Later, my wife and I also watched him salmon fishing on his Lower Crathes beat of the Scottish Dee. Wading deep, he wielded his heavy fly rod with one arm. To play a fish, as we watched him do successfully, he inserted the butt of the rod into a leather socket fixed to his belt. Guts!

Meanwhile, my shooting life had been further enhanced by the Sopwiths, who invited me to many of the splendid pheasant days they staged on their superb Compton estate. Like her husband, Lady Sopwith was an accurate shot and so keen that when, being over eighty, she needed an electronic heart-pacemaker, she insisted on having it inserted into her left side so that she could get her gun up to her right shoulder.

Not long before she died, aged eighty-six, she insisted on coming out with us to a stand I shall never forget. She waited in her Range

Rover until the really high birds began to arrive, got out, pulled off a splendid right and left and went home to rest.

Not only were the Compton pheasants of special quality but so were some of the guests, who often included statesmen like Harold Macmillan, judges, chiefs of staff and, frequently, Lord Mountbatten. Living so close by, 'Dickie' Mountbatten attended as what Lady Sopwith called 'a day-boy'. One morning he had arrived too early and when I took my dog out of the front door for a pre-breakfast walk (the dogs of visitors spending the night there always slept in the bedrooms) I found him leaning against the wall, sunning himself. I had not seen him since he had been seriously ill for some months and I congratulated him on looking so fit, as, indeed, he did. 'I look fit because I am fit,' he declared. 'And it's all down to ginseng. Barbara Cartland put me on to it. It is very good for the balls!'

There had been rumours of an affair between the handsome Dickie and the prolific novelist. Did his remark resolve the mystery?

On the last occasion I saw him – at a Sopwith lunch – he was telling us about his love for Classiebawn Castle in Ireland, where he holidayed with his family. When asked about his security arrangements there with regard to the IRA he answered, 'Who would want to kill an old bugger like me?' The answer came in August 1979 when he was assassinated by the IRA with a bomb secreted in his boat, which had been tied up without a guard or any routine search.

Yet again, I was indebted to the dear Sopwiths for my introduction to grouse-shooting, as they owned a moor at Arkengarthdale in North Yorkshire with a lovely old house. To be in a grouse-butt on a sunny day, scanning the heather, with shotgun at the ready and the wind in your face, is to be in another world. With the wind behind it, alternately flying then gliding up and down as it follows the contours at speeds up to 60mph, a grouse is the most difficult target shooting has to offer. I have many memories of such glorious days but one of them was not quite so pleasant.

I have been gifted with an outsize nose ever since my adolescence when what had been a normal proboscis began to enlarge. It was straight and symmetrical but did nothing for my looks. However, when I took up investigative journalism in 1946, it became something of an appropriate hallmark for someone who was quickly notorious in Whitehall and Westminster for sniffing out secret information. Sadly, its symmetry was to be shattered in a way which, possibly, has made it unique in the world.

I was waiting in a butt at Arkengarthdale, loaded gun in hand, with my loader, a local man, ready with my second gun as we faced the stiff wind, peering for the first sight of an approaching covey, spurred into flight by the beaters who were still over the horizon. Suddenly, we spotted about eight grouse approaching at speed and I shot the first well out in front to give me time for a second barrel at the next one. As I was concentrating on the second grouse, the dead bird, hurtling forwards under its momentum, struck me plumb on the nose, breaking it and blackening my eyes. It bounced off with sufficient force to knock my loader sideways.

Having established that I still had a face, and stuffing bits torn from my handkerchief up my nostrils to stem the blood flow, I carried on shooting. When the drive was over some twenty minutes later, the man in the next butt, Charles Hughesdon, rushed over shouting, 'Are you alright?' When I explained what had happened he said, 'Thank God! I thought you had been shot.'

A few years later, while shooting on another North Yorkshire moor, many miles away, my loader, who was new to me, asked me to repeat my name and then exclaimed, 'Oh, you must be that feller that was 'it on't nose by't grouse!' Fame indeed!

Considering the time I have spent standing in a line of guns, some of whom were insufficiently safety conscious, I suppose that I am fortunate that my broken nose was my only penalty. I did, however, have a near miss when I witnessed an accident that appears in most shooting manuals as the classic error to avoid.

I was standing at a pheasant shoot about thirty yards from a stranger, a judge, who was accompanied by his young son who was learning to shoot. The judge was shooting with the usual 12-bore shotgun while the son had a smaller and lighter 20-bore gun. If an easy pheasant came over, the father left it for the boy to shoot. For 'safety's sake', the father had the 20-bore cartridges in one of his pockets and reloaded the boy's gun when necessary. Unbelievably, he had inserted a 20-bore cartridge into his own 12-bore gun and, being of smaller diameter than the 12-bore cartridge which he should have put in, it had slipped halfway up the barrel and lodged there. So when he next fired that barrel nothing happened. Assuming that he must have forgotten to insert a cartridge of any kind, he loaded in a 12-bore cartridge. When he eventually fired it at an oncoming pheasant it exploded the 20-bore cartridge stuck above it with appalling results. The barrels were shattered and the heavy breech-block was driven towards his son's head at fatal speed. By extraordinary luck, it only grazed his chin and the judge escaped with the loss of only the top joint of his left little finger.

Both were rushed to hospital and eventually reappeared, with the father's arm heavily bandaged and, hopefully, a lesson learned.

The only other accident I witnessed was the result of even greater stupidity. One of those standing in the line, again a stranger to me, had needed to adjust his clothing and, while doing so, rested the barrels of his gun on his left foot, seemingly unaware that the gun's safety catch was in the firing position. Suddenly, as the gun fired, we were all running towards the prostrate form of the shooter – with one exception. The Cabinet minister Reginald Maudling, who was noted for his laziness, never moved, even when the victim was rushed to hospital with serious injuries.

At the Sopwiths' Hampshire home, I even encountered my old foe Harold Macmillan in the shooting line and we both stayed overnight. He liked to gossip round the table and shook with laughter as he told how, when visiting the White House accompanied by the atomic guru Sir William Penney to discuss the East–West balance of nuclear weapons, Penney had been asked by the US President, 'How many Russian H-bombs would be needed to knock out Britain?' In his deceptively lackadaisical voice, Penney had replied, 'I think five would finish us but let's say eight to be on the safe side.'

Attending so many of the same shoots, Macmillan and I eventually became friendly enough, despite our past grievances, for him to invite me and my wife to his home at Birch Grove, in Sussex. We arrived to find the house deserted but spotted through a window the old gentleman immersed in a book in his library. We tapped on the window and he shuffled to the front door explaining that the servants were all out and apologised for an awful black eye he had sustained that morning, when he had fallen and hit the fender.

As there was nobody to make the tea he offered us whisky – at 4 p.m. – which we gently declined. After the small talk, I managed to get the conversation round to a former head of MI5, Sir Roger Hollis, who I had long suspected of being a Soviet agent. Hollis had been well known to Macmillan, who raised his famous sloping eyebrows and said, 'Ah! Hollis! He was a marine, wasn't he?'

'No, no,' I replied, 'it was Major General Sir Leslie Hollis – no relation – who was the marine. I'm talking about the head of MI5, Sir Roger Hollis.'

'Oh!' he replied, with an air of innocence, and immediately changed the subject, rambling away. I felt sure that all was lost but, by some miracle, I got the conversation back to Hollis when his immediate response was, 'Ah! Hollis! He was a marine, wasn't he?'

I smiled at the old fox and gave up trying but his memoirs would show he had known plenty about the Hollis case and the secret uproar it had caused in high places had he wished to talk.

A more straightforward personality I met through shooting with the Sopwiths was Jim Joel, the diminutive and exceptionally kind member of the South African diamond and gold-mining family, best known in Britain for their horse-racing interests. Any sight of Phyl Sopwith in her emerald-green shooting clothes always reminded me of Jim because her lapel was adorned with a diamond brooch in the shape of an owl which he had given her.

Jim, who lived near St Albans, invited me to what he called his 'drawing-room' shoot appended to his house. There were so many pheasants on the final drive that several of the guns, who all had loaders, could not cope with them and sat exhausted on their shooting sticks.

Close to Ewhurst, near Bramley in Surrey, was the estate which most closely approximated to my ideal. Owned by our friends Peter and Ann Hutley, the manor house, Wintershall, dated from at least 1227 and sat in fields and woods of outstanding beauty, its hills,

ravines and dells providing challenging pheasants. I shot there for
many years, meeting many of the Hutleys' distinguished friends
who, regularly, included Viscount (John) Slim, a former chief of
the SAS, and the Attorney General Sir Michael Havers, who was
gloriously indiscreet, being informative on major issues over many
years, as later chapters will detail.

Shooting also strengthened my friendship with Julian Amery,
then the Air Minister and a keen shot, who organised an exciting tour in 1962 of the RAF's Middle East bases for me, providing
a small transport plane with a high-ranking pilot who, starting in
Cyprus, took me to Aden in the Yemen on the south coast of Arabia
where there was a large RAF airfield. Having explored Aden, also
an important port, I was flown northwards to various places in the
very wild Yemen to meet various tribal chiefs including a delightful
young man called the 'Naib' who had a small palace. As with the
other chiefs I met, I observed the rule regarding coffee on which I
had been briefed – accept a second cup or he will be offended but
decline a third or he will think you are greedy.

We then flew low along the south coast of Arabia to Oman, landing in the capital, Muscat, where the buildings then were mainly
built from mud. From there we flew to the Omani island of Masirah
where, in the twilight, I was taken to watch giant turtles laying their
eggs in the sand. On each stop I filed a report of my adventures for
my newspaper.

From Oman we flew along the Persian Gulf visiting each of the
main towns of what were then known as the Trucial States – Dubai,
Abu Dhabi and Sharjah, each of which was small but harboured
an RAF station. To see Dubai and Abu Dhabi now, as I so often do
on television, amazes me as I recall how modest they were just fifty
years ago.

On a later occasion, when Amery was seeking a way of publicis-
ing the atomic capability of the RAF, I suggested that a photograph
of me leaning against an H-bomb, which no outsider had ever seen,
would be helpful. A few days later he asked me to visit an airfield
where an official photographer was waiting. We were taken to a
hangar from which was wheeled a trolley bearing the RAF's biggest

megaton bomb and the photograph duly appeared, exclusively, in the *Daily Express*. The vital need for secrecy can be very elastic when it suits a political purpose.

Early in September 1972, I was telephoned by Julian, then Minister of State in the Foreign Office. He told me that a very important Arab, who was visiting Britain, had inquired about a day's duck-shooting. Did I have any ideas? My only possibility was my neighbour, Alan Bristow, the forceful founder of Bristow Helicopters, who had a nearby sporting estate called Baynard's Park with a large lake.

Alan was keen to oblige when he learned that the VIA was Sheikh Zayed, ruler of the then oil-rich Abu Dhabi and the elected spokesman for the United Arab Emirates as the Trucial States had become in 1971. He scented business for his helicopters servicing the off-shore oil-rigs, so, as his reared mallard ducks were not ready, he offered an evening's flighting of wild mallard and, hopefully, wild geese. The Sheikh accepted and I too was invited. Sadly, no ducks or geese appeared in quantity before darkness fell and Alan was deeply embarrassed.

So well mannered was the Sheikh, however, that next morning he personally telephoned Alan with his thanks and asked to be invited again. Determined to take no further chances, Alan offered a partridge shoot, though his large stock of reared birds was not really ready. The Sheikh accepted also on behalf of three other important Arabs who were with him. Again I went along.

When the Arabs arrived they were in their long robes and head-dresses, the only concession to the field being green wellies, which were just visible. There was also an Italian in attendance, in an electric-blue suit, who was the Sheikh's official photographer.

Whenever a partridge flew towards the line, whether low or high, every Arab fired at it, which did not surprise me because, having spent some time with Arab tribesmen in the Yemen, I knew that there is nothing that the desert Arab enjoys more than letting his gun off. As each bird rose, the beaters made themselves as flat on the ground as possible. The all-round danger of the situation was exacerbated by the young son of one of the Arabs who ran out to pick up the bird every time his father shot one. The accolade for courage went to the Italian photographer who lay on his back in front of the Sheikh taking action shots.

The break for lunch was staged in a large tent which Alan had set up in a farmyard to make the guests feel at home. Imitation palm fronds sprouted from the poles. There were dozens of colourful scatter-cushions on the floor. Outside, a whole sheep was being roasted on a spit. All that was missing were the belly-dancers.

Billee, who had been invited to lunch along with Alan's partner, was seated next to the Sheikh and did her bit for Britain by feeding grapes to him as he reclined. After the roast lamb, the Sheikh insisted on providing Arabian-style coffee, which he had brought. It seemed to have some special potency because, after we banned the ladies from the field on safety grounds, they spent the afternoon falling about in giggles on the scatter-cushions.

By the end of the day, three beaters and a keeper had been slightly peppered with shotgun pellets but, when lavish compensations were handed out, it was the unscathed who felt aggrieved. Alan ended in lucrative business with the Sheikh, whom he thenceforth referred to as 'Sheikhy Baby', though anybody less infantile would be hard to imagine.

The Foreign Office was delighted on all counts. My eventual reward from Alan was a beautifully bound volume with gold lettering entitled 'Highlights in the Sex Life of Chapman Pincher'. It was filled with blank pages.

I met many self-made rich men shooting with Alan Bristow but none had made their fortunes more dramatically than a young, unassuming wartime sailor with whom I have remained in mutually affectionate touch for more than half a century. Born in Streatham, and with no sea-faring background, Donald Gosling joined the navy in 1944 aged fifteen as an able seaman and fell in love with it and, particularly, with his warship, the cruiser *Leander*. He was heartbroken when forced to leave because of the peacetime reductions.

With a £200 gratuity he walked the London streets wondering what to do and conceived the idea of using a cleared bomb-site as a car park. He consulted the relevant London council official,

Ronald Hobson, with whose guidance he set up his first parking facility. Hobson, who also had a £200 gratuity for his wartime army service, joined him in the venture, which later became National Car Parks, the biggest operation of its kind in Britain or Europe. By 1997 it was valued at £750 million and employed many thousands!

Ever grateful to the navy, Don has devoted much energy and support to the White Ensign Association, which finds jobs for retired naval and marine personnel, becoming its president, and to several other naval charities. In 1976 he was knighted for 'services to HM Forces' and created KCVO in 2004. In 2012, his charitable foundation gave £25 million towards the upkeep of Nelson's flag-ship, *Victory*.

Until 2012, Don rated as his greatest honours his promotion to honorary captain of the Royal Naval Reserve in 1993 for his charitable efforts for the navy, then to rear admiral, then vice admiral, which required him to carry out ceremonial functions in full uniform. Then, in 2012, at a private lunch in his honour at Windsor Castle, the Queen awarded him the ancient title of Vice Admiral of the United Kingdom, directly subordinate to the Lord High Admiral of the United Kingdom, who is the Duke of Edinburgh. A very able-minded seaman!

Don attributes his success to the impact of his beloved navy on his character. He says that it taught him the values of work, discipline and teamwork. It also taught him to trust others, as one needs to do on a fighting ship. He and Hobson never had a written agreement in their car park partnership, trusting each other totally from the outset. They still keep an office in London but Don spends much of his time afloat on his magnificent yacht, inevitably called *Leander*.

He also continued to shoot pheasants, which was how we had first met, and, for many years, he rented the Mountbatten shoot at Broadlands in Hampshire, where I was a regular gun – usually along with several admirals! After age required me to retire from shooting, my wife and I still attended the usually hilarious shoot lunches there. (On one occasion Don, who loves to laugh, entered the room seemingly in a cage carried by an enormous gorilla. He had seen the clever trick at a London party and hired it.)

As recently as February 2013, Don sent me a letter attributing his success to his first day, in 1943, onboard the *Arethusa* training ship. For a certain administrative task he was selected to be in charge of twenty-four other boys, recalling, 'It gave me an immense feeling of power and I believe it really all started from there!'

Alan Bristow himself also owed his first success to one idea, so outrageous that I put it on record as he told it to me. He had learned to fly helicopters while serving in the Fleet Air Arm during the Second World War and became so captivated by the possibilities of hovering flight that he decided to centre his life around it. In 1949, he was in French Indo-China (now Vietnam) hoping to sell helicopters to the French forces, who were trying to stave off a determined attempt to end their colonial power. In one demonstration, he managed to rescue several French soldiers who were surrounded by the enemy, for which he was awarded the Croix de Guerre.

He then moved to the Antarctic where a Greek shipping magnate was operating a whaling fleet. During the four years he worked there, Alan demonstrated the power of the helicopter for finding whales and learned so much about them that he conceived the idea of a humane harpoon to be fired from a helicopter.

First, to his great surprise, he found that he could hover low over a whale without disturbing it. The whale simply ignored the machine. This gave him the idea of developing a harpoon which would instantly kill the whale with a powerful electric shock generated by equipment on the helicopter and passing through a wire attached to the harpoon. Having no barbs on it, the harpoon could then be withdrawn and wound back on to the helicopter.

Then he not only demonstrated that his idea would work but found that the shock made the tongue of the whale block the opening to its lungs so that the carcass always floated and could be collected by the mother whaling ship later. In all respects, his humane harpoon was far less cruel than the standard barbed harpoon fired into the body with all the consequent struggle.

So in 1951, having patented his equipment, he set up a company called Air Whaling with every intention of selling it. He managed to do so to a Dutch whaling company. The company, which had an office in London, insisted on paying him in cash and, after receiving it, Alan found himself on an Underground train carrying a suitcase containing £1 million in banknotes!

Not long afterwards, the International Whaling Commission banned hunting by helicopter because it was so efficient that it would rapidly deplete the whale population.

With his new capital Alan set up Bristow Helicopters, which was quick to exploit the oil boom, servicing rigs at sea. The company was such a huge success that when Alan finally lost it in a takeover battle, he received so much in recompense that he came to my house to tell me and my wife, 'I'm not just a millionaire, now! I'm a multi-multi-multi-millionaire!'

Our last meeting, shortly before he died in 2009 aged eighty-five, was at the Vineyard hotel in Newbury where, sitting in a wheelchair, he and his wife Heather gave lunch to my wife and me. He was as irrepressible as ever as we recalled old experiences, one of which was an encounter with a TV presenter called Reginald Bosanquet. While I was standing in the line next to Bosanquet, a woodcock came towards us and I shot it without comment from anyone. Many years later, I was sitting in the waiting room of a TV studio when Bosanquet drifted in. Pointing a finger at me, he cried, 'There's the bugger who shot my woodcock!' It had rankled with him all those years.

At one of Alan's shoots I met the property developer Harry Hyams, who lived in Ramsbury Manor in Wiltshire, where he then ran a small but demanding shoot providing some very high pheasants. It was a fluke that Kintbury, to which we moved in 1980, is close to Ramsbury and it cemented our friendship and, though Harry 2 (as he calls himself) is very reclusive, he has kept in touch with Harry 1 (as he calls me).

The friendship led to an invitation to Billee and me to accompany him, along with several others, on his first voyage on the *Shemara*, the luxury cruise ship he had acquired and refurbished. We greatly enjoyed ourselves during a week-long cruise in the Mediterranean.

I could tell many tales about Harry 2's relationships with women but he is, happily, still with us. However, there is one I cannot resist as it is so typical of his humour. He and his wife attended a large party at our old Surrey house and, as usual, he had arrived with a second lady. Eventually, when I went outside with them to see them depart, he slammed the back door of the car into which the second lady had climbed, remarking in a loud voice, 'Always carry a spare!'

The outstanding room in Ramsbury Manor is the saloon, panelled in walnut. Above each of the four corner doors there was a plain rectangular panel and, one day, when Billee and I were there, I noticed that one of the panels was missing. Hyams explained that an art expert had noticed signs of a painting underneath the brown surface. A few weeks later, the panel was back in place bearing a landscape of the type painted by Claude Lorrain in the mid-seventeenth century. Eventually, all four panels were found to bear such a landscape while the huge brown panel over the fireplace yielded a splendid portrait of a young boy garbed in classic style – probably a former scion of the house.

The immediate question was, 'Who could have been guilty of such vandalism in having them over-painted?' A few years later the mystery was revealed by a man who had overseen the dreadful act, much to his disgust. The wife of a relatively recent owner had wanted all the panelling 'to match'.

Harry 2 was an assiduous collector of the finest porcelain, silver and the rarest antique clocks, his collection being valued at £60 million – an estimate made for a tragic reason. In February 2006, while Harry and his wife Kay were away, thieves broke into Ramsbury Manor and stole most of his collection thereby committing Britain's biggest-ever burglary from a private house. Five members of a well-known gang of thieves were imprisoned for the crime but Harry doubted that they alone were guilty. Having no children, his collection was especially significant for him and the last time we spoke by telephone he said, 'We don't go to Ramsbury much these days. It doesn't seem like home anymore.'

Early in the 1970s, on arrival at Ramsbury Manor to shoot, I recognised one of the other guests as Rupert Murdoch, who I had met in 1953 in Adelaide. One evening, while dining in a restaurant there with a local girl called Pam, a tall, pleasant-looking chap in his early twenties drifted in causing Pam to exclaim, in the slightly cockney accent which was common in Australia then, 'Hello Rupert!' Her friend came over and was introduced as Rupert Murdoch, who owned and ran Adelaide's *The Advertiser*, a newspaper previously owned by his father. Having decided to devote his life to the media business, young Murdoch acquired other papers in Australia for a parent company he called News Corporation, which he expanded into Britain by acquiring *The Sun*, in 1969, converting it into a highly successful tabloid.

He either remembered me or affected to do so when I shook his hand at Ramsbury and noticed that he was wearing an obviously new knickerbocker suit and had a brand new shotgun. On the way to the first drive he asked me what we were supposed to do, explaining that he had never experienced driven pheasants before.

I felt appalled for him because we were opening with the Plantation Drive where the pheasants always came very high and fast. So, I had time only to advise him what *not* to do – which was not to shoot at birds going to other people. Predictably, he hit nothing. However, by the end of the day he was shooting surprisingly well. Clearly he was a man determined to succeed at whatever he attempted.

At lunch, Murdoch told me that he was not enjoying Britain because of the snobbish attitude of many people, especially to his wife, Anna. He was, therefore, thinking of moving his base to the US. He did so, acquiring his first American newspaper in 1973. Later, he bought the *New York Post* and the *Wall Street Journal*, also acquiring the British *Times* and *Sunday Times* in 1981.

With remarkable foresight for technological advances, he introduced electronic production of newspapers in Britain and, with great courage, broke the power of the print unions, which had long held the UK newspaper industry to ransom. In the US, where he became a citizen in 1985, he moved into television, investing heavily in satellite TV. He became worth more than $6 billion and became rated one of the world's most influential people. (Knowing so many of the self-made super-rich, why did I never learn how to join them?)

The recent public vilification of Murdoch and his son through the 'phone-hacking affair' by MPs incapable of creating anything except noise has saddened me, especially as my phone has been hacked by government departments all my investigative life.

The Hyams shoot was frequented by many other men who would now be dubbed celebrities, the racing driver Graham Hill being a regular. There, I also encountered Sir Charles Clore, the highly successful businessman, financier and philanthropist, who invited me to his house and shoot at Stype, near Newbury. He liked to do everything on a grand scale (including his most generous charities) and I recall joining him for tea at the end of an enjoyable day's pheasant shoot when the gamekeeper handed him the score-card, which read 'Pheasants 486'. Charlie threw down the card in disgust saying, 'No bloody good!' He liked 1,000 or thereabouts, especially when he had special guests like the Duke of Marlborough, known to his friends as Sonny.

I stayed at Stype on several occasions in the Duke's company, always being impressed by his elegant style and marksmanship. I remember an occasion when, at a stand where many pheasants were expected, the keeper put his master behind the Duke to share in the feathered fray. At the end, we all heard Charlie complaining loudly, 'What's the point in putting me behind the Duke? You know he never misses anything.'

CHAPTER 12

A LIFE-CHANGING SHOOT

In the 1970s, while I was still in Fleet Street and living in Surrey, I was asked regularly by my friend Norman Angel to a small but exceptionally pleasant shoot called Radley Bottom, about a mile from Kintbury, of which I had never previously heard. Lunch with the farmer of the land, Ivor Gore, and his wife and son Trevor was always a delightful and, usually, hilarious bonus and Billee, who accompanied me to pick up with my dog, shared my enjoyment. It became our habit, at the end of the shoot, to slip into Kintbury to visit the bakery to buy a delicious confection called a 'lardy' cake.

To be within a mile of Radley Bottom after our move to Kintbury in 1980 was another bonus as I was shooting there almost every week during the game season. Inevitably, I met many new people there, including two foreign 'royals' – Prince George of Denmark and the former King Constantine of Greece (inevitably known to us as 'King Con'). Prince George, who was attached to the Danish embassy in London, became a friend who visited our house, where he would, unusually, tap the base of his empty sherry or wine glass gently against the table until it was refilled.

One day, while being transported in King Con's Range Rover between pheasant drives, my wife, who was sitting in front with him, idly pressed an odd-looking button on the dashboard. A cavity containing a loaded revolver was exposed.

'You should not have done that,' King Con remarked, 'but as you are so curious, press the next one.' She did so and the vehicle and the land round it was quickly covered in a cloud of black smoke – all part of the security the ex-king regarded as a worthwhile precaution.

The shoot was also attended by Major General Hashim Said Hashim, who had been chief of the Saudi Arabian Air Force and, while still being based in Jeddah, where he had major businesses, owned a fine house close to Radley Bottom. One day, in between drives, King Con asked Hashim why he had retired from the air force so young. Hashim explained that he had already been a major general by the time he was thirty-two. With a grin and a wink, King Con replied, 'I was a field marshal when I was twenty-one.'

I learned a great deal about the Arab and Muslim mind from Hashim (described by my wife as 'a cross between Clark Gable and Omar Sharif'). His family, who had lived in Mecca, claimed direct descent from the Prophet and he gave big parties attended by other Arabs. Now living in Lebanon, Hashim still calls on us when he visits the UK to shoot.

Radley Bottom was also regularly frequented by Air Vice Marshal 'Johnnie' Johnson, the RAF's official top-scoring wartime fighter pilot (three DSOs and two DFCs), accredited with shooting down thirty-eight Luftwaffe planes over Britain and France with many more 'possibles'. As was true of several other distinguished pilots I met during and after the war, such as Douglas Bader, Johnnie was an unforgettable character, tough, determined, a born survivor and with a good sense of humour. He had gone to great lengths to meet and correspond with his opposite number – the Luftwaffe's top-scoring ace, General Adolf Galland, who was officially credited by the German authorities as having destroyed 104 enemy aircraft, mostly British.

Johnnie had regaled us with many stories of his once arch-enemy, whom he always called 'Dolfo' as, in fact, he was known throughout the Luftwaffe. It transpired that while Johnnie, a Spitfire pilot, had never been shot down, Dolfo, who flew Messerschmitts, had been shot down four times and had always survived to fly again. Whether Johnnie had shot him down remained uncertain but they had established that they had tried hard to kill each other in at least one dogfight.

Having told us so many Dolfo stories, we were excited to learn that the German superhero had been invited to shoot and had accepted.

'Dolfo can tap 'em,' Johnnie assured me when I asked if he was a good game-shot. Galland turned out to be quiet, modest and charming to talk to. Like Johnnie, he had an excellent shot because both had learned the art of deflection, firing their guns in front of their targets, as is required with a shotgun when shooting fast game. Dolfo certainly had the killer instinct. While Johnnie let the low-flying birds pass, considering them too easy targets, Dolfo downed anything off the ground as was, and still is, common European practice. My wife, whose first husband had died during the Battle of Britain, said nothing but could not help wondering whether the nice guy 'tapping 'em' had been responsible for making her a widow at the age of twenty.

We later discovered that the circumstances all fitted that grim possibility. Her young husband had been shot down over the Channel in an area patrolled by Galland. So, understandably, Billee's views about the experience remain mixed. To me, to have stood in the line with two such war superheroes, now both dead, was an exciting privilege I would always treasure.

Another famous war hero with whom I shot at the same location was David Stirling, the founder of the SAS, whom I had first met at Bruce McKenzie's house in Kenya, playing his eccentric version of snooker. After commando training in 1940, David had been posted to the Eighth Army in the north African desert to assist in the battle against the German forces led by the brilliant General Rommel. Bored by the slow pace of the British weapons build-up, he conceived the idea that a small mobile team in American jeeps fitted with machine guns and carrying small bombs and demolition charges could inflict great damage on enemy airfields, dumps and bases through surprise raids in darkness. Gaining access to senior officers by a ruse, he secured permission to seek volunteers for his group of night-raiders, which was given the deliberately deceptive title of First Special Air Service Brigade.

After a disastrous start, this prototype of the now-superlative SAS was eventually credited with the destruction of 250 aircraft, hundreds of enemy vehicles, munitions dumps and communication centres. Leading from the front, Stirling guided his unit in darkness across many miles of desert, suddenly attacking the target and inflicting maximum damage before escaping. Field Marshal Montgomery, who eventually defeated Rommel, is on record as saying that Stirling was 'quite mad' but, nevertheless, appreciated the results of his madness.

Inevitably, Stirling was captured by the Germans in January 1943 and, inevitably, escaped but was recaptured, ending up in the Colditz fortress, where he was to remain until the war's end when the SAS he had founded, with its slogan 'who dares wins', rapidly achieved worldwide respect.

I have a strong mental picture of this extraordinary man standing alone with his gun in a field of cabbages at Radley Bottom. I also recall a story about him that certainly fits his character. While staying with a certain duke, who required each of his shooting guests to plant a sack of daffodils, David was allotted the area beneath the window of one the main rooms. In the spring his flowers spelled an unmistakeable two-word message to His Grace.

Though David and I met regularly in London, he discouraged being questioned about his exploits which, I discovered later, were being duplicated in Kenya where he was assisting Bruce McKenzie to set up an SAS-type unit, which scored some notable successes against terrorists.

After the war, David had set up an arms-sales outfit called Watchguard. Then in 1974, when the power of the unions was threatening a general strike, he applied his leadership and expertise to an organisation called Great Britain 75 to keep Britain up and running, to which I gave welcome publicity. The reaction from highly qualified people prepared to assist in keeping the power stations and other essential services running was almost overwhelming. All too belatedly, David was knighted in 1990 when, reluctantly, the seemingly indestructible warrior confessed that he was suffering from 'shallow breathing'. He died later that year, aged seventy-four.

Beyond Radley Bottom, on the edge of the little town of Hungerford, is another, much larger shoot where I also was privileged to raise my gun and whose owner, Sir Peter Michael, was to be instrumental in saving my wife's life.

We had visited Peter's splendid house, Eddington, but had not known him long when he heard that my wife had been diagnosed as having colon cancer. He telephoned me immediately and I told him that we had made arrangements for her to undergo surgery at a hospital in Reading. He insisted that I must cancel my arrangements, explaining that the most successful specialist in colon operations was a friend of his who he was sure would operate without delay. He named the man as Bill Heald, who operated at the Hampshire Clinic near Basingstoke, and would brook no argument when I protested that I had already seen the Reading surgeon. 'Leave it all to Bill, who will make all the arrangements,' he insisted.

Having such respect for Peter's achievements in so many enterprises, I accepted. (Then in his mid-forties, Peter had founded Quantel, a pioneer electronics company which invented most of the TV graphical tricks and special effects which we now take for granted, and, eventually, had sold his holding for £60 million. Pursuing the decision taken along with his wife, Maggie, that they would 'never have all their eggs in one basket', he co-founded the radio station Classic FM. He has also bought and still runs two successful hotels and has founded and built up a highly profitable wine business in northern California. He was recently listed as being worth £185 million.)

I was, therefore, not surprised when he proved to be right about Bill Heald, whose operation on my wife was totally successful. In the process, Bill and his wife, 'Bounce', became new friends and we have had happy times together, especially during joint visits to a marvellous villa in the south of France then owned by Peter.

One day, shooting at the Sopwiths', I had encountered Henry Porchester, son of the sixth Earl of Carnarvon. I told him that I had been the tenant of Milford Lake and how I had been sacked when he had moved into the house there. His amused response was to invite me to fish there again and we became close friends. Henry was one of the best and most elegant pheasant shots I had ever encountered and he invited me to shoot at Highclere, his family's 5,000-acre estate near Newbury, now famed on TV as *Downton Abbey*.

Billee and Henry's delightful lady Jeanie already knew each other through their services to the nearby Newbury Spring Festival, of which I, too, became an active supporter, attending all the concerts. Another regular attender, who was an acquaintance of mine through game-shooting, was Sir William Mount, a very private country squire who was to achieve posthumous distinction by being the grandfather of a Prime Minister – David Cameron. When Sir William gave up shooting he came to pick up pheasants with his dog at the nearby shoot of which I was a member. He stood behind me several times and I made his acquaintance. Anyone more remote from politics, and especially Downing Street, would be hard to imagine. Sir William was a countryman to his marrow.

I sat in front of him in Newbury's St Nicholas Church at a performance of Mozart's *Sinfonia Concertante*, which features forceful counter-play between the violin and the viola, with the two performers standing close together and fiddling away furiously and competitively in turn. When, at the end, I asked Sir William what he thought of it, he replied, 'It reminded me of a couple of cock pheasants having a go at each other.' Surely a unique interpretation which, I think, would have amused Mozart, who had an earthy sense of humour.

One of the many virtuosi who performed at the festival was the outstanding French cellist Paul Tortelier. Through our friendship with Jeanie Porchester, my wife and I were honoured with a private performance by him in the confines of our Kintbury home where he not only played but sang!

After his festival performance, Tortelier was scheduled to spend the night with the Porchesters but Jeanie fell ill and asked us to accommodate the great man, along with his two cellos. Next morning, over breakfast, he began to question me about the anti-atomic 'Peace Women' encamped on nearby Greenham Common, with whom he expressed sympathy, suggesting that I might take him there to play for them.

He then announced that he had composed both the words and music of a *Hymn to Peace* in English and insisted on performing it. In the confines of our modest hall he produced a cello and, to his own accompaniment, sang to my wife and me until the arrival of the daily help, who was startled to see a tall, lean stranger with a mop of hair fiddling away and singing, stridently, under the grandfather clock. The maestro insisted that she delay her chores and listen as he restarted the hymn.

He sang less tunefully than he played but, in his very French way, got his message across in several forceful verses – a unique performance to remember.

Henry Porchester's father, the Earl of Carnarvon, known to his friends as 'Old Porchie' and who I had also met through the Sopwiths, lived in the enormous house and he, too, regularly invited me to shoot. Small in stature but larger than life, Old Porchie had an imperious voice and an outstanding capacity to engender laughter and make his guests, male or female, feel special. Once, when I managed to bring down a very high pheasant, he yelled, 'You'll remember that bird all your life!' He was right.

When he could no longer raise his gun he watched the drives from his car to ensure that each of his guests had a fair share. His other joy was horse-racing and he would whisper such lore as, 'Razorsharp in the 3.30 – he's worth a fiver!' So that he could attend parties and be with the standing drinkers, rather than sidelined on a chair, he fitted his shooting seat with a soft rubber ferrule.

In his old age, when he was living alone in Highclere Castle, I would take him a trout and find him sitting on a sofa, sporting bright red braces, and he would chat about his many female conquests and those that had eluded him. When my wife spotted him sitting in the Iron Stand at Ascot, as he always did, he explained that it was reserved for 'boys who had been naughty'.

Though Highclere was only a short drive from Kintbury, he insisted that we should stay the night with him for a shoot next day and we noted his habit of switching off the lights at every opportunity to 'prevent waste'. He was punctilious about beginning meals on time and leaving the table as soon as possible so that the servants could finish. If there were thirteen to lunch or dinner he would have his meal on a separate table one inch from the head of the main table.

One of the regular guests at Old Porchie's shoots was Christopher Soames, who had married Winston Churchill's daughter Mary. One of my deepest journalistic regrets is never having met

Churchill, the greatest Englishman of the twentieth century, but
through Christopher Soames and two other of his close relatives
– Duncan Sandys, who had married Churchill's daughter Diana,
and Churchill's grandson, who was also called Winston – I heard a
few Churchillian anecdotes worthy of record.

Churchill's French was always fractured and Sandys told me
that he was present at a wartime meeting chaired by the great man
and attended by the French leader-in-waiting, General de Gaulle,
who, though having no real power or effective authority, was being
his arrogant self, objecting to this and that. Suddenly, the furious
Churchill stood up, looked de Gaulle in the eye and shouted, '*Si vous
m'opposerez je vous get riderai!*'

Soames told me of his first meeting with de Gaulle in 1968,
when he began a four-year stint as British ambassador in Paris.
Still installed as the French Prime Minister, the vengeful de Gaulle
peered at Soames and said, slowly and almost menacingly, '*Nous
savons qui vous êtes*'.

When discussing his grandfather's habits with Winston junior, I
expressed surprise that, as he had always seemed to have a glass of
whisky and had smoked so many cigars, he had lived to be ninety.
'He was a bit of an old fraud in both respects,' Winston replied.
'The cigar and the whisky were media trademarks. He didn't puff
the cigar much and drank little of the whisky.'

In fact, the war had taken a vicious toll on the great states-
man's health. He suffered two minor strokes in 1949, when he was
seventy-five, and a massive one in the summer of 1953, while he
was still Prime Minister. With the help of Beaverbrook and other
newspaper barons, his condition was withheld from the media and
the public. Churchill recuperated hidden away at Beaverbrook's
villa near Monte Carlo, and did not resign until 1955. During the
ten more years that he lived he was having increasing difficulty
getting to his seat in the Commons but that, too, was not reported
out of respect for our wartime debt to him.

I became friendly with Duncan Sandys when he was Defence
Minister in the late 1950s and needed media support for the many
post-war changes he made. I found him to be as cool under political

fire as he had been when fighting the Germans in Norway in 1941 when he had received a severe wound which gave him a permanent limp. On one occasion, I needed to alert him to a scandalous situation which I imagined would cause him deep concern. It involved Margaret, Duchess of Argyll, whose unusual sexual activities had been publicly revealed in court in 1963 when sued for divorce by the Duke. As evidence, the prosecution had produced some devastating pictures of the Duchess, one of which showed her wearing only a pearl necklace while in an encounter with a naked man, whose head did not appear on the photograph which had been taken to enhance the excitement.

There was a Fleet Street scramble to identify 'the headless man' which quickly required me to telephone Sandys in his ministerial office in Whitehall to warn him that there was a growing newspaper belief that he was the culprit. I will never forget his cool response – 'Don't worry, dear boy! There's safety in numbers!'

By contrast to Old Porchie, his son Henry was tall, handsome and serious, being an outstanding mediator and conciliator, chairing the Hampshire County Council, the South East Regional Planning Conference, the Standing Conference on Countryside Sports and the Agricultural Research Council. He, too, was interested in racehorses but more seriously as the Queen's racing manager and close friend. Her Majesty enjoyed the informality of her many visits to Milford Lake House, especially on shooting days.

A complete countryman, when Henry had been in active army service in Italy during the war he had dreamed of his safe return to Highclere to run the estate and to do as much for other country people as he could. He was also listed among the twelve best shots in the UK and to watch him deal with the most challenging pheasants and partridges, as I was so often privileged to do, was to witness near-perfection.

During the many years that my wife and I visited Henry and Jeanie we watched the progress of their three children – Geordie, who is the present Earl; Harry, who now runs a racing syndicate; and Carolyn, whose life was to become the nearest thing to a fairy tale that I have ever encountered.

I recall sitting with Old Porchie at a large reception to meet Carolyn's young husband, John Warren, the son of a greengrocer from Harlow in Essex, who had been a stable lad where, we were told, he had developed a rare 'eye for a horse'. We met his parents and the good-looking John, who clearly had an engaging personality. Nevertheless to Old Porchie, as to me, it did not seem to be a union likely to succeed. We could not have been more mistaken.

Warren's 'eye for a horse' proved to be so real that he and Carolyn have happily set up and run Highclere Thoroughbred Racing, which has prospered. More impressively, he has become bloodstock adviser to the Queen, succeeding his father-in-law as the Queen's racing manager, overseeing her racing and horse-breeding interests. As such, he has become a national figure regularly seen on television as the millions who watched the Ascot Gold Cup race on 20 June 2013 are unlikely to forget. As the Queen's horse Estimate won the Gold Cup, the TV cameras were trained on Her Majesty and Warren as in close proximity they expressed their joint excitement and joy.

Old Porchie died in 1987 and, after sixty-three years as Lord Porchester, Henry became the seventh Earl of Carnarvon. Tragically, he died in his prime, unexpectedly, in 2001.Over so many years, I have had the privilege of watching Henry's successor Geordie mature and take over command and am specially delighted that the public interest created by *Downton Abbey* has eased his daunting task of coping with the enormous upkeep of Highclere, which he and his wife cherish.

A genuine abbey where I enjoyed memorable shooting and hospitality was Woburn in Bedfordshire, then the enormous abode of Robin and Henrietta Tavistock. My first day there was enlivened by a wallaby which hopped in front of the shooting line, being a descendant of one of the several wild creatures freed on to the estate by Robin's eccentric grandfather, the Duke of Bedford. Even more memorable, as we spent the night at Woburn, was to dine surrounded by Canalettos, ingeniously illuminated as though by the Venetian sun.

Another major landowner who, justifiably, I would call our

local Lawrence of Arabia and who I met through shooting near Kintbury, was Brigadier Sir Timothy Landon, whose astonishing financial success – he left a fortune in excess of £500 million when he, so sadly, died in 2007 aged sixty-four – remains a source of wonder. He lived just a few miles up the road from my home in Kintbury in the little village of Faccombe, where he invited me to enjoy the testing pheasants and partridges on his 4,000-acre estate many times. Generous, gregarious and outgoing, he also regularly invited my wife and me to parties, dinners and lunches and to the concerts and operas he staged in the magnificent entrance hall to Faccombe Manor.

Born in Vancouver in 1944 to a Canadian mother, his father having been a British brigadier seconded to the Canadian Army, he was sent to the army officer training centre at Sandhurst, where one of his fellow students was Qaboos, heir to the ruler of Oman, a large country south of Saudi Arabia on the Arabian Sea. They became close friends, a chance association which was to condition his life.

In 1962, thanks to Julian Amery, I had visited Oman, where the RAF had air bases for defence of Britain's Middle East interests. I met the ruler, Sultan Said, in his summer palace in Salalah and found him living in a medieval backwater with no intention of changing. He was cutting off the hands of thieves and stoning women to death for adultery. Large oil reserves had been found in Oman and he was converting the income to gold bars and spending nothing to improve the poor living standards of the people. Inevitably, there was a Communist-inspired rebellion which the UK needed to defeat. (The day I arrived in the capital, Muscat, a grenade was thrown into the electricity plant there.)

By coincidence, it was Tim's regiment that was sent to Oman. There he found his friend Qaboos under house arrest – his father did not trust even his own son. Tim, who quickly learned the language, was made an intelligence officer, forging links with MI6 which lasted for life.

In July 1970, with British connivance, Qaboos ousted his father in a bloodless coup in which Tim, then twenty-seven, was deeply involved. The old Sultan was exiled to London where he lived in the Dorchester Hotel until he died. (When once asked if he had any regrets, he replied, 'Not having Landon shot!')

Tim resigned his UK commission and joined the Omani army as a brigadier, his main purpose being to help Qaboos use the oil revenues to convert Oman into a modern state, which was rapidly achieved with great success. Oman is prosperous with a contented people sharing its affluence. In the process, visiting Oman regularly, Tim amassed a great fortune through grateful gifts from Qaboos, who still reigns, and from contracts in building up substantial defence forces, with British firms securing many of them. Both Oman and Britain are greatly in his debt.

In 1977 he married Kata, a member of the famed Hungarian Esterhazy family. They had a son, Arthur, who figures in the annual 'Rich List' as worth £200 million. I lunched with him and his mother recently and, like his father, he is unspoiled by his wealth.

When Sultan Qaboos visited Britain in 1982, Tim was made a Knight Commander of the Victorian Order by the Queen for his service to the nation but could never use the title because he remained a Canadian citizen.

I was too young to have known my father's hero, Lawrence of Arabia, or even to read his *Seven Pillars of Wisdom* when it was published in 1922. What a biography Tim could have written! Instead, as a good intelligence officer should, he obeyed what he might have called *Seven Pillars of Silence*. I feel greatly privileged to have known him.

Meanwhile, my heavy costs of shooting at high level were totally defrayed through articles I wrote for the *Shooting Times*, *The Field* and other magazines and by the exclusive news I picked up from some of the other guns. By serious application, I improved my shooting prowess and considered myself reasonably proficient, though aware that I still had much to learn. As my flow of luck continued, I was suddenly gifted by an extraordinary role model and mentor who was, probably, the greatest bird-shot of all time and with whom my professional life would become entwined.

CHAPTER 13

JOE

In its 2011 *Hunting, Shooting & Fishing Guide, Tatler* unknowingly paid me a fine compliment. Among its five all-time 'shooting heroes' it – rightly – named my old friend Sir Joseph Nickerson and among its five all-time best books about shooting it named Joe's biography, *A Shooting Man's Creed*. What it did not know was that I wrote every word of that book and even devised the title. Joe paid me, handsomely, to ghost his memoirs and the deal included his right to mention my name if he wished. He decided not to do so and few have known of my authorship. I put it on record now because Joe has been dead for more than twenty years and his family are fully aware of my role.

I was introduced to Joe by Charles Forte when were all shooting pheasants at Ickworth, which Charles rented from the Marquess of Bristol. Over lunch, as a former botanical geneticist, I was astonished to learn that Joe had set up a research centre at his home village of Rothwell on the Lincolnshire wolds, and had staffed it with well-qualified scientists to plan and carry out trials of new varieties of wheat and other cereals with greater yields and improved resistance to disease. This was highly expensive research usually restricted to stations sponsored by governments or universities.

When he heard of my interest in genetics, Joe invited me to visit Rothwell and also to bring my gun for a day's shooting. The quality of the staff he had recruited was exemplified by the mycologist – the specialist on fungal diseases of cereals. A few months after my visit, he was appointed to a chair at a major university!

It transpired that Joe, who had left school at fourteen, had inherited a small business which sold and delivered coal in the winter and seed-corn in the spring, a common combination then because it used the same vehicles. Without any scientific training, he became fascinated by seed-corn and the possibilities of improving yields of wheat, oats and barley by experimentation and the importation of varieties from other countries. So, having made some money buying and selling farms, and borrowing more, he secured the sole rights to importing and selling new breeds of cereals, especially from France, and then set up his own breeding station, Rothwell Plants Breeders, and, also, the Nickerson Seed Company. Soon, he was dominating the British cereals market. Later, he also secured a monopoly on importing the Desirée potato.

Just how and why he had achieved so much was demonstrated to me by a most memorable personal experience. While pheasant-shooting with him at Rothwell, we were walking together between drives when he remarked, 'I'm thinking of breeding a mini-duck.'

'Why?' I responded.

'Well,' he replied, 'people have made a fortune out of the poussin so why not a mini-duck?'

Having by then known Joe for several years, I knew that anything he said had to be taken seriously but I expressed doubt that there would be enough meat on a mini-duck. Unimpressed, Joe passed the idea to his geneticists, who quickly agreed with me but, knowing that he would be expecting a full report, they made a study of the duck market. They found that because ducks varied so much in weight when they became marketable they were sold at different prices, having to be weighed in the shops for each customer. They realised that what the big food stores, like Marks and Spencer, and the new supermarkets needed was a steady supply of ducks which were all the same weight, within an ounce or two, so that they could all be sold at the same listed price. After reporting to Joe, they set in train the research to produce such a bird, carefully regulating the food supply so that all the ducks reached the required weight at the same time when they could be mass-marketed. The result was a new company called Cherry Valley Ducks (and later Cherry Valley Farms), which became the biggest duck-producer in Britain, even exporting breeding stock to China!

All great businesses, on which modern civilisation depends, originate as a new idea in some individual's mind and I had witnessed such a moment.

Later, as a further adventure in animal genetics, Joe bought the Cotswold Pig Development Company and built it into the UK's leading producer of breeding pigs, becoming a major exporter of breeding stock. Eventually, he sold his genetics research enterprise to Shell in a deal in which I played a modest part by introducing Joe to Shell's chief scientist, Lord Rothschild. For 'services to agriculture' Joe was, most deservedly, knighted in 1983.

Joe's business acumen was outstanding but his prowess in the shooting field was truly awesome. He very rarely missed even high-flying birds at extreme ranges and to witness his action was to watch perfection. Having shot his first bird, a magpie, at the age of nine, he had vowed at seventeen to set aside 100 days a year for sport but, in the result, did far more. He had a record of every item of game he accounted for subsequently. They totalled more than 250,000 but he was able to claim that, through rearing and conservation, he had put far more game into the environment than he had taken out. As a farmer, he regarded game birds as a crop which, like any other, vegetable or animal, has to be harvested. (In September the pheasant is almost certainly the most numerous game bird in Britain and most shoots manage to kill only about 50 per cent of the birds they rear.)

Joe's eyesight and mental power of observation were phenomenal. Standing next to him at the partridge shoot he had founded near Toledo in Spain, I saw him kill a high partridge which fell into thick bushes. When the Spanish pickers-up, who traditionally did not use dogs, failed to find it (and clearly doubted that it was there) Joe insisted on continuing the search and forecast that, when the bird was found, it would have one or two pellets on the left side of its head. A dog was sought and found the bird, which had been killed by one pellet near the left eye! (Joe always looked at the target's head and not at the whole bird, as most shooters do.)

Unlike almost all other game-shooting men I have met, Joe never suffered from being 'off form'. My own performance was dogged by the infuriating eccentricities of 'form' all my shooting life and, as it affects most professionals in all sports, I am surprised that so little research has been devoted to it. I have discovered only one attempt, which was sponsored by the British Medical Research Council, to probe its mysteries. Scientists used clay-pigeon shooting as the medium, because it could be easily controlled, and reported – as I and so many others could have told them – that 'form' did not depend on fitness or mental attitude. I have gone to a shoot feeling great and shot badly while on days when I set off feeling unwell I have surprised myself and others by my accuracy.

A perfectionist to the point of eccentricity, Joe always planned and executed a day on any of his several shoots with military precision. On such a day, 3 October 1952, on the Rothwell shoot Joe and five other guns bagged 2,119 wild partridges, a record never likely to be broken.

While most shoots usually had eight or nine guns in the line (which was why shooting was such a good medium for meeting new people), Joe preferred no more than six and regularly cut that down to five, four or even three. In 1988, when I shot with him on his partridge shoot in Spain, we were only five guns, compared with the usual twelve or more on Spanish shoots. (That, I suspect, was one of the reasons why the King of Spain liked shooting with Joe.) So, his guests' imperfections – whether through ineptitude or 'poaching' neighbouring guns' birds – were more than usually apparent and I experienced the rough edge of his tongue for the latter fault on several occasions. However, that criticism was more than neutralised by occasions when, after a few poor shots, I would down a really difficult bird and Joe would respond with a lusty shout, 'That's the bloody ticket!'

'JN', as his staff all called Joe, expected his guests to be smartly dressed as he always was himself. He had the habit of wearing white spats, especially on his grouse moors, where all aspects of his expertise were on display. Instead of a shooting stick, which one could sit upon while waiting for a drive to start, Joe always had a thumbstick, long and strong enough to lean on. Eventually we all acquired one and, for many years, I have not been seen outside in my village without mine, a splendid blackthorn, which, in my old age, has saved me from a few falls.

Joe preferred over-and-under shotguns rather than those with side-by-side barrels and, to increase the demand on his accuracy while also being able to mount and swing his gun more swiftly as he aged, he switched from 12 bores to the smaller 20 and, later, to tiny 28s. When past seventy, he had a pulley with ropes inserted in the ceiling above his desk so that while working there he could keep his arm muscles in trim.

To watch him deal with grouse coming with a strong wind at about 60mph, and moving up and down with the contours of the heather, as I did many times on his beloved Wemmergill Moor in North Durham, was, inevitably, to sigh for one's own ineptitude. Assisted by one of his loaders, who were more skilled than any I have seen elsewhere, he would regularly kill two grouse in front and two behind from any covey unfortunate enough to approach him. As the politician Jim Prior (now Lord) witnessed, Joe once shot every grouse in a covey of eight – four in front and four behind – a brilliant combination of accuracy and swift movement.

Politicians were frequent guests and included the late William Whitelaw (later Lord), who, on a grouse moor, had the sad distinction of accidentally shooting Joe, who was rushed to hospital where he was shown the X-rays of his injuries. Not only was one side of his body heavily peppered by pellets which had to be dug out, but a grave-looking doctor warned him that he might have to undergo internal surgery because there were pellets in his gut. With customary presence of mind, Joe told the doctor, 'I do eat a lot of game so let's leave it for a few hours.' Further X-rays then showed that, indeed, the gut pellets were *en passage.*

Mortified, Whitelaw vowed to give up shooting but Joe convinced him that he must not make that sacrifice and invited him again. Nor would he ever talk about the event or have it mentioned in his memoirs.

The biggest riddle surrounding Joe was how he managed to amass such a large fortune while spending so much time in the shooting field. After three exacting days shooting grouse at Wemmergill, he would be motored back to Rothwell to rise early next morning to shoot wildfowl, attend to business in the afternoon and then be motored back to Wemmergill to shoot grouse there the following day. Sometimes when he woke on a non-shooting day he would feel an urgent need to have a few shots and would make sudden arrangements for two or three drives of grouse or pheasants over himself with no other gun present.

He owned the duck flighting rights on an island in the Humber estuary and, perhaps having shot six days at Rothwell or at the many shoots to which he was invited, would spend Sunday downing ducks. Or he might shoot wood pigeons, which, being an agricultural pest, can be shot all year. It was the challenge of difficult targets, not a killer instinct, which motivated him. To enhance the challenge, Joe went to great lengths to ensure, whenever possible, that the birds came with the wind behind them, boosting their speed and difficulty. As with ships, the bigger, the faster the bird, and with a strong wind behind it, a pheasant can exceed 60mph while, in still air, it averages about forty. The grouse comes next for speed and then the red-legged partridge followed by the grey.

I was grouse-shooting with Joe at Wemmergill shortly after he had reached seventy and asked him how long he expected to continue with such a punishing schedule. He looked across the heather and said, 'I'll shoot another five years, God willing, and then I'll try to do more if I can. You see, with me, shooting is a religion.' (It was from that remark that I eventually coined the title *A Shooting Man's Creed*.) What Joe meant was that, as all religions do, shooting, as he conceived it, requires discipline, reverence, ritual and, above all, love.

Joe really loved the countryside and expressed his special love for moors and their grouse in 1985 by setting up the Joseph Nickerson Heather Improvement Foundation with a large personal donation. It is not generally realised that, unless cared for, heather, on which the grouse depends for its food, declines and is replaced by scrub. Joe also maximised the grouse population by putting out grit, which the birds need to digest heather shoots, and by other means.

So how did he find time for work? He would leave written instructions for his staff every evening and would dictate ideas while travelling to and from shoots on a tape-recorder. On his return home he would call in senior staff for progress reports and discussions. I met and grew to know several of these seniors and they remained with him for many years, enjoying their work and clearly having the highest respect for their employer. Joe attributed his success mainly to his ability to choose the right staff, and his confidence in delegating his requirements and leaving them to pursue them.

To ghost the biography of such an extraordinary man was clearly going to be arduous and we intended to have many meetings when I could question him. Inevitably, as I should have guessed, he was never available because he was away shooting, often in the US where he pursued quail. So I had to depend largely on his staff, especially the efficient lady whom he called his literary secretary and his archivist, who had access to his copious records. Joe and I also exchanged letters. The biography, with a foreword by the Duke of Westminster, was published in 1989 with a launch party in London and was well received. My presentation copy is inscribed, 'Harry, thanks a lot. Joe.'

Larger than life in so many ways, Joe lived with his wife Eugenie in fine style at his two main homes – Rothwell and Middleton House in North Durham, his centre for grouse-shooting. As the self-made squire of Rothwell (even the pub was called the Nickerson Arms) he had the responsibility of choosing the vicar. When candidates came for interview Joe made sure that it was on a shooting day so that any obvious anti-bloodsporter could be eliminated. They were required to come out and watch a shoot and would then be asked to pick up a few shot birds. The day I witnessed that exercise the candidate was a rather ethereal young man who, I sensed, was doomed the moment I saw him bringing back a pheasant holding it, rather distastefully, by one leg.

Joe's food, wine and everything around him was of the best. Sadly his love of good living resulted in obesity problems which proved intractable because he enjoyed his food so much that he would rather face the added risk than diet seriously. Joe died of a massive heart attack on 3 March 1990 aged seventy-five, while on holiday in Palm Beach, Florida.

He had left instructions for his shooting friends that if they had already accepted a shooting date on the day of his funeral they were to shoot and, in the course of the day, fire two wild shots as a gesture of farewell. However, he had conveniently died in the closed season so, with scores of others, I attended his funeral, flying to it with Charles and Rocco Forte. Joe was particularly associated with the partridge, which even appeared in his coat of arms, so, after his burial, a cage containing a covey of wild grey partridges was placed on the grave and opened. As the birds escaped into the fields it seemed that Joe's soul was flying with them.

If he is in Heaven I fear for the fate of the angels or anything else there with wings.

CHAPTER 14

DOG MAN

In one important aspect of life I was not at one with Joe Nickerson – his attitude to dogs. Joe had the best gun dogs I ever saw. He would have two, or even three, big black Labradors untethered by his stand or in his grouse-butt and, with birds falling all round him, they would never move until he sent them. How they had been trained to that standard I never knew but one aspect of their master's canine discipline was that under no circumstance were they ever allowed in the house. For me, the prime purpose of a dog is as a companion and I like it to be near at hand at all waking times. No other animal so closely resembles man in temperament. So, a writer sitting long hours in a study is never alone with a dog and when the going is tough, as it becomes increasingly with age, there is little that is more welcome than an intruding snout. Outdoors, in the country, I have rarely been seen without a dog.

For most of my shooting life I had a succession of springer spaniels, Honey, Scat and Scoop, which roamed the house and slept in the kitchen. There, they were well placed to fulfil their other function of warning us by barking at the sound of any intruder. Also my dog's enthusiastic welcome in the morning when I open the kitchen door has always been a delightful start to the day as we renew our bond.

Many times in the shooting field I was asked why I did not have a Labrador, being assured that I was depriving myself of the 'Labrador experience'. I was soon to appreciate what that meant. After my last springer, my beloved Scoop, had died aged almost fourteen, there was such desolation in our house in Kintbury that our need was quickly on the bush-telegraph. So, one summer afternoon, when I was in our living room giving a TV interview about spies, a girl who needed to dispose of an eighteen-month-old chocolate Labrador before emigrating to Australia knocked on our door. My wife hurriedly seated her and the dog in her study while I finished the interview. Then, as the producer wanted an introductory shot of me walking through the churchyard with a dog, I seized the Labrador and we duly appeared together that night on national television. Clearly, we were destined for each other.

It was mutual love at my first sight of her broad head and muzzle, her otter-like tail and magical brown eyes, and at her first sniff of me. When I saw how delighted my wife was with the canine, I could not wait to hand over the purchase money. Dido, as she was called, responded by casing the joint and telling herself, 'I've landed!' She guzzled her meal and, within five minutes, learned to negotiate the two dog flaps from the kitchen into the walled garden, where she began to hoover the crumbs knocked off the bird tables, teaching us that outside every slim Labrador there is always a fat one trying to get in. We were relieved to find, however, that she was totally honest and never stole anything, however tempting.

Being a pack animal, any dog feels insecure when alone, because that was a dangerous situation in the wild, inherited from its wolf ancestors, but Dido had a particularly low threshold for loneliness and whenever my wife and I came downstairs in London attire, her glumness was immediately apparent. On our return, we would find my cap, a slipper and items of clothing on her kitchen beanbag, where she had collected them as comforters, consoling herself that she would soon be back in our pack of three. In return, she would often declare our bond by offering me her best thing – her favourite toy or the remains of the current bone. My wife and I are deeply in debt to her infectious happiness.

On our first shared morning, I took her down to the Kennet to fish, expecting to have to peg her down but she never left my side, being fascinated by the river and my fly-casting, perhaps because of the breed's strange history. Dogs are not usually associated with fishing but Labradors were bred by Canadian cod-fishermen to retrieve fish falling off their long-lines, baited with hundreds of hooks, as they were dragged into the boats. It was only after Labradors were seen showing off their retrieving skills from a Canadian boat in Poole Harbour, where it had been delivering salt cod, that some were imported here and converted to bird dogs.

Dido was always with me on the river bank watching the fly as I cast it upstream, being wildly excited when I hooked a fish and staring at me, accusingly, if I lost it. So it was fitting that what I will always regard as a canine miracle should have happened to Dido while we were fishing.

On a summer evening I was standing, with Dido by my side, on a bank of the River Kennet at Littlecote when, casting into a deep pool, I hooked a trout which jumped and threw the fly from its mouth. As the fly swung in towards me Dido snacked at it. I quickly opened her mouth and was horrified to see about ten inches of the nylon thread cast, to which the fly was attached, round her teeth with the fly itself apparently stuck out of sight in the back of her tongue. Dido was quickly trying to spit out the fly while snatching at grass and swallowing it, presumably to make herself sick.

Deciding that it was a veterinary emergency, which would probably need a general anaesthetic, I cut the nylon cast and walked Dido to my car, with her snatching at more grass on the way. By the time we reached the car she had ceased to shake her head and I could see no sign of the fly or the nylon. She seemed to have swallowed it all so there was no point in seeking the vet at that stage. Throughout that night I remained deeply worried that the hook would stick somewhere in her gut with the added danger of some entanglement there caused by the nylon. So I visited Dido, downstairs, several times. All seemed well but I needed to be reassured and early the following morning, I decided to carry out the obvious examination the circumstances demanded.

As was Dido's wont, she had been out into the walled garden through her dog doors and had deposited the necessary specimens, which I dissected with short, sharp sticks. The investigation proved negative and looked like being the same on the following morning until I reached the last specimen. Within it I found a neatly folded rectangular packet of grass, about the size of a postage stamp, with something bulging inside it. A gentle douse with a watering can washed away the grass to reveal my fly with the nylon neatly coiled round it and covering the hook, which had then been incapable of penetrating anything. How this had been accomplished remains a mystery beyond my comprehension.

I carried my find upstairs, where my wife was reading the papers in bed, and dangled it triumphantly, declaring, 'We are going down to the river to catch a fish with it.' We duly did so, returning with a trout which must have been unique in piscatorial history, having taken a fly which had passed through a dog.

In the ensuing seasons, whenever I hooked a trout, Dido came running but never barked. On a salmon river, she always barked when the reel began to screech and if the ghillie was out of sight, down he came to assist! Though she loved Scotland, her favourite fishing venue was a small idyllic lake built by my friend Raleigh Place, whom she greatly liked. Sometimes she would break off her mooching in the reeds and run from the other side to where I was fishing just to give me a 'wuffle' – taking my fingers into her mouth in the softest of soft bites – which could only mean, 'Isn't it marvellous here?' One of the greatest services dogs do for us is to remind us, as they bounce about or roll, legs in the air, of the privilege of just being alive.

Dido had not been trained as a gun dog but she accompanied me to shoots where I kept her pegged down during drives and induced her to retrieve the odd pheasant, but her heart was on the river, where she expressed her joy with a couplet – 'Oh! Kennet Banks are fair and wide with lots of reeds and tufts, I'd rather roam with my Chap there than reign the Queen of Crufts.'

The Labrador experience was to change my life professionally. With Dido being so magical, I thought we might collect enough interesting anecdotes about her to make a children's book, *The Adventures of a Chocolate Dog*, but, while watching the popular TV programme *One Man and His Dog*, I conceived the title *One Dog and Her Man*, which would be Dido's unexpurgated account of the dog–man relationship and what life is really like down there near ground level.

So, over several months, Dido and I conferred in my study, on our walks and on the river, which was a pleasant change from writing about spies to a world free from treachery, disinformation and dirty tricks. Dedicated 'To the Greater Glory of Dog' the book recorded, fearlessly, her views on the human species, especially about 'her Chap' and his wife – 'the Boss' – with their manifold faults and deficiencies. In twenty-four chapters, Dido bared our souls as well as her own. Like me, she revelled in being an only dog in the household because it also meant that she was top dog.

Exploring and explaining the canine predicament, there were chapters headed 'Beauty is in the Nose of the Beholder', 'Sex and the Single Dog' and 'The Rights of Dog', with much to say about human wrongs, and the literally soul-searching 'Can Eternity Belong to Me?' – the question of whether or not a dog has a soul. The book duly appeared in June 1991 as written by Dido with my assistance. It was published by my old friend George (now Lord) Weidenfeld, to whom I owe so much.

One Dog and Her Man was serialised over three days by the Daily Mail with colour photographs showing the joint authors at the computer. The book quickly reached No. 11 on the Sunday Times list of bestsellers and the paperback rights were sold to Bantam Books. This led to demands for her to do book-signings with her paw print, which was kindly facilitated by a local dentist. He made a cast of Dido's right front paw which was then mounted in the form of a stamp that could be anointed with brown ink. She opened fairs and fetes and appeared on television, including The Big Breakfast, where she demonstrated her method of cutting a ribbon to open an event: one end of two long ribbons was threaded through a slit in a cooked sausage so that when Dido grasped the banger on the command 'Open!', the two ribbons fell apart.

In January 1991, by invitation from the Kennel Club, Dido appeared in the Parade of Dog Personalities at Cruft's and was interviewed by Angela Rippon. She was photographed opening her own bank account for her royalties at Lloyds, in Hungerford, her picture appearing in the local paper under the heading 'Barking all the way to the bank'.

Acquiring Dido so fortuitously had been yet another major stroke of luck for both of us. As Dido expressed it, 'There is a tide in the affairs of dog and I took it at the flood.'

Her fan mail filled several box-files and she received more Christmas cards and treats than I did. Over the years, we gave countless lectures on the dog–man relationship but Dido's finest publicity coup was to ambush the Queen, who had accepted her first book and had sent a letter of thanks. When Her Majesty was visiting Kintbury church for a ceremony in memory of the great jockey Sir Gordon Richards, it was arranged that Dido should be standing outside the gate when she emerged. This gave my wife, who accompanied Her Majesty, the opportunity to say, 'Oh, look, there's Dido!' As cameras flashed, the Queen said, 'Oh, that's Dido, is it? One doesn't see many chocolates.'

I was quickly cut down to size as her ghostwriter, presenter, secretary, interpreter, minder, chauffeur and general amanuensis. 'Are you the man who owns that famous dog?' I was asked at parties, to which I replied, mournfully, 'No. She owns me.' In her mind she did, because the possessions in her territory, which she guarded bravely when necessary, included us.

One Dog and Her Man was translated into German and Japanese, selling so well in Japan that a Japanese reporter was sent from Tokyo to interview and photograph Dido. Following the sale of 50,000 hardbacks in Japan and 250,000 paperbacks she barked for Britain when the Foreign Office used her image to promote British goods and tourism there.

In 1991 we took part in a Chocolate Labrador Field Day near Banbury where we encountered a fine stud dog called Downfarm Bugler. Convinced that Dido's genes were special, a union was arranged and consummated. Nine weeks later, to the day, she produced seven chocolate pups which were so winsome that press photographers queued to take pictures of Dido in the big wooden box where she suckled her young, with the title of her next book, *A Box of Chocolates*, composing itself.

In her third book, *Life's a Bitch*, a collection of bone-dreams concentrating on the rights of dog, published in 1996, Dido scathingly rejected the theological dogma that, along with all other animals, dogs have no soul and are therefore barred from Paradise. This followed replies to letters I had forwarded on her behalf to the Pope, the Archbishop of Canterbury and the Chief Rabbi, who all insisted that man, the only species made in God's image, is unique in possessing a soul.

In 2000, our vet had numbered Dido's days after a malignancy recurred, but she kept going so gamely that I felt confident she would make 2001. On the morning of 14 December she delighted me by eating every scrap of her morning meal but then horrified me by indicating that even a short walk was beyond her. Anxiously, I watched her wandering in the garden and when she rubbed against me, clearly asking, 'What's happening to me?' I knew we had to bite the bullet.

Aware that I would make an exhibition of myself, my wife bravely offered to drive her to the vet, with whom I had made hurried arrangements, and I took the coward's way out. With my wife stroking her head, Dido finally closed her eyes, lying peacefully on the back seat of the car where she had spent so many hours on the way to exciting places.

As a soldier's son, and a wartime soldier myself, tears have always seemed unmanly, but the last of the many things which Dido taught me was that age engenders emotional, as well as physical, fragility.

Raleigh Place offered to inter her by his lake but I declined because visiting it would have been upsetting for me. Instead, she was cremated and her ashes were thrown into the river. She was widely missed in the village, where our inseparability had become something of a joke. Children would shout, 'Hello Dido, written any good books lately?' Should I be seen slipping up to the post office without her, people would ask, 'Is Dido alright?' Their sympathetic concern was most kind.

I still sense her wherever I look in our house. Admirers sculpted her in bronze, painted her in watercolours, etched her on perspex and embroidered her on cushions. There are pictures of her on my study wall. They help me to think that Dido has resolved the riddle about her soul and I visualise her looking at me from above and saying, as she so often seemed to when I had told her (wrongly) that she was barking at nothing, 'See! I told you I was right!'

'Brothers and sisters, I bid you beware of giving your heart to a dog to tear,' warned Kipling but our emptiness demanded a quick replacement. We decided that we could not cope with a puppy, and would not be tempted by viewing any litters. We needed a house-trained, reasonably obedient, chocolate bitch, two to four years old and used to walking on a lead without pulling. When a newspaper feature about Dido's death, which I wrote, brought scores of letters and telephone calls of condolence, we felt sure that we would soon be told of a suitable replacement. One candidate brought to our notice was a two-year-old male called Tom, who had always lived in kennels and a paddock and had never seen the inside of a house. He was available only because he had been neutered, after judges had ruled him genetically unsuitable for breeding, a deficiency of advantage to us, for he would have no urge to stray. We decided to see him, as he was only a few miles away.

Tom was so like Dido, with a broad muzzle, magical brown eyes and bushy tail, and was irresistible on so many other counts, including an affectionate nature, that we decided to take him, especially when he jumped on to the back seat of our car with such alacrity.

Tommy, as we usually called him, had so many of Dido's endearing qualities, along with some of his own, that all sadness quickly evaporated and that particular happiness which only dogs can generate soon reigned as fully as it did before. His powers of accommodating to such a different environment were most instructive regarding canine intelligence. He was intensely curious about the carpets and every piece of furniture, examining each item in every room to which we gradually introduced him. He did not interpret furniture legs as handy trees, as we thought he might, especially with Dido's scent all over the place. This was just as well for Tommy had a habit I have never seen in any other dog. Usually, when a dog has sniffed out a selected target, he cocks his leg, makes his mark and moves on. Almost invariably, Tommy would anoint the spot then turn round and do the same again, thus delivering a right and left.

We showed him the swinging dog flaps, which lead from the

kitchen to the conservatory and thence to the walled garden. Dogs are supposed to be dumb at solving puzzle-boxes but he worked it out after two demonstrations. We then put him out by a different door and could almost hear the canine cogs going round as he stood and pondered then ran to the outer dog flap and was through into the kitchen.

Never having seen stairs, his reaction to ours, which are steep, was entertaining: apprehension then determination to explore. With a few slips he made the landing but was terrified of coming down. Eventually, when even a proffered biscuit was ignored, we had to drag and push him to the bottom, learning how powerful a young male Labrador can be. After that, he was up and down like a yo-yo.

He made only two liquid mistakes before going out through the dog doors or asking to be excused if we were in another room. He did no damage whatever, either on those occasions or subsequently.

For a dog which had spent so much time alone or in the company of other dogs, he craved our companionship as much as Dido did and followed me around like my shadow. While Dido just looked miserable when I left the room, Tommy whimpered, which massaged the remnants of my ego. While Dido was essentially my dog, Tommy bonded himself to us both, displaying total trust and being happy so long as one of us was there.

I took him down to the river and the Labrador history in his genes was quickly evident. He was intensely interested in my activities, watching the fly as Dido did and with an additional service on offer – he loved to carry a fish in his mouth back to the weighing hut.

In his bid to emulate Dido's literary success, Tom (with my assistance) produced a book called *God's Dog*, the result of asking the question 'Does God have a dog?' In pursuit of an answer, Tom is recruited to the Celestial Intelligence Service (CI6), targets Satan and discovers his astonishing secret, which has eluded theologians down the ages. We have published it as an electronic book available on Amazon where Tom can be seen on the book-cover wearing his hoped-for halo.

Among those of us who find existence without canine companionship seriously deficient, it is commonly believed that, in a lifetime, we are gifted just one really great dog, which outshines all our others but Tommy broke that rule. When he reached fourteen and a half, which is beyond the usual life-span of a Labrador, and we were two old codgers together, we conspired to depart in a photo finish. Shortly after I had written this account of our long association in June 2013, however, Tommy died with little advance notice of any serious ailment. I was – and remain – grief stricken, especially as in my 100th year I cannot, sensibly, consider any replacement. I have often been 'dog-tired', now I am 'dog-desolate'.

Some years ago a newspaper front-page headline announced: 'The cat is ousting the dog as man's best friend.' In a published response I pointed out that, while there may be more cats than dogs in the UK (an estimate in 2012 indicated that there were eight million of each), they are loners by nature and are constitutionally incapable of providing the degree of friendship naturally given by a pack species like the dog. Whoever heard of guide cats for the blind, hearing cats for the deaf, guard cats, sniffer cats, police cats, tracker cats, mountain rescue cats, gun cats, sheep cats, hunting cats or racing cats?

Dogs have earned the title 'man's best friend' by centuries of devoted duty and companionship which have made them indispensable. Neither cats nor any other species can oust them from that proud position.

CHAPTER 15

ROYAL ENCOUNTERS

My first propinquity to a member of the royal family occurred when I was eight years old in Aldershot, where my soldier father was stationed. My mother and I were watching some military event to honour King George V and were seated just a few rows behind him. I noticed that he was very knock-kneed and conveyed my observation to my mother, who hushed me up.

I had an even closer view of his successor, Edward VIII, but only after he had abdicated and become the Duke of Windsor, living in exile. At the end of a garden party at the British embassy in Paris, we arrived, together, at the cloakroom. The person in charge had awful difficulty in finding the Duke's grey top hat. 'I do hope you find it,' he said. 'I would hate to lose it because it is a memento of happier days.' He sounded rather wistful.

I greatly admired but never met King George VI, who I heard giving a post-war talk about radar and other inventions which he delivered with seemingly little difficulty in spite of his stammer. Unforgettably, I met his lovely wife, Queen Elizabeth the Queen Mother, on an intimate occasion – just eight of us round a lunch table in a garden on a sunny summer's day. The lunch was staged by the late Gerald Ward, owner of the Chilton estate near Hungerford, and his wife, Amanda. Our mutual friend, Brigadier Andrew Parker Bowles (former husband of Camilla) and his new wife Rose were present, as was my wife, Billee. The Queen Mum's partner for the lunch was her old friend Jack Profumo, who had survived the furore of his parliamentary and public disgrace.

Before the lunch I was given the opportunity to talk to Her Majesty, who was already 100, about her favourite sport – salmon fishing, especially on her favourite river, the Royal Dee in Scotland. I asked her if a story I had heard while fishing the Dee was true. Allegedly, the Queen Mother was fishing the Dee when a man on the other side foul-hooked a salmon, played it and, feeling that the presence of the Queen Mum required him to do the sporting thing with a foul-hooked fish, returned it to the water after beaching it. Sound carries easily across water, especially on such a narrow stretch, and the Queen Mother was heard to observe to her ghillie, 'Bloody fool! Putting a fresh fish back!'

Her Majesty laughed and would not confirm the story but did not deny it. We exchanged a few more words round the lunch table but HM was more interested in discovering how my wife had come by the name 'Billee', first observing, 'You couldn't possibly have been christened that.'

Happily, I have enjoyed several close encounters with the present Queen Elizabeth. The most memorable was the occasion in March 1995 when Her Majesty unveiled a plaque in Kintbury Church in honour of Sir Gordon Richards, the great jockey who had lived in the village. Billee, who had raised £33,000 for the project, accompanied the Queen throughout and we have a full photographic record of the occasion. As the Queen departed she was quite moved when a girl in the crowd called out, spontaneously, 'Thanks for coming!' As she told her lady-in-waiting, that had never happened before on any occasion, large or small.

I have been completely alone with the Queen only once, during the interval of a music festival in Newbury which she attended. My friend Henry Carnarvon, who was her racing manager, asked me into a small room where the Queen was standing alone and left us for about five minutes. Taken aback by the unexpected situation I was, for once in my life, lost for words so I was inclined to ask her about a recent encounter of which I had been told in great secrecy but felt that she would be embarrassed and, therefore, desisted.

Normally, Her Majesty has remained as aloof as possible from weapons of mass destruction because of their political sensitivity but, during a visit to the USA in the 1980s, the Queen's plane put down for refuelling at the Strategic Air Command HQ at Omaha.

By previous arrangement, she then witnessed the excitement of the scramble as fully loaded nuclear bombers took to the air in a mock retaliatory attack on the Soviet Union. She even spoke by telephone to the SAC commander, who was airborne in the control plane. Had this become public at the time, the media would have had a field day with guaranteed repercussions from Moscow. With the Soviet Union long gone, I put it on record now.

On 17 October 1956, I witnessed the moment when the Queen made history by pulling a lever which directed electricity into the National Grid from the world's first nuclear power station, Calder Hall in what is now West Cumbria. As I and many others reported, it seemed that Britain was poised eventually to produce most of its power that way but, for various reasons, including nuclear accidents which released radioactivity (enabling political protestors to exploit the danger), nuclear electricity has been disappointing here. Meanwhile the French have made a huge success of it, producing so much that it provides 75 per cent of the national need at very low cost and it is now a major export. I wonder if Her Majesty has ever expressed her disappointment at what has, clearly, been a massive cock-up here when originally we had led the world.

My favourite story about HM was told to me by Sir Charles Forte, who, being of Italian origin, had been chosen to be with the Queen when she and Prince Philip met the leading singers from the La Scala (Milan) opera company at Covent Garden, following a performance of *La Cenerentola*.

A large, over-enthusiastic baritone was commenting so profusely and with so many gestures on Her Majesty's qualities and, especially, on her 'beautiful smile' that Sir Charles guided her away but she broke free and returned to the Italian with, 'You were saying – about my smile…' Sadly, few people dare to take the liberty of paying her the compliments which are music to any woman's ear.

While the Queen never wanted to shoot, she has experienced life-long satisfaction from 'picking up' game with her dogs, usually behind her husband, Prince Philip, on the royal shoots and on those which they visited as guests. Her Majesty usually picked up with two

Labradors, working with a whistle and hand signals, and sometimes changing for another pair in the afternoon.

After becoming Queen, Her Majesty, assisted by the Scottish dog-handler Bill Meldrum, built up the Sandringham Labrador kennels, with the emphasis on working ability. Meldrum told me that she visited the kennels regularly, taking a close personal interest in the genetics, inspecting the puppies, deciding on which should be retained and keeping tabs on the working careers of those which were sold or given to friends. The most famous royal field trials champion was a yellow Labrador called Sydney, who had such a mind of his own on shoots that the Queen suspected that he regarded her purely as his chauffeur. According to Meldrum, the dogs in the kennels knew when the Queen was arriving at the Sandringham gates and started barking, which they did not do for anyone else.

On the grouse moor the Queen often used spaniels and was rarely beaten, even by a strong distant runner (a bird that can run but not fly), being persistent with her hand signals, sending a dog back repeatedly, or even, especially, when keepers advised quitting. She did not take kindly to defeat and at a pheasant shoot in Suffolk, when one of the Labradors supplied from Sandringham would not work for her, she claimed that it must have been trained to a man's voice and dispensed with its services.

With most canine misdemeanours, however, her sense of humour came to her rescue, as it did when Margaret Thatcher visited Balmoral for the first time, accompanied by her husband, Denis. One of the corgis under the dining room table generated a smell so powerful that it could hardly be ignored. 'Are you alright, Denis?' one of the guests (Gerald Ward) inquired, solicitously. Nobody laughed more than the Queen.

Her Majesty also attended shoots alone, especially at Highclere, where she is remembered for her fussless informality. (A farm worker, under a broken-down trailer there, looked up to see a small, head-scarfed lady with a dog and a thumbstick asking, 'Can I help?') The informality of her visits to Highclere, where she stayed in the

Carnarvons' unpretentious, lakeside home, Lady Carnarvon being a close friend, was a great joy to her for she could relax there with minimum security. Unlike many monarchs, wherever the Queen stayed informally, which was usually for shooting, she is remembered as an easy, undemanding guest with a minimal retinue.

While the Queen missed little in the shooting field, she rarely commented on shortcomings, the notable exception being her remark to Lord Mountbatten after a Broadlands day in the 1960s, when the bag of pheasants exceeded 2,000. 'It's obscene, Dickie!' she observed and it was surprising how quickly and, in some cases, effectively, news of her displeasure spread among the owners of big shoots.

The last time I saw HM she was to give me a look which clearly meant, 'What are you doing here where you should not be?' I was attending an event at Windsor Park and noticed Valerian, the Duke of Wellington, among a small group of men and one tall lady. As my wife and I had recently lunched at his country home, I went over to greet him and found that they were all laughing at a hilarious display by gamekeepers of what not do at a shoot, especially with loaded guns. I joined in the laughter and a small lady who had been enjoying the fun from a closer vantage point suddenly decided to join us. It was the Queen and I realised that, inadvertently, I had joined a royal party, the tall lady being the lady-in-waiting. After frowning at me, Her Majesty continued to laugh at the keepers' antics, so I joined in, eventually appearing in a colour photograph of the whole group which appeared in *The Field*.

For a feature which I wrote about the Queen and her dogs for *The Field* in 1997, HM kindly answered a series of questions about her eight companions – corgis and dorgis (a cross between a corgi and a miniature dachshund). Her information was transmitted to me by her private secretary, Sir Robert Fellowes (now Lord), who I had first met in Barbados. He also sent me some photographs from Her Majesty's private albums. The Queen always tries to feed her dogs herself, giving them one meal in the afternoon plus dog-chocs and other treats, but, to prevent contention, no bones. They are all admitted to the family dining rooms of the various residences and receive surreptitious titbits there. Contrary to some magazine cartoons, they have never slept in Her Majesty's bedroom but in a 'dog room'. The Queen exercises the dogs herself whenever possible and, when moving between residences, the pack, or a selected few, usually travel with her in her car. All Her Majesty's dogs have been buried in the royal pet cemetery at Sandringham, with a headstone.

Queen Elizabeth II will be remembered in history as an outstanding monarch who could be regal when it mattered and never put a foot wrong through more than sixty years of tumultuous change. Her Majesty is, beyond question, the most experienced statesperson who has ever lived. In her reign she has met so many heads of state and heads of governments and seen them go. Yet by nature, she is a warm-hearted woman of common touch and simple tastes with which others can identify. Some weeks after Her Majesty loaned me the personal snapshots of her dogs, her secretary telephoned me to seek their return, explaining, 'The Queen is going on holiday and would like to put them back in her albums and lock them away, safely, in her cupboard before she leaves.' I hurried to obey such a delightfully expressed royal requirement.

Since then, in 2012, the year of her Diamond Jubilee and the London Olympic Games, we have all witnessed her physical and mental powers of endurance, which remain quite phenomenal for a lady of eight-seven.

I have long admired HRH Prince Philip, the Duke of Edinburgh, for the splendidly supportive role he has played which could never have been easy for such a highly intelligent man with a strong personality. My first contact, in the 1950s, was indirect through Joe Fallon, a mutual friend based in Sydney. Joe was descended from an Irish political convict who had been transported to Australia in its days as a penal colony, and was so proud of his ancestor that he had mounted his handcuffs in a glass case on a wall of his fine house in the exclusive area of Vaucluse. It was rumoured that the convict had been given a plot of land on one end of which Sydney Harbour Bridge was eventually built. So it had earned his successors a pile of money.

The generous Joe had befriended the lonely, young Greek, Prince

Philip, when he had been a junior naval officer on a destroyer visiting Australian ports. They had remained in touch and there was a filing cabinet containing the many letters which had passed between them. One day when I was lunching with Joe – always a bibulous occasion as he had a fine wine cellar – he needed a nap. To my surprise, he pointed to the filing cabinet, saying, 'If you were to look in there while I was asleep I wouldn't know, would I – though you must never use any of it.' I took the hint and spent an enthralling hour reading intimate material which would have made international headlines. Presumably Joe destroyed the letters before his death.

Whenever the royal couple, or the Duke of Edinburgh alone, visited Sydney, Joe was always contacted. On one occasion, as the weather had been unbearably hot, the Queen had wished to swim in privacy and Joe had been asked to provide the facility of his pool. As he was unwell he had not bothered to clean out the pool so, at his request, the fire brigade did so in a hurry and Her Majesty swam. Journalists who disliked Joe learned that the pool had been spruced up at public expense but not why, so they hounded him for an explanation which, loyally, he never gave.

On the next royal visit, Joe answered his doorbell to find the Duke and an aide urging him to accompany them to a grand house close by, which was giving a reception. He demurred on the grounds that the owners disliked him and that he would not be welcome, especially after all the bad publicity. Nevertheless, the Duke persisted and, on arriving at the reception, announced, 'This is my friend, Joe Fallon!'

I met the Duke casually at several functions and soon learned that he had a private club of friends who met regularly for dinner at Buckingham Palace. While his public image has been of an abrupt, and even abrasive, personality, the Duke loves constructive conversation and, for that purpose, he ran the dining club for many decades – a remarkably well-kept secret. There were about a dozen permanent members, all of whom were close friends of the Duke. The Duke would choose a topical subject for discussion in advance and each member was required to bring one guest, usually selected from different professions and walks of life. After the meal, the participants remained at the table for a lively, no-holds-barred discussion. Most of the regular members were keen field-sporters, among them Lord Mountbatten, Sebastian de Ferranti, Lord Carnarvon, Lord Brabourne and Lord Buxton. As members died, they were replaced by other friends.

As Lord (Henry) Carnarvon was a friend of mine, he asked me to attend one of the dinners as his guest. Sadly, the subject was the Common Market (as it was then), which was out of my field of interests, and I did not distinguish myself.

In 1999 I spent a whole morning with the Duke of Edinburgh at the beautiful seventeenth-century Frogmore House, half a mile south of Windsor Castle, where I interviewed him for a profile published in *The Field*. Arriving early, I was left alone in a magnificent room with a large table bearing scores of Victorian trinkets. I picked up one of them and the rest were, suddenly, on the move. To prevent pilfering, they had all been tied together with near-invisible nylon thread and I had great difficulty rearranging them before my royal subject arrived. We discussed many pastoral issues, especially HRH's concern about the decline of songbirds at Sandringham, and even touched on Joe Fallon (though I did not mention the letters). A memorable interlude with a fine man.

Barred, by protocol, from active participation in political or professional life, the Duke of Edinburgh owes a deep debt to the countryside and its opportunities for the action which his nature and talents have demanded. Though he has shared many interests with the Queen in their long, close companionship, horse-racing, Her Majesty's great love, is not one of them because he is essentially a doer rather than a watcher. He has always been a hands-on man preferring to do something, even if only moderately well, rather than watch anybody else do it brilliantly. In fact, he has performed ably at everything that he seriously attempted – polo, yachting, shooting, fishing, stalking and carriage-driving.

Like many former naval officers, the Duke is, essentially, an open-air man, spending as much time outside as his royal duties allow. When not involved in sport he is a serious birdwatcher and an active participant in the conservation projects undertaken to improve the royal shoots at Sandringham, Windsor and Balmoral. He has been deeply concerned by the general decline of our songbirds over the last few decades, which is noticeable both at Sandringham and at Windsor, where fewer and fewer species visit his bird tables and stocks of lapwings, yellowhammers, goldfinches and firecrests were sadly depleted. While he admires the eagles and peregrine falcons at Balmoral, in spite of their impact on the grouse, he is convinced that the increasing population of sparrowhawks and the ban on culling them are partly to blame for the songbird decline.

His serious interest in wildlife and natural history in general began during a trip aboard the royal yacht *Britannia*, across the Pacific and skirting Antarctica where he saw seabirds which he had never encountered before. Then, encouraged by his friends Peter Scott, the bird-artist, and James Robertson Justice, the actor, who was a falconer, he became increasingly conservation conscious. The continuing worldwide decline in wildlife has grieved him deeply and he has remained committed to any cause which might halt or delay it.

He was introduced to shooting by Lord Mountbatten, his uncle and ardent promoter, and became highly proficient, with a natural eye and a graceful stance, which, with his height and lean, handsome looks, made him 'pretty to watch', as I have heard more than one keeper say. He has taken a personal interest in the royal shoots and especially the conversion of Sandringham's pheasants into an all-wild stock. While extra feed was necessary to maintain numbers and prevent straying, all the birds hatched naturally from wild nests. To provide nesting sites and foods for chicks, the Duke oversaw the development of conservation headlands, beetle banks, new hedges and permanent strips of cover. He was at pains to point out to me that such environmental improvements benefited all wild birds, which are always more numerous on well-keepered shoots because of the feed put out for the pheasants and the control of crows, magpies and foxes.

Inevitably, he has suffered, more than most, from media censure of the human paradox that it is possible to admire and promote wildlife yet engage in country sports involving killing birds and mammals, the truth being that artificially boosted game populations need to be culled. Those opposed to field sports concentrated their fire on such an easy target, so much so that Buckingham Palace's public relations officials were deeply worried about media reaction when I went to interview him about his country activities and asked me to avoid questioning him about shooting. When I warned him of that concern, he dismissed it: 'Pay no attention! Certain newspapers and the antis will twist what I say on anything!' He then commented at length on his love of shooting, especially grouse and partridge days, and his debt to it for so much pleasure and friendships in the field.

His field companionships have included that of dogs. Though never as keen on the corgis as the Queen, he loved his Labrador gun dogs, often naming them after motor cars, like Minx, Mini and Maestro. He used them for picking up around his peg or butt, leaving the runners and long-distance birds to his wife, who usually stood well behind him with her Labradors or spaniels.

The Duke expressed his competitive spirit in polo and carriage-driving. Again, it was Lord Mountbatten who introduced him to polo, which he greatly enjoyed for many years and was a sport he shared with Prince Charles. It also provided a joint equine interest with the Queen, for he did not often ride out with her. He ceased playing when he was fifty, preferring to quit when he was still reasonably competent rather than put on an inadequate performance which would penalise the team. He was aware that, because of his position, a team would find it difficult to drop him and he was firmly set against using that advantage. His guiding principle throughout his field life was to give up when a sport clearly became too taxing physically, his advice being that the body will indicate when abandonment will be wise and that ignoring it is not clever. That was why he gave up stalking, which he loved, when he reached sixty. He liked being out on the hill with one ghillie but, once a long, crawling stalk became exhausting, he bowed to the combined ravages of time and then expressed his love of the Scottish wilderness in painting, a substantial skill which he shares with Prince

Charles. Giving up any sport always caused him sorrow and he reckoned that apart, perhaps, from pain, the worst penalty of the ageing process is having to strive increasingly hard just to stay at the same level of performance.

After quitting polo, the Duke of Edinburgh decided to continue his equine interest with competitive carriage-driving, starting with ponies while he learned the technique of a difficult sport which is not without its dangers from upsets and broken poles. They were Fell ponies transferred to Windsor from Balmoral, where they were used to carry shot stags down from the hills. Perhaps they reminded him of his stalking days, but, satisfied with his competence, after assiduous practice on obstacle courses, he switched to horses and became a tough and successful competitor, driving four-in-hand at events throughout the country and abroad. He served the sport as president of the International Equestrian Federation for twenty-two years, being instrumental in introducing many changes. Sticking to his rule, he switched back to ponies when he reached sixty-five and, knowing that he was unlikely to win with them, continued to compete as an outlet for his energy, to keep himself fit and because he had learned to love the challenge and the carriage-driving company.

With shooting, it was possible to taper off by attending fewer days and he continued to fish, an activity which brought him particular pleasure perhaps because of its solitary nature. He had been introduced to it while at Cheam School by the games master there, Jack Malden, my fishing friend whom he remembered with affection. He deplored the decline of the salmon, especially on the Dee, where the Balmoral beat was once productive fly water, as well as being scenically delightful to wade, and, seeking action at all times, he ceased fishing there because, as he put it, 'I can see no point in casting at what is, almost certainly, not there.' In that connection, he held strong views about the effect of the explod-ing seal population on salmon stocks and, for private circulation, rejigged an official report on the widely accepted need for the cull-ing of red deer by simply replacing the word 'deer' throughout it by 'seals'. The spoof, expressing his mischievous sense of humour, made perfect sense because the Duke, a president of the Zoological

Entering the flying car with inventor and pilot, Bob Fulton. July 1948.

Preparing to fly with the RAF over the Yemen in 1962.

ABOVE With Lord Beaverbrook, the proprietor of the *Daily Express*, at Cherkley in 1963.

'The Beaver', as Lord Beaverbrook was known. © Press Association

LEFT Klaus Fuchs, the German-born physicist accused of betraying western atomic secrets to Soviet Russia. After covering his case Chapman Pincher became the paper's 'spy man'.
© Press Association

RIGHT The Profumo affair was a huge scandal. Pictured here at the Cliveden pool is Stephen Ward, with Christine Keeler (right), Mandy Rice-Davis (left) and Paula Hamilton-Marshall (centre).
© Press Association

LEFT An extraordinary man: intelligence operative in Kenya, Bruce McKenzie.

RIGHT The last Shah of Persia with his wife and family, whom Chapman Pincher would meet at the Shah's palace in 1972.

ABOVE Pheasant-shooting at Beaulieu with Sir Max Aitken, Lord Beaverbrook's son and successor as the owner of the *Express* (second from the right), racing driver Graham Hill (third from the right) and others.

The author in his mid-fifties.

© Press Association

LEFT With Sir Marcus Sieff, head of Marks and Spencer, at a joint book-signing session.

RIGHT The subject of *Their Trade is Treachery*, former head of MI5 Sir Roger Hollis. © Press Association

At home, shortly after *Their Trade is Treachery* was published.
© Press Association

Joking with Lord (Hartley) Shawcross, the former Attorney General.

Meeting ex-President Nixon with Lord Longford and, left, William Armstrong, of the publishing firm Sidgwick and Jackson.

With Sir Thomas Sopwith, the aircraft pioneer, and Lady Sopwith at their country home.

Chapman Pincher with Duncan Sandys, the Minister of Defence.

With Sir Charles Forte during lunch at the Forte pheasant shoot near Ripley, Surrey.

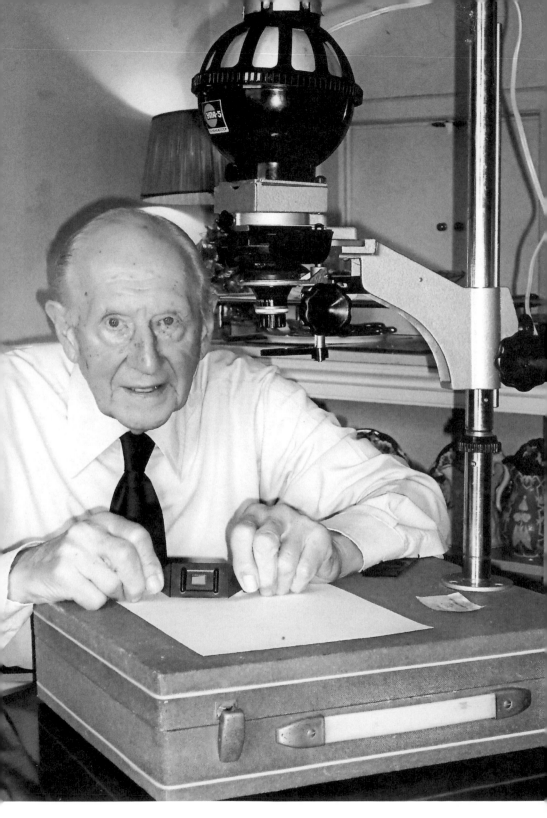

The author with the Russian-made 'darkroom-enlarger', an espionage device used by Soviet agents. Brigitte Kuczynski gave it to Michael Butt with instruction to dispose of it.

Society, knows what he is talking about before he gives tongue on any subject involving animals.

When salmon were reintroduced to the Thames, he jokingly pointed out that Windsor had a beat but he never fished it. Instead, he pursued the small, wild trout in the Highland lochs, fishing from a boat, alone or with a ghillie. He tried to recruit Princess Anne, with whom he had a warmer relationship than with his sons, to trout fishing but with no success.

During a long discussion I had with him when he was seventy-eight, in which I commented on his fitness, he demurred in a way suggesting that he felt that it was not all that it seemed and that perhaps he might not last long. Happily, he was wrong about that.

I also had several close encounters with the Prince of Wales when he was young and we were both shooting guests, staying overnight at the Hampshire home of Sir Thomas Sopwith. It was the custom there for one's dog to sleep in one's bedroom. HRH had a lively black Labrador which occasioned cries from the royal bedroom of 'You!' Before breakfast we often ran our dogs together in the garden.

On one occasion, when we were about to leave the house for the shooting field, the prince's host, Tommy Sopwith (junior), who was rounding us up, asked, 'Where is His Royal Highness?' The question was answered, loudly, by another guest, Dick Wilkins, a well-known financier in the City. 'He's on the throne.'

Once, when Mountbatten had been unable to attend, the prince had dined and spent the night at the Sopwiths', as I usually did. The young man, then in his early twenties, had to contend, alone, with nine elderly guests during the table conversations. I was so impressed by the ease with which he contributed, constructively, to all the many subjects that, when I wrote to Mountbatten expressing my regret at his absence, I mentioned the prince's performance, saying that he had so much confidence that he would do well in his public relations when he came to make speeches. Mountbatten replied (in a letter which I still possess) that he had shown my letter to the Queen, who had remarked – as any mother might – 'He must be better than we thought.'

I have stood in the shooting line next to Prince Charles on three occasions and, on one of them, incurred his displeasure by 'wiping his eye', i.e. shooting a high pheasant which he had missed with both barrels. He told me that, in his view, a bird which had survived two shots had run its fair share of the gauntlet but, in doing so, imparted his message with charming diplomacy. On another occasion, while standing next to him, I wounded a high pheasant with my first barrel and did the same with the next. Having shot it dead behind me, the prince walked over to apologise.

Around that time, in 1971, the prince, then twenty-two, acquired the newspaper description of 'Action Man' because of his determination to experience the risks taken by his fellow cadets at the Cranwell RAF college. I managed to secure advance details of his parachute drop into the sea which led the *Daily Express* front-page in July, shortly before the prince received his wings. Later, in January 1972, when he was in the navy, I was able to report in advance on a mock escape from a stricken submarine which Charles was required to make in a huge practice tank before going on patrol in a nuclear submarine.

On one occasion when I spent a weekend in Prince Charles's company, I was deprived of what turned out to be a scoop by the reticence of other guests. I arrived late for dinner because of thick swirling fog, and took my place next to the prince. When I explained the reason for my lateness nobody mentioned that the prince had also been held up by the fog. We spent the whole of the next day, a Saturday, in the shooting field and the subsequent evening in the house. On the following Monday I was startled to read a story in the *Daily Mail* reporting that Prince Charles had had a narrow escape from death on his way to a shooting weekend. A car had almost collided with his in the fog and had swerved into a ditch. The prince had made sure that the occupants were safe and had spent some time helping to make arrangements for their car to be extracted. I did not tell my editor that I had spent the weekend with the prince and had been soundly scooped.

The prince's public image has since been sadly distorted by the failure of his marriage to Diana Spencer and the repercussions of her tragic death while being driven through a tunnel in Paris on 31 August 1997. The public reaction to that event was the strangest I have ever witnessed in nearly 100 years.

Thousands took to the London streets, standing for hours holding candles or fixing on railings pictures of Diana, messages and other symbols of affection and piling up tons of flowers. The throngs seemed stunned as they stood or knelt, speaking in whispers with some quietly weeping and hugging each other. There had never been such a massive display of mourning or of the need to be seen mourning, which was alien to the customary British reserve and reticence during bereavement.

Fuelled by the media, the phenomenon reached such proportions that many serious observers believed that it marked a fundamental change in the 'national psyche'. Headlines described Diana's death as 'the event that changed the world' with claims that 'things will never be the same again'. This mass response to the sudden disappearance of an iconic figure, whose real nature was very different from that imagined by most of the mourners, induced several writers (including me) to ask: 'Have we all gone mad?'

The further the event recedes, the more extraordinary the reaction seems. So what were its causes? Much of the genuine grief was the age-old human reaction to the wasteful sacrifice of youthful beauty in seemingly mindless circumstances. There was also deep sympathy for Diana's two boys but most of the mass response was the result of the image of a wronged princess created by the media and to which millions could relate – a down-to-earth royal regularly seen on London streets in trainers and short pants, determined, in spite of stuffy protocol, to 'do her own thing', a role model emotionally vulnerable and fallible like themselves but good, kind and deeply sympathetic when, in reality, the 'People's Princess' was unstable, capricious and sometimes vindictive.

The image which Diana had actively cultivated through her excellent charitable work and regular contact with the media was largely a fantasy which ensured that she was visualised as a victim, not just of fate, but of unfair treatment by the royal family, who had driven her to seek romantic comfort elsewhere – an eventuality which had led to her death. Diana's own admitted adultery was dismissed as the consequence of her victimisation.

With the benefit of hindsight, I suspect that the prime motivation for the Diana phenomenon was a deep-seated mental factor common to us all. The sudden death of someone so fit, so vibrant and so ubiquitous in the media focused everyone's attention on the uncertainty of life and the propinquity of death. In their candle-lit vigils people were quietly and communally expressing their own anxious helplessness and their mutual behaviour brought them comfort.

In spite of the quickly proven facts about Diana's death, which showed that it was the result of a driving accident perpetrated by a driver under the influence of alcohol, many people suspected that it was contrived in the long-term interests of the monarchy by some secret conspiratorial organisation. Yet all they needed to do to settle their doubts was to ask themselves a simple question.

Could they really conceive a situation in which distinguished men of integrity and with prestigious careers at stake could sit round a table, somewhere in Whitehall, and coldly plan such an appalling crime in a foreign country? The only agency which could, theoretically, have been responsible was MI6, which is responsible for covert operations abroad. MI6 is firmly under the control of the Foreign Office and no such mission could have been sanctioned without the agreement of the Foreign Secretary. Can anyone in their right senses think that any British Foreign Secretary would have agreed to such a crime? One only needed to consider the catastrophic effects of its exposure on international relations to appreciate that no such conspiracy could ever have been seriously considered.

The brain's requirement to avoid undue anxiety by dwelling on the inevitability of death may explain, in part, why Diana's image faded so fast in spite of efforts by tabloid newspapers to keep it shining. Along with TV networks, they anticipated the first anniversary of her death as an occasion for a resurgence of national grieving but it did not happen and the 'Diana industry' disappeared. Statements that her death would change society proved to be credulous drivel.

In retrospect, the Diana phenomenon was a rather frightening exhibition of mass irrationality.

For several years Prince Charles was heavily censured for his relationship with Camilla, the wife of his friend Andrew Parker Bowles, who is also a friend of mine. I can throw some secret light on the true history of that relationship, given to me by the late Gerald Ward, a man of integrity who was a friend of all four of us and so close to Charles that after he suddenly died at seventy, the prince was the main speaker at the memorial service, which I attended.

Gerald assured me that, between 1981 and 1988, Charles had no affair whatever with Camilla. They occasionally met socially when her husband was also present and they exchanged Christmas cards but otherwise there was no relationship.

While Gerald's main home was at Chilton, near Hungerford, he also had a house in Scotland called Balmacneil, on the River Tay, where he had a good stretch of salmon fishing. Then, in 1988 (by which time Diana was having extra-marital affairs), Gerald invited Andrew to fish at Balmacneil and to bring Camilla with him. Unexpectedly and at very short notice he was unable to do so and Camilla came alone. Prince Charles had also been invited to fish and it was on that occasion that his affair with Camilla was ignited after his marriage to Diana had irretrievably collapsed.

Diana's psychiatric problems, to which she confessed on *Panorama*, sometimes drove her to assault her husband and Camilla was the only person in whom he could confide when at his wit's end. He also turned to Camilla for advice and help when Diana mutilated her own arms and legs or deliberately injured herself in other ways. The emotional quirks already in her nature before the marriage contributed as much, if not more, to the wreck of the royal marriage as did Charles's attitude to his immature wife.

Central to the problem was Diana's obsessive urge to draw attention to herself by hysterical outbursts, self-mutilation and rampant bulimia – a habit which the sensitive Charles found extremely unpleasant. When asked by Charles and other royals to moderate this pathological need Diana's response had been to claim that she was being sidelined by 'the enemy' who were 'ganging up' on her.

While Camilla avoided media attention (including from myself), declining all comment, Diana encouraged and manipulated it while blaming it for damaging the marriage. Few have shown more skill in manipulating the media to her advantage through direct contact with selected members or through well-briefed friends.

After Andrew Parker Bowles had divorced Camilla he assured me and my wife, while we were visiting him and his new wife, Rose, at their home near Malmesbury, that Camilla had no wish to be Queen. Nevertheless, Camilla was convinced that the particular emotional support which she alone had been able to provide could be helpful to Charles in his future role as King. In short, she envisaged herself in a consort role for which she is having excellent experience as Duchess of Cornwall, apparently to the great satisfaction of the rest of the royal family and, perhaps even more so, of the public.

In 1999 I interviewed Anne, the Princess Royal, for *The Field* at her 1,300-acre estate, Gatcombe Park in Gloucestershire. She was still out picking up pheasants in torrential rain when I arrived at 4 p.m. Apologetic for being late, she dried and fed her two bull terriers, which had been with her for exercise, and settled them in front of the Aga before seeing to her own comfort. For the next couple of hours the princess, who laughs a lot, could not have been more down-to-earth or less regal.

The birds had flown high and, with a countrywoman's attitude to the weather, HRH had enjoyed herself. Her two black Labradors, which lived with the keeper, had not let her down. 'Labradors are more businesslike if kept in kennels,' she explained. 'I like to think I'm controlling mine with my whistle and hand signals but they know more about finding game than I do and just get on with it.'

With a heavy list of official duties, not fully appreciated by the public because she does them unobtrusively, the princess enjoyed relaxing in the casual comfort of Gatcombe, which overlooks a deep hollow. As the princess's husband, Timothy Laurence, was in the navy, having recently been promoted to commodore (he is now

a retired vice admiral), it was the mistress's eye that was overseeing
Gatcombe Park.

Like her mother, HRH has been captivated by horses for as
long as she can remember. 'I rode in pony club trials when I was
small, then took up competition after I left school – show jumping,
dressage and cross-country riding,' she explained. 'Later, I rode in
races and won a few on the flat and one over fences. Now I ride
almost every day when I'm here. It's a better way of supervising
the estate than from a vehicle. It is surprising what you see from
a horse.'

The princess agreed with me that the British thoroughbred horse
is the most beautiful animal species on the planet – its proportions
and the conformation of its limbs, body and head being as close
to perfection as can be imagined. She also agreed that the horse's
relationship with man and its effects on his history down the ages
have also been unique and too little appreciated these days.

My encounters with Her Majesty's younger sister, Princess
Margaret, were less than regal. Lord Beaverbrook's grandson,
Johnny Kidd, a leading show jumper, had an old house in Ewhurst
where he staged large parties. At one of them, Princess Margaret
was sitting on a throne-like chair when the gossip columnist the
late Nigel Dempster seized an ancient sword adorning a wall and,
kneeling before HRH, offered the hilt, crying, 'Knight me now for
being the biggest shit in Fleet Street!' HRH declined to go through
the motions but fell about laughing.

Later, in Cowes, while staying with my newspaper proprietor, Sir
Max Aitken, I was detailed to drive Princess Margaret from a yacht
in which she had arrived to attend lunch at his house. I had my car
radio tuned quietly to a Mozart piano concerto and she, imperi-
ously, switched it off.

There were eight of us at lunch sitting on two highly polished
benches, with HRH's husband, Lord Snowdon, me and my wife,
and two large, rumbustious men on one of them. Suddenly, the two
over-grown schoolboys made a concerted lunge to the left, pushing
me along the bench and depositing Snowdon very roughly on to
the wooden floor. Long lame from polio, he had difficulty getting

up while HRH, far from complaining, just looked at him, rather contemptuously, both my wife and I thought.

Incidentally, I learned that it was Princess Margaret who was, unintentionally, responsible for the 'dorgis', which are now an established component of the royal pack of house dogs bonded to the Queen. They were the result of an unintended union between an enterprising long-haired miniature dachshund belonging to Princess Margaret, which had its way with one of the Queen's corgi bitches. The rather odd result found such royal favour that the cross-breeding was continued.

My shooting acquaintance Angus Ogilvy was a frequent guest at the Sopwith shoot in Hampshire and once his wife Princess Alexandra, who accompanied him, decided to join the beaters for the exercise. The keeper then insisted on paying her a beater's wage. Far from being insulted, she pocketed the money, complaining, 'All the years I've beaten elsewhere and I've never been paid!'

I have enjoyed two small lunch parties with the Duke of Kent, who is a good and amusing conversationalist, but the only royal I would dare to call a friend is the Duke's younger brother, Prince Michael of Kent. I first met him when we were both shooting guests of Harry Hyams at Ramsbury. Then, in the late 1980s, I was invited to a dinner of intelligence and security officers at the Cavalry Club in London and found myself sitting next to the prince. To my great surprise, he was in charge of the proceedings as he had been secretly involved in intelligence issues in the Defence Ministry for several years. Present were senior figures from the secrets world, even including the CIA, who all held him in the highest respect. Since then, he has kindly invited me to lunch with him in London on several occasions.

He also asked me to his apartment in Kensington where I met his wife, with whom I have also corresponded regarding advice about the bad press they tend to attract, unfairly in my opinion. Prince Michael's letters to me always began 'Dear Friend'.

A cousin of the Queen, Patrick (Lord) Lichfield, who made a world-renowned reputation as a photographer, became a lasting friend during my brief career as a consultant to J. Walter Thompson, the advertising agency for which he, occasionally, worked. Endowed with good looks, an engaging manner and an exceptional talent for portrait photography, he had welcome access to a broad range of subjects from royalty to film stars, pop stars, boxers and almost anyone who took his fancy as a subject.

The ancestral seat of the Earls of Lichfield, the family name being Anson, was Shugborough Hall in Staffordshire, which I visited several times. On the last occasion, he invited my wife, Billee, and me to lunch and staged it, nostalgically, in the house nursery, regaling us with many stories. One I recall centred on the island of Mustique, where he and Princess Margaret had houses. Ever an opportunist, Patrick had encountered an interesting girl and made a brief date on an evening when he was due to dine with Princess Margaret. After the meal he told HRH that he wanted to go out for a short time to take some pictures in the moonlight. After he returned, her observant comment was, 'Patrick, can you explain why you have sand on your forehead?'

He died, still a working photographer, suddenly in 2005 aged only sixty-six.

A foreign royal, whose friendship gave my wife and me much pleasure, was Crown Prince Alexander of Yugoslavia, who, when a young man, told us the extraordinary details of his birth in Claridge's Hotel in Mayfair. This happened shortly before his exiled father, King Peter II, was stripped of his titles, palaces and estates by the Communist dictator, Tito. For the Crown Prince to retain a claim to the throne he needed to be born on Yugoslav soil, so the Home Office arranged for a suite in Claridge's to be declared Yugoslav territory! A few years later, when UK citizenship was introduced, another gimmick had to be sought so that he could remain in Britain as a citizen. As he was a great, great grandson of Queen Victoria, he could claim connection with the Hanoverian line, which, under some ancient law, qualified him. After education at Gordonstoun and service in the British Army, the Crown Prince and his wife Princess Katherine, who we also met, settled in London where I occasionally visited him in his office.

Much as he loved Britain, in 2000 the Crown Prince saw it as his duty to move to Yugoslavia, having been offered citizenship there along with the restoration of the former royal palaces and other family property provided he avoids active politics. He now lives in Belgrade and, aged sixty-eight as I write, still nourishes hope that, one day, the government will decide to adopt a constitutional monarchy in the British style.

CHAPTER 16

THE BEAVER

While still a schoolboy, I knew that the *Daily Express* had been founded by an extraordinary Canadian called Lord Beaverbrook because my father had been greatly impressed by a book he had published and which he induced me to read as an example of a man who had made fame and fortune starting with nothing.

On joining the *Express* in 1946, I was surprised to find that the owner, who was generally referred to as 'the Beaver' or 'the Chief Reader', did not visit the Fleet Street building and, indeed, would never do so during the whole thirty-four years I was to serve there. The staff were regularly reminded of him on entering the rather garish front hall of the *Express* building where, mounted on a plinth, was a bronze head of his Lordship sculpted by Epstein. Otherwise his influence was exerted directly on the editor and the managing director mainly by telephone calls, dictaphone and through occasional summonses to Beaverbrook's London flat in Arlington House or to his country home, Cherkley Court, on a large estate near Leatherhead in Surrey.

Unless one was called to the presence, which was such a rare event that, for most, it never occurred, journalists and other staff members saw their proprietor only at the occasional 'tea party' he staged at the Savoy Hotel, where there was everything to drink but tea. Newcomers of note were introduced to him but only briefly because a bodyguard of senior executives made sure that they absorbed most of the Beaver's time. I was disgusted at the way so many of my colleagues swilled down the drink because 'it was on the Beaver' and were tipping waiters to slip them bottles of whisky which they took home. I vowed that I would never attend such a gathering again and never did.

Against the day when I might be called to the presence, I had acquainted myself with a brief summary of his early political life, already knowing that, as the wartime Minister of War Production (later Supply), he had played an essential role in the Battle of Britain by keeping enough Spitfires and Hurricanes in the air through his ruthless, round-the-clock search for spare parts and by ensuring that they got to where they were needed. He had also been instrumental in building up Bomber Command through his unrelenting personal drive. He, therefore, had a special interest in defence and, in particular, in the atomic weapons and long-range missiles dominating post-war East–West politics. As defence editor, I soon began to receive messages from him, first through the editor and then directly. Eventually, in the early 1960s, he discovered that my home, Lowerhouse Farm, was not far from Cherkley Court and I was asked to lunch with him there.

There was no resident lady at Cherkley Court then. In 1906 he had married a Canadian girl, Gladys, but, after producing a daughter and two sons, she had died in 1927. So, often, early on Saturday, the phone would ring and a rasping voice would say, 'Ah gotcha! Come to lunch.' The phone would then go dead. Anything I had planned, such as a day's shooting, had to be abandoned. It was often infuriating but, in retrospect, I wish it had rung more often.

Lunching with this little dynamo with a large head and staccato Canadian voice was exciting but quite an ordeal. He would always sit in the middle of his long dining table where he could command all the conversations. His guests had to remain alert as he could, suddenly, call on anybody for an opinion. In doing so, one needed to be succinct. A drawn-out statement would be met with 'When does the train get in?'

Sometimes the victim would be a new guest whom I had suggested and it was important to me that he should shine. In that respect, I recall being anxious about George Brown, the Labour politician and future Foreign Secretary, who could be unpredictable after a few drinks and whom I accompanied to lunch at Cherkley

Court. Lady Dunn, the widow of a Canadian financier, had been explaining to Brown's gentle, over-borne wife, Sophie, her difficulties in coping with the huge interest flowing from the $9 million her husband had left her – a really huge figure in those days. George's brash response, which gave the Beaver a belly-laugh, was, 'Blimey, to Sophie just five hundred quid would be a Godsend.'

I recall asking Enoch Powell if he would like to meet Beaverbrook. 'No!' he answered. 'I like to recognise evil but not to embrace it.' His was the view of many people who did not know the subject they were condemning. All who knew him well, as I came to, found him to be an intensely politically aware, pro-British idealist and entertaining with it.

Everything about the Beaver was in a style of his own. He always wore a black tie with an enormous loose knot. When he ate a pear he put the fat end down on his plate, cut the fruit across then scooped out both halves with a small spoon as though he was eating a boiled egg. Even the way he poured wine was individual. He was able to grasp a champagne bottle by the base and refill his guests's glasses by pointing the bottle at them and pouring from a distance. I never saw him spill a drop.

Several of his *Express* employees are alleged to have been subjected to what became known as 'ordeal by lavatory'. A senior writer or executive would be summoned to his London flat at short notice and, when he arrived, the butler-valet Albert would announce that his Lordship was in the bathroom and would see him there. The Beaver would be on the throne and would continue his function while engaging his visitor in conversation. Presumably it was an expression of how valuable his time was. Happily, I was never subjected to it.

When the Beaver learned that I was a keen fisherman he told me how the sport had sparked his success. As Maxwell Aitken, the son of a Scottish Presbyterian minister, he had emigrated to Canada with his family. On his twenty-first birthday in 1900, he had been fishing a lake from a boat with nothing biting. Beset by an overwhelming feeling of futility, he had barked, in the accent which never left him, 'Ah to Hell with it!', packed up and left to make his fortune. Canada was booming and people had savings to invest, so Aitken decided to make money quickly by selling bonds. He was a millionaire by the time he was thirty after cornering the cement market.

Moving to Britain in 1910, he entered British politics as MP for a seat near Manchester. In 1916, he was made a peer, taking the name Beaverbrook to commemorate and emphasise his Canadian origin. He never tired of poking fun at aristocrats who had inherited their titles – especially the 14th Earl of Home – formerly Sir Alec Douglas-Home, with whom I eventually became acquainted and greatly admired. Sending me a thank-you note for a salmon I had sent him from Scotland, the Beaver could not resist remarking that 'only a salmon caught by the 14th Earl could be better'.

He regularly raved about the dangers of 'the European entanglement', as he referred to the Common Market, which, he foresaw, would inflate itself with the inevitable takeover of the UK's parliamentary and legal powers by 'European bureaucrats' – a stance since fully justified by events.

In 1958, Beaverbrook decided to visit an international scientific exhibition in Brussels along with several prime ministers from maritime provinces in Canada, who were his guests. When he was invited to tour the Soviet pavilion, which featured atomic exhibits, I was bidden to fly over and join him as guide. Because of his wartime admiration for Stalin, the Russians were all set to make political capital out of his visit and, when we were invited to a private room for caviar and vodka, who should be waiting for us but the very astute Boris Belitsky from Moscow Radio. He asked many loaded questions but the Beaver, with his trilby hat pushed back on his balding head, cleared every possible trip-wire in a bravura performance.

In the evening, when we were all at dinner in the restaurant at the Metropole Hotel, the Beaver spotted the very sexy Italian film star Sophia Loren, with a substantial entourage. Though he had never met her, he was over at her table in a trice and brought her back to sit at ours.

At one of my early lunches at Cherkley I met his old Canadian friend Sir James Dunn, who had also made a fortune, and his wife, Christofer, who was of Greek origin, her name being Marcia Christoforides. When Sir James died in Canada in 1956, his widow, to whom he left his fortune, went into isolated mourning in the style of Queen Victoria. Beaverbrook, who regularly visited Canada, dragged her out of solitude and Lady Dunn, as she was known, made her home at Cherkley Court. When Beaverbrook became ill he would refer to her as 'my nine million dollar nurse'.

In the early 1960s, the Beaver took a deep dislike to overweight journalists on the principle that a fat body meant a lazy mind. Fortunately, I have always been slim. Among the first to be dismissed was the news editor, Morley Richards, who was a good friend of mine. I was even more horrified to discover that his Lordship wanted me to be Morley's successor in the totally misguided belief that, as I was effective in finding news in my fields, I would be good at direct-ing others in theirs. When the editor, then Edward Pickering, called me in to offer me the post I declined it on the grounds that I had no executive ambitions. Being desk bound in a London office and living life only by reading about it on bits of paper written by others was not for me. I remained an investigative reporter throughout my jour-nalistic career because I resisted all efforts to promote me to executive status. 'Putting the paper to bed' was night work and I relished the daytime chase so much that I never wanted to lose its opportunities.

As nobody had ever refused the news editorship of the *Express*, I was summoned to Cherkley Court to be told that I was 'running away from promotion'. To my surprise, I had no difficulty in convincing the Beaver that I would be unable to pass on my precious contacts to anyone else and they would be lost to the paper. He responded by giving me a salary rise.

There was one downside to being so close to the Beaver – it deprived me of several scoops, one of them being the best-kept secret in military history. In 1959, I had lunch with Air Vice Marshal Kingston McCloughry, who had served on the Beaver's wartime staff in the Supply Ministry, and we fell to talking about Field Marshal Montgomery, who happened to be ill at that time. I was comment-ing on the brilliance of Monty's actions in defeating Rommel, ending in the great victory at El Alamein, and Kingston remarked that Monty could never lose because he always knew in advance what Rommel was going to do. He then explained that the British Intelligence Service had gained complete knowledge of the codes in which Rommel signalled to Berlin and to his subordinates.

I reported the details to Beaverbrook in a long memo, of which I have a copy, telling him that I would be making further inquiries but he responded by instructing me to 'leave Monty in peace' and not pursue it further. Stupidly, I complied and it was not until 1974 that the public learned the great story of 'Ultra' – the breaking of the Germans' codes generated by their ingenious Enigma machines by the brilliant team at Bletchley Park – and its decisive influence on the outcome of the war. Perhaps, already knowing all about Ultra from his war service, Beaverbrook feared that the leak might be attributed to him.

Few of his employees dared to disagree with the proprietor but I often did so concerning technical issues. If I worsted Beaverbrook in argument he would invariably respond, 'You mustn't be hard on a poor old man.' Anything less like a poor old man would be hard to imagine.

One day, I was informed that I was going to Düsseldorf to write a story about someone there who had discovered a way of making cement out of rubble. The editor told me that Lord Beaverbrook had telephoned him with that exciting news, declaring, 'I always said that some young feller would find a cheaper way of making cement. The Germans have millions of tons of rubble. All those bombed-out buildings!'

I immediately told the editor that the story must be wrong. Being a keen stone-wall builder – I erected many at Lowerhouse Farm – I knew that cement had to be carefully compounded of specific substances with adhesive and setting properties. I pointed out that rubble contained brick-dust, wood, plaster, broken glass, old nails and other metal. Nevertheless, I was advised to go to Düsseldorf. Instead, I consulted an expert at Portland Cement who confirmed that the idea was crazy. I informed the editor, who agreed to telephone the Chief Reader with my findings, asking me to leave his office while he did so and muttering, 'God help us all!'

When he called me back he was smiling broadly. 'You don't have
to go,' he announced.

'What did he say?' I inquired.

The editor replied, 'He said, "I knew it was bloody nonsense all
the time." Then he slammed the phone down.'

I also managed to disobey him on another issue – his hatred of
Lord Mountbatten. He was forever agitating the editor and me to criticise Mountbatten in the newspaper. On one occasion, Mountbatten
asked me to lunch with a long-retired Canadian politician who
regaled me with a wartime story about a substance called 'pykrete'– a
frozen mixture of water and sawdust. A UK scientist had developed
the idea of building huge unsinkable aircraft carriers from pykrete
on the principle that any bomb or torpedo damage could be quickly
repaired by refrigerating more ice and sawdust. Taken with the idea,
Mountbatten explained it to an audience of experts, including the
Canadian politician, and had a large cube of pykrete on a table.
Suddenly, and without warning, he produced a revolver and fired
six shots into the cube, which absorbed them without splitting. Both
the Beaver and his friend regarded this as evidence of Mountbatten's
irresponsibility because a ricochet might have killed someone in the
audience. I realised that Beaverbrook wanted me to print the story
but, as Mountbatten was a powerful force in the Defence Ministry
and a source of information to me, I evaded doing so.

It was common knowledge that the Beaver and Mountbatten had
once been good friends as one of Beaver's mistresses, Jean Norton,
had been a close friend of Mountbatten's wife, Edwina. So, I asked
Mountbatten what had soured the friendship. He claimed not to
know, saying that suddenly at a lunch one day Beaverbrook had
shouted, 'Between you and me, Dickie, from now on it's war! It's
war!' I suspect that, as an Empire crusader, he despised the role
Mountbatten had played as Viceroy during the partition and
handover of India by the post-war Labour government.

Beaverbrook made no secret about his succession of mistresses
and continued the casual conquest into old age. He would reminisce
about them, one being a favourite tale harking back to 1921, when
Lloyd George had been Prime Minister. He had been dining in a

Piccadilly restaurant with two obliging American actresses, called the Dolly Sisters, when a messenger appeared and summoned him to Downing Street. Knowing that Beaverbrook was an ardent Presbyterian, Lloyd George offered him the honorary post of high commissioner to the General Assembly of the Church of Scotland. Beaverbrook wanted it but, reminded of his sinful habits by his current contact with the Dolly Sisters, he felt himself unworthy and declined the honour.

Lloyd George then declared, 'Then Geordie gets it', 'Geordie' being the Duke of Sutherland. Beaverbrook raced back to the restaurant, intending to make the most of his sacrifice and, as he recalled it, 'Who should be dancing with one of my Dolly Sisters but Geordie Sutherland!'

He expressed his attitude to casual sex more forcibly in 1963, when we were discussing the Profumo affair. 'Why in God's name should a great political party tear itself to rags and tatters just because a minister's fucked a woman?' he asked me. Why, indeed?

I do not think that anyone would have judged Beaverbrook to be physically attractive to women but he demonstrated the common fact that if a man is famous and rich, and especially if he has a title, many women are flattered by his attention and keen to be seen in his company, and the rest follows.

Occasionally, Beaverbrook would contact the *Express* editor and ask for an office secretary to be sent to Cherkley Court for a couple of days. The chosen girl, who would always be selected mainly for her looks, would find that her bedroom was next to the Beaver's, with which there was a connecting door that was open. If the girl left the door open, the Beaver wandered in at night. If she shut the door he did not. Very civilised!

He enjoyed talking about sex with intimate friends but never about his own conquests. Once when we were discussing the influence of a lady, well known in Fleet Street and with whom he (rightly) suspected I might be involved, as I was single at the time, he puckered his face into a leery smile and declared, 'I bet she's got a big bush!' (When I told the lady what he had said, her only comment was, 'But isn't that a good thing?')

The Beaver's taste in the films he showed in his private cinema at Cherkley was odd for such an intelligent man. His favourite star was Betty Grable, whose only notable feature was her legs. However, the content of the film was usually of small importance for his Lordship tended to talk right through it.

Born into the Presbyterian faith, his father being a preacher, he sometimes talked about it and would describe it as 'terrible – all fire and brimstone'. He liked to tell a story about a Scotsman, another Presbyterian, who died and found himself in Hell. On looking up from the pit, he saw God looking down on him and said, 'Oh God, I didna ken, I didna ken.' Grimly, God replied, 'Well, you ken noo!'

When I joined the *Daily Express* in 1946 those who controlled the paper's general policy had assumed that the Chief Reader accepted what they thought to be the Presbyterian belief that the world had been created in about 4000 BC. They, therefore, refused to publish anything about the concept of evolution, as I discovered when I submitted a story about a fossil fish believed to be 200 million years old. Determined to change such a stupid policy I persevered but managed only a few minor triumphs until a living fossil, the coelacanth fish, was dredged up off Mozambique. The editor and the Beaver had to admit defeat or fail to print the intriguing news. After that I was permitted to write about evolution.

In the spring of 1962, when salmon fishing on the Dee and staying at the Raemoir Hotel, I drifted into the bar before dinner and was introduced to a famous radiologist who was drowning his lack of success that day with whisky. After asking me how Beaverbrook was and hearing that he had seemed OK when I had seen him recently, he staggered me by declaring, 'He'll be dead in six months! He has inoperable cancer of the prostate. I've seen the X-ray plates.'

I recalled that Lord Beaverbrook had raised my suspicions by telling me that he was having 'cobalt bomb' treatment for lumbago, with Lady Dunn pointing out that, while the 'cobalt bomb' was used against cancer, their doctor had assured them that it was also 'good for lumbago'.

On my return south, I went to Cherkley Court to see Lady Dunn, who was horrified and insisted that nobody else should know, least of all 'the Lord', as she called him. She then told me that, because of his many financial interests, 'the Lord' had told his doctors that they must always tell him the truth about his life-expectation, believing that he could face death with equanimity. However, when they told him that he had an incurable malignancy, he had been so 'cast down', as he said it, that she had induced the doctors to change their verdict and attribute the pain to lumbago.

Beaverbrook had a splendid home at Cap d'Ail near Monte Carlo and invited me there as a lone guest along with Lady Dunn. He enjoyed singing hymns and as Lady Dunn and I were helping him to walk a considerable distance, she holding him on one side and with me on the other, he burst into song but stopped as he reached the end. Lady Dunn asked him to finish but he declined, saying, 'I don't like the last line.'

'Please sing it, dear,' she insisted and he obliged with, 'Until I come to Thee', adding, 'Who the hell wants to go to Him? I don't. At least not yet.'

Beaverbrook also enjoyed listening to what he called 'jingles' on old gramophone records. On one occasion he wanted to let the editor know his views about some American enterprise being favoured by the Prime Minister, Anthony Eden, whom he disliked. So, he telephoned the editor from Cherkley Court and told him to: 'Call me back in ten minutes and I'll give you the title for the leader column for tomorrow's paper.' The editor did so and all he could hear was the Beaver urging on Albert, the butler, to wind up the gramophone. Eventually, he heard the reedy strains of a song, 'Working for the Yankee Dollar'. Then the phone went dead.

One day, in 1963, on being bidden to Cherkley Court, I was told by Lady Dunn that 'the Lord' was a bit off colour but would appear soon. Alone with her and knowing how ill he really was, I said, most sincerely, 'I don't know what he would do without you', to which she replied, 'Oh, I do no more than any woman would do for her husband.'

Seeing my astonishment, she explained, 'We were married yesterday at the Epsom Registry Office.'

I asked her if the wedding was to be kept secret and she made it clear that she would prefer the world to know but insisted that I must get the Lord's permission. All he would say when he joined us was, 'Ah, you don't want to be writing about things like that.'

I pointed out that the *Express* would be deeply embarrassed if the news first appeared in another newspaper but all that elicited was, 'If any young journalist gets a scoop on it then good luck to him.' I informed my editor, then Bob Edwards, who agreed that nothing could be done. The news eventually appeared in a Canadian magazine and then in the *Daily Mail*.

When the Beaver approached his eighty-fifth birthday in 1964, his close friends were all pushed to find him a present that would mean much to him. Again, my lucky streak came to my rescue. While visiting the country home of Lieutenant Colonel Sammy Lohan (who would later figure rather prominently in my life), I spotted the original visitors' book belonging to Cherkley, which the parents of Lohan's wife had originally built. I persuaded Sammy and his wife to sell me the book and I have a letter from Lord Beaverbrook saying that it was the present which had pleased him most.

Lady Beaverbrook's present had involved much more effort. She had bought an old barrel organ of the kind which, in my childhood, was used by Italians to patrol the streets of British towns, virtually begging. She had spent a great deal having it restored and altered, the glass panels being repainted with scenes from 'the Lord's' Canadian childhood. She planned to play it by winding the handle as the Lord descended the stairs on his chairlift on his birthday morning and had even hired a donkey and an organ-grinder's monkey. Sadly, the Lord did not respond as expected.

'Get rid of that donkey,' he shouted. 'It'll do its business on my Bokhara carpet. And get that ape outta here, it'll give me asthma.'

Later, Lady Beaverbrook turned the handle of the organ as she told me the sad story – surely she was the only multi-million-dollar barrel-organist.

A big dinner in Beaverbrook's honour at the Dorchester Hotel had been arranged by Lord (Roy) Thomson, a fellow Canadian, and, on my next visit, Lady Beaverbrook told me that the end was so near that the festivity was almost certain to be cancelled. She had withdrawn all the invitations to women because she believed they were likely to waste money on dresses. However, by a most admirable effort of will, the Beaver not only attended the dinner, in a wheelchair, but made a splendid speech in a strong voice which, I remember, ended with the statement, 'All my life, I have regarded myself as an apprentice with lots still to learn. I shall continue to be an apprentice in another place, sometime soon.'

He then joined a few of us for an hour's talk after the dinner then went back to his bed at Cherkley Court where he died eleven days later, aged eighty-five.

A few of what Lady Beaverbrook called 'his favourites' were invited to say farewell to the embalmed corpse. I went into the room containing the open coffin with Michael Foot, the Labour firebrand, who the Beaver had always liked. Lady Beaverbrook stood at the Lord's head watching our reactions as we viewed the corpse, which seemed very small and had a slightly mischievous smile. I recalled the Beaver's invariable comment whenever I had mentioned the word 'rest' to him – 'You'll rest long enough in that little box!'

About eight of us then stayed on for an early evening wake at which I was instructed by Lady Beaverbrook to make them laugh. It was, in fact, grimly hilarious without my help. Michael Foot and his wife had been in a serious car accident and had their arms in slings. Another guest had a black patch over one eye making him look piratical. I had injured my right leg and, limping badly, was carrying a knobbly blackthorn thumbstick. As we sat down, as though on cue, a violent thunderstorm broke over the estate.

Beaverbrook had been given a huge, square birthday cake and his widow had placed it on the lawn outside the French windows where we could see a crowd of jackdaws and starlings pecking at it. Beyond the lawn, illuminated by the lightning flashes, we could also see a huge white cross which Beaverbrook had erected early in his tenure of Cherkley Court as a symbol of his religious belief.

My last service for my beloved master, who had so enlivened my life, was as an usher at his memorial service in St Paul's Cathedral.

I kept in touch, briefly, with Lady Beaverbrook, who soon became entranced by horse-racing and -breeding, employing the former great jockey Sir Gordon Richards as her chief trainer and adviser. As I attended only one race a year – the Oaks, as a guest of Harry Hyams, who took a box for it – that was the only annual occasion on which I encountered her Ladyship.

Having devoted most of her widowhood to philanthropic causes, mainly in Canada, she died in 1994 aged eighty-five.

CHAPTER 17

THE BEAVER'S PROGENY

Happily, my personal relationship with the Beaverbrook family would continue for many years mainly through my close association with two of his children, his daughter Janet and his son Max.

Again, solely by good fortune, Janet moved into a large house with a small stud farm called Slythehurst, on the edge of Ewhurst, less than a mile from Lowerhouse Farm. She was then married to a Canadian wartime soldier, Major Edward Kidd – known to all as 'Cappie' – whom Janet, being a true daughter of the Beaver, dominated rather ruthlessly. We quickly became regular visitors to each other's homes and she and Cappie brightened the lives of me and my wife in many ways. She introduced us to the world of showjumping, where her son, Johnny Kidd, excelled, and we became regular visitors to such events, especially at Hickstead, the show ground developed by the remarkable Douglas Bunn, who became an entertaining friend.

Her greatest gift was to invite us, over many years, to Barbados, where she would spend half the year in her splendid former plantation house, Holders. We were well served by the staff, which always included five 'mini-butlers' – young black boys whom she trained, which meant that, eventually, they could find employment in the island's bustling hotel business. Beautifully dressed with bow ties, they loved their jobs and one of them, Wesley, was to stagger me. Wesley was so good as chief butler that when Janet returned to Slythehurst she would bring him with her to serve there.

One weekend in the early 1960s, Janet telephoned us to join her at lunch to help entertain a black gentleman visitor called Errol Barrow, who was Prime Minister of Barbados. He was there with his son, whom he was delivering to Oxford University later in the afternoon. I found him delightful company, especially when I learned that he had served in the RAF from 1940 and had taken part in forty-five bombing missions as navigator. During the lunch, we noticed that Wesley, then in his twenties, was in a bad temper, slamming dishes down.

With the lunch over, and the Prime Minister and his son out of the room, Janet asked Wesley, 'What the hell's wrong with you?' to which he replied, 'I'm sorry, ma'am, but I can't abide serving niggers.'

In view of the present racial objections to the use of that word (now generally referred to only as the 'n-word') I put this astonishing reaction on record as Barrow, of whom Wesley should have been so proud, sadly died in 1987 after serving as Prime Minister for five years.

With the Beaverbrook genes forever on display, Janet was assertive to a degree I have never seen in any other woman. In her sixties she learned to fly a helicopter and won flying competitions. On one occasion, visiting our house for coffee, she had arrived by helicopter, landing by the swimming pool. The wind from the blades of the machine had stripped all the blossom from my precious rose-beds and blown them, with much else, into the pool, which I had laboriously cleaned. When I remonstrated with her, Janet responded in true Beaver style: 'If all you ever have to worry about is rose petals in your swimming pool you'll be damned lucky.'

When she could no longer fly for medical reasons she took to two-in-hand horse-driving and, again, was good enough to win competitions. She would regularly drive to our house by horse.

I was with Janet at Slythehurst in 1971 when A. J. P. Taylor, the historian writing the massive biography *Beaverbrook*, came to check the proofs with her. Janet criticised him for failing to show what she called 'the dark side' of her father's nature and, particularly, to what she called 'his cruel streak'. 'I never liked my father after the incident when, at the age of eleven, I went with my mother to see him at the Hyde Park Hotel and we found him in bed with Jose Collins, the music hall star,' she said. However, she did recall that when his wife had died her father had been really heartbroken.

She then recalled how, at the age of eighteen, she had married Ian Campbell, later Duke of Argyll, an inveterate gambler who believed she was rich, when, in reality, her father had always kept her short of money. As a wedding present, she had received an emerald and diamond tiara from a rich lady and Campbell had pawned it for £1,000. Janet stole the pawn ticket from her husband's trousers and induced her father to redeem the tiara. Finding that it came apart to make a necklace and brooches, Beaverbrook had kept it and had given the parts away to women friends.

Janet had also been disgusted by her father through his treatment of Jean Norton, whom she had liked so much that she had hoped he would marry her. Instead, Beaverbrook had become involved with Lily Ernst, a ballet dancer. For appearances' sake, Mrs Norton was housed in a cottage on the Cherkley Estate and when, in 1945, he had decided to give a party to which she was not invited, he asked her to move out for one night to provide extra accommodation for his guests. She did so and later found out that her home had been occupied by Lily Ernst. When Jean Norton returned to the cottage she died of a heart attack.

Taylor responded to Janet's views of her father by saying that he had loved the old man so much that he could not put such stories in his book, whereupon Janet made me promise that if I ever wrote reminiscences about her father I would do it 'warts and all'.

Sadly, we lost close contact with Janet after we left Ewhurst for Kintbury in 1980. Geography can be a mortal enemy of friendship. She died in 1988.

I first encountered the Beaver's son, Max, at the Fleet Street *Daily* and *Sunday Express* office where, aged thirty-six, he had taken over command as chairman of Beaverbrook Newspapers (with persistent interference from his father) in 1946. I knew that he had a brilliant record as a fighter pilot in the wartime RAF, winning the DFC and DSO and ending as group captain, after which he had been an MP for a short time. Like his father, he was impressive – but in a different way. He was well built, handsome and energetic with a straightforward manner and, through shooting in particular, we became good friends. With a few others, he rented a shoot at

Beaulieu on the estate of Lord Montagu and I enjoyed many days there meeting his companions.

Max Aitken's main post-war recreations were yachting and power-boat racing, at which he excelled, to the annoyance of his father, who considered it all a waste of time. 'Where've ya been? "Yattin" I suppose,' was the Beaver's regular greeting.

I witnessed an oddity of Beaverbrook's attitude to his son while staying at Cap d'Ail. One evening, he had asked me to be present with him at 9 a.m. on the following day, when he duly telephoned his son in London. He then proceeded to criticise Max's handling of the newspapers in most savage terms. As soon as he put the phone down he said that he would not need me again until lunchtime.

He had not let Max know that I was listening so whatever extra satisfaction he had secured by my presence remained a mystery though it would seem to have been some variety of sadism. As, by then, Max was not only my chief but a shooting friend, I felt embarrassed but said nothing.

Max fell under the spell of the outstanding lawyer Arnold Goodman, who was a brilliant negotiator and troubleshooter employed, in particular, by Harold Wilson. Shortly before the white Prime Minister of Rhodesia, Ian Smith, declared the country independent from British rule in 1965, Wilson asked Goodman to go there and negotiate with him. As Max had met Smith when both were serving in the wartime RAF, Goodman suggested Max should accompany him on the trip. The expedition was a flop but there was one aspect which Max enjoyed recalling.

The project was so secret that Max and Goodman could not be seen entering No. 10 Downing Street to receive their final briefing from Wilson. So arrangements were made to take them in, separately, through a back entrance. Max described to me how he had been required to stand, with his umbrella up in heavy rain, outside a certain door near the top of Whitehall where he was, eventually, picked up by a car and taken to the back door. After the briefing by Wilson in the Cabinet Room he and the physically large and very recognisable Goodman were escorted out of No. 10 together via the front door!

I was to have many brushes with Goodman, mainly concerning my newspaper attacks on Wilson. One afternoon, I was sitting in the office of Jocelyn Stevens, a managing executive at the *Express*, discussing a very damaging potential story about our joint shooting acquaintance Angus Ogilvy, the husband of Princess Alexandra. Stevens had picked the story up from 'Tiny' Rowland, the boss of conglomerate Lonrho, who wanted it published to get revenge on Ogilvy for some misdeed. I was opposed to writing it as it was not in my field of interests and I would receive the backlash from Ogilvy's friends. The situation was suddenly resolved by an unexpected telephone call from Arnold Goodman – speaking from Buckingham Palace! Stevens rapidly lost his interest and the story was never published.

On the morning of 21 August 1968, I was able to do a small service for Max, which I know he appreciated. We were both enjoying a week's prime grouse-shooting as guests of the Sopwiths on their splendid moor at Arkengarthdale and I awoke early to the totally unexpected news that Soviet troops had invaded Czechoslovakia to crush the freedom reforms which had become known as the Prague Spring. Realising that, as the defence reporter, I needed to be in Fleet Street with all speed to cover a most serious situation, I was making my apologies when Max appeared. 'Do you think I need to be there, too?' he asked. I will never forget his smiling look of relief when I assured him that he did not, as I promised to keep him informed by telephone.

When Lord Beaverbrook died, his son inherited both his father's baronetcy and the barony. He chose to be known only as Sir Max, declaring that there would be no other Lord Beaverbrook in his lifetime.

Max told me how he had promised his dying father hat he would burn all his secret papers – of which there was a large pile – which the Beaver wished nobody to see. He did so, rather reluctantly, realising he was burning history, especially as Beaverbrook had been a close friend of Winston Churchill and had assisted him financially. There were enough other documents left to form the Beaverbrook Library in London's St Bride Street.

Once in charge without interference, Max proved to be a good chairman. He brought in some of his old friends such as Hugh 'Cocky' Dundas, a wartime RAF fighter ace, who had served under Douglas Bader. As Bader was then, occasionally, visiting our house (I have a vivid mental picture of this extraordinary legless war hero swinging his way, without a stick, over our living-room carpet on his false legs), Cocky and I had much to talk about in the office. I was also able to give him an old signed photograph for his family archives.

The head of the Dundas family is the Marquis of Zetland, whose family seat is Aske Hall, near Richmond in Yorkshire. My paternal grandmother's sister, Julia Chapman, who never married, had a house in Pottergate – then a narrow road leading into Richmond from the direction of Aske. From it she sold sweets, including a special toffee she made called Tom Trot, which I recall as short, dark brown sticks which were delightful to suck. In the early 1900s, the then Marquis of Zetland used to ride into Richmond on horseback and was in the habit of calling at my great aunt's shop for some Tom Trot. Eventually, presumably in gratitude for the toffee, he gave her a photograph of himself wearing long buttoned-up leggings and signed 'Zetland' which is now in the family archives at Aske.

Max also recruited to the managerial staff a distinguished submariner called Johnnie Coote, who became a useful source to me because he had taken part in many electronic spying missions on Russia's coastal defences.

Having escaped from the teaching profession, I did not expect that I would ever be required to address a large gathering of boys again but in 1970, or thereabouts, Sir Max had been approached by the then headmaster of Eton to ask me if I would give a talk there about spies. I was rather surprised because that disreputable, though intelligent, member of the Foreign Office, Guy Burgess, who had revealed that he was a Soviet agent by defecting to Russia in 1951, was an Old Etonian and nostalgically wore his Old Etonian tie in Moscow. So it would be impossible for me to avoid mentioning him in my talk.

I accepted gladly because I knew little about the school and I was curious even just to see the inside of such an historic establishment. I was told that, traditionally, while many boys attended the morning religious service in the splendid chapel, they were given the choice of attending 'the Alternative Assembly', which was a talk given by a visiting speaker in a large hall.

I was thrilled to learn that, for my convenience as my talk was at 9 a.m., I was invited to spend the previous evening and night as a guest of one of the housemasters and to have dinner and breakfast with some of the senior boys, when we discussed many subjects. In that short time, and during my address (well received), I was unforgettably impressed by the quality of the staff and pupils and by the whole ambience of the college. As a former teacher with a Teacher's Diploma, I could see that the education offered there was superb. No doubt, with my genial acquaintance William Waldegrave now the provost, it remains that way. So, when sour-grapes left-wingers pour scorn on a great British institution, at least one old grammar school boy vigorously responds, 'Floreat Etona!'

(Once my name became well known through the newspaper, I often received calls for favours and resolved them by applying a simple principle – 'Duty, pleasure, cash or credit' – meaning: Is it my duty? Is there any pleasure in it? Is there any cash? Is there any credit? If the answer to all was negative, I declined.)

Normally, Max did not interfere with the day-to-day running of the newspapers and I was surprised to be summoned to his office to be ordered to stop attacking Harold Wilson. Goodman had been working on him for some time and I now suspect that he had told him, in confidence, that Wilson was showing the first signs of Alzheimer's Disease, which would eventually lead to his resignation from politics. Being unaware of that, at the time, I thought it was Max who was losing his reason.

Max began to record a true history of his father but was overtaken by illness and died in 1985. I continued my friendship with the family through his most likeable son, Maxwell, the present Lord Beaverbrook, and his wife Susie, both of whom I first met shooting with Harry Hyams at Ramsbury Manor.

I was also in regular touch with a great nephew of Beaverbrook, Jonathan Aitken, who had all the potential for an outstanding political career but was to end up in prison. The son of Sir William Aitken, a former MP, and a former pupil of Eton and Christ Church, Oxford, Jonathan was outstandingly handsome, tall and with a speaking voice which commanded respect. Through some rich Arab, he had an interest in a leisure centre in Kintbury and, when visiting it, he and his wife Lolicia would call and see us. My wife and I regularly visited his rather grand London home for parties where an occasional visitor was Arthur Martin, a distinguished former MI5 officer whose leaks to his host would eventually reach my ears in a career-changing way.

Aitken had distinguished himself in international journalism and was elected to Parliament in 1983 at the age of forty-one. I recall lunching with David Owen when his party was in opposition and we talked about who might succeed Margaret Thatcher as Prime Minister. He regarded Aitken as the likeliest contender. Instead, John Major was the Tory Party's choice and Aitken became a Cabinet minister in his government in 1994.

He lost his seat in the 1997 election and, two years later, following some visit to Paris in connection with his Arab interests, stupidly became involved in a libel case in which, on a trivial issue, he committed perjury. As a result, he was sent to prison for eighteen months, serving seven of them.

Shattered as we were by the tragedy, my wife wrote Jonathan an affectionate letter while he was awaiting sentence. His reply in March 1999, before he was sentenced in June, showed that he was remarkably composed. He wrote, 'Disgrace, divorce, impending bankruptcy and jail are four horsemen of the apocalypse yet I am far from down-hearted. I shall make my time in prison a positive experience. I am hoping to study computer skills and theology – a felicitous combination of God and Mammon.'

He emerged a dedicated Christian and is now, at seventy-one, the president of Christian Solidarity Worldwide. He has written some successful books and is still in active journalism.

As I have commented so many times on so many peculiar circumstances, 'It's a funny old world.'

CHAPTER 18

THE JEWISH CONNECTION

There were not many Jews in Darlington and district, where I spent my youth, and there were few chances of meeting any as, in those days, they 'kept themselves to themselves', as the saying was. The only one I can recall was a girl, called Raphael, with whom I occasionally walked home, as our houses were close. One day, I asked her what would happen if she should marry a man who was not a Jew. 'I would be ostracised,' she replied primly. 'And quite right, too!' That remark summarised the clannishness of most Jews who, understandably, tend to prefer the company of their own race and religion.

It was not until I was forty-nine that I became closely acquainted with any Jews, through a moment which was to have far-reaching consequences for the rest of my life. As I have mentioned, while dining with Hugh and Antonia Fraser I had met a German-Jewish immigrant called Peter Adam and both I and my wife Billee became very friendly with the Adam family, especially Peter's Polish wife, Ushy. Through them we met Israel Sieff, who became a particularly interesting friend. His full name was Israel Moses Sieff, which he recalled, rather plaintively, had caused great mirth when first read out by the headmaster of Manchester Grammar School during the welcoming of the new pupils. In fact, he would prove to be most aptly named because he was to be involved in the creation of the state of Israel.

Billee usually accompanied me to the pheasant shoot run by Peter Adam and did so four days after we had married on a Tuesday in mid-November 1965. The shoot lunch was attended by Israel, who had just been honoured with a peerage, and he remarked, 'Didn't you two get married this week? I thought you would be on your honeymoon,' to which my wife replied, 'This is it! You don't think that Harry would miss a big shoot, do you?'

'No honeymoon!' Israel exclaimed. 'That won't do! I'll have to think of something.'

Next day he telephoned us to say, 'As a wedding present, I am sending you both to Israel – all expenses paid. There is a snag, however. I'm coming with you!'

It meant being abroad for nearly three weeks because so many events had been organised by the Israelis to celebrate Lord Sieff's peerage, as he had donated so much to the young state and helped it in other ways, but my editor agreed that the chance of meeting the Israeli leaders in such circumstances should not be missed.

We had never visited the Holy Land, as Christians used to call that territory, and just to see a signpost pointing to Nazareth or Bethlehem was spine-tingling. Jerusalem, with its extraordinary history, could not fail to excite. Neither did Meggido, the site of that predicted final battle, Armageddon, nor any other of the many Biblical locations which we encountered. (While roaming the ruins of Ashkelon, I learned that the Crusaders had so enjoyed the local onions that they brought some back to Britain, where, in that context, 'Ashkelon' became corrupted to 'escallion'. I then realised why, when I was a boy, spring onions were known in the north as 'scallions'.)

We attended the many festivities, which involved visits to various kibbutzim as honoured guests, my wife being unforgettably serenaded at one of them by the superb violinist David Oistrakh, who played a Beethoven romance.

At a big lunch at the home of Teddy Kollek, the new mayor of Jerusalem, who would earn the description 'the greatest builder of Jerusalem since Herod', I was seated next to a little man whom I vaguely recognised but could not name. He turned out to be David Ben-Gurion, Israel's first Prime Minister. His most recognisable feature had been his white hair, which stood out from his head like an aurora borealis but some politician had offended him and to show his anger he had cut all his hair off!

We also heard many Israeli jokes such as the claim that Moses should be routinely booed for making a cardinal blunder when leading his people to the Promised Land – if he had turned left, instead of right, Israel would have acquired the oilfields.

During our visit I met all the Israeli leaders and many generals, including the chief of Mossad, the legendary intelligence service with which I forged a relationship, bringing me many scoops and a warning from Scotland Yard that I was on a Palestinian hit-list!

Perhaps our most memorable experience was to be driven to Masada by our ambassador to Israel, Sir Michael Hadow, a Christian who years later was to marry into the Sieff family. Masada is a flat crag which, on one side, drops 1,300 feet into the Dead Sea. To stand on it was to witness history as it happened nearly 2,000 years ago for there, in AD 73, the last of the Jews holding out against the might of Rome staged a heroic act of defiance. Below, to be seen with astonishing clarity, were the camps and siege works of the 10th Roman Legion, which, under the leadership of General Flavius Silva, was determined to reduce the fortress. With a force of 15,000, including many Jewish slaves, Silva built a wall, which is still to be seen, round the entire rock to prevent any escapes. Then they built a ramp of stones and earth 200 yards long reaching to the summit. With a battering ram the Romans breached the walls when, rather than be captured, the defending Jews killed their wives and children and drew lots to decide who should kill the men, with the last committing suicide. When the Romans entered Masada it was a burning ruin with more than 950 corpses lying there. That defiance seems as strong as ever in modern Israel where, to show it, soldiers now take their oath of allegiance on Masada to defend their hard-won country to the last. Having met many of them, from commanders in Jerusalem to artillery men in their bunkers on the Golan Heights, I know they mean it.

On a second visit to Israel we also visited – by helicopter – the Santa Caterina Monastery at the foot of Mount Sinai, where Moses is supposed to have received the Ten Commandments. There we were shown the burning bush which, it was solemnly claimed, was still the original bush encountered by Moses and, while burning, 'was not consumed'.

I took a walk in the desert around the heavily fortified walls of the monastery but was hurriedly recalled by the commander of an Israeli army contingent who warned me that the local Arabs of the occupied Egyptian territory were quite likely to use me for target practice.

On our return to London, I made friends with the military attaché at the Israeli embassy, Brigadier Zvi Zamir, and began to receive useful inside information for my newspaper. I knew that Zamir was held in such regard that he was scheduled to return to Israel to become the Mossad chief. So, I was understandably elated when he telephoned me to ask if I would like an exclusive interview with General Yitzhak Rabin, who was passing through London to become ambassador in Washington. The time was December 1967 – six months after the Six-Day War, in which Israeli forces, headed by General Rabin, had achieved spectacular victories in what Israel claimed to be a pre-emptive strike against threatening Arab forces. In the process, Israel had taken control of the West Bank and East Jerusalem from Jordan, the Golan Heights from Syria and the Sinai Peninsula and the Gaza Strip from Egypt. The Israeli capture of Sinai had given it control of the Suez Canal, which was within Israeli artillery range. As a result, the Suez Canal had been closed.

Foreign Office diplomats led by the Labour Foreign Secretary, George Brown, were putting all the pressure they could on the Israeli government to allow the canal to be reopened because its closure was costing Britain millions. The ebullient Brown was confidently predicting success but my Israeli sources were predicting otherwise, as I intimated in my newspaper, to Brown's increasing annoyance.

In a meaty interview in a private room in the Hyde Park Hotel, Rabin assured me that not only did the Israelis want the canal kept shut but that the American government was backing them strongly in that resolve. He stressed that the US government was the only one capable of exerting effective pressure on Israel to reopen it. Brown could bleat as much as he liked but he would have no impact.

Rabin then explained to me why the Israelis wanted the canal closed indefinitely. So long as they remained in control of Sinai, the Egyptians would be forced to keep their Russian-supplied fighter planes on airfields out of Israeli artillery range. That meant that the planes would not have enough range to bomb the major Israeli cities. The Israeli defence line against Egyptian tank attack could also be much shorter and there were other tactical advantages.

Rabin then revealed that the secret American interests in keeping the canal shut were strategic. The Russians could not use it to ship arms to Vietnam, as they had been doing before, and it also blocked their easy route to the Red Sea and the Indian Ocean, where Britain had recently left a power vacuum with abandonment of control of the port of Aden.

Without, of course, revealing my source, my front-page report stated categorically that the canal would remain shut indefinitely – probably for years – because the US did not want it opened. It was roundly ridiculed in Parliament by Brown, who forecast that it would be reopened 'within weeks'. The canal remained closed for eight years!

In the whole field of investigative journalism there is little that is more satisfying than triumphing, publicly, over a great department of state and its civil service mandarins and senior politicians with whom one has been in open conflict. The incident, which still warms my old bones, also highlights the extent to which events of the greatest international importance are so often governed by factors unknown to the general public.

Through Israel Sieff I regularly renewed my acquaintance with the Israeli leaders on their visits to London. Another spin-off was my introduction to Israel's son, Marcus, a forceful personality who was to succeed his father as the chief of Marks and Spencer, having made his mark by founding the food department there. In the process, he would be honoured with a knighthood and then a peerage. Our wives became great friends and we paid many visits to Marcus's town and country homes.

On the shoot there was an interesting stretch of the small Enborne River and I encouraged Marcus to keep it stocked with trout. He became a keen angler, regularly being my guest on the Kennet. Through Marcus and Lily Sieff we met many other distinguished Jews, including Lord (Victor) Rothschild, a strange, elusive, unknowable character who would have a rather dangerous impact on my life.

I also met David Susman, a South African member of the 'M and S' board, who, with his wife Anne, had a country home in a lovely old rectory close to Kintbury. Billee and I managed to wheedle him into our fishing club on the Kennet and, being exceptionally pleasant company, he enlivened our lives for many years.

At various parties I had also met the remarkable Jewish immigrant from Vienna, George Weidenfeld, who ran the publishing company Weidenfeld & Nicolson. Weidenfeld, later Lord, was famed for the parties he staged in his Chelsea flat and elsewhere and I met new sources there, including Harold Wilson's political secretary Marcia Williams (now Lady Falkender). In 1965, George published my first novel, *Not with a Bang*, which was a success, and, much later, *One Dog and Her Man*.

Meanwhile, in different circumstances, I had met Jimmy Goldsmith (later Sir James), with whom I shared political views, especially relating to the danger threatened by the Soviet Union. I first met Jimmy in Paris where he had been born in 1933. His Jewish father owned the Scribe Hotel there, where I stayed. Baptised a Catholic on his Catholic mother's insistence (as I had been), Jimmy was an exceptionally handsome young man and we eventually became close friends through our joint interest in the Institute for the Study of Conflict, which had been founded by the polymath Brian Crozier in 1970 to record and publicise the massive efforts being made by the Soviet Union to undermine democracies, and the United Kingdom in particular. Crozier was generous with his information over several years.

My newspaper reports on these efforts, especially about the Communist influence on powerful unions – in some cases amounting to control – which was aimed at destroying whole capitalist industries, had long been dismissed as 'Reds under the beds' paranoia. So, in 1985, I published *The Secret Offensive*, which was a full account of what the Russians called 'active measures', including sophisticated techniques of deception, forgery, blackmail, subversion and the promotion of violence. In that venture, which opened many eyes and enraged those in the Kremlin, I was greatly assisted by Goldsmith, by then Sir James, who gave me access to a mass of documents he had acquired for his defence of a libel action against him which had collapsed.

Jimmy, who (eventually) had made a great fortune in various food businesses, had received his knighthood in Harold Wilson's notorious resignation honours list, Wilson having been impressed by Jimmy's intellectual powers and drive. He was, however, by nature a gambler and one of his close friends was John Aspinall, who ran a gambling club in London. I recall giving them lunch at the Café Royal when, discussing Jimmy's vast wealth, he remarked, 'It could all go in the next throw, you know.' I think he meant it.

Jimmy eventually settled in France on a large estate and we kept in touch by letter. In fact, I possess – and treasure – the last words he ever wrote, sent to me by his secretary for that reason. In 1997, I had heard that he had an illness but had not realised that it was terminal and wrote to cheer him up, reminding him of the fun of our joint enterprises. Shortly after signing his brief reply he died, aged only sixty-four.

Peter Adam, too, was to die even younger, from the first case of Alzheimer's Disease I had encountered. Thank you, Peter, for so much.

CHAPTER 19

CONNECTIONS WITH CRIME

My work as a scientific reporter occasionally required my attendance at trials – usually at the nearby Old Bailey – when forensic evidence was likely to be important or there were other technical aspects, as with the case of the ex-German atomic scientist Klaus Fuchs.

In 1950, I attended the Old Bailey trial of Donald Hume, a thirty-year-old car-dealer who was accused of murdering Stanley Setty, a wealthy businessman, and of cutting up the body and disposing of it. Hume was, indeed, the killer. A qualified air pilot, he had dropped the head and legs into the Channel, where they sank, and on a second trip had dropped the torso, which floated and had been found washed up in the Essex marshes. Hume had cooked up a story that others had killed Setty and had paid him to dispose of the body, to which he pleaded guilty. To my amazement, he was acquitted of murder – then a hanging offence – and served just eight years in jail.

In March 1958, soon after his release, Hume came to my Fleet Street office with an astonishing story for which he wanted payment. While in prison he had become a close friend of Fuchs, who was serving a twelve-year sentence for systematically passing the secrets of the atomic bomb to Russia. Hume had repaid Fuchs's friendship by organising the smuggling in of new scientific books and playing chess with him. Fuchs had also taught Hume to speak some German.

As proof of his claims, Hume had a mass of notes and had some of Fuchs's own calculations made on the back of prison laundry lists. There was even a sheet of prison toilet paper on which Fuchs had sketched for Hume the principle of the Hiroshima bomb. (Later, I secured Fuchs's copious notes for a course of seventeen lectures on atomic physics, including how the H-bomb works, which he had given to his fellow prisoners.) Hume also supplied me with copies of poems about religion written by the atheistic Fuchs, along with his private views on the inefficiency of MI5, the security service which he had been able to fool for so long.

My editor agreed to buy Hume's story so long as we could keep the papers as proof of its authenticity. I consulted them to write this recollection, also checking the articles I was able to write about my encounter with Hume, which record that I interrogated him for two weeks. The articles were of special interest because Fuchs was soon due for release and there had been argument about whether he would be too rusty to be of use to Communist East Germany, where he had decided to settle. Hume's evidence showed that Fuchs had kept his mind and knowledge in good fettle.

Shortly afterwards, Hume, who told me that he would kill anyone for money, approached another newspaper and, in return for £10,000, confessed in print to Setty's murder, giving all the horrific details. The police were powerless because, having been acquitted of that crime, Hume could not be tried again.

When Hume had spent that money he held up a bank at gunpoint and shot an official, escaping to Switzerland, where the German which Fuchs had taught him proved useful. He then robbed a bank in Zurich, killing a taxi-driver who tried to stop him. He was caught and sentenced to life imprisonment. He returned to Britain as a mentally ill old man and was held in Broadmoor until he died in 1998, aged seventy-nine.

Of all these memories of such a villain, who was proof that entirely evil people do exist, the one that haunts me is Hume's leering statement when we were briefly discussing the Setty murder before he had confessed to it: 'They never found the 'ead, did they?' Ugh!

Hume had, certainly, been very dangerous to know but his crimes were totally outweighed by those of John Christie, a serial killer in London whose trial I had attended in June 1953. That insignificant creature standing in the dock had murdered at least eight women.

It was to be the only time I would witness a judge putting on a black cap to deliver the sentence that the prisoner should be hanged by the neck, as he duly was.

It was not, however, the first time that I had seen a condemned man. Previously, I had been asked by a charity to give occasional talks to criminals in various prisons. On one occasion, at Pentonville prison, I noticed that one member of my audience was sitting away from the rest in what looked like a small tent accompanied by two warders. Later it was explained to me that he was to be hanged in a few days' time.

I never imagined that I would, myself, be suspected by Scotland Yard of being a mass-murderer but that was the case for a few days in the spring of 1965. A team of detectives had been baffled for months by five Jack-the-Ripper style murders of London prostitutes whose naked bodies had been dumped mainly in the area of Shepherd's Bush after being subjected to a peculiar sexual assault. After the discovery of a sixth, Scotland Yard appealed to the public because they had a new clue – the victim had been seen being picked up by somebody in a dark blue car near one of the gates of Hyde Park.

The Yard quickly received a brief, anonymous telephone message, from a call-box, giving the number of the car, which proved to be a Jaguar owned by the *Daily Express*. The outstanding crime reporter of the *Daily Express*, the late Percy Hoskins, spent most of his time with Scotland Yard detectives so they had no difficulty in establishing that the car was allotted to me for my work and that I was the likely driver. Their immediate problem was how to get hold of it for forensic examination.

I was not available because my wife and I were on holiday salmon fishing in Ireland, having left the car in the garage at Lowerhouse Farm. My schoolgirl daughter, Pat, however, was at home with a couple who lived at the house and, with Hoskins's help on the telephone, the detectives convinced her that they were from the *Express* and needed to take the car away because it might have a dangerous problem with its brakes. The car was duly examined and, as soon as the detectives opened the boot, they felt that they had their serial killer for they saw exactly what they were looking for – the dark blue, plastic lining of the boot was heavily stained with large patches of recent blood! While forensic scientists went to work in the laboratory, the detectives powdered the car in search of the victim's fingerprints.

I have always regretted being unable to see the investigators' faces – first when they saw the stains and, second, when tests quickly showed that the blood was not human. The bloodstains were those of several hares which I had recently brought back from an annual farmers' hare-shoot in Essex.

The car had been returned by the time I reached home and, when my daughter told me about the brakes problem, I dismissed the incident. A little later, Hoskins told me the truth, with much mirth, and when I looked closely at the dashboard in front of the driver's seat and inside the glovebox I could see lots of white finger-print powder. Shortly afterwards, the whole Scotland Yard team, which was led by the very able and affable John du Rose, took me out to a conciliatory dinner – they seemed to be satisfied that the murderer had been a policeman who had since committed suicide.

Regarding the anonymous phone call, they seemed sure that it had been made by someone in my private life with a personal grudge and who had certainly been dangerous to know. I was fortunate that none of my Fleet Street rivals got wind of the story in its early stages.

Percy Hoskins had developed exceptionally close relations with senior officers in Scotland Yard through a unique arrangement which he had organised, with the newspaper's financial support, over many years. He had an expensive flat in Park Lane, the living room being a well-stocked bar open to his Scotland Yard contacts whenever they felt like a change from the office or when on their way home. Inevitably, in their conversations they would talk 'shop' and update their host on the latest developments or answer his queries, all of which gave Percy a regular advantage over his rivals.

Through Percy I met several of the Scotland Yard 'top brass' over the years and visited some of them there, being taken on one occa-sion to see the Black Museum with its fascinating, and sometimes grisly, exhibits – not often open to the public. The most vicious was a crudely made pair of binoculars which had been mailed, anonymously, to a pretty young woman. When she had opened the parcel, her father had chanced to twist the focusing wheel without putting them to his eyes and a pair of spring-loaded penknife blades had sprung out of the eye pieces. The police had never been able to prosecute the sender.

One of the Metropolitan Police Commissioners was Sir Robert Mark, an outstanding man who, after his resignation in 1977, honoured me by being my guest at lunch at the Café Royal. He told me of his battle to reduce corruption in the Metropolitan Police where so many officers had been taking bribes from criminals running protection rackets and prostitutes for many years. On taking command in 1972, his greatest surprise had been aroused when a senior officer, who was not corrupt, advised him to leave the situation as it was because the process of abolishing corruption would be 'so bad for morale'.

I met Sir Robert's most able successor, Sir David McNee, socially at several of the lunches and dinners given by our mutual friend, Charles Forte. Sir David was a mine of inside stories including one about Lord Mountbatten, who had visited Scotland Yard for advice about anti-robbery precautions at Broadlands in Hampshire. McNee told him that the Metropolitan Police could not possibly become involved and then asked Mountbatten why he had ever thought they could. 'The Queen suggested it,' Mountbatten replied, whereupon McNee telephoned the Hampshire Chief Constable, who was at Broadlands the next morning.

Unexpectedly in February 1987 I received a telephone call from the Serious Crimes Squad at Scotland Yard warning me that I was being investigated and would have to be subjected to interrogation. The conversation ended with the caller stressing that the matter was 'serious'.

The inquiries arose from the fact that, five years previously, a renegade MI5 officer called Peter Wright had blown all his secret work to me so that I could publish a book called *Their Trade is Treachery*, which had caused a political furore, as I will describe later.

Wright, who was living in the safety of Australia, from which he could not be extradited, had shared half the royalties earned by my book, which had been a bestseller, but wanted more. So, without consulting me, he had written an extended version, called *Spycatcher*.

The UK government was trying to stop him publishing it with a court action in Sydney in which Wright had made a long confidential statement about my activities which Scotland Yard, alerted by the Crown Prosecution Service and spurred on by several Labour MPs, needed to investigate. A few weeks earlier the Attorney General, Sir Michael Havers, who was a friend, had warned me at a pheasant shoot that to placate the demands of some MPs he might 'have to do something'.

So, on the afternoon of 12 February, a detective chief superintendent and an inspector of the Metropolitan Police knocked on my door in Kintbury and, after stating that I was not under arrest, began their questioning. Using the mendacious allegations in Wright's statement, they interrogated me for about two hours, which were interrupted by the appearance of Billee with tea and scrumptious cakes and jam – all eagerly devoured by the detectives.

They quickly made it clear that they were confident that they were dealing with a definite prosecution and told me they intended to interview the several distinguished people named in Wright's statement. As one of these was Sir Arthur Franks, the former chief of MI6, who I had long known as 'Dickie', I predicted that for reasons of state secrecy they would not be allowed to meet him. They politely disagreed and pressed on.

I endured two further long interrogation sessions during which they made it clear that they were convinced that I still possessed documents sent to me by Wright though I had assured them that I had destroyed them all, as Wright had asked me to do.

At the end of the last session, the detective chief superintendent produced a search warrant and demanded to inspect my safe. When I assured him that I had no need of a safe he demanded to see my private files. On seeing the extent of them – shelf after shelf of box-files filled with documents – he suggested taking away a small selection, which I helped him to make. I ensured that it included the fat folder marked 'Havers' containing all the details of his numerous indiscretions to me which made me very dangerous for him to have known. For good measure, as the situation did indeed seem serious, I also supplied folders recording the indiscretions of other eminent politicians and some Whitehall 'mandarins'.

A few days later, the detective chief superintendent phoned me, in some anger, to say that they had been called off the case and all the inquiries had been ended. The whole episode had been a waste of police time as well as of my wife's cakes. I am convinced that my documents, which were returned to me, had played their part because they showed the kind of information I was capable of revealing in my defence, with the resignation of more than one high-level political figure being inevitable.

On 8 July, the Attorney General told Parliament that there was no evidence to justify any proceedings against me. A few days later, Havers, who in the previous month had become Lord Chancellor, invited me to lunch at his London club, the Garrick. To celebrate further, I invited the two detectives to lunch at the Café Royal in London and, to my surprise, they accepted.

Sadly, after only six months in the peak post of Lord Chancellor, Havers was forced to resign 'because of ill health', which may not have been the real cause. The detectives told me that some of my impounded documents had been copied before being returned to me. Had some of the contents been reported to Prime Minister Thatcher, including those about herself? That could have made me especially dangerous for Havers to have known.

CHAPTER 20

CONNECTIONS WITH COURTS

When, at eighteen, I left home in a North Yorkshire village for university life in London and then, hopefully, an academic career, my father gave me various items of worldly advice which included, 'Stay away from doctors and lawyers!' In the sense that he meant it, I have managed to do both to a remarkable degree in view of my vulnerable circumstances.

When I became, among other things, the medical correspondent of the *Daily Express* I had to meet leading doctors and surgeons in the line of duty but the more I learned about them the more determined I became to stay out of their professional clutches. At ninety-nine, which included five war years in the army, I can recall only one night spent in hospital and that was just for a bad nosebleed.

In my later years, that good fortune has been nobly assisted by the several NHS doctors in Kintbury and their dedicated staff. I have also appreciated their humour, such as the observation, when I had complained of some ache, 'Your body parts were not designed to last ninety-eight years.' Or, better still, from a since-retired doctor who had become a friend of mine, 'If you were a horse you'd have to be shot.'

So far, my wife, now aged ninety-four, has needed the help of the NHS much more than I have so I pay grateful tribute to that service for us both. Whatever arm of the NHS we have ever required, it has functioned close to perfection, often at the shortest notice.

On the legal front, I have weathered sixty-five years of journalism and authorship of a nature which put me in frequent peril of being sued for libel or prosecuted under the Official Secrets Acts, neither of which, happily, ever happened. I have to admit that it was my personal friendship with certain lawyers which helped me to avoid the clutches of others in their profession. The most important was the resident office lawyer of the *Daily Express*, Andrew Edwards, who happened to be a fishing friend. Every Fleet Street newspaper employed a full-time lawyer to check written copy before it was printed and I never submitted anything without first having it cleared by my friend. Sometimes a simple change of wording eliminated the libel risk.

Labour MPs were the biggest libel threat to me, especially when I was attacking their leader Harold Wilson. The employment of the formidable lawyer Arnold Goodman managed to prevent publication of several important scoops of mine purely by him telephoning my editor and threatening dire consequences.

After I had appeared in court as a witness for Lord Russell of Liverpool, who won substantial damages for being libelled by the scurrilous magazine *Private Eye*, I was regularly attacked by it, being accused of various defects, the alleged worst being reserved for the final thrust 'and friend of Harry Hyams!' Though, as a result, I could sometimes have sued for libel myself, I refrained from any action mainly on the advice of another legal friend, a libel lawyer called Peter Carter-Ruck, who warned me, 'Always remember that going to law is like going to war: the only certainty is the cost.' The more I thought about that wisdom the more I took it to heart. Also, I felt that those, like myself, who almost daily dished out criticism of others, should take any against themselves on the chin. However, there came a time when I was ordered to institute libel proceedings by my boss, Sir Max Aitken. My intended victim was none other than *Private Eye*.

In those less technological days, to make a London telephone call from a country home it was necessary to call the local exchange and state the required number. The number of the *Daily Express* was Fleet Street 8000 and, one Sunday, when I needed to dictate a story to my newspaper, the exchange man quite inadvertently put me through to Fleet Street 3000, which happened to be the number of the *Daily Mail*. I asked for the news editor and found myself talking to our fiercest competitor. I – and he – quickly realised the situation and I ended the call with laughter on both sides.

At that time the *Daily Mail* employed the spiteful gossip columnist Nigel Dempster, who also supplied titbits to *Private Eye* – there soon appeared a statement in the magazine that Sir Max Aitken ought to know that Chapman Pincher, one of his most highly paid journalists, was trying to sell information to the *Daily Mail* on the side. After I had explained the facts to Sir Max and secured a statement from the telephone exchange admitting its error, he insisted that I must sue *Private Eye* for libel.

With the help of the office lawyer I did so and the magazine stumped up £1,000 damages – then a substantial sum. I celebrated victory by presenting the office lawyer with a new fishing rod and by providing what my wife has always called 'the *Private Eye* mink coat', a beautifully tailored, ankle-length garment. Sadly, not long afterwards, under pressure from animal rights fanatics, it became not only unfashionable to wear any animal fur but even dangerous. So, as the coat has languished in a wardrobe with presumably little monetary value, *Private Eye* had the last laugh.

In 1985, when I published a book *The Secret Offensive*, using a great deal of information supplied by the very rich Sir James Goldsmith, I quickly received libel claims on behalf of two people who smelled easy money. As soon as they learned that I had a written indemnity from Goldsmith so that, in effect, they would be suing him rather than me, the claims were withdrawn.

My first serious involvement in a legal situation commanding widespread publicity occurred early in 1963 following the prosecution for espionage of John Vassall, a clerk in the Admiralty. At the age of twenty-nine, Vassall had been of established homosexual habits when he was sent to Moscow to work in the British embassy in 1954. His vulnerability was quickly spotted and exploited by KGB officers who set him up at a drunken, homosexual party and took incriminating photographs. Under threat of exposure, and with the additional offer of money, Vassall agreed to become a Soviet agent, supplying the KGB with secret documents, first in Moscow and then in London, to which he returned in 1956. There, to the

KGB's delight, he was attached to Naval Intelligence where he dealt with the in-trays and out-trays of naval officers and civilians of the highest ranks. With his previous training as a photographer in the RAF, he copied abstracted documents at his flat in Dolphin Square during lunchtime and handed the photos to KGB officers.

Vassall was arrested on 12 September 1962 and his confession has recently been released into the National Archives. When sentenced to eighteen years' imprisonment, it was obvious that he had inflicted great damage over a long period.

Under parliamentary pressure for a public inquiry into how Vassall had been able to spy for so long, and to clear the names of ministers who had been accused of negligence by some newspapers, the Prime Minister, Harold Macmillan, set up a three-man tribunal headed by Lord Radcliffe, a Lord of Appeal, with powers to require witnesses to appear and give evidence on oath. It opened proceedings in London on 17 January 1963.

I had previously disclosed that Vassall had been betrayed by a KGB defector to the US and I was, therefore, required to give evidence. By previous agreement, I was enabled to name the source of my information about the defector – Lieutenant Colonel L. G. (Sammy) Lohan of the Defence Ministry press office. I had consulted him in advance and had secured his permission to name him. Lord Radcliffe had, secretly, been advised not to press me about the defector's name because the Russian, called Anatoli Golitsyn, was secretly in the UK assisting MI5. (Later, I was told that after briefing by MI5, Radcliffe had ensured that I would not be pressed when in the witness stand into revealing any more details about the defector.)

Two other journalists from other newspapers who had written false accusations about other matters and declined, or were unable, to name their sources were sent to prison for contempt of court and their careers were ruined. As I had escaped unscathed, I was referred to by some other writers as 'the Artful Dodger', which, I suppose, seemed fair enough.

When Vassall came out of prison I met him twice for long interviews over lunch and he was such an obvious passive homosexual that he should never have been sent to the British embassy in

Moscow and left alone there, as he was, being an obvious target for the KGB.

I was to renew my association with Lord Radcliffe in a way which would cause the most widespread publicity of my career, recorded in many books and with long-lasting political repercussions, particularly on the career and reputation of the then Prime Minister, Harold Wilson.

I had first met Wilson, at his invitation, shortly after he became Prime Minister in 1964. Sitting alone with him at the Cabinet table in No. 10, we discussed defence policy, especially about his pre-election promise to get rid of the deterrent submarines armed with Polaris missiles carrying H-bomb warheads. I soon realised that he had never had any intention of fulfilling that promise, which had been entirely to bamboozle his left-wing colleagues, such as Michael Foot, and the left-wing voters. I found him charming and humorous and, after a long talk, I left convinced that the nation's defences were in safe hands. (He was, quietly, to invest millions of taxpayers' money in improving the Polaris warheads!)

I saw Wilson again after a Czech defector fingered the Aviation Minister, John Stonehouse, as a Soviet Bloc spy. In my library there is a novel called *Ralph*, inscribed: 'To my dear friend and master Harry Chapman Pincher with warmest regards, John Stonehouse. 16 April 1982.' The cover carries a photograph of the handsome and charismatic author and states that he was an MP for nineteen years, joined the Labour government in 1964 and served as Minister of Aviation, Minister of Technology and Minister of Posts and Telecommunications. It does not state that he had served a prison sentence for fraud. Nor does it state that he had been a Soviet Bloc spy as his 'dear friend and master' was, eventually, able to establish.

There are various reasons why talented men are prepared to betray their country. With Stonehouse it was purely for money. I first met him at a rather grand country house where his behaviour made it obvious that he greatly envied the lifestyle of the owner. We then met regularly and he became a useful source of political 'leaks' to me, especially when he was Aviation Minister.

In July 1969, Josef Frolík, a Czech intelligence officer, defected to the CIA and claimed that Stonehouse had been recruited by sexual entrapment, followed by blackmail threats, while visiting Prague in 1957 and had been on the payroll ever since. The CIA informed MI5, which warned Wilson, who was horrified by the political impact of such an exposure. In 1964 Wilson had forbidden any surveillance of MPs by MI5. He declined to let MI5 investigate Stonehouse and assured Parliament that Frolík's allegations, which had leaked to the media, were unfounded. Stonehouse remained in office for another year.

Then, after founding a bank and other businesses, which all collapsed, Stonehouse faked his death in 1974 by leaving his clothes on a Miami beach, implying that he had drowned, and fled to Australia. There, he called himself Muldoon and set up a bank account in that name, but was soon identified following an unforeseeable twist of fate. The world was looking for a missing murder suspect – Lord Lucan, whose disappearance from London had caused a sensation which has never been resolved. The Australian police thought that Muldoon was Lucan, questioned him and discovered the truth. Stonehouse was eventually extradited and convicted.

As I had written to him in prison, he asked me to lunch at a London restaurant on his release and I tried to question him about the Czech intelligence claims. 'Why don't we both go to the States and interview Joe Frolík?' he asked, with a smile, clearly indicating that he had known him as 'Joe'. He wrote three books then died from heart problems in 1988, aged sixty-two.

In January 2006, having secured new information, I published evidence that Stonehouse had been a spy and, while Aviation Minister, had provided the KGB with details of the Concorde supersonic airliner which enabled the Russians to build a replica, inevitably known in the West as the Concordski. I was then invited by the *Mail on Sunday* to visit Prague to try to induce Czech intelligence to release Stonehouse's file. I declined, knowing that they would refuse to do so, but the enterprising newspaper made inquiries in Prague and found someone who had a microfiche copy of the file – all 1,000 pages of it. They showed that he had been codenamed Kola, then Twister, and would meet a Czech contact in a London street and hand over information, receiving money in exchange. He was the first proven traitor inside any British government. A sad story of a talented man driven to self-destruction by greed.

Years later, after Stonehouse had been jailed and his treachery was also certain, I asked Wilson, 'Did you know that Stonehouse was a spy?'

'No,' he replied, 'but I always knew he was a crook.'

'Why, then, did you make him a minister?' I asked.

'It's surprising what you have to do to keep the party happy,' he said with his disarming smile.

In the ensuing years, through Denis Healey, Wilson's Defence Minister, I felt that Labour was doing dangerous harm to the nation's defence requirements in the continuing Cold War. Being regularly fed evidence of the damage by high-level forces sources, I attacked the policy in print so fiercely that Wilson was to describe me to a Royal Commission on the press as 'a prominent journalist known for his virulence of opposition to the Labour government'.

While admiring Healey's tough personality, as I still do, I missed no opportunity to attack his actions with such effect that, once, when he spotted me in a corridor of the Defence Ministry, he caught up with me and said, sourly, 'Why don't you stick to writing about fishing?'

I responded: 'In the national interest I will make that sacrifice if you will stick to photography.'

He was not amused and, a few years ago when we were reminiscing, amicably, he recalled, 'You were always so savage!' Maybe I was.

Meanwhile, as Christopher Andrew's recent *The Defence of the Realm: The Authorized History of MI5* has revealed, Harold Wilson had become so deluded about me that he was convinced that MI5 was feeding me with secret information to undermine him. He summoned the MI5 chief to Downing Street and, in a fearful row, refused to believe his honest denial.

While newspaper-readers claiming to have secret information were, usually, time-wasters, one of them, early in 1967, was to spark the most bitter and politically charged intelligence incident of my lifetime – the so-called 'D-notice affair'. My informant, who drifted into the office off the street, said that he had worked for two cable companies and that, every day, all private cables along with telegrams sent from Post Offices were being made available for scrutiny by the security authorities.

A spokesman for the Defence Ministry denied the allegation to me but a fishing companion, Turlough O'Brien, who headed the Post Office press department, confirmed it, explaining that while all the cables were available only those selected were sent for scrutiny to the security authorities. I deduced that the main authority concerned was GCHQ, the radio-signal interception station near Cheltenham, looking for coded messages to and from foreign intelligence agents.

I then telephoned Lieutenant Colonel Sammy Lohan, my old Defence Ministry friend who had succeeded Admiral Thomson as D-notice secretary. He assured me that there was no D-notice to interfere with the publication of such a story. However, next day, having consulted the Foreign Office, he telephoned me asking me not to print the story as it would cause a diplomatic furore. I later discovered that there was a most secret American aspect. Certain cables were being supplied to the US National Security Agency in contravention of the American constitution and the US President (then Lyndon Johnson) was aware of it and was, illicitly, condoning the practice.

I agreed to lunch with Lohan so that he could make a final appeal to prevent the *Daily Express* from running the story. He produced two D-notices saying that they were the only two that could possibly apply and, in his view, neither did so. He then asked me to give my editor, then Derek Marks, his direct appeal to suppress the cable story, which I promised to do.

After deliberation with me and the office lawyer, the editor decided to print the story which I had written and it dominated the front page on 21 February. It and the follow-up stories caused a tumultuous collision between Wilson and the entire media, which lasted six months and caused him permanent political injury – so much so that he would later describe his behaviour as his 'worst self-inflicted wound'. As his political secretary Marcia Williams (later Lady Falkender) recorded in her book *Inside Number 10*:

Now began the time when Number 10 was dominated by the D-notice affair. We all became obsessed with the matter. The whole lamentable affair hung like a heavy cloud over us for many months. It had sapped the energies of the Prime Minister and his morale.

Wilson reacted immediately by telling Parliament that my disclosure had put men's lives at risk, which proved to be untrue. He insisted that the practice of cable-vetting, which, it transpired, had been going on for many years, was officially secret and was covered by a D-notice which I had breached. So, he set up a three-man committee, again under Lord Radcliffe, to examine all the circumstances and, hopefully, discredit both me and Lohan, who stood accused of failing to veto my story about the cable-vetting, though Wilson had admitted that it was true.

Over eleven days, I, Lohan and other witnesses gave evidence to the committee, of which the other members were Selwyn Lloyd, an eminent Tory, and Emanuel Shinwell, a staunch Labour MP who, Wilson believed, would be hostile to the *Daily Express*.

To Wilson's angry astonishment, the final report, fully supported by the admirable Shinwell, exonerated me and the *Daily Express* completely – a victory that was hailed throughout Fleet Street as a triumph. The verdict stated that my account of the cable-vetting had not been inaccurate and had not breached any D-notice. It also showed that, under instructions from the Foreign Office, a Defence Ministry spokesman had given false information to the press. (I treasure a letter from the late Sir John Junor, the *Sunday Express* editor, stating, 'There may have been greater triumphs in Fleet Street but, if so, I have never heard of them.')

Unable to admit that he had been wrong, Wilson rejected the findings of the committee he had set up and cobbled together a White Paper which upheld the Foreign Office and Defence Ministry statements. It also attempted to show that I and Lohan, to whom Wilson had taken massive dislike, were both villains. There was unanimous outcry from the press, epitomised by a cartoon which showed cricket batsman Wilson with all three stumps and bails sent flying declaring that he was 'not out'. His inability to admit that he might have been wrong destroyed his credibility.

A long review of the D-notice affair by Lord (Hartley) Shawcross, the former Labour Attorney General, stated: 'Petulant and maladroit false steps led Mr Wilson deeper into the mud.'

Having failed to ruin my reputation, Wilson, who a few weeks previously had handed to me the award of Reporter of the Decade, concentrated his anger on Lohan and had him followed, an unusual move later extended to me.

The civil service set up an inquiry into Lohan's behaviour which resulted in his resignation, though he stated that he had, in fact, been sacked. I deeply regret my unwitting role in his downfall and disgrace. I paid a heavy price myself because, over the years, Sammy had leaked scoop after scoop to me during our many meetings, both in restaurants and at our homes – some, I suspect, at the request of ministers or senior officials – and that prime and totally reliable source had been removed.

Equally reprehensible was the treatment of Turlough O'Brien, who had made the mistake of admitting the truth to the tribunal. He was prematurely retired, while officials who had lied and encouraged others to lie were promoted. For both Sammy and Turlough, I certainly had been catastrophically dangerous to know.

PhD theses and books are still being written about the D-notice affair and it is an event which will always loom large in my memory. The story was set on official record in 2009 by the publication of *Secrecy and the Media: The Official History of the United Kingdom's D-notice System*, superbly written by Rear Admiral Nicholas Wilkinson, a former D-notice secretary. Even more revealing on the subject was Dr Moran's book, *Classified* (2013), as he had access to recently released documents and other information.

Following my D-notice victory I was dubbed a man of the year at a function at the Savoy Hotel where the others so named were Jack Hawkins, the handsome actor and film star, and Topol, who headed the cast of the successful play *Fiddler on the Roof*.

For more than half a century, my *Who's Who* entry has recorded one of my hobbies as 'ferretting in Whitehall and bolting politi-cians'. In that splendid sport no quarry gave me more satisfaction than Harold Wilson. Tragically, he developed early symptoms of dementia and, unlike several other prime ministers who knew that they were seriously ill but chose to remain in power, he was patriotic enough to resign in 1976, knowing that to continue in office might be dangerous. Understandably, he declined to give his reason, lead-ing to all manner of nasty theories when, in fact, he had made a noble sacrifice.

In 1978, Lord Weidenfeld, a mutual friend of Wilson and me, invited me to his Chelsea flat, after saying that Wilson would be there and wanted to bury the hatchet. Wilson, who was most affable, volunteered, 'I'm sorry we fell out. It was all my fault.' Staggered that any Prime Minister could ever bring himself to apologise to a journalist, I shook his outstretched hand.

After that we lunched together several times – always with his former secretary, Lady Falkender, in attendance. On one occasion I happened to mention that I was a Yorkshireman, like himself.

'Eh! I wish I'd known that,' he exclaimed. 'It would have made a difference, you know.' I feel sure that he meant it.

CHAPTER 21

INSIGHTS INTO THE PROFUMO AFFAIR

everal high-ranking politicians, with whom I was in regular contact, ruined their careers through sexual scandals which I then had to cover journalistically. The common factor responsible for all those tragedies lies in what I rate as the best 'story' I have ever heard. It concerns God's first conversation with Adam:

> Well, there you are, Adam! I have created you in my image for my purposes and it is up to you to get on and fulfil them. To enable you to do that I have equipped you with two special gifts. I have given you an organ called the brain and with that you and your descendants will be able to civilise the world. I have also given you an organ called the penis and with that you and your descendants will be able to populate the world. There is, however, an important limitation, Adam, to which I must draw your attention – you can't use them both at the same time.

What I call the Adam paradox has been a major factor in world history and always will be. Due to the hormone testosterone, most men are saddled through most of their adult life with a demon rider spurring them to sexual activity and politicians, however ambitious, are no exception. The same applies to many women whose sexual availability has been hugely increased, compared with former times, by what I call the Three Ts –Time, the Telephone and Transport. There is also the Flattery Factor. Many women are so flattered by the attention of a man who happens to be famous (and especially if he has a title) that they are willing, and even keen, to oblige sexually.

The first sexual political tragedy with which I was closely involved, and the severest of political consequence, was the 'Profumo affair', which has been the subject of a stream of books, television documentaries, and even a musical show. It has always been of special interest to me because Jack Profumo was a friend, with whom I remained in touch until his death in 2006 at the age of ninety-one. Further, in covering the case journalistically, I met several of its other major figures.

The saga began on the evening of Saturday 8 July 1961, when Profumo, the Secretary of State for War (then the name for the Army Minister), and his wife, the former film star Valerie Hobson, were weekend guests of Lord and Lady Astor at their Thames-side country home, Cliveden. On an after-dinner stroll, the Astors, accompanied by their guests, wandered to the swimming pool, where Astor knew that a party from a cottage on the estate were bathing. As they did so, a pretty nineteen-year-old girl, called Christine Keeler, emerged naked from the water to general amusement all round.

The cottage was occupied by a very accomplished osteopath and physiotherapist called Stephen Ward, who was treating Astor for muscle problems so effectively that he had been granted the use of the cottage for himself and any friends he cared to invite. Ward was a sexual voyeur and encouraged Christine, then working as a hostess in a night club, and several other nubile young girls to visit his London home, 17 Wimpole Mews, where he often entertained his patients. The girls served the patients with coffee and generally enlivened the scene.

Ward had dared Christine to remove her bathing costume, which he had then hidden. Later, when Christine was dressed and they had all repaired to the house, Profumo showed her around and flirted with her.

On the following afternoon, there was a formal bathing party attended by the Astors and their guests and Ward and his guests, who included a Russian 'diplomat', Lieutenant Commander Yevgeni (Eugene) Ivanov, an intelligence officer for Russia's military intelligence agency GRU, registered as assistant naval attaché in the Soviet embassy. During a convivial afternoon, Ivanov and Profumo swam races, which the Russian would have been able to report with some kudos to the GRU centre in Moscow. As a military figure, the Army Minister would have been a potential GRU target.

On that same Sunday evening, Ivanov drove Keeler back to London and they enjoyed what she recalled as 'marvellous, passionate love'.

Smitten by Keeler's youthful beauty, the 48-year-old Profumo secured her telephone number from Ward, who then encouraged her to see him. A sexual liaison developed that lasted, on and off, until the end of 1961.

Previous to the bathing incident, an MI5 informant inside the GRU had listed Ivanov as a Soviet intelligence officer, so he was tailed by MI5 watchers, who found that he was visiting Ward's home. Being aware that Ward had many distinguished patients, including several prominent MPs and Lord Astor, MI5 had sent an officer to warn him that Ivanov might use him to gain access to some of them. Ward had promised to be careful and to inform MI5 of any developments.

During the period of Profumo's illicit affair, the US government was planning to supply the West German army (then part of NATO) with a medium-range ballistic missile, called Sergeant. Its nuclear warheads, designed to blunt an attack by massed Russian tanks, were to be kept under American control until an emergency, when the German troops would be empowered to use them. This plan was open knowledge as part of the deterrent policy, but the date when the missiles were to become operational in Germany was still secret. On 12 July, shortly after the Cliveden bathing party, Ward told MI5 that Ivanov was trying to find out the delivery date of the Sergeant warheads.

On 11 November 1962, George Wigg, a Labour backbench MP and old soldier specialising in army affairs, was lunching with his political agent in his Dudley constituency. The telephone rang and a muffled voice said, 'Forget about the Vassall case! You want to look at Profumo!' The line then went dead.

For many years, Wigg and I regularly kept each other informed, either through meetings or telephone conversations, and we discussed the possible identity of his caller. He became convinced that the caller was Vitali Lui, a KGB agent posing as a freelance Russian journalist who, under the name of Victor Louis, frequently contributed to a London evening newspaper. Lui could have been informed by Ivanov, who knew about Profumo's affair from Keeler, and on whose behalf he could have then tipped off Wigg.

The vindictive Wigg, widely known as 'Big Ears', ran a private intelligence system to gather damaging information about his Conservative opponents and he soon learned how Profumo had become entangled with Keeler, though the War Minister had imme-diately distanced himself when eventually warned of his danger. To do so, Profumo had written an off-putting letter to Keeler which was later to prove extremely damaging to him because it began 'Darling'.

Wigg hated Profumo because he felt he had been slighted by him in Parliament and revelled in settling scores. He was keen to expose the 'scandal', which had been confirmed to him by a Labour MP to whom Keeler had confided details of her affair. However, as a married man with a steady mistress himself, Wigg told Harold Wilson, then leader of the Labour opposition, that he knew so many Labour MPs who were having illicit affairs that it would be dangerous to pursue the War Minister on moral grounds. Wilson agreed and they decided to concentrate on the security aspects of the affair, once they knew about the involvement of Ivanov in it.

There was a specific security factor which eventually came to light. Allegedly, Ivanov had asked Keeler to try to induce Profumo to tell her the date when the Americans would hand over control of the Sergeant missiles to the Germans. When Wigg heard that he realised that his grounds for pursuing Profumo on security charges could be fully justified in Parliament. With Wilson's agreement, Wigg decided to wait for the right moment to strike.

On 22 January 1963, Keeler, who needed money, signed a contract with the *Sunday Pictorial* newspaper to tell her story and provided the letter from Profumo, in which she was addressed as 'Darling'. Alerted to his imminent danger by Lord Astor on 28 January, Profumo asked the director general of MI5, Sir Roger Hollis, to see him in the hope that some D-notice might be issued to prevent publication of the story and limit speculation. Hollis told him that was impossible. In the course of the conversation, Profumo told Hollis some details of how he had first met Keeler at Cliveden.

An MI5 secret source had also stated that the Russians were so certain that a major scandal was about to break that Ivanov was to be sent back to Moscow prematurely. Ivanov fled the following day, 29 January, giving Hollis the excuse to declare no further interest in his case.

While the *Sunday Pictorial* withheld its scoop, Fleet Street soon learned of what Keeler had to tell and I was immediately involved. In common with the other newspapers, the *Daily Express* withheld publication, mainly on the advice of office lawyers worried about libel.

On 7 February, the commander of Scotland Yard's Special Branch went to MI5 with a report showing that, on 26 January, Keeler had told police that there had been an illicit association between her and Profumo. She had also stated that she had met Ivanov several times and that Ward had asked her to discover the nuclear warheads' delivery date.

On returning on 4 February from a brief trip to Italy, the Conservative Prime Minister, Harold Macmillan, was warned of the rumours by his private secretary. By that time, the chief whip – a senior MP responsible for party discipline – had confronted Profumo, who had denied the allegations of sexual misconduct. Macmillan accepted the assurance.

Then, on 8 March, a political newsletter called *Westminster Confidential* published some of the information including the possible connection between the War Minister and a Soviet attaché. It was soon widely rumoured that Keeler would be in bed with Profumo and Ivanov on the same day but, later, she was to insist that she had intercourse with Ivanov only on the one occasion. Nevertheless, they had continued to meet each other at Ward's homes.

On 15 March, the *Daily Express* ran a front page bearing the headline 'War Minister Shock', claiming that Profumo had offered his resignation to the Prime Minister. On the other side of the page, seemingly by chance but quite deliberately, was a picture of Keeler headed 'Vanished Old Bailey Witness', referring to her disappearance after her involvement in an unrelated criminal case.

On 21 March 1963, Wigg raised the issue in Parliament, in full knowledge of its explosive mixture of high-level politics, sex and espionage. He demanded that the House be told the truth about the rumours. Next day, after a night during which Profumo had been roused and questioned by the chief whip and fellow ministers, he delivered a statement to a packed House of Commons declaring that 'there had been no impropriety whatsoever'. He also threatened to sue for libel if provoked and eventually did so, giving to charity the damages paid by two foreign magazines.

As soon as Profumo had made his statement to Parliament, Hollis knew that he had lied because MI5 had known the truth about the relationship since at least 28 January. Nevertheless, he still did not warn Macmillan. He just sat back and waited for the time bomb to explode.

A few days later, I received a copy of a long statement which Keeler had made to a *Daily Express* reporter in Spain, where she had fled to avoid involvement in the unsavoury court case. From the details she described, there could be no doubt that she was telling the truth and I felt that Profumo should be warned immediately. My easiest route was through his chief civil servant, Sir Richard 'Sam' Way, who was a friend. After seeing the report, Way agreed that his minister had lied and should be warned but his courage failed him. Instead, he consulted Profumo's chief soldier, General Sir Richard Hull, who agreed with him that to tell their boss that he had lied would be too embarrassing. Had they told him, the affair might have been settled more swiftly and with less collateral damage. Way later told me that he had made a bad error of judgement.

Shortly afterwards, Profumo asked me to lunch at the Savoy Grill along with his chief press liaison officer, Gilbert Monckton. As we savoured aperitifs in the ante-room, Profumo made a point of calling over everyone he knew as though he wanted them to realise that he could not have anything disgraceful to hide because, otherwise, he would not be consorting with a journalist specialising in disclosures.

At the lunch table his response to my questions about the alleged scandal was, 'I love my wife and she loves me and that's all that matters. Anyway, who is going to believe the word of this whore against the word of a man who has been in government office for ten years?'

'But what about the letters?' I asked, having heard that Keeler possessed several from him.

'Letters?' Profumo said. 'There are no letters.'

A few minutes later, Monckton brought the lunch to an abrupt end by stating that Profumo had an early appointment.

In May, the bubbling situation was brought to the boil by Stephen Ward, who, on learning that his activities were being investigated by the police, provided information to the Prime Minister's office indicating that Profumo had lied to Parliament. Profumo was questioned again by the chief whip and, again, denied that he had lied. On 31 May, Parliament went into recess for Whitsuntide and Profumo and his wife left for a short holiday in Venice, their favour-ite city. There, his conscience forced him into confessing to his wife and they decided that he must return to London and admit the truth. On 4 June, he resigned from the government and as an MP.

Soon afterwards, Monckton asked me to lunch to explain why he had ended our Savoy meeting so abruptly. When Profumo had assured me that there were no letters from him in Keeler's posses-sion Monckton had realised that he was on dangerous ground and had told him so on their way back to Whitehall. Profumo's pathetic response had been that it was true because there was only one letter.

When Parliament reassembled on 17 June, Harold Macmillan faced a debate on the whole affair, which I attended, noticing the hunched figure of Sir Roger Hollis sitting in the Distinguished Visitors' Gallery. With Profumo gone, Wilson and Wigg concen-trated their assault on Macmillan over his inept handling of the affair. Macmillan blamed Hollis, repeatedly, for failing to inform him of the security aspects of the Keeler–Profumo relationship. To cries of 'Oh!', Macmillan declared that MI5 had kept him ignorant about the relationship between Profumo and Keeler and about her requirement to discover the nuclear weapons' date. He revealed that Hollis's explanation, on each count, had been that he had not considered the issues 'as of great importance'.

In helping to prepare Macmillan's defence, the law officers had relied on a brief prepared by Hollis. It contained the suggestion that Ivanov had posed no security threat because he was just an accredited diplomat even though MI5 knew that he was a professional GRU intelligence officer. Macmillan repeated his regret at Hollis's lack of action and threw himself on the compassion of the House. No sympathy was shown by some of his own MPs, who demanded a new and younger leadership. When the House voted, twenty-seven Tories abstained from supporting their leader. His reduced majority and his admission that he had not known what was going on were extremely damaging and I watched 'Supermac' leave the Chamber crestfallen and dispirited.

On 21 June, Macmillan appointed the senior judge Lord Denning to investigate and report on the whole Profumo affair and especially on the security aspects. It seemed clear that his career was near its closure.

Interest in the Profumo affair was regenerated on 22 July by the trial of Stephen Ward on a trumped-up and totally untrue charge of living on the immoral earnings of his call-girl friends. In a public trial, widely regarded as being staged and an outrageous abuse of the judicial system, he was found guilty and compounded the whole tragedy by committing suicide on 3 August.

On 9 August the *News of the World* began publication of Keeler's story, for which they had agreed to pay £23,000, then a large sum.

Coming on top of the many spy scandals, the Profumo affair left Macmillan mentally shattered. Suddenly stricken by prostate problems, he underwent surgery and the consequent weakness induced him to retire from the premiership on 18 October 1963.

A year later, after the brief premiership of Sir Alec Douglas-Home, the Conservatives were defeated and a Labour government led by Harold Wilson came to power with an overall majority of only four seats. Later, I discussed this narrow victory, separately, with Wigg and Wilson and, later, with Macmillan and Sir Alec. They all thought it likely that it was the Profumo affair which had swung the balance.

Through being in the know, from that anonymous phone call,

George Wigg had won but, with poetic justice, his own reputation was to be nastily besmirched by a sex scandal. After being elevated to the House of Lords by Wilson, he was charged by the police with kerb-crawling in search of prostitutes. Again, I was involved, appearing as a witness at his trial.

Wigg was always impatient to know the news and had discovered that, through some special arrangement, a newspaper vendor standing at the entrance to Marble Arch Underground station was regularly selling the next day's *Daily Express* soon after 10 p.m. One late evening, when I was chatting with Wigg in his flat, he asked me to accompany him to Marble Arch to secure a paper but when we reached the news vendor's stand he had not yet arrived. As it was not permissible to park there, Wigg drove round nearby streets doing two or three circuits before the vendor was in position. As soon as Wigg pulled up in front of him he brought the paper to the car window and took the payment which Wigg had ready. It was clear to me that this had happened before, perhaps on many occasions.

Eventually, when Wigg was charged by the police with kerb-crawling he claimed that he was simply killing time as I have described. I therefore gave evidence of my experience to the court at Wigg's trial and, for that and other reasons, the magistrate abandoned the charge. Typically, Wigg suspected that the police had set him up at the behest of his old friend Wilson, with whom he had fallen out. As *The Authorized History of MI5* states, Wilson had, in fact, hired private detectives to follow Wigg.

My old friend and foe, Wigg, who died in 1983, left a mass of papers to the London School of Economics where, I am told, there are many references to me. I have never bothered to look at them for, Wigg being such a fantasist, they are hardly likely be complimentary, even though I did help to save him from conviction.

During the Profumo uproar, I had met Christine Keeler briefly during a visit she paid to the *Daily Express* office when she was accompanied by another of Ward's girls, Mandy Rice-Davies. Soon afterwards, while giving evidence in a court case, Mandy had uttered a statement which caused worldwide mirth and has become a historic one-liner. Pursuing a statement that Lord Astor had enjoyed her sexual favours, his Lordship's lawyer had told Mandy that Lord Astor denied any such relationship, to which she had replied, 'He would, wouldn't he?'

I was to encounter both girls again when they were rather more mature. In the 1980s, I was invited by a Spanish television company to appear on a programme about spies. One of those taking part was Philip Agee, a former CIA officer who in 1973 had defected to Communist Cuba, where he had written a damaging book, *Inside the Company: CIA Diary*. I had previously met Agee, a short, long-haired figure, in London and had disliked him as a person but was keen to argue his case with him in public.

Arriving at the studio in Madrid, I was surprised to see Christine Keeler, who had also agreed to take part in the programme, during which I had to explain to the presenter that she had never been a spy, as he had imagined. Afterwards, my wife and I had dinner with her and she seemed a sad figure with an uncertain future.

Mandy reappeared in quite a different way. In the 1990s, my shooting friend Norman Angel invited my wife and me to a dinner near Virginia Water in Surrey. First, we called at a rather splendid apartment to pick up another couple of guests. The wife proved to be Mandy, who showed me round her impressive library where there was a novel which she had written herself. It became clear, in the course of the evening, that Mandy was highly intelligent and cultured and had made a success of her life with a happy marriage to a rich and charming man.

I remained in occasional touch with Jack Profumo. Not long after his disgrace, when he was doing penance through charitable works, I was a fellow guest at a partridge shoot and, before he arrived, our host urged us to avoid any topic which might embarrass him. I asked him about his work in prisons and he told us about his first day as a visitor to Grendon prison, where he was required to 'welcome' a dangerous criminal with helpful advice.

'Who the bleedin' hell do you think you are?' the prisoner had responded. 'You should be in 'ere yourself for what you done to the country.'

Jack told the story with gusto.

My final encounter with him was at an intimate lunch for eight at which the chief guest was the Queen Mother. Her partner for that occasion was her old friend, Jack Profumo, as I have already recorded. After the lunch, as Her Majesty waltzed up some steep garden steps towards her waiting limousine, with me and Jack struggling up behind her, he pointed with his stick and whispered, 'Oh look! Her stocking's falling down!' which, indeed, it was. At nearly ninety, Jack still had a roving eye.

CHAPTER 22

MORE 'AFFAIRS' OF STATE

My journalistic activities were to embroil me in two more major sex scandals in the field of defence with sad political consequences. They both involved men whom I knew and admired – Lord Lambton and Lord Jellicoe.

I first met Tony Lambton round Lord Beaverbrook's table because he was then a regular contributor to the London *Evening Standard*, a Beaverbrook newspaper. He was tall, rather gaunt with a ready smile and a languid, aristocratic air which, with his blue-tinted spectacles, made him memorable. I had also heard that he was a brilliant game-shot, as I was to witness much later when we shot together. He was the only man I have ever seen who could nail high pheasants while running.

I judged him to be highly intelligent and an amusing conversationalist. As Tory MP for Berwick-on-Tweed, which he became in 1951, he was also highly ambitious. So much so that when he inherited the Earldom of Durham, on his father's death, he declined the title so that he could remain in the Commons. So I was not surprised when, in 1970, he was appointed Minister for the Royal Air Force.

Through our previous acquaintance and because he knew that I was deeply interested in the RAF and its welfare, he developed the habit of visiting my flat, then conveniently in Mayfair, to read me speeches which he had prepared. I helped him to anticipate the press reaction and suggested ways of dealing with it.

It was common knowledge that Lambton, who was married, was attractive to women who were often seen dining in his company. Knowing some of the women, I had little doubt that he enjoyed some extra-marital sex but was genuinely surprised when it became known that he patronised prostitutes dignified by the name 'call girls'.

The girl who brought about his downfall, Norma Levy, had a criminal husband who not only encouraged his wife's adultery but was in the habit of taking surreptitious photographs of her in action with the prospect of selling them to newspapers when prominent men were involved.

Stupidly, Lambton had paid Norma by cheques with his full name and title on them so he was a prime target for her husband, who was intent on exploiting his good fortune as he looked at his pictures of the two in bed smoking cannabis. Knowing Lambton's political position, Norma became seriously worried and felt that she needed advice.

As she sometimes worked as a hostess in a London night club, she asked the 'madam' who controlled the hostesses what she should do. That lady was equally concerned and told Norma that the government – meaning some senior minister – should be warned of the danger and that she knew how that might be achieved.

She was aware that one of her occasional customers moved in political circles and, at the first opportunity, told him the facts. He was none other than my old shooting friend Sir Joseph Nickerson, who, after his usual analytical consideration and being the stalwart Englishman he was, contacted another field acquaintance, James (now Lord) Prior. The delightfully straight-forward Prior, known to his many friends as Jim and with whom I reminisced about the situation recently, was then the Agriculture Minister in Edward Heath's government. He informed Heath without delay.

Spurred by recollections of the Profumo affair, the sexless Heath asked Prior to interrogate the 'madam', which he did in his Whitehall office with a senior civil servant present. Meanwhile, inquiries by the police and MI5 were set in motion.

Heath then confronted the fifty-year-old Lambton, who admitted all and resigned from Parliament in 1973, disappearing to his country estate in Durham.

Purely by chance, during the police inquiries a building with the word Jellicoe in its name had been mentioned. The building had

been named in honour of a former member of the Jellicoe family.
It so happened that Lord (George) Jellicoe, son of the famous
First World War admiral and an outstanding Second World War
commando himself, had entered politics and was serving in Heath's
government as Leader of the House of Lords and Lord Privy Seal,
having previously served in the Admiralty.

For no sensible reason, on hearing that the name Jellicoe had
been encountered, Heath sent for George and asked him if he
was involved in the Lambton case in any way. Jellicoe firmly and
honestly denied any knowledge of Norma Levy or anyone else
connected with the case.

That should have ended the matter but, such was Jellicoe's
honesty and integrity, that, having brooded about it overnight, he
saw Heath and confessed that, though what he had said was true,
he had patronised a Mayfair 'escort agency'. Explaining that to me
later, George described how, so often, he found himself at a loose
end in London for a couple of hours and would spend it at his flat
with a call girl.

That information, which applied to other politicians of my
acquaintance, was irrelevant in the circumstances but Heath
showed that he was so worried by it that Jellicoe offered his resignation. Heath accepted it and thereby extended the harmful publicity
quite unnecessarily.

Several of Heath's ministers told me that they were infuriated by
his behaviour concerning Jellicoe. The puritanical Enoch Powell
reserved his judgement. His only comment to me concerned the
'madam' whose patriotic action had led to Lambton's disgrace –
'That woman's a good Tory!'

After Lambton had resigned, I remained in touch with him. He
was shattered at having lost his political career but blamed nobody
but himself. He admitted that 'any man who has access to secrets
and goes to bed with a woman looks like a security risk' but never
really came to understand why he had been victimised. 'Surely,
most men patronise whores,' he insisted. I had difficulty trying to
convince him that he was exaggerating the true situation.

Heath and I had mutual friendship with Sir Jack and Rosslyn

Lyons, a most pleasant Jewish couple who had a beautiful house with grounds in the centre of London. On the evening after the announcement of Jellicoe's resignation, my wife and I were guests there along with Heath and others. Just as we were seated for dinner, I was told by a servant that I was wanted on the telephone by Lord Lambton.

The name electrified those at the table as there was some concern about Lambton's state of mind and what he might do. In fact all that Lambton wanted to know was how Jellicoe had become involved. I told him that there were Fleet Street rumours about two more of his former colleagues, at which he declared, 'It will soon be clear that Heath is the only member of the government who can't do it.' I assured the other diners that they need not worry about the state of Lambton's health.

Eventually, Lambton left his wife and his estate, buying a house in Tuscany where he lived until he died in 2006.

My last contact with George Jellicoe was in 2005, when he visited my house in Kintbury accompanied by his biographer, because he thought that my memory of certain events was likely to better than his, which he knew to be fading. His biographer, Lorna Windmill, called the book *A British Achilles*, indicating that George, who died in 2007, was a brave warrior with a weakness – women.

It is an odd fact that almost all the public figures who became involved in sexual scandals specialised in defence issues. I mentioned that one Saturday evening in 1994 in a warm-up speech at a private party to introduce the Minister for the Armed Forces, Jeremy Hanley, who was the main speaker. Amid some mirth, I warned Hanley of the special danger which his association with weapons might pose. To everyone's astonishment, the following morning's newspapers were full of the sad but spicy news that the current Chief of the Defence Staff, Marshal of the RAF Sir Peter Harding, had become embroiled with a lively lady. His resignation smartly followed. Another good man driven to disgrace by the demon rider. Do macho men seek association with weapons? Or does association with weapons make men more macho?

Of course, basic to all the sex scandals involving ministers and others with access to secret information was the possibility – stressed by MI5 – that they might be blackmailed by the KGB should that ever-active agency get wind of a compromising situation. That possibility had been publicly highlighted in 1965 by the sad experience of Commander Anthony Courtney, a former naval officer who had been elected a Tory MP in 1959 after a distinguished career. While in Naval Intelligence, he had learned to speak Russian and, having retired, regularly visited Moscow in a job promoting East–West trade. There he had become involved with a woman, Zina Volkova, who invited him into her hotel bedroom, which was set up so that the KGB could photograph the proceedings.

The KGB waited until Courtney made several anti-Soviet speeches in Parliament and, when he continued to do so after being warned by the Soviet embassy to desist, it sent copies of the incriminating photographs to newspapers, various ministers and his wife. Courtney's political and private lives were shattered.

I duly met Courtney, who in 1968 put his story on record in a book, *Sailor in a Russian Frame*, and found that he had been a friend of Sir Roger Hollis. He kindly gave me a couple of photographs showing Hollis with him on a visit to West Germany when Courtney had still been in Naval Intelligence. In one of them, taken on a boat trip on the Weser River, the hunched, shirt-sleeved figure of Hollis was wearing his badge of office – his large, black homburg hat.

When my book *Their Trade is Treachery* was published in 1981, causing the commotion which I will detail later, the pictures duly appeared, and I experienced a rather different Anthony Courtney. He telephoned me demanding £1,000 – a large sum in those days – because some journalist seeking a picture of Hollis had told him that photos of the MI5 chief were so rare that his paper would be prepared to pay that sum. When I explained that photographs were paid for by the publisher and that he would duly receive the going rate – probably £100 – he threatened me with legal action, claiming that his lawyer had always been 'very successful in the past'. After I told him that he would then, in fact, be suing the publisher, who, effectively, was Sir Charles Forte, I heard no more from him. He died in 1988 aged seventy-nine.

The power of the demon rider was publicly demonstrated again in the late 1960s by the experience of the British ambassador in Moscow, the late Sir Geoffrey Harrison. The KGB had infiltrated an attractive prostitute into his residence as a maid and His Excellency had quickly succumbed to her charms. When threatened with photographs of his activities, taken by a hidden KGB camera, he had, wisely, reported his predicament to London and had been hastily withdrawn.

The case was hushed up and the erring envoy's stupidity was duly awarded with the GCMG. When his behaviour eventually came to light he excused it by saying, 'My defences were down', inevitably leading to the comment that they were not the only things that had been down.

CHAPTER 23

ENOCH

The most controversial figure among the many politicians with whom I became friends was Enoch Powell, who was driven by an intense sense of duty and almost fanatical determination to succeed at whatever he decided to do. I can best describe those drives by two particular conversations I had with him.

He told me that in 1930, at the age of eighteen, he had been forced to make a crucial, lifetime decision: whether to pursue a career as a university academic in Greek or to become a concert clarinettist. He chose Greek and at the age of only twenty-five, by dint of unremitting intellectual effort, became professor of Greek at Sydney University. An amazing achievement, but what staggered me was his statement that, knowing that he had been outstanding on the clarinet, he never played the instrument again, having decided that he could not spare the time.

When the Second World War began, in September 1939, Enoch quit his beloved professorship and returned to England to join the Royal Warwickshire Regiment as a private infantry soldier. In 1944, aged thirty-two, by sheer brilliance and drive, he had become the youngest brigadier in the army. Usually, when visiting his London home near Eaton Square, we talked in the upstairs sitting room but, once, he took me to his study where I noticed a glass frame on the wall behind his desk containing his army epaulettes bearing his brigadier's crowns and pips.

'You kept your epaulettes!' I exclaimed, to which he replied, 'I've kept my whole uniform. I'm going to be buried in it.'

'With your red hat on?' I asked.

'Yes!' he replied, solemnly. 'With my red hat on!'

While bowing to his intellectual superiority, I had quickly realised that we had much in common on which to base a lasting friendship, both being self-drivers who enjoyed acquiring new information and possessing the kind of memory to store it. We were also, consciously, devoted to the land called Britain (he preferred to call it England, having been born in Birmingham) and committed to the concept of nationhood, as we had experienced and enjoyed it in our youth.

After Enoch had entered politics, in 1950 as Tory MP for Wolverhampton, his target, as usual, was the summit – the leadership of the Conservative Party and the eventual premiership. I heard him speak in Parliament where he was a brilliant debater. His main rival became Edward Heath, whom he outclassed intellectually, but it was Heath who became party leader in opposition in 1965 having beaten Enoch, though he remained a threat to him.

Enoch's position in Heath's shadow Cabinet was shadow Defence Minister and he disagreed with the party's policy of requiring British forces to remain in their bases east of Suez, like the Aden air and naval base, those in the Persian Gulf and Singapore, to retain Britain's influence there. As the *Express* defence reporter, and having visited Aden and all the Persian Gulf bases, which he had not, I had long talks with Enoch on the subject, and he judged that, sadly, the nation could not possibly sustain the costs.

He was right and, when the Labour government withdrew from the bases, he appeared to be supporting Labour – an odd situation for a man who had declared, 'I was born a Tory and I will die a Tory.' (Labour's action was also reluctant because at my first meeting with Harold Wilson on becoming Prime Minister he had said, 'I am an east of Suez man.' Both he and his Defence Minister, Denis Healey, were driven by sheer lack of money.)

Another basic on which Enoch and I agreed was the biggest menace of all – the growth of the world's population. With the human biomass totalling about 300 million tons and set to double, the over-riding problem faced by the whole world was over-breeding. I remarked to Enoch, 'It used to be said that the pen is mightier than the sword but it is really the penis.'

'No, no,' he cried with force. 'It's the uterus! The uterus!' Whether this implied a touch of misogyny I do not know but he always treated his wife, Pam, with love and respect.

Enoch was moral to an extent which many might regard as excessive. For example, he refused to accept any pay rise which MPs had voted themselves until the following general election when the voters could renew their contract with him on the new pay terms or reject it if they wished.

Because of such respect for others, whoever they might be, it was always ridiculous to regard Enoch as a 'racist'. He had spent most of his war service in India where he admired the people and their way of life, even learning the Urdu language (one of eleven that he studied), and, at one time, thought of settling there. It emerged that his first political ambition had been to become viceroy of India!

It was the over-population problem and its grimly foreseeable consequences that underlay his attitude to immigration and his honest and sensible views about it, which have been misinterpreted to the grossly unfair detriment of his memory. We agreed that the attitude to countries where, in spite of existing poverty and starvation due to sheer lack of food, the men and women refuse to limit their copulation, the slogan should be, 'If you can't feed 'em, don't breed 'em.' Instead, by temporarily solving their problems with hand-outs, at great expense to taxpayers, we increase the pressure on them to come to Britain, which is already grossly overcrowded by any sensible standard.

Why have so many foreigners decided to settle here? The most potent factor has been and remains the simple fact that the English language is the most widely spoken throughout the world and emigrants prefer to go to a country where they can understand and be understood. Now, with the Human Rights Acts and the European Union, which have spawned a huge industry of charity groups, Britain has become a landing place soft beyond belief. Recently, a Somali family found itself housed with 'benefits' in a large London house rented by the local authority – a symptom of national insanity, as historians will see it.

Most of the present population have little idea of what Britain

was like before the Second World War when we were a homogene-
ous white society or of the initial factors leading to the change. On
my first visit to the United States of America in 1953, I had been
unpleasantly surprised by the extent of the bad feeling between
whites and blacks and, on the return journey, consoled myself that
we did not have that problem. Shortly afterwards, we quite deliberately imported it.

It all began in the late 1950s with a shortage of London bus-
drivers because the wages being offered for this onerous and
highly responsible task were too low. The Conservatives were in
government and someone conceived the idea of offering the jobs to
Caribbeans who would be invited to live in Britain and be trained.
In they came, soon to be joined by the rest of their large families.
Once the barrier had been lifted it became politically difficult to
exclude others.

Macmillan had been Prime Minister at the time and, years later,
at his home, Birch Grove, his explanation to me was, 'We just never
imagined that they would want to come here in such numbers.' I
then asked him why they had not solved the bus-driver problem
simply by offering better pay. He replied, 'That would have meant
putting up the bus fares which would have made us very unpopular
and cost us votes that could have been crucial in marginal seats.'

In the mid-1960s when my Kenyan friend Bruce McKenzie was
motoring me round Mombasa, we passed through an area inhabited
by many Asians who had emigrated there. 'You are going to get all this
lot,' he declared, explaining that the Kenyan leader, Jomo Kenyatta,
would force them out because he wanted all the jobs and space they
were filling for his black African supporters. Sure enough, in 1967
they began to pour into Britain and Enoch Powell loudly opposed
their acceptance. The Kenyan Asians had been issued with British
passports but they were of a limited kind, giving no right of abode in
the UK. Nevertheless, they were allowed in and Enoch foresaw that
it was the opening of floodgates, as he described it to me.

In late 1972, the Ugandan dictator Idi Amin decided to expel his
country's 30,000 Asians, who were mainly from the Indian subcon-
tinent, because they were too successful in competing with Africans

in trading and in business. Again, Enoch drew my attention to the fact that many of them were issued with UK passports by the local British passport office in Kampala to enable them to travel but the documents specifically carried no right of abode in the UK, as I reported in the *Daily Express* as forcefully as I could. They could have been required to return to their countries of origin but were allowed into Britain.

Meanwhile, in 1968, at a Conservative Association meeting in his home town, Birmingham, Enoch had delivered what, quite falsely, has become known as his 'rivers of blood' speech. Speaking about the inevitable effects of the ever-increasing influx of immigrants he said, 'As I look ahead I am filled with foreboding; like the Roman, I seem to see the River Tiber foaming with much blood.' As a classical scholar he was quoting the poet Virgil.

What he foresaw, and had the courage to declare, were the outrages which, inevitably, would be inflicted on the indigenous British people by extreme, fanatical 'jihadist' Muslims driven by the belief that any not of their faith should be killed. I recall the dreadful bomb outrage on the London Underground in 2005 which killed many citizens. I realised, then, how uncannily accurate Enoch's prophecy had been. It had been wrong by only two letters. For 'Tiber' read 'Tube'.

As a devout Christian and, eventually, the author of *Evolution of the Gospel*, Enoch was unusually well informed about the atrocities previously inflicted on each other by Roman Catholics and Protestants in Britain. He foresaw that, once Pakistanis and other Muslims had settled in Britain in large numbers, such horrific turmoil could be repeated. Since then, MI5's main target has become the scores of Muslims, mainly now British born, who travel to Pakistan for training as suicide bombers. Many more atrocities have been prevented only by the arrest of the fanatics before they could complete their bombs. In the week in 2012 that I wrote these words, the director general of MI5 was driven to break with usual silent practice and warn the public of the increasing number of British-born Muslims going abroad for terrorist training.

Such is the attitude of some Muslims that they are prepared

to serve as suicide bombers to inflict mass murder on those who differ from them in interpreting *their own faith*, as witness the regular outrages involving appalling casualties in Iraq, Pakistan and other Islamic states. Small wonder that such fanatics are prepared to kill those of different faiths.

Enoch was also aware that the citizens of some parts of the Islamic world are governed by Sharia law – a legal system controlled by the equivalent of priests – and many of them would prefer to see it imposed in any country which they occupy.

In spite of the public service Enoch had bravely achieved by his Birmingham speech, he was branded a 'racist' by the left-wing press and what he came to call 'the race relations industry'. Heath used the outcry as an excuse to sack him from his shadow Cabinet and never spoke to him again. Yet a national opinion poll on the subject showed that 74 per cent of the indigenous population agreed with Enoch. There were spontaneous marches of workers bearing 'Don't knock Enoch' placards.

Enoch's warnings that the Home Office estimates of the numbers of immigrants and their birth rates were pitched too low proved to be correct. In 1972 an opinion poll voted him the most popular politician. I did all I could in my newspaper columns to support Enoch.

There are now English towns where the indigenous population is outnumbered. The 'race relations industry' has striven, with considerable success, to convince people that a 'multi-cultural society' carries great advantages which neither I nor Enoch could ever see. Most politicians have been driven to agree, whatever their true thoughts, because they need the immigrant votes.

As part of his ecclesiastical interests Enoch enjoyed visiting churches and, after lunching with us in Kintbury, I showed him round the 1,000-year-old churchyard. He then said that there was a church at Avington on the Howard de Walden estate, about two miles away, which he had always wanted to see. I secured permission to visit it and Enoch showed me round the charming building of which I, a near resident, had been unaware.

It proved to be our last meeting as I then became totally involved in intelligence and espionage affairs for unexpected reasons I will describe. Sadly, Enoch developed Parkinson's Disease and I was dismayed to see and hear him on television with his once-commanding voice weakened and highly pitched. He died in 1998 and, sure enough, was buried in full uniform wearing his red hat in his regiment's graveyard in Warwick.

CHAPTER 24

MORE UNUSUAL PEOPLE

Early in 1972, I was approached by a friend of His Imperial Majesty the Shah of Persia (now Iran) to be asked if I would do HIM (as he was invariably referred to) a special service. The Shah was to come to Britain to stay with the Queen at Windsor and attend the Ascot races but his main objective was to pave the way for large arms purchases. So, it was essential for HIM – and for our export industry – that he be well received. HIM was perturbed by a barrage of severe criticism he had been receiving in the British media over the alleged excesses of his secret service, Savak, against those opposed to his determination to westernise Persia.

In short, he needed some good publicity and, provided he had something new and interesting to tell me, I was keen to take advantage of this unprecedented opportunity to meet a monarch with near-absolute power. I was put in touch with an intermediary, Shapoor Reporter, a UK citizen who had been a friend of the Shah since their childhood and lived in the Persian capital, Tehran.

In mid-June, the amiable Reporter conducted me to the Shah's Niavaran Palace in Tehran. At every turn of every corridor there were uniformed Savak guards and civilian bodyguards who all stared, stonily, but remained silent. Eventually we entered a large room where, on a raised dais, HIM, a most pleasant man aged fifty-two and not looking at all imperial, was working at a desk in a dark western suit and tie. He shook my hand, directed me to a seat and asked me to pose any questions I wished.

As he sipped milkless tea from a silver tumbler, I was quickly in awe of his total recall of facts and figures – from oil production down to the details of the modern weapons with which he was equipping his army and air force following the withdrawal of British forces from the Persian Gulf. Speaking perfect English, HIM explained that he was unwilling just to rely on his country's oil reserves and was building an industrial base to replace the ancient pastoral economy and drag his country into the modern age free from the religious fanaticism of the ayatollahs. The Persian women already had voting rights and wore western dress if they wished, as most in the capital certainly did.

He had fostered a huge increase in university students to create an intellectual and scientific base but was beginning to suspect that he had overdone it as some of them (as students always do) were rebelling, especially about the growth of Savak. (My wife and I appreciated their point when, returning to our hotel one evening, we found ourselves looking down the barrel of a Sten gun.)

After telling me more than enough to fill two pages of my newspaper (as it eventually did) the Shah asked my advice about which ministers to meet in London. I agreed to consult them and pave the way for HIM but had to deter him from his planned request for a team from Savak to visit Northern Ireland to see how the UK dealt with terrorists! Gently, I explained that for any minister to arrange such a facility would be political suicide if the media found out as we, assuredly, would.

On my return to London I briefed Lord Carrington, then the Defence Minister, about the Shah's requirements, pointing out that special attention should be paid to Mr Reporter, who would be with him. My inquiries had shown that Reporter had already been involved in placing arms orders in the UK worth £800 million! On hearing that, another minister, Jim Prior, who had breezed into the room, cried, 'We'll give him a gong!'

In the next honours list Mr Reporter was elevated to Sir with a KBE. My ongoing reward was a regular Christmas gift of three bottles of champagne and a large can of the best caviar, delivered to my office from the Iranian embassy.

Sadly, the Shah was deposed in 1979 and supplanted by the Ayatollah Khomeini, resulting in a repressive, fanatical and dangerously isolated mess. Still, not many Englishmen can say that they took tea with the Shah of Persia.

His departure also put paid to my champers and caviar from the Iranian embassy but not before another unforgettable experience.

Whenever the caviar had arrived at the *Express* my secretary would put it in the office fridge until I collected it to take it home in the evening in my briefcase. There, it went into our fridge until we devoured it all at a small party of special friends who always included Janet Kidd, Lord Beaverbrook's daughter.

One year, we summoned Janet and the other lucky ones to the annual party and all was ready, including the chopped boiled egg and the rest, when the Chinese servant we then employed came in holding the opened tin with the shocking news, 'Not caviar, madam! Pistachio nuts!'

I grabbed the tin and, sure enough, it was filled with nuts. I could not read the lettering on the tin which, as with the caviar tin, had been in the Persian language, but realised that the tin was far too light in weight for it ever to have been caviar. So, how could I and the others who handled it ever have thought it was? Simply because, being convinced in advance that it was caviar, our several brains fooled themselves and failed to register the light weight of the tin.

This strange quirk of the brain was demonstrated in an even more extraordinary way more recently when I was visiting a highly intelligent and well-known nobleman whose identity I will not reveal to save him embarrassment. My wife and I spent a day with him on our way to a week's salmon fishing in Scotland and he chanced to mention that one of his hobbies was wood-carving in soft wood. He then produced, with some pride, a wooden salmon about three feet long which he had carved meticulously, with all its fins perfectly spread as though in action.

While admiring his skill, I spotted that he had made a glaring mistake and decided that, hurtful though it might be to him, I had to make him aware of it.

The salmon has a pair of fins behind the gills on the underside of the body – one on each side – called the pectoral fins. These had been carved perfectly. Further back in the centre of the underside is another pair, the ventral fins. These too were superbly carved. Further back still, near the anus, is a single anal fin which assists in balance but has no propulsive powers. Sadly, instead of a single anal fin, my host had carved another pair of fins like those in front of them. When I pointed out his error he appreciated it immediately and was totally at a loss to understand how, while working on the carving for so many hours, he had never spotted it. Also, being a keen salmon fisher himself, he had handled scores of them.

The simple truth is that, wonderfully ingenious though the human brain is most of the time, it has an in-built capacity to fool itself. I have studied this quirk for many years and, recently, published my findings as an e-book on Amazon called *Out of This World*. It shows that, without some degree of credulity, which expresses itself in many ways (such as dreams for example), the brain cannot function properly. So, we are all capable of fooling ourselves on occasion.

While dining with my shooting friend Charles Hughesdon in Ripley, Surrey, I met the phenomenally rich, humourless American oil tycoon Paul Getty, who lived in the nearby Tudor mansion, Sutton Place. Later my wife and I visited him there and saw, on the main landing, a huge, red pay-as-you-call phone box which guests had to use to make any call. Getty explained that guests had been making long, expensive calls from their bedrooms, from which he had since removed the phones.

Years later, in 1998, we were invited to lunch by Getty's son, Sir Paul, who was also hugely rich but of entirely different temperament, being full of fun and outstandingly generous. Californian bred, he was then British and had been awarded the KBE for his philanthropy, which had included £50 million to the National Gallery alone. To anglicise himself, he had bought the 2,500-acre estate of Wormsley Park, set in a valley of the Chilterns. The house there was Georgian and Sir Paul had added a library, built in the Gothic style, to hold his collection of rare books and ancient manuscripts.

After lunch he showed me the library, where I noticed there were several desks with reading lamps. He explained that academics came there to study and that one of them had written a whole original book about one of his volumes, *The Faerie Queene*, a huge epic poem which had been published by Edmund Spenser in 1590.

As *The Faerie Queene* was so well known down the centuries – even I have a copy – I asked how anybody could have found enough new in it to write another book. In smiling response, he passed me his treasured volume, which was very thick. On looking at the title page I saw the name of its first owner, who had written it in small but easily readable script – Ben Jonson! I felt a frisson of excitement for this was the towering playwright and poet whose epitaph in Westminster Abbey simply states 'O Rare Ben Jonson' and who had been a contemporary of Shakespeare, with whom he is said to have had many arguments in London's Mermaid Tavern.

I turned the pages and on almost every one of them there were marginal comments and criticisms written by Jonson about 370 years previously. I was lost in wonder.

As part of identifying himself with Britain, Sir Paul, a former baseball fan, had become entranced with cricket, to which he had been introduced during his wayward youth by the rock star Mick Jagger. He had, therefore, enhanced his estate with an ideal village cricket ground with a thatched pavilion and incomparable views. He established the Getty XI, which took on about twelve formidable sides in the season with many other matches being played there. Happily, my wife and I were invited to several of them each year, lunching at Sir Paul's table and encountering there not only celebrities from the cricket world like Fred Trueman, Richie Benaud, an old friend whose home in Australia I had visited, and Dickie Bird, but retired politicians like Lord Carrington, Sir John Major and Jack Profumo, along with former defence chiefs and many other notables such as the world's first four-minute miler, Sir Roger Bannister.

I was particularly grateful for the opportunities to meet Peter Carrington again as I had such respect for his political integrity and enjoyed his sense of humour. We had often met when he was Defence Minister and, once, while sitting in the waiting room outside his office, I was reading the latest issue of *Private Eye*, which had just been added to the several magazines there. The front cover was a photograph of an elegant lady dancing with Ted Heath and saying (in a large 'balloon' issuing from her mouth), 'I do so love your Tory balls!' I was laughing when Peter appeared to call me in and when I showed it to him he cried, with great mirth, 'Oh look! It's Mother!' That was his name for his beloved wife.

When in 1979 I told him I was retiring from Fleet Street, Peter exclaimed, 'I can't bear it', and took me out for a farewell tea at the Ritz.

Like everything Sir Paul did, his hospitality was prodigious and the spectators sipped champagne, which was regularly replenished by itinerant waitresses, while their children had access to a free ice-cream parlour as we watched the cricket, sometimes enlivened by the rare red kites he had introduced.

Sadly, Sir Paul's hippie-style youth, which had involved drugs, took its eventual toll and in my last memory of him, shortly before he died in 2003 aged seventy, he was in a wheelchair joking with Keith Miller, Australia's greatest all-round cricketer, who was also wheelchair bound.

O Rare Paul Getty!

As a Fleet Street defence correspondent, I often attended lectures by forces chiefs at the Royal United Services Institute in Whitehall, which has long been the leading forum for defence and security studies. Between 1968 and 1973 my visits there were more frequent because the then director general, Air Vice Marshal 'Paddy' Menaul, was a close friend who I had first met while we were both involved in atomic bomb tests in Australia. We had many reminiscing chats in his office, where there was a single oil painting which I much admired.

It was a head and shoulders portrait of a truly great, but little-appreciated, old gentleman called Lord Howard of Effingham, who, as the wooden label on the oval, gilded frame stated, was the Lord High Admiral of England during the reign of Elizabeth I. He was in charge of the Battle of the Armada in 1588 and was chiefly responsible for the victory for which Sir Francis Drake, who was his second in command, usually gets all the credit. He was at sea during the battle, had visited every ship before it to boost morale and had confidently forecast victory.

Surviving letters show that he had also been astute enough to keep warning Elizabeth that, while the Spaniards appeared to be negotiating peace, they were assembling a massive invasion fleet which would have to be assaulted.

The portrait, which showed a benevolent-looking, white-haired and white-bearded old chap in a white ruff and wearing a lace cap, was part of a huge collection of paintings of military or naval significance – some of them large battle scenes – which had been bequeathed to the RUSI over the years and was housed in a building close by.

One day in 1973, when visiting Paddy, I found him in sombre mood. The Crown authorities had decided that they could no longer permit the RUSI to pay a peppercorn rent for its Whitehall premises. So, to meet the increased demand, the council had decided to sell off all the pictures to create a fund. Even the Lord High Admiral would be under the hammer.

After the sale, while sitting in Paddy's office, I asked how much the great man had made. 'Nothing!' he replied. 'He was painted on a thin, wooden panel and some idiot took the panel out of the frame, whereupon it split into two parts. So we had to withdraw it.'

He opened a large, deep drawer in his desk and produced the two sections, whereupon I asked what he intended to do with them. 'Probably nothing,' he replied despondently. 'It would cost too much to have it restored.'

I wasted no time, as I then owned a Tudor house and thought that, even with the split in it, the picture would grace one of my panelled walls. 'I'll give you £200 for the bits and the frame,' I offered.

'OK. I'll put it to my council,' he responded after brief thought. The council duly accepted my offer. I simply put the two wooden sections back in the frame and hung the picture on a wall, feeling that the restoration costs would be heavy.

A few months later I was lunching in the boardroom of a company in London where the only person I had not previously met introduced himself as Arthur Lucas. 'I am the chief restorer at the National Gallery,' he added. I lost no time to tell him of the Lord High Admiral's sad plight, whereupon he volunteered,

'That is a painting of historic interest. Bring it to me at the National Gallery and we'll restore it for nothing.'

The experts there did a near-perfect job, giving me the occasional privilege, which I still enjoy, of giving the Lord High Admiral of England a naval salute to thank him for our national deliverance more than 400 years ago.

The recent screening of an excellent programme about the 'Dambusters' regenerated memories of those in that courageous operation whom I was privileged to know – Guy Gibson, who led the raid, and Barnes Wallis, the engineer who made it possible. The gentle, quietly spoken, Barnes, who I met journalistically when living not far from his home at Effingham, Surrey, looked and sounded the unlikeliest person to be involved in devising bombs to kill people. Yet, he had been the first to propose really massive bombs to eliminate specific German targets. His first mega-bomb, codenamed Tallboy and containing six tons of TNT, could penetrate up to seventy feet of concrete before exploding. In November 1944, Lancaster bombers armed with Tallboys sank the German battleship *Tirpitz* sheltering off Norway. Wallis followed up with Grand Slam – a ten-tonner to destroy targets protected by concrete so thick that it was rated impregnable.

Earlier, in 1942, he had developed a unique weapon which came to his mind from the way pebbles thrown on to the surface of a river can skim the water and bounce several times, covering a considerable distance. This gave him the concept of a 'bouncing bomb' which could be used to destroy the huge dams generating electricity for the German war effort, with the bonus of causing devastating floods in the areas below them. Most RAF planners rejected the idea as a pipedream but the RAF commander-in-chief, Sir Charles Portal, supported it and over-ruled them.

During experiments on British reservoirs, Wallis also devised a way of giving the drum-shaped bomb backspin so that when it struck the face of a dam it would climb down to its base before exploding there doing maximum damage.

Early in 1943 the air chiefs decided to use the bomb to attack and, hopefully, destroy three large dams serving the Ruhr, the heartland of German industry. In 'Operation Chastise' a fleet of nineteen Lancaster bombers fitted with bouncing bombs was to be led by Wing Commander Guy Gibson who, aged only twenty-four, was the RAF's most experienced bomber pilot. I had met him at his Lincolnshire base of Scampton, which was not far from the army unit near Newark, where I was then serving. As I have previously described, my very social commanding officer made a practice of liaising with nearby Bomber Command bases and usually took me with him. Gibson was always hospitable but had an aura of arrogance which I found understandable in view of his achievements when so young.

Operation Chastise was, clearly, going to be extremely dangerous as the bombers would have to approach the dam walls at only sixty feet if the bombs were going to work. As the dams were heavily defended, it would have to be done at night in moonlight. On the night of 16–17 May 1943, the bombers breached the Möhne and the Eder dams. Eight Lancasters and fifty-three crew were lost but Gibson returned and was awarded the Victoria Cross. In September 1944 he crashed in action and was killed. He was twenty-six years old and had carried out 174 operations over Germany.

After the war a grateful government awarded Wallis £10,000, which he gave to his old school, Christ's Hospital (the 'Bluecoat School'), to set up a trust to enable children of RAF personnel killed or injured in action to attend it. His ever-curious mind then generated a new concept for a plane capable of speeds up to 1,800 mph either as a bomber, which could reach Moscow in one hour, or a passenger plane reaching New York from London in two hours and Australia in eight. Codenamed Swallow, it could fold its wings back in flight. There were no ailerons, tailplane or flaps. The jet engines, which were on pivots, did the steering. As Wallis was being starved of funds to build a prototype I supported him with publicity and often visited his office near Weybridge.

The project was killed off in the 1957 defence cuts but Barnes continued to develop it, having 'a better idea' each time I visited him. When he came up with an even faster plane with wings like a Venetian blind even I had to admit that he was over the top.

He then concentrated on wood-carving, at which, inevitably, he was superb.

Throughout the Second World War, the most pulse-quickening word ever to come over an Allied airman's earphones was 'Messerschmitt!' implying the sudden appearance of the pride of the German Luftwaffe's fighter force – a Messerschmitt 109 or, worse still, especially if the airman was in a heavy bomber, a group of them.

This German counterpart of the Spitfire and the Hurricane fighter planes had not only been designed by an ingenious engineer called Willi Messerschmitt but his company, Messerschmitt AG, had also built it. Willi was one of those phenomenal men – like the American Henry Ford – who combine inventive ability with capacity for big-scale industrial organisation. As such, he had been one of the main springs of Hitler's 'total war' because the Me-109 was the most produced fighter in history – 35,000 having been built and flown.

Later, Willi designed and built the Me-209, which broke the air speed record, and the Me-262 – the first jet-powered fighter, which came just too late to affect the war.

After the Allied victory in 1945, he was prosecuted for using slave labour, which he may have been forced to do, and served two years in prison. Being a fighter himself, he then immediately resumed his position as head of his company, which was based near Munich, but was forbidden to make aircraft. I was later astonished when his irrepressible energy quickly produced a strange little three-wheeled motor car, a few of which were imported to Britain. I decided to fly out to Munich to meet Willi at his factory and see for myself what made him tick. When I did so, in June 1949, I was not disappointed.

He was lanky, lantern jawed, soft voiced, and very pleasant to talk to – I will never forget his joyfully loud '*fünfzig!*' when I asked him his age. He said that the name Messerschmitt translates as 'maker of knives' so he seemed to have been destined to make something. He had fallen in love with aircraft when he had flown in a glider at the age of fourteen and then trained as an engineer. He had designed the Me-109 in 1934 then, with government backing, had manufactured it.

Of course, what he wanted to make after his release from prison was more aircraft – transport planes much needed to help rebuild the German economy – and was bitter about the way the Americans, in particular, had treated him. While he had been in prison, they had stripped his factory and laboratory of everything that was movable as war reparations. I could see little sign of the sewing machines he was also making as they were just side-lines. True to form, Willi was mass-producing something that the Fatherland needed more desperately – pre-fabricated houses for more than fifty towns rubbled by Allied bombs and artillery. He had bought a dozen books on house-building and had quietly gone to work on the drawing board. Soon, he was churning out homes elegantly designed to be permanent, as I saw for myself when taken to see some of them. After 1955 he was permitted to restart making airplanes for the West German Luftwaffe, retiring in 1970 and dying eight years later.

Though he had been a most dangerous enemy, I feel privileged to have met a man who, having been knocked off a pinnacle of power, could pick himself up, dust himself off and start again and whose name in the history of aviation and in the history of war will resonate down the ages.

Among unusual people I have met none was more unpredictable than George Brown, the Labour politician who became Foreign Secretary in Harold Wilson's government in the 1960s. For me, he was the epitome of an MP with a drink problem, being frequently described in the media as 'tired and emotional', which was a kindly way of saying 'drunk'. There were also stories of social gaffes, some perhaps apocryphal, such as George, in his cups, having insisted on dancing with some high-ranking papal visitor because he was wearing a skirt!

His drink problem arose from two mental quirks, the first being an inferiority complex about the poverty in which he had been born and reared. He had been delivered in 1914 in a grim little flat in one of London's Peabody buildings, built for the poor by the

Peabody Charitable Trust, and seemed to think that everyone was holding that against him. He was driven to talk about it so much that I suspect he drank to help himself forget it. His second quirk was an allergy to alcohol which, after just a couple of drinks, made him aggressive and inclined to insult people, hardly a good quality for a Foreign Secretary. It was sad because, basically, he was kind and astute.

George also lacked the flow of luck which politicians need to be successful. After one of our little tiffs (though we were friends we had them often) in 1974, I walked to my table in a London restaurant and noticed George sitting with three other men at the next one. I did not know whether to nod or to cut him when he shouted 'Harry!' and we shook hands. My guest happened to be another Harry – Harry Hyams, of Ramsbury Manor – and, after Brown emerged from the cloakroom following his lunch, I introduced them. He was affable but I saw that he was standing rather awkwardly.

At our next meeting George explained what had happened. He had been lunching with his lawyers (the three men) in the break during a court case in which he was eventually convicted of driving with an excess of alcohol in his blood. While he had been in the cloakroom misfortune had struck again. The zip on his flies had broken and he had faced the prospect of appearing before a woman judge, who already appeared hostile to him, with his flies open or risk further displeasure by being late if he had gone home to change his trousers. Eventually, a fresh pair of trousers had been rushed to the court just in time for him to change there.

Poor George! But he did end up in the House of Lords as Lord George-Brown. Not bad for a lad from Peabody buildings.

CHAPTER 25

FOREIGN TRAVEL

My wonderful old friend Sir Thomas Sopwith was a fount of wisdom and one day he offered me the following advice: 'Always do your travelling when you are young because, when you are old, you won't want to go. And always do it at the expense of some organisation. That way you will travel in better style.' As usual, he was right – since I turned eighty I have had no wish to stray out of Britain and, after ninety, little desire to leave my village where, happily, friends and new sources are prepared to visit me.

As a senior journalist on Beaverbrook's *Daily Express*, I was already acting on Sir Thomas's advice because so many of the international scientific and medical conferences which I chose to attend in search of news were held in enthralling cities like Paris, Rome, New Orleans, Stockholm, Geneva, Vienna and – best of all – Venice, which became, and remains, the city of my dreams.

In my halcyon days, senior journalists of the *Daily Express* always travelled first class with a wad of travellers' cheques and one was not seriously expected to return many of them. Because most of my reports emanated from sources based in Britain, I never liked being abroad for more than a week, which was usually the length of time of the conferences which I chose to attend. A detailed account of how the money had been spent was eventually required by the accounts department but, provided sufficiently printable copy had resulted from the visit, not much art was needed to justify it.

Journalistically, it usually paid to stay in the best hotels, along with the conference 'big shots', and I particularly recall residing in the hotels in Paris and Athens where my friend Harold Watkinson, then Defence Minister, was staying. On each occasion, he called me for a drink with him in his room to give me exclusive briefings which produced much-envied scoops.

Looking back, I have enjoyed many of the world's finest hotels, my favourite being the Gritti Palace in Venice. From the Gritti, one can stroll into San Marco Square or just sit on its balcony on the Grand Canal, admiring the gondolas and other traffic against a backdrop of unique architecture. (For lunch, though, my favourite has to be the roof restaurant of the Danielli with its stupendous view over the Venetian lagoon.)

At the Ritz in Madrid, my wife and I enjoyed an almost royal suite. We were the guests of Sir Charles Forte, who then owned it, and were told that our splendid suite of rooms had, once, been occupied by the Duke of Windsor (formerly King Edward VIII) and his wife, the former Mrs Simpson.

A fine hotel which, for me, is particularly nostalgic is the Grand Hotel in Stockholm as it was my first experience of a really good hotel on my first foreign assignment for the *Daily Express*. This occurred in the autumn of 1946 in response to an intriguing report from Sweden that missiles, apparently launched by the Russians, were being test-fired through Swedish air space and were, presumably, ending in the North Baltic Sea. The Swedes called them 'spookbombs' so I flew to Stockholm to interview the Swedish anti-aircraft chief, who confirmed his belief that they were 'winged Russian missiles' being test-fired. The major mystery was why so many of them were being fired every night.

The mystery was never resolved but my journey introduced me to Sweden, which had been neutral during the war, and the Swedes, who I liked so much that I developed scientific contacts which enabled me to make regular and productive visits there over many years. I have to confess, however, that my biggest thrill on that first visit was to see large shops and stores packed with food and every other item which was still rationed in Britain. I returned with my bags stashed with goodies.

Later, attending an international conference in Stockholm, I made a friend of Professor David Katz, a psychologist at Stockholm University, whose various research projects were always newsworthy.

If I needed an excuse to visit Stockholm all I had to do was contact Katz, who enjoyed the publicity and, invariably, came up with a good reason to visit him.

Whenever I was in Stockholm I stayed at the Grand and made many Swedish friends in the newspaper world there. Happily, I still have a Swedish friend to remind me of those happy times – a British-based businessman called Claes (pronounced 'Class') Bourghardt, who I met shooting and taught fishing, at which he is now highly competent. He is a favoured companion of the King of Sweden, to whom he has introduced me, and they fish and shoot together, sometimes at Highclere.

Claes, who lives in a fine manor house close by my village, is the only man I have met to have achieved a 'MacNab' – a quickly caught salmon before breakfast, a stag stalked and shot on the hill, followed by a brace of walked-up grouse – all on the same day.

After I had left Fleet Street, I was occasionally invited to take part in foreign conferences about espionage, along with my wife, all expenses paid. One of the most memorable, in the 1970s, took place in Cattolica, a seaside resort on Italy's east coast not far from Rimini. We found the conference dull but, happily, it was enlivened by the presence of the distinguished actor, writer and film director Bryan Forbes, and his lovely wife, the actress Nanette Newman. We spent much time with them and took Nanette with us to see the magnificent mosaics of Ravenna on a day when Bryan was busy. I spent much of my time answering the whispered question from other tourists, 'Is that Nanette Newman?'

Both were endowed with an unusual sense of humour, Nanette, for example, remarking that her first name was 'too reminiscent of frilly knickers'. Bryan, who went on to ever-increasing fame as a script-writer and film-director, realised that I might be useful to him as an information source and we remained in touch by telephone. Sadly, he developed a long and devastating illness and died in 2013.

My foreign birth (in India) had caused me no travel problems because, in the days of the vast British Empire, all people in it were simply 'British', but in 1951 I suffered something of an emotional crisis when, having recently served five years in the wartime army,

I was officially informed that I could no longer call myself an Englishman and was, in fact, stateless. In 1948, a conference of Commonwealth countries had decided to introduce the concept of citizenship and when the UK was driven to follow suit with a British Nationality Act, which came into force early in 1949, the geographical peculiarities of my birth disqualified me. I could have qualified if my father had been born in the UK but he had been born in what is now Eire because his father's regiment happened to be stationed there then. So I was stateless, though it was suggested that I could apply for Indian citizenship!

I was not given the dreadful news until 1951, when I tried to renew my passport. All my life I have felt a particularly firm attachment to that part of the earth's crust called Britain which may derive from my ancestry as my parents, and the few other males I have been able to trace, lived mainly as Yorkshire farmers or miners who worked the crust or as soldiers who protected it. For me, Walter Scott's 'Breathes there the man with soul so dead / Who never to himself hath said / This is my own, my native land!' speaks volumes and I can think of no worse penalty than to be banished from it.

The new laws almost made my father an Irishman but, after much argument, I was told that if his father had been born in the UK – as he had been – I might qualify if I was prepared to sign a form, then make a solemn declaration before a commissioner for oaths and pay a small fee.

When I told my father, who had served through both World Wars, he turned purple and his language reverted to the barrack room. However, with no alternative, I swallowed my pride and went through the ludicrous motions. It was worth it for the privilege of calling myself an Englishman again.

One of the many advantages of working for a national newspaper lay in the fact that it had an office with a resident reporter in most of the major cities of the world. So, on my travels I usually had access to an expert who really knew the place. That way I learned a few fascinating things usually denied to the ordinary visitor and recall three such 'secrets' which are worthy of wider record.

The first, which seemed grossly unlikely, was that the best apple strudel in the world was on the daily menu of the café at the Kunsthistorisches Museum (equivalent to our National Gallery) in Vienna. My wife and I went there and decided that the claim was justified. The strudel was superb. So we paid a second visit – just for the strudel.

The second concerns Venice, where there is a sixteenth-century statue which goes unseen by most visitors though it is close by one of the most visited sights – the Rialto Bridge over the Grand Canal. Known as *Il Gobbo di Rialto* – the Hunchback of the Rialto – it played a long and sinister role in the strange history of that ever-astonishing city. In the days of the Doges, with their dreaded 'Council of Ten' (1310–1797), those convicted of serious crimes were executed in San Marco Square near the Doge's Palace. Those judged guilty of lesser crimes were offered the alternative of grim imprisonment or a run, naked, by any route of their choice, from the square to the Gobbo. The snag was that, on the way, any citizen – and there were usually many lined up to enjoy the event – had the right to strike the criminal until he had touched the Gobbo when, if he survived the journey, he became a free man.

To see the Gobbo, one must walk over the Rialto Bridge from the San Marco side where there is a small square called Campo San Giacomo, usually full of market stalls. Behind the fruit stalls under a lean-to shelter on the far right is the kneeling figure of the Gobbo, which one can touch while sparing a thought for the thousands of bloody miscreants who took such a terrible beating.

My third – and best – secret seemed incredible when I heard it. Our Rome correspondent assured me that deep inside one of the holiest buildings in the world – the great Basilica of St Peter itself – there was a public bar, not very far from the Great Altar, where anyone who knew how to find it could buy the cheapest booze in the Eternal City. His instructions were as follows: bear left after entering St Peter's through the massive main doors and you will soon encounter a sign saying *Tesoro* – the Treasury, where the Basilica's most precious objects are stored. Close by, there is a small room where, in the left-hand far corner, there is a ticket-office where one can buy a pass into the Treasury. Instead of buying a

ticket go to the far right-hand corner where there is a short passage
with a closed door at its end. Open that door and walk through the
short passage.

I did so and found that I was in a coffee and drinks bar being
patronised by several off-duty priests and basilica officials. My presence caused no concern as the couple behind the bar made me a
coffee, using one of the standard machines. The priests were drinking something stronger and were joined by others who entered
from a different door – presumably the main entrance. I did not
check the price of the drinks but my coffee was the cheapest I ever
encountered in Italy.

On another visit I took my wife there and the situation was similar, as she vividly remembers. Over several years I passed the secret
to a few close friends who all enjoyed the facility. Then, in the late
1980s, when we took two friends to find the St Peter's bar, we found
that our path was blocked. The whole entry to the Treasury had
been altered by new wooden structures. I sought guidance from a
uniformed official who looked at me as though I was blasphemous
to suggest that there had ever been such an indignity in St Peter's.
A young American priest studying at the Vatican laughed me
to scorn.

So has St Peter's Bar been closed? Or has it just been barred
to the general public with those who know the other entrance still
enjoying their tipple-break? Sadly, I am too old now to find out but
it would make a noble research project for someone younger.

For various journalistic reasons, I was able to visit Rome on
many occasions which are entrenched in detail in my memory. My
travels have enabled me to witness many great performances of
opera in many cities, but the one I recall most vividly was of *Aida*,
staged in the ruins of the Baths of Caracalla in Rome, an evening
event which my children have never forgotten, its highlight being
the arrival of the hero in a chariot drawn by four cantering white
horses to the rousing sound of Verdi's haunting trumpet theme.

On my travels, I have been within hand touch of some of the
biggest weapons of mass destruction, such as the giant Minuteman
rocket I inspected deep down in its underground silo in wildest

America, but the most sinister weapon I ever encountered at close quarters was the smallest and it happened on another of my visits to Rome in that paragon of peace, the Vatican.

The story began in Chilton Foliat near Hungerford, in Littlecote House, then the home of Sir Seton Wills and his wife Gillian, with whom my wife and I were dining. Following the discovery of Roman remains in the Littlecote grounds, including a magnificent mosaic, the conversation turned to Rome, which, it transpired, our hosts had never visited. As I was familiar with the Eternal City, we decided to holiday there together with myself acting as guide.

Having arrived there, I contacted a Polish friend who was domiciled in Rome for advice about any special venue. He said that he had a Polish acquaintance who was a priest in the Vatican and could arrange a visit to those parts of the Vatican gardens closed to the public. As the weather was sunny we met the priest, who operated under the name of Father Flavian, and he gave the four of us a conducted tour of the Pope's private gardens, including a little building where His Holiness, then the much-admired John Paul II, meditated. Pope John Paul, who, too, was Polish, preferred to confess his sins in his native language and Father Flavian had become his confessor, which gave him a special aura in our eyes. In the course of our conversations I told Father Flavian that I had been baptised a Roman Catholic but was 'totally lapsed'. He had made no comment.

As a final treat, he invited us to see his 'cell' but it had to be 'men only' as no woman was allowed there. Our wives waited in the garden while Seton and I viewed the 'cell', which, contrary to our expectation, was a superb Renaissance room with a splendid fireplace surmounted by a bulging chimney-breast bearing an unusual crucifix. The cross was black, of ebony, about eighteen inches long and ten inches wide with silver mounts. Unusually, it was oval in cross-section instead of square. The delicately carved Christ was of ivory, yellowed with age.

Father Flavian took it down, explaining that it was English, dated 1632, and had been used when Catholics, especially priests, were being hunted down by the Protestant authorities. While

Seton watched, he asked me to kneel and make to kiss the cross as he presented it towards me. As I did so, he swiftly pulled away the section above the Saviour's head. It was the handle of a long dagger, razor edged on both sides, the lower part of the cross being its scabbard, and the priest went through the motions of bringing it down close to my outstretched neck.

Even to the lapsed Catholic, the crucifix seemed outrageously sacrilegious. Equally sickening was the realisation that some Christian authority had ordered it and that some English craftsman, fully aware of its purpose, had toiled for many days in making it.

My defence responsibilities spawned many trips to Washington, where I developed valuable new contacts, mainly in the US Air Force, most of whom were based in the Pentagon, where I visited them. Just being in that colossal building, which accommodated more than 30,000 people, was memorable in itself, especially on the occasion in 1966 when I interviewed its chief inhabitant, Robert McNamara, the Defense Secretary. Before doing so, I had taken the precaution of being briefed by my old friend Solly Zuckerman, then the chief scientist in the UK Defence Ministry, who 'marked my card' and debriefed me on my return.

Las Vegas, the gambling centre of the US, was not a place I would have chosen to visit but I was taken there courtesy of the US Air Force. Until they developed long-range missiles which could reach Russia from American soil, the US defence chiefs needed to base their short-range missile, called Thor, in the UK. So, to encourage British defence journalists to support that requirement, the US Air Force organised a conducted tour of the American factories and testing grounds where Thor was being developed. I enjoyed the facility, especially watching a test-launch of Thor at Vandenberg Air Force Base in California, and it made a good story for my paper, but the organisers felt that we needed a rest and we were all taken to Las Vegas in Nevada for a two-day break.

As we touched down, our guide announced, 'Well, here we are – Lost Wages!' How apt that name was quickly became apparent when, in the casino hotels, I saw the massive arrays of 'one-armed bandits', roulette tables, poker tables and the many other means of extracting the money of visitors most of whom seemed happy to oblige. They did not extract even a token dollar from this visiting Yorkshireman.

As our trip covered so much of the US, we were also given a break in New Orleans where so much of the charming old French quarter had been preserved. I visited it several times later and particularly recall delightful dinners in an open-air restaurant called the Court of Two Sisters. (Not quite so wonderful as a dinner in the Piazza Navona in Rome, but nearly.)

On another trip, the US Air Force flew us to secret bases in Alaska and Greenland where I met my first Eskimos, though, apparently, it is now 'politically correct' to call them Inuits. (I wonder if the great epic poem is now called *Inuit Nell*.)

Later, when American scientists had developed much larger missiles, I was to pay many visits to the launching site at Cape Canaveral in Florida. There, I witnessed several successful launchings, always being enthralled by 'We have lift-off!' and always impressed by the courage of astronauts, calmly sitting atop these flaming rockets when being launched into space. I had the honour of meeting and questioning several of these gallant space pioneers, one of whom was to lose his life in one of the rare accidents.

In the late 1980s, my wife and I made several more visits to the US, sometimes as guests of friends, the most memorable, for me, being to Epcot, a huge theme park near Orlando in Florida, built as an adjunct to the Disneyland there. It is a magnificent tribute to technical innovation, celebrating human achievement worldwide with many countries having their own pavilions.

We could not, of course, resist a day at the nearby Magic Kingdom to meet Mickey Mouse and his entourage, recalling memories of our distant youth.

Usually, I took the quickest air-route to any destination but there was one journey, in 1971, on which my wife and I took the longest. It was also memorable because it involved Harry Messel, one of the most remarkable men I have ever known and, over many years, I have come to know him well. He is a Canadian turned Australian and when I first met him he was professor of physics at Sydney University. He had invited me to speak to his students on science and the media and, instead of a fee, the reward was first-class air travel tickets for me and my wife by any route we cared to choose. As I was on vacation, we made the route circuitous, taking in many places such as the country of my birth, India, staying in Delhi, then moving to Johannesburg, Mauritius, Singapore (staying at the famed Raffles Hotel) and a few other places which caught our fancy.

I had already met Messel in London and had been impressed by his direct, no-nonsense, if sometimes crude, manner of speaking. During the war, he had served as a paratrooper with the Canadian forces and, in 1952, being a very bright specialist in mathematical physics, he had been appointed physics professor at Sydney where he was appalled at finding the department so poorly equipped. Until Harry arrived, the bright students who wanted to take a PhD went to Britain or the US to do so and their talents were lost to Australia. In what he always called his 'pursuit of excellence', Messel realised that much money was needed to establish advanced science in Australia and he set about raising it.

He did so by personal contact with rich Australians, bullying them and, in some cases, shaming them, into investing in Australian science, beginning his onslaught with 'Australia's done a hell of a lot for you. What have you done for Australia?' Once, when he was visiting London, I took him to lunch. He had needed to visit a dentist and he showed me a cheque for £400 – a tidy sum then – which the dentist had given him.

Eventually, he raised $130 million, enabling him to establish a Nuclear Research Foundation, import a giant computer – the first in Australia – and build radio telescopes and other advanced devices which induced distinguished British scientists to join him. He even established an environmental group for the study of Australian crocodiles.

His personal sacrifice was to reduce his sleep to five hours, arguing, 'When you are asleep you might as well be dead.' However, I usually managed to encourage him to take a little more on the occasions when he stayed with us at Lowerhouse Farm on his many travels, greatly impressing my children, who remember him vividly.

Concentrating on the young, the indefatigable Messel established international science schools and wrote textbooks. When he retired from Sydney in 1987, aged sixty-five, he became chancellor of Bond University on Queensland's Gold Coast and in 2006 was awarded his country's highest honour – the Order of Australia. In April 2013 my daughter, Pat, who was visiting Australia, called at the Messels' home and found both Harry and his wife to be in good shape.

I am proud to have known this dynamo, now ninety-two, who is still trout fishing, a sport we shared, and we still keep in touch.

CHAPTER 26

MOMENTOUS LUNCHES

For extracting secret information from prime sources there was nothing so productive as a long, relaxed lunch in a fine restaurant. My favourite venue was the Ecu de France in London's Jermyn Street as it was equidistant between Fleet Street and the Whitehall–Westminster complex, where most of my sources were based. More importantly, against one wall it had a long row of red, double banquette seats where, it seemed, two people could talk in absolute privacy. For more than twenty-five years, several times a week, my guests there included defence chiefs, senior civil servants, intelligence officers, ministers and captains of industry, who usually rewarded me with some newsworthy indiscretion.

In June 1964, when the Tories were in office, I gave lunch to the Navy Minister, Lord Jellicoe, and it was soon clear that he had come prepared to give me a major scoop for my newspaper.

He told me that, after all the years of animosity between Britain and Spain's Fascist dictator, General Franco, a historic arms deal had just been concluded with the Spanish government. Spain was to build several frigates of British design under licence from the Defence Ministry, paying royalties for the privilege. Spain would also be buying most of the equipment to be fitted in the ships from British firms, thereby creating hundreds of jobs in many areas – always good news for any government.

The initial order would be worth £14 million but follow-on orders worth £100 million or more – a huge sum in those days – seemed highly likely. As George pointed out, 'Buying a warship from another country is like a marriage – you are stuck with it for years.' During that time it seemed likely that relations between Britain and

Spain would become closer through the technical contacts, and the rebuilding of the Spanish fleet would increase Spain's qualifications for membership of NATO.

Jellicoe was particularly pleased that he had managed to preserve total secrecy about the deal for many months because he knew that if Labour MPs and their extremist supporters heard of it they would try to scupper it, so great was their hatred of Franco, who, whatever his faults, had saved Spain from becoming another Communist state operating under Soviet influence – a European Cuba. I was, therefore, urged to make sure that the contract had been signed before making it public and I agreed to check with the navy press office that the deal was absolutely firm.

I was in no doubt about Jellicoe's purposes. He wanted his ministry to get the credit for the deal, with himself and his close colleagues bathing in the political glory. He also needed to take the sting out of the parliamentary row with Labour, which was inevitable. That was a common reason for political leaks to me. If the deal had been announced first in Parliament, the uproar from the Labour benches, especially from firebrands like Michael Foot and the many Labour MPs who were really Communists, would have been tremendous.

I duly telephoned the navy press officer, who consulted the office log book where a confidential entry enabled him to confirm officially that the order was firm. I then visited the press office to make absolutely certain that it was safe for me to proceed and was assured that was so.

The following day my story covered most of the front page of the *Daily Express* under the headline: 'British ships deal. Frigates for Franco earn £14 million – and row looms.' Harold Wilson, Foot and others tabled a motion calculated to end the contract and Labour's general reaction was so insulting to Spain that Franco cancelled the deal, which, contrary to what I had been told, had not been finally signed.

The Defence Minister, Peter Thorneycroft, eased my conscience by telling Parliament that I was not to blame because I had gone through all the right proceedings. However, it is a scoop I still regret.

For Jellicoe, Thorneycroft and the nation I had, on that occasion, been dangerous to know.

The lunchtime leak which caused the greatest upheaval was given to me for the most trivial reason and, I think, the most reprehensible. In 1953, Sir Archibald Rowlands, the highly respected Permanent Secretary of the Ministry of Supply, which dealt with all manner of weapons including atomic bombs, retired and, while at lunch with him, I asked if he could remember any area where I might profitably dig, to which he replied, mysteriously, 'Ask the Ministry of Supply about Nomination.' Realising that it was a codeword I had never encountered, I questioned the Supply Ministry's public relations chief, who, after prolonged inquiry, assured me that the name was unknown. Other evasive responses convinced me that there was a cover-up so I eventually produced a small report about a secret committee called Nomination which appeared to arouse no interest. In fact, my inquiry had caused such a response that I was subjected to surveillance to discover the source. Rowlands's successor, Sir James Helmore, then called me in to say, 'I must tell you that whoever gave you that information is a traitor and it is your duty to give us his name.' After declining to oblige, I assured him that the source could not possibly be a traitor and that, had the ministry been honest with me, instead of burying its head in the sand, I would never have mentioned Nomination.

Years later, when giving a lecture to selected officers on the war course at Greenwich, I was seated at lunch next to Professor R. V. Jones, whose wartime intelligence adventures have been recorded in his classic *Most Secret War*. 'However did you find out about Nomination?' he asked. 'It was more secret than the atomic bomb itself.' As Rowlands had died, I enlightened him. Jones then explained that it had been an MI6–CIA group set up to exchange intelligence about Russia's atomic activities and, on the day after my report appeared, was about to hold a meeting in Washington. The American reaction to the leak had been fierce, especially in my direction.

What had Rowlands's motive been? All that we could suggest

was that he wanted to cause grief to his successor, Helmore, with, perhaps, a dash of vanity thrown in.

After that lunch Reg Jones became a friend and, over many years, my salmon-fishing guest in Scotland, where he was a professor in Aberdeen, still with access to secrets.

I owe so much to lunches that maybe I should have changed my name by deed poll to Chapman Luncher.

Being such a regular customer at the Ecu, I became friendly with the restaurant's senior director, a delightful Spaniard called Rafael Calzada who had become a patriotic Briton. Sometime after the Ecu closed down in the 1990s (it is now a shop) Calzada asked me to lunch at his club, so that he could offload something on his conscience. He told me that, early in the Second World War, MI5 had approached him for permission to bug the table-talk of senior foreign diplomats of neutral countries, many of them being Ecu habitués, as some of them might not really be as friendly as they seemed. As Britain's plight was so precarious, he felt he could not refuse, so, in the dead of night, microphones were installed in the backs of all the banquette seats and were linked to a room on an upper floor where an MI5 officer could sit, listen and make notes (tape-recorders were not then available).

After the war's end, Calzada expected that the bugs would be removed but MI5 pressed for their continuation because of the Cold War and its atomic aspects. Intelligence officers of the Soviet Union and its satellites, like Poland and Czechoslovakia – all posing as diplomats – were also using the restaurant and their table-talk could be revealing. Again, under pressure of patriotism, Calzada gave way. The microphones were upgraded and tape-recorders installed in the upstairs room. They stayed there until the Ecu closed down, having functioned during the whole of my tenure of a banquette seat, for which Calzada profusely apologised.

Calzada told me that MI5 chiefs valued the information supplied by the bugs so highly that they had tried hard to induce him to keep the Ecu going, even offering money from its slush-fund, but without success. When they sent in technicians to remove the bugs and wires before anyone discovered them they were shocked to find that the seats had also been bugged by the KGB! An MI5 inquiry showed that an Ecu employee with Communist leanings had probably allowed in Russian technicians at night.

While I was wondering how to expose this personally appalling disclosure, Calzada telephoned me in some panic to say he would be in deep trouble with his old MI5 friends if the bugging was revealed in his lifetime. Foolishly, he had told them of his confession to me and they were horrified. He died a couple of years later, relieving me of my restriction, and I immediately put the situation on record in *The Spectator*.

Since then I have spent much time wondering whether any of my sources suffered as a result of their leaks to me though most of them were far too senior to be admonished without causing a scandal. The situation had certainly made me potentially dangerous to know for any of my talkative guests.

Fortunately, while MI5 wanted to know everything for its files, it rarely took any action against a culprit because to do so might reveal the source of their information, which, regarding my Ecu guests, was a hidden microphone. So long as the information was in the files that seemed to be all that mattered to MI5.

I am certain of only one Ecu guest against whom MI5 took any action – my old friend the bibulous politician George Brown, who I knew had been quickly identified as my informant about the secret crimes of the KGB spy George Blake.

With hindsight, I should have realised that my table-talk was bugged because Brown had told me that he had been called in by Harold Wilson, who had asked him to stop seeing me. When he had declined, Wilson had said, 'We have full accounts of all your conversations with Chapman Pincher, you know.' Both Brown and I assumed he was talking about telephone conversations as I knew my phone was bugged.

In the secrets world one lives and learns.

Sometimes my guests preferred another lunch location and I always obliged them. George Wigg, for example, enjoyed the Hunting Lodge in Lower Regent Street and we had many productive meetings there. (Whether he had been tipped off about the bugged seats at the Ecu I will never know.)

Wigg had joined the army in 1919 and so enjoyed the disciplined life that he stayed there until 1937, rising to sergeant major. He had rejoined in 1939, serving in the Army Education Corps as an officer and rising to the rank of colonel. In 1945 he became MP for Dudley in the unexpected popular swing to Labour which ousted the war-winning Winston Churchill. At heart, he still remained a soldier. 'Ring me at Reveille!' he would tell me, meaning 6 a.m.

In Parliament he specialised in army matters, building up a private intelligence service to discover issues he could raise. He cultivated me as a source and we traded information which sometimes provided revelations for my newspaper. Often, during our lunches, he would declare, 'I think I'll have a bet!' and leave the table to telephone some bookmaker.

Another characteristic was the sadistic pleasure he derived from creating and pursuing grudges. He cut me off several times, sometimes for months, after I had published items attacking Labour defence policies. Then my phone would ring, with George explaining, 'I enjoy inflicting wounds but I don't like to see them fester.'

After his political victory in the Profumo affair and Harold Wilson's accession to power in 1964, they both feared that the Tory opposition would seek some kind of revenge. So Wilson put Wigg in charge of counter-measures as his security adviser, in the sinecure post of Paymaster General, with a new, unique relationship with MI5. The director general of MI5, Sir Roger Hollis, was called to No. 10 to be told by Wilson that he must give Wigg regular access and supply him with advance information about any incipient scandal affecting Labour ministers.

On Wilson's accession to No. 10, he had set up what became known as his 'kitchen Cabinet' of cronies. Wigg was a member with direct access to Wilson through a locked door into No. 10 to which he had a key, once taking me into the Cabinet Room by that route. He became known to other ministers as 'Harold's Rasputin', his many machinations being called 'Wiggery Pokery'.

Another major member of the kitchen Cabinet was Wilson's

political secretary, Marcia Williams, who had served him for many years. Initially, Wigg admired Marcia but they quarrelled after he told Wilson that she had access to too many secrets without proper clearance. Marcia, who I came to know quite well, is said to have responded by putting her large handbag under Wigg's nose and declaring, 'Secrets! I have enough secrets in here to bring the government down!'

Wigg became enraptured by the atmosphere of secrecy and conspiracy in MI5 and any criticism I made of that incompetent machine was dismissed with, 'Bollicks, mate, bollicks!' It quickly became apparent that what Wilson had really done was to place an MI5 spy inside No. 10.

In 1967, 35-year-old Marcia, having fallen in love with the Fleet Street political journalist the late Walter Terry, decided to have two children by him quickly. She understood that Terry would be divorced by his wife and marry her. When her pregnancies became obvious, the No. 10 staff attempted to conceal them in devious ways which led to Fleet Street speculation that the Prime Minister had fathered them. This sparked searches for the birth certificates, copies of which are available to anybody at the Records Office, but nobody found them because Marcia had registered her two sons under deliberately confusing names.

Eventually, during a lunch at the Hunting Lodge, Wigg triumphantly presented me with copies of both certificates, which had been found by his researcher. Having no intention of writing about them myself, I gave them to my editor, then Ian McColl, to put in his safe against the day when they might be useful.

A few days later, I chanced to board a bus with John Junor, the editor of the *Sunday Express*, and, for something to talk about, told him about the birth certificates. Next day – a Thursday – I was summoned to lunch with McColl, who told me that Junor had walked into his office and declared that, unless McColl printed the story about the birth certificates within the next two days, he would do so on the following Sunday. McColl had decided that he could not be scooped that way, so the *Daily Express* would run it. Further, as I had been responsible for bringing the certificates in, I would have to write it.

I was horrified because, by then, Walter Terry had joined the *Daily Express* as political correspondent and I would be seen to be shopping a colleague. I reminded McColl that our chief, Sir Max Aitken, had recently instructed both of us to reduce our attacks on Wilson and his entourage.

McColl countered my warning by saying that Sir Max was airborne on a long journey and could not be contacted and the story had to be printed that night to beat Junor's threat. So, on our return to the office, I wrote the story so clearly intended to lead the front page, accompanied by pictures of the certificates, while McColl called Terry in to warn him of his fate. Terry immediately alerted No. 10, where there was consternation.

At 6.30 that evening, the office lawyer, Andrew Edwards, and I were in the editor's room when there was a telephone call. It was Arnold Goodman, Wilson's lawyer, who had managed to contact Sir Max and urged McColl to get himself to Goodman's office. On his return Edwards and I were told that the story would not be printed that night, nor would it appear in the *Sunday Express*. We were greatly relieved. It never appeared in either paper.

I made my peace with Marcia and I visited her home where we decided to co-author a book of political revelations, even securing a contract with my publisher, Sidgwick and Jackson. Sadly, for history, Marcia never got around to producing anything.

I would eventually become friendly with Goodman, and found him amusing company. He asked me to lunch at his modest country home near Oxford where the only other guest was the Countess of Avon, widow of the former Prime Minister Anthony Eden. The event reminded me of a previous lunch I had enjoyed with her and her husband in what I have always called the Garden of Eden.

Eden, Britain's most handsome Prime Minister, had escaped my journalistic attention because of the Fleet Street convention that premiers and foreign secretaries (as Eden had been) were the rightful preserves of the political and diplomatic reporters respectively. As the defence reporter I did not poach on their territory any more than they did on mine (though if I felt I had been attacked unjustly I was prepared to fight back!). Nor did I happen to meet him socially through game-shooting or salmon fishing as I did with many other politicians.

So it was not until the 1970s that we met – in Barbados. Lord Avon, as he had become in 1961 after retiring from politics in 1957, owned a beautiful old plantation house on that sunny Caribbean island. As I have recorded, my wife and I had the regular privilege of holidaying in another plantation house belonging to Janet Kidd. So it was inevitable in that relaxed and hospitable climate that Janet would introduce us to Lord Avon and his wife, Clarissa, and that, one day we should lunch together. He had lost none of his famous charm and I found him in a talkative and reminiscent mood as we ate and drank at his home in the sunshine.

He recalled that in 1953 his health had been shattered by a disaster during what was normally a routine operation for the removal of stones from his gall bladder. The surgeon had sliced through his bile duct, requiring a repair involving the insertion of a metal tube to rejoin the duct. What the unfortunate patient always referred to as 'my old tin tube' occasionally leaked, causing a debilitating fever with temperatures up to 106 degrees F, but, happily it was behaving itself during our meeting.

Inevitably, I switched the conversation to his dealings with MI5 and MI6 and his reaction was vitriolic. 'Anything to do with spies almost always reveals a cock-up which rubs off on the political leadership,' he said. 'So, I kept clear of the security and intelligence people as much as I could.' His brow then darkened as he added, 'But there was one horrible occasion when I had to approach them and they disobeyed my orders so blatantly that I should have sacked the lot of them.'

He was referring to his very sensible move, late in 1955, to reduce the dangerous tension between Britain and the Soviet Union by inviting the Russian leaders Khrushchev and Bulganin to pay a goodwill visit to the UK, which had been accepted.

The Soviet delegation decided to arrive in April 1956 in some style on the latest Russian cruiser, the *Ordzhonikidze*, which was known to have some secret advantages, especially concerning its screws. Immediately, naval intelligence wanted to examine the screws surreptitiously when the ship would be moored in Portsmouth Harbour while MI5 wanted to bug the private talk of the Russian leaders. Eden responded with a firm order banning any illicit activities as they might imperil the talks.

My host bridled as he recalled how his political initiative had been ruined by a branch of MI6 which had secretly hired a free-lance frogman, Commander Lionel Crabb, to examine the cruiser surreptitiously. The frogman had been spotted in Portsmouth Harbour by the Russians before he accidentally drowned and the whole operation caused a public scandal which ruined the initiative.

Eden had then fired the head of MI6 but told me that he should have sacked several others who were involved in other breaches of his order, MI5 having bugged the conversations of the Russian leaders while they were staying in London at Claridge's Hotel.

The senior KGB security men aboard the cruiser had been fore-warned by a British traitor of the frogman's mission at least two weeks in advance of their arrival in Portsmouth. Very few people knew of the venture and it seems likely that one of them was the traitor.

More recently, I have learned from an impeccable Russian source who had been involved in the operation that the KGB even knew the frogman's full name. Still fewer people knew that because Crabb was generally known as 'Buster'. One of them was the MI5 chief, Sir Roger Hollis.

One lunch which I was hoping might prove to be momentous was at an especially beautiful private house in Berkshire owned by an unusual friend, Gerald Benney, then Britain's foremost living silversmith, who had, literally, made his mark as a result of a clumsy accident. While working on a piece of silver in 1963, he picked up a hammer with a head that had been damaged. To his annoyance, he found that his blows had made some striations on the metal but then realised that he had stumbled on a new way of decorating silver. By continuing the hammer blows, he found that the striations ran together beautifully producing a textured surface offering an unusual alternative to smooth finish.

The finish had wide appeal among customers and collectors, including Benney's other lunch guest, Edward Heath, our former

Prime Minister, whom I had never questioned though I had been introduced to him at parties staged by mutual friends. I had known all I needed to about him through my friendship with his parliamentary private secretary, Sir Timothy Kitson, MP for my beloved Richmond in Yorkshire, with whom I occasionally shot grouse and met regularly on a parliamentary committee which he chaired and on which I served as an adviser.

It was a hot day and Heath had arrived in a white linen suit and white shoes. I did my best to push the ball of conversation around but, apart from confirming that he was writing his memoirs, he had nothing of interest to say. We had witnessed his musical skill as a conductor at the Newbury Music Festival and knew of his expertise as a yachtsman but, basically, he seemed to be a dull loner. As my wife, who was also present, observed on our way home it was evident why he had always remained single – he simply had no interest in women. There was nothing 'gay' about him.

I recall one lunch encounter which was momentous in the literal sense as it lasted only a moment. I had been invited to White's, the exclusive old club in St James's Street, and was in a small queue lining up at a table to help ourselves from some cold food. I recognised the man in front of me as Sir Norman Brook, the Cabinet Secretary, who had motivated many of the leak inquiries into my exposures. As I introduced myself, he instinctively grasped my outstretched hand then, without a word, dropped it with a pained look of horror.

CHAPTER 27

THE NOVELIST

I have already recorded how in 1965 my interest in the study of the ageing process, gerontology, induced me to write my first novel, *Not with a Bang*. Not having an agent, I negotiated a publishing contract with my friend George Weidenfeld, of Weidenfeld & Nicolson, and he made a success of it, securing publication in the US and Germany and later in paperback. The book was serialised in the *Daily Express*, bringing both author and publisher some instant return, and there were good reviews in magazines though most newspapers were disinclined to praise the work of a journalist in such ruthless daily competition with them.

The experience whetted my appetite for fiction and I decided to watch for topical areas of my knowledge which I could exploit for more novels. So, two years later, I produced *The Giantkiller*, a story of two outstanding men – one a psychiatrist, the other a trade-union leader – who set out on well-meaning crusades to benefit society but pursue them so ruthlessly that the conflict can be ended only by the destruction of one of them. On rereading it recently, I was pleasantly surprised by its originality and the quality of the dialogue, as the build-up of personalities through their dialogue is so essential in fiction. However, it was not a big seller.

In 1970, I tried my hand at an espionage thriller based on the extraordinary situation called Mutually Assured Destruction (MAD) in which, to maintain peace, the UK and the Soviet Union were deploying nuclear submarines armed with long-range missiles fitted with H-bomb warheads capable of destroying each other's major cities. To ensure accuracy I managed to induce some senior Whitehall officials and service chiefs to vet the text.

I called the book *The Penthouse Conspirators* as it was essentially an intelligence battle between opposing secret service chiefs housed in penthouses on top of their headquarters in London and Moscow. It was serialised in the *Sunday Express* with great publicity and enthu- siastically reviewed.

Eventually the MI6 chief Maurice Oldfield asked me, 'How the hell did you hear that there had been a project to install me in a penthouse on top of the MI6 headquarters? It was top secret.' In fact, I had invented the entire concept.

A British film-producer took out a year's option on the film rights but, as with several of my later novels, the option lapsed without further action.

In the early 1970s I was in Rome to cover a conference and was invited to lunch by the British ambassador at his splendid resi- dence, the Villa Wolkonsky, near the ancient Porta Maggiore. The Renaissance-style villa had been built by the rich Russian Princess Wolkonsky in 1840 but it was the eleven-acre garden that was really impressive. The garden's high north wall had been a section of an ancient aqueduct where, at one point, some previous resident had cemented in an arm from an old marble statue, which looked rather macabre.

Over lunch, the ambassador told me that in July 1954 a skeleton had been found by labourers repairing the wall near where the arm protruded and it had proved to be not ancient Roman, as first thought, because the teeth had gold fillings. During the Second World War, the villa had been the Nazi Gestapo headquarters and it was feared that the skeleton might have been a victim of some atrocity. This possibility had created a politically difficult situation as it could be exploited by those opposed to the entry of West Germany into NATO, which was under serious international consideration.

The more I thought about the facts the stronger became my urge to use the situation as the foundation of a novel – inevitably called *The Skeleton at the Villa Wolkonsky*, which I published in 1975. It was well reviewed, being described by the *Liverpool Daily Post* as 'a rattling good thriller' and by the *Oxford Mail* as 'a beautifully constructed labyrinth'.

The current concern that Islamic terrorists might gain access to an atomic weapon and explode it in a British city recalls an incident around 1973 when, for a short while, there was a terrific scare in Whitehall that several British nuclear weapons had fallen into the hands of the IRA. The circumstances which had made this possible were so ludicrous that those responsible went to extraordinary lengths to conceal them. However, the facts were eventually told to me, over a good lunch, by the late Victor Macklen, the Defence Ministry's atomic expert.

In 1967, when the navy took over responsibility for the nation's nuclear deterrent by replacing the RAF's airborne bombs with Polaris missiles carried in submarines, the Sea Lords decided that atomic warheads were just another weapon and should be treated that way. It had long been standard practice for the navy to use its auxiliary service of little ships for transporting munitions in harbours and around coasts. Using a vessel classed more as a merchant ship than a warship meant that, in the event of mechanical trouble or bad weather, it could seek refuge in a civil port. So the Admiralty decided to continue that practice for the nuclear warheads of their Polaris missiles, carried in submarines based at Faslane, in Scotland.

In those days, the fuses and trigger-mechanisms of the warheads needed to be checked regularly and that could be done only at the Royal Ordnance Factory at Burghfield near Reading. So, for several years, little unarmed ships brought nuclear warheads from Faslane to Portsmouth, whence they were taken to Burghfield, and then ferried the refurbished weapons back to Faslane without incident. Then, one dark and dirty night, a small ship called *The Throsk*, carrying refurbished warheads from Portsmouth to Faslane, went missing in the Irish Sea, having failed to report by radio. Because Cardigan Bay was in regular use as a missile-firing range, *The Throsk* had to travel close to the Irish coast. Further, it had permission to seek shelter in Irish ports. Suddenly, there were real fears in the Admiralty that the ship might have been hijacked by the IRA with appalling possible consequences.

A destroyer was dispatched to find *The Throsk*, did so and discovered that the trouble had been a breakdown of radio equipment.

There was enormous relief all round but the Sea Lords, whose decisions were not to be questioned, decided to continue the practice until the chief scientist at the Defence Ministry found out about it and insisted on a change for safety reasons. Since then, nuclear weapons have been transported by air or by road under heavy guard.

By the time I learned the story it was too old to be told in a newspaper so I used it as the basis for a nuclear hijack in a novel I published in 1976, called *The Eye of the Tornado*. It was serialised in the *Sunday Express*, was well reviewed, went into paperback and caused a considerable row in Parliament, which is always good for sales.

At the book launch staged by the publisher, then Michael Joseph, I met the retired naval officer who, after consulting superiors, recommended which books should be supplied to the libraries aboard naval ships. I asked him what his superiors had said about *The Eye of the Tornado*, to which his answer was 'Watch it!' meaning that it was not to be recommended. The naval chiefs had no intention of letting their sailors know what idiots they had been.

During my many visits to the entrancing city of Venice, I had, literally, spent hundreds of happy hours poring over its inexhaustible treasures of which the four ancient bronze horses in the alcove on the façade of St Mark's Basilica provided the greatest fascination because of their extraordinary history.

The proudly stepping stallions, each six feet high with one hoof raised, mouth half opened, nostrils flaring, were once part of a quadriga – a chariot driven by four horses, the driver having probably been Apollo. They are the remains of the last surviving quadriga of antiquity – about 2,300 years old. How they became separated from the chariot and what happened to them after that involved me – and my wife – in much travel.

My research told me that they were probably made for Alexander the Great around 330 BC, the original sculptor perhaps having been being the great Lysippus. The quadriga had, certainly, been mounted in front of a building in Corinth, then the most beautiful city in Greece and Alexander's administrative centre for the country he had conquered.

In 146 BC the Roman general Lucius Mummius, who had 'liberated' Greece, shipped the quadriga to Rome where it was gilded, signs of the gilt still remaining on the horses. Around AD 60, as an Oxford historian assured me, the Emperor Nero set them atop an immense triumphal arch built close by the most sacred location in Rome – the Temple of Jupiter on the Capitoline Hill, which had shocked the Senate. The new driver was a figure of Nero himself.

After Nero was deposed and had killed himself in AD 68, his arch was demolished, the quadriga was dismantled and the chariot and its driver melted down. About 250 years later, the Emperor Constantine took the horses with him to Constantinople, his new capital (previously Byzantium), where he set them up – a pair on each of two towers in his new chariot-racing Hippodrome. There they stayed for 900 years when what was supposed to be the Fourth Crusade stopped at Constantinople in 1203 and sacked it. The Venetian contingent, led by the old Doge, Enrico Dandolo, took the horses as part of his spoils.

Eventually, in Venice, they were hoisted into their alcove – the Loggia dei Cavalli – on the front of St Mark's Basilica where they stayed for nearly 500 years until Napoleon conquered Italy and Venice. In 1797 he shipped the horses to Paris where they were set up, attached to a new but empty chariot, on another triumphal arch – the Arc du Carrousel on the Champs Elysées. After Napoleon's fall the horses were returned to Venice in 1815 and reinstalled exactly as before. What a history, crying out to be told in a novel! Even the title was ready made: *The Four Horses*.

To give the book topicality, I invented a couple of opening chapters in which Palestinian terrorists had occupied the horses' alcove and threatened to destroy them unless various demands were agreed to by Israel. There were also four final chapters in which the situation was ingeniously resolved by Mossad. The book was published in 1978.

Sadly, my invention proved to have been a bad mistake. The Italians and lovers of Venice generally resented the whole terrorist concept and the book did not sell.

Happily, in 1978 I had published a very successful documentary book, *Inside Story*, about the 'pursuit of power', as I had witnessed it among politicians, civil servants, forces chiefs, ambassadors and secret servicemen. It had been published by Sidgwick & Jackson, a thriving company bought by Charles Forte to help out the former owner, who needed to sell it. Charles suggested that I should switch to S & J and, having met the dynamic managing director, William Armstrong, and the chairman, the delightfully eccentric Lord (Frank) Longford (father of Lady Antonia Fraser), I was happy to do so.

In 1980, as *Inside Story* had sold so well, being serialised in the *Daily Express* and being well reviewed, S & J published my next novel, *Dirty Tricks*, which was a serious account based on real cases of the deception techniques used by intelligence and counter-intelligence agencies. It went into paperback and was bought by an American publisher.

For many years I had been a lunch customer at London's Café Royal near Piccadilly and had become fascinated by its history when the Domino Room (later, the Brasserie) had been the haunt of Oscar Wilde and his cronies like Lord Alfred Douglas, writers like D. H. Lawrence and Max Beerbohm, painters such as Whistler and Augustus John, rogues like Horatio Bottomley and personalities like Frank Harris, Lillie Langtry and a host of other eccentrics. It seemed to be an ideal setting for a novel and eventually I developed the idea of having a regular attendee who, through increasing deafness which had afflicted him at an early age, had learned to lip-read. That way he had compiled a massive collection of written notes of remarks and conversation which I had, allegedly, acquired on his demise.

So, in 1982, after much research, I presented his account under the title *The Private World of St John Terrapin*. I had wanted to call it *Right Royal Days*, which I thought would have wider appeal, but the publisher prevailed. It involved a massive amount of work and though Charles Forte launched it with a big party at the Café Royal, it did not sell well. Maybe the concept was too far fetched.

For the next seven years I was to be totally involved in real-life documentary books as, at ninety-nine, I still am. Not until 1989 did I have the time to produce another novel, which I called *Contamination* and was described as 'a state of the art thriller about the intelligence war as it was still being fought between East and West' immediately prior to the collapse of the Soviet Union. It was really a way of projecting a lot of super-secret information I had acquired over the years without falling foul of the Official Secrets Acts.

By then, my name was heavily publicised because of my documentary books about real-life spies. The attention lasted several years and *Contamination* – my ninth and last novel – did quite well.

Looking back, I had clearly lacked the 'golden touch' possessed by some novelists, like my friend Robert Harris, whose home is separated from mine only by the village's small churchyard. Every book he produces is not only a bestseller but is usually made into a film which, as he puts it, is 'where the megabucks are'.

Perhaps some lack of judgement also lay behind my strange encounter with another phenomenally successful author.

Round about 4.30 p.m. used to be a particularly busy time for a Fleet Street journalist, as I then was, because I would be trying to complete the news story or feature that I was writing for the following morning's paper. The editors and sub-editors who 'put the paper to bed', as the saying was, came in at 6 p.m. and wanted to start looking at the morrow's material as quickly as possible and I always tried to oblige them.

So, I was not best pleased when around 4.30 on a sunny afternoon in 1968, the phone of my excellent secretary Yolande rang and she told me that a Mr Forsyth had presented himself in the front hall, unsolicited, to see me as he had an article which, he thought, would interest me and which the newspaper might like to buy. As I knew no Forsyths but was very aware that the editor expected his own staff to fill the paper and was averse to spending money on outside contributors – there was a permanent economy drive at the *Daily Express* – I asked Yolande to go down and politely get rid of the caller. Instead, being a kind soul, she returned with him and three cups of tea.

Stuck with this slim, rather pale stranger, at least until we finished the tea, I quickly disposed of his offer because the story was definitely not of the kind we published and I advised him to try further up the street at the *Daily Telegraph*. I then asked him about his background and he explained that he was thirty-one and had been a foreign correspondent for the Reuters news agency, working in France and other countries, and then for the BBC, but had left and was working as a freelance. I grimaced, knowing how tough life was for a freelance in such a ruthlessly competitive place as Fleet Street, and felt some sympathy for him.

He then told me that he was writing a novel, to which I responded by saying, 'Oh, I write novels! What's yours about?' He told me that it was about the attempted assassination of General de Gaulle.

As the French leader had been dead, from natural causes, for nearly three years, I did not think much of the idea and when Forsyth had gone, I said to Yolande, 'Poor sod! That novel's bound to fail. In fact, I doubt that he will find a publisher.'

Yes, you have guessed correctly. It was Frederick Forsyth and the novel was *The Day of the Jackal*, which was a justifiably stunning, worldwide success making the author a millionaire. He has since repeated his triumph with many more bestsellers. My judgement could not have been more at fault but he had not told me the title – which would have impressed me – and, in fact, several publishers did reject the book.

Eventually, Freddie and I became good friends and we have often joked about that first encounter, his letters always being amusing and on the ball.

In similar circumstances I encountered another 'character' who would also become famous. One sunny afternoon a stranger wearing white trousers and a white shirt breezed into my office unannounced, sat himself in the armchair and said, rather grandly, 'I'm Christopher Hitchens. I'd like you to introduce me to some of your contacts.'

As I had only vaguely heard of him and being astonished by such a ludicrous request, I quickly convinced him that he was wasting my time and his and I never saw him again. Eventually, he moved to the US where he became well known as a speaker and writer on religion and other contentious subjects, sadly dying in 2011, aged only sixty-two.

In saying farewell to my life as a novelist I have an odd confession to make – when looking through the copies of my nine novels to write this chapter, I could not remember a single name of the scores of characters I had created. Maybe that says a lot!

CHAPTER 28

TWO TELEPHONE CALLS

I was due to retire from the *Daily Express* on my sixty-fifth birth-day – 29 March 1979 – and, soon after I had passed sixty, had firmly decided to do so. Sales of the paper had been falling and the financial situation was precarious because Beaverbrook, in his will, had left the company too little money, instead lavishing it on Canadian charities. Also, it seemed clear that with the rapidly expanding inroads by television into both advertising and news presentation, the golden age of newspapers was reaching its end.

In pursuit of new readers, the *Express* policy was to take it down-market, concentrating on trivia so that it had less interest in what I regarded as serious news. To this end, Max Aitken had brought in the former magazine owner Jocelyn Stevens (later Sir) to assist him. Stevens and I had met several times, socially, in the shooting field and I disliked him.

In 1974, they hired a new editor, Alastair Burnet, the TV broad-caster and editor of *The Economist*, who brought in TV cronies such as George Ffitch, who became the features editor. In eighteen months their hapless policies reduced the readership by a further 340,000 and, realising he was a failure, Burnet quit.

I have always been short in financial acumen and have hated haggling about money, with the result that I had been seriously underpaid considering my contributions in so many fields over the years. Journalism was unique in that it was quickly possible to assess an individual's output by looking at his cuttings, which were all kept in boxes in the office library, and mine were more voluminous than anyone else's. So, as my pension would be based on my last year's salary, it was clear that I would have to continue to work after leaving Fleet Street, which, being a workaholic, I would have been driven to do anyway. Then in 1973, out of the blue, my life-long run of luck was to ease my problem.

I received a telephone call from Vere Harmsworth (later Lord Rothermere), the owner of the *Daily Mail*, who I had met socially, inviting me to lunch at his home. It had long been understood between the *Express* and the *Mail* that, in their joint interests, they would not poach each other's staff. So I was surprised when he offered me more than twice my salary to move to the *Mail*. He also indicated that I would not be obliged to retire at sixty-five.

Recently, the government had, temporarily, imposed a national freeze on wage increases so Vere told me he was confident that Max Aitken would be unable to retaliate by offering me more. He then made a psychological blunder by making it clear that his main motive was to take revenge on the *Express* for poaching the *Mail*'s most prominent woman journalist, Jean Rook, who was being heavily promoted in the *Express* as 'the First Lady of Fleet Street'. I did not take kindly to being used as a pawn in anybody's vendetta but, as the increase would also more than double my pension, I could not ignore the offer. I told Vere that I was interested and would need a couple of days to consider it, to which he agreed.

I went to see Max and Stevens, told them the circumstances, including the Rook aspect, and Max asked me to give them a couple of days to consider the position. They then offered me an even bigger package, getting round the wage-freeze problem by promoting me to chief defence correspondent of Beaverbrook Newspapers, which in essence I had already been, and putting me on the management board.

Not wishing to move so late in my career and being a personal friend of Max, I accepted his offer though I felt sure that his, and Stevens's, main motive had not been to retain me but to thwart Harmsworth.

When I telephoned Vere to tell him my decision he was furious about the phoney way the 'freeze' had been circumvented and said that if I would change my mind he would also give me 'a piece of the action', whatever that might have meant. I was not tempted.

I soon found that the meetings of the management board under Stevens were a waste of my time. Further, they were held on a Wednesday, which happened to be the day when Harry Hyams held his shoots at Ramsbury Manor. So, before the shooting season started, I resigned from the board and each day that I lined up with Graham Hill, the racing driver, and others with news to impart, I knew that I had made the right choice.

The way that my continuing luck was to take me in quite a different and more stimulating direction would prove that I had made the right decision to retire in 1979.

On the sunny afternoon of 4 September 1980, shortly after we had moved to the village of Kintbury in West Berkshire, I received another unexpected telephone call from Lord (Victor) Rothschild, to whom I had been introduced by my fishing friend the second Lord (Marcus) Sieff. He told me that an overseas acquaintance, who was visiting him at his home in Cambridge, wanted to meet me. So, he offered to send a chauffeured car to take me there for dinner and to spend the night.

Rothschild, who had served in MI5 during the war, was a brilliant man but was introverted, deviously disinclined to give a straight answer to any question and prepared to lie, even about trivial things, if it suited him – but, out of curiosity, I accepted the invitation. The consequences were to engage the attention of the media for years and lead to major changes in regulations governing official secrets – and they still rumble on.

When I arrived at his home, Rothschild explained that the visitor, whom he called 'Philip', was a retired member of MI5 domiciled in Australia. He showed me a slip of paper bearing the names of many alleged spies and asked me if I would be interested in talking to his friend about them. I certainly was, especially as Sir Roger Hollis, the former director general of MI5, was one of them. I was already interested in Hollis because five months previously the Tory MP Jonathan Aitken had told me of the official suspicions about him which he had been researching. In a conversation with the CIA intelligence officer James Angleton, Aitken had been made aware that within MI5 itself Hollis, who had retired in 1965 and had died in 1973, had become deeply suspected of being a Soviet agent. Aitken then received more detailed information from Arthur Martin, a former MI5 officer who had been involved in the official inquiries into Hollis's behaviour.

So, early in 1980, he had written to the then Prime Minister, Margaret Thatcher, to warn her of the situation, which might become public. Having received a reply stating that she was already aware of the allegations, Aitken had shown his letter to me.

The visitor, who told me that his real name was Peter Wright, was a frail-looking, white-haired man in his sixties leaning on a stick. I had never met or heard of him before. He explained that he had become so concerned about the Soviet penetration of MI5 and the way it had been covered up that he had begun a book about it but, after completing only ten short chapters, could not proceed through illness. He also stressed that he urgently needed £5,000 to prevent the bankruptcy of a small Arab horse stud farm he had started on his retirement in Tasmania. On leaving MI5 in January 1976, his pension was only £2,000 a year as he had joined the service rather late in life and achieved only modest rank. He therefore suggested that I should write the book, for which he would supply the information, on some profit-sharing basis.

As nobody from MI5 had ever told its secrets before – except to the Russians – I provisionally agreed but only on condition that I would never be responsible for paying any money to him. That could have laid me open to a charge of bribery. So, I insisted that he would have to be paid directly by the publisher, if I could find one. To my astonishment, Rothschild volunteered to set up a banking arrangement so that Wright's identity could be kept secret from the publisher and from everyone else.

At Rothschild's, Wright was prepared only to whet my appetite for his revelations, stating that to receive his information and take notes, which would take at least two weeks, I would need to visit his home in Tasmania, where he and his wife had moved to be near their married daughter. He assured me that though he would be breaking the Official Secrets Act and the individual pledge to secrecy he had signed on his retirement, he could not be prosecuted in Australia nor extradited from there on that account.

I realised that by acquiring so many top secrets, as Wright had promised, I would be putting myself into a possibly dangerous situation but my policy has always been to get the information first and then worry about using it. So, in October 1980, I duly arrived in Cygnet, the pleasant Tasmanian village in which Wright lived. While staying in a small hotel, I was shocked to find that Wright and his wife Lois were living in a shack. Though he was taking many pills for a blood disorder, there was no sign of the walking stick and it soon seemed that he had been exaggerating his infirmity during our meeting in Cambridge, perhaps to stress his difficulties in finishing his book himself.

In a small extension of the shack, I spent nine days taking notes as Wright talked, thereby becoming the first journalist ever to be taken into the confidence of an MI5 officer prepared to tell everything he knew. The breadth of his knowledge was exceptional because as MI5's only man with a scientific background he had been involved in an unusually large number of cases.

Wright showed me nine of the ten short chapters he had written. The missing one had dealt with Rothschild's career in MI5 and contained embarrassing details about his private life and that of Lady Rothschild, Tess, which he had discovered mainly when interrogating the MI5 traitor Anthony Blunt, who had long been an intimate friend of both Rothschilds. At Rothschild's request, Wright had undertaken to omit the damaging chapter and tell me nothing about it. There was disappointingly little meat in the other nine chapters, from which I had to make notes because Wright would not let me take away anything that might be traceable to him. There was nothing about the Hollis case as he had not reached that far in his narrative. He had to tell me all the details, which I noted down. The most startling among these was the extent of the suspicion inside MI5 that Hollis had been a Soviet spy. The suspicion had arisen mainly because so many MI5 activities against Soviet espionage had failed that it seemed that the Russians had some internal MI5 source who was regularly warning them. Though the wartime treachery of Anthony Blunt had already been exposed, he could not be the culprit because he had left MI5 in 1945.

Wright told me how Hollis, shortly before his retirement, had learned that he was the chief suspect and had joked about it. He also told me how Hollis had been recalled from retirement to be interrogated for two days during 1969 when he repeatedly claimed poor memory for the answers to awkward questions – just as the MI6 spy Philby had done.

Wright then revealed that in 1974 a former MI6 officer called Stephen de Mowbray, who had been involved in the Hollis inquiries, went to see the Cabinet Secretary, Sir John Hunt, who was so impressed by his allegations that he set up a further inquiry to be carried out by his predecessor, Lord Trend. Over a year, Trend reviewed the previous inquiries, questioning witnesses including Wright. Neither Wright nor any other of the witnesses were allowed to see the final Trend Report, which, in 2014, is still classified as top secret, allegedly for security reasons. Wright believed – wrongly as it transpired – that Trend had concluded that the case against Hollis was firmly based.

In the course of our talks, Wright told me that MI5 had a paid informer inside every Fleet Street newspaper. When I asked him why MI5 had never tried to recruit me, he replied, 'We considered it but decided that you would be uncontrollable.' He was dead right.

I arrived home on 24 October and started work on the book immediately, having already decided on its title – *Their Trade is Treachery*, which was the title of an insider MI5 booklet written for government officials to warn them of the wiles of the KGB. The 'authorities' had gone to great lengths to prevent me from publishing parts of it when I had secured a copy, some years previously, so it would be satisfying to use their title and publish a more entertaining version.

Meanwhile, I had made a provisional publishing deal with William Armstrong, the managing director of my publisher, Sidgwick & Jackson, and secured a rapid payment of £5,000 for my unnamed collaborator.

I wrote the book in less than four months and delivered the typescript to the publisher's office on 13 January 1981 when I recall discussing its possibilities with the delightfully eccentric Lord (Frank) Longford, who was a director of the company.

The finished book exposed many astonishing secrets of which the most sensitive was the fact that Sir Roger Hollis had been seriously suspected by some of his own officers of being a GRU agent throughout his twenty-seven years of service and had been recalled from retirement to be interrogated.

In that connection, the book presented previously unknown evidence of the existence of an important GRU spy inside MI5 operating under the codename Elli. As the next chapter will describe in detail, Wright revealed that there was strong evidence for suspecting that Hollis was Elli.

Armstrong had the courage to accept the Official Secrets Act risk but insisted on vetting by a lawyer for libel danger and, as a result, various names had to be omitted from the hardcover edition, which saddened me. One of them was Michael Straight, an American who had been recruited by the KGB while at Cambridge in the 1930s and had eventually been responsible, in 1963, for revealing that the art historian Sir Anthony Blunt had spied actively for the KGB during the war years when he had worked in MI5. I was allowed to refer to him only as 'a middle-aged American belonging to a rich and famous family'.

Another was an Englishman called Leo Long, who had knowingly assisted Anthony Blunt over several years. A third was Jack Jones, of the Transport and General Workers' Union, who was described in the book only as 'one major union leader of recent times who was under regular surveillance by MI5 and was seen in contact with Soviet intelligence men'. My book also stated that 'defectors have named him as a KGB agent'. The culpability of Jones, including evidence that he had taken small sums of KGB money, was put on official record in 2009 in *The Authorized History of MI5*, six months after he had died.

Armstrong decided that, because the book would cause a political sensation, he would have to discuss it with Sidgwick & Jackson's owner, Sir Charles Forte, who numbered among his friends leading politicians, including Margaret Thatcher. Perturbed by the security, legal and political implications, Sir Charles decided that he needed confidential advice before agreeing to publication.

So, as he happened to be a golfing friend of Sir Arthur ('Dickie') Franks, the then chief of MI6, he showed him a synopsis which I had produced for him. Neither I, nor Armstrong, knew that he had done so. Later, when explaining his action to me, he said, 'You are a dear friend of mine but my country comes before my friends.' It was a sentiment with which I fully agreed.

Sir Arthur alerted senior colleagues in MI6 and MI5 but without mentioning his source, as he had promised never to do. He then told Sir Charles that he could not offer a worthwhile view without seeing the full text. Before supplying it, Sir Charles had secured a firm undertaking that neither I nor the publisher would be at risk if any objection was taken to it. He had also secured a solemn agreement that nobody else should know how and from whom Franks had received the typescript. Because the secret service was involved, Sir Charles felt that he could not tell either William Armstrong or me what had happened.

Copies of my script were quickly made and distributed to MI5 and the Cabinet Office. Wherever it was read it caused consternation, especially concerning the suspicions about Hollis, which had international implications, particularly regarding the United States.

The crucial advice on action or inaction about the book was finally left to the legal advisers of MI5, who agreed that there was no point in seeking any specific deletions or other changes in the text because every page offended the Official Secrets Acts. They then decided – in agreement with the Treasury solicitor – that it was not in the interests of MI5 or MI6 that the book should be restrained in any way because, if I fought the decision in court, they would have to make too many damaging admissions!

Margaret Thatcher, the Home Secretary and the Cabinet Secretary, Sir Robert Armstrong, all wanted the book suppressed but felt constrained to agree with the MI5 legal advice, while being fully aware that the book, which Sir Robert later publicly described as 'a bombshell', would cause a furore.

The whole scenario was like a tale told by an idiot because the decision was to lose the government an eventual costly court case against Wright in Australia and lead to the publication of his own even more damaging book, *Spycatcher*, in 1987, in a blaze of adverse publicity. Clearly neither Mrs Thatcher, nor anyone else, had been told that all that was needed to stop the book was a telephone call to Sir Charles Forte. Instead, he was told that the book could safely be published without deletions. With a clear conscience, he instructed Sidgwick & Jackson to press ahead.

Many people have asserted that the 'authorities' simply decided to take the opportunity to dispose of all the skeletons in MI5's closet because other investigators were on their trail. The true reasoning behind the government's decision is almost farcical and is a prime example of what excessive secrecy can engender.

The book was cleared because the MI5 legal advisers did not, themselves, know the name of the person who had supplied the script. They had been told that the source had been assured that it would never be revealed to anyone under any circumstances. They assumed that an injunction would be needed to restrain the book, that I and the publisher would fight it and that, in the process, legal argument might require the supplier of the text to be exposed. At that stage, even Sir Robert Armstrong was told by an MI5 official that the script had been obtained 'on conditions which made it impossible to take any action about it'.

When Lady (Val) Hollis disappeared from her cottage at Catcott, Somerset, on the eve of the book's newspaper serialisation in March 1981, it became clear to me that the security authorities already had wind of its contents. MI5 had organised her removal to a 'safe house' for an indefinite period so that she would not be troubled by reporters pursuing the revelations about her late husband. The next event was a deception operation by Sir Robert Armstrong (now Lord).

On the Monday that the *Daily Mail* began to serialise *Their Trade is Treachery*, four days before its appearance on the bookstalls, William Armstrong was telephoned by Sir Robert, who said that he urgently needed a copy of the book because the Prime Minister would be required to make a statement to Parliament about it. My advice to William was to supply a copy only if Sir Robert would give a written guarantee that the government would not prevent its publication. To our delight, he agreed to do so, immediately sending a letter by hand.

Later, in 1986, during the *Spycatcher* trial in Australia, Sir Robert was to admit that the letter was a deception to cover the government's possession of the script and, while denying that it was a lie, he made the comment, which was to haunt him, that he had been 'economical with the truth'. All he had needed to do, had he been better advised, was to tell the court that he had needed the book because it might have been different from the script as a result of possible redrafting by me. That would, in fact, have been correct because of the omissions demanded by the publisher's lawyer.

Since then Sir Robert and I have joked about the way I inadvertently saddled him with the doubtful achievement of having introduced a new one-liner into the language. To that extent I had been dangerous to know. He has forgiven me and we are on the best of terms.

Their Trade is Treachery was a number one bestseller and was described by critics like Malcolm Muggeridge as a 'watershed book' breaching the barriers of excessive secrecy for the first time. The book made headlines round the world and was reprinted successively, in hardback and paperback, until 1988, each issue being updated as new information came my way. The reviews and other media responses were so numerous, so varied and continued for so long that they filled five thick cuttings books. Having reread them for this biography I cannot recall any documentary book that produced such a massive and ongoing reaction.

One unpleasant result, as I have already described, was pressure from backbench Labour MPs for the prosecution of Rothschild and me under the Official Secrets Act, which, for both of us, eventually resulted in visits from Scotland Yard's Serious Crime Squad. That did not worry me unduly because I was fit and quite enjoyed the experience but for Rothschild it really was serious as he was suffering from a severe arterial disease and took the ordeal badly.

Sometime after Victor Rothschild had died in 1990, I encountered his son and heir, Jacob, who I already knew and admired. He was talking to the artist Lucien Freud, to whom he introduced me, then asked, 'Why did my father introduce you to Peter Wright?'

In all honesty, I replied, 'I have no idea.' Since then, I have become convinced that Wright's omitted chapter, divulging damaging details of Tess Rothschild's long relationship with Anthony Blunt, played its part. I suspect that Wright had told Rothschild that he intended to publish the details and that, in return for an introduction to someone who would write the book for him, had agreed to omit them – behaviour not far short of blackmail.

What is certain is that after Wright left the Rothschilds' house following his introduction to me, neither Victor nor Tess ever communicated with him again. Much later, I had reason to mention Wright to Tess in a telephone conversation. Her bitter response was brief: 'Fuck him.' (With both Rothschilds, the F-word was never far away, the intellectual Victor having the foulest mouth of anyone I have ever met.)

Once the hardback version of *Their Trade is Treachery* had been published, a *Daily Mail* reporter working in the US was sent to confront Michael Straight, who admitted his folly, eventually recording it in detail in a book, *After Long Silence*. Straight and I became friends and met together several times in London when, after my own experience of Communist recruiters at university, I was able to appreciate his behaviour. As a result, I was permitted to name Straight in the paperback version of *Their Trade is Treachery*, which appeared in 1982. Straight died in 2004.

Leo Long was, also, eventually questioned by journalists and freely admitted his past treachery and close association with Blunt.

CHAPTER 29

THE ELLI RIDDLE

On 5 September 1945, Lieutenant Igor Gouzenko, a 26-year-old Red Army cipher clerk, left his office in the Soviet embassy in Ottawa and changed the history of the world. After two years in Canada, with its freedom, high living standards and open society, Gouzenko and his wife Svetlana had hated the thought of their imminent return to Moscow, where Igor faced severe disciplinary action for some minor lapse of duty. He therefore defected with 109 secret telegrams hidden in his clothing and a mass of startling information in his head.

Gouzenko was a member not of the KGB, the widely known and much-feared Soviet intelligence and security service, but of the GRU, which specialised in military intelligence. His indisputable evidence soon convinced the Canadian, British and American security authorities that the Soviet Union was waging seriously menacing espionage and subversion against its trusting wartime allies in anticipation of an eventual military showdown between Communism and capitalism.

The shock in Ottawa, Washington and London was so intense that if historians need to fix one day when both sides consciously became embroiled in what came to be called the Cold War between East and West, which was to affect the whole world for forty-five years, then 5 September 1945 is probably it.

A memorial plaque erected by the Canadian government to Gouzenko's memory in 2004 states: 'The Gouzenko Affair brought the realities of the emerging Cold War to the attention of the Canadian public.' It also brought it to the public attention of the rest of the world.

Gouzenko exposed more than twenty Canadians who appeared to be working as agents for the GRU, which had taken over the Canadian Communist Party and was using it as an intelligence tool. He also named a British scientist, Alan Nunn May, who was working on the allied atomic bomb project in Canada and had supplied the GRU with details of the first atomic bomb test in America, along with samples of uranium explosive, and other information. This was the first proof that the Russians had been actively trying to penetrate western atomic secrets and it caused particular concern as both the US and Great Britain were hoping that their atomic monopoly would last substantially longer than it eventually did.

Before he had defected, Gouzenko had told his wife that if he were to be captured by his Russian colleagues she was to tell the Canadian police of the existence of a GRU spy inside the British security agency, MI5. The codename of that 'mole' was Elli. Recently, a crucial Russian document provided by the former KGB officer Alexander Vassiliev has confirmed that a GRU agent codenamed Elli definitely existed and worked inside British intelligence.

Because there was so much British interest, MI5 decided to send an officer to Ottawa to learn all that he could and report back to London HQ. The chosen officer, heavily recommended by Kim Philby, a Soviet spy inside MI6, was Roger Hollis, who was told everything that Gouzenko had revealed to the security specialists of the Royal Canadian Mounted Police (RCMP), who had interrogated him. That included the claim of the existence of Elli. Being so involved with leads to so many Canadian Soviet agents, the RCMP left the British Elli lead entirely to Hollis, who did not manage to meet and question Gouzenko personally until 21 November 1945.

Sitting with Peter Wright in Tasmania in 1980, I learned all the information about Elli that Hollis had gleaned and reported on his return. As Gouzenko confirmed to me, years later in several long telephone conversations and in letters, he had eventually learned six details about Elli, who had to be British born to be an MI5 officer at that time.

First, in spite of the feminine sound of his codename in English, Elli was male.

Second, the GRU centre in Moscow, where Gouzenko previously worked, had rated Elli so highly that to protect his identity personal contacts with him were forbidden unless absolutely necessary and, only then, with the centre's express permission. His couriers should communicate with him through *duboks* – hiding places where messages could be left or collected, also called 'dead-letter boxes' or 'dead-drops'.

Third, Elli's information was usually sent in code to the centre in Moscow by the military attaché in the Soviet embassy in London, who was always a GRU officer. So Elli had a courier who collected his written information and had direct access to the embassy and took it there, or gave it to someone who did so.

Fourth, Elli was in a position to consult and to remove those MI5 files that dealt with Russians suspected of involvement in espionage in London. In late 1942, when Gouzenko had first heard about Elli, all those files were located in the MI5 registry at Blenheim Palace near Oxford, where most of the agency had been evacuated to escape the London bombing. It would, therefore, seem likely that Elli was based in Blenheim and his GRU courier, who picked up his information, lived nearby.

Fifth, some of Elli's messages were so important that they were passed to Stalin by the GRU chief, who had direct contact with the Soviet dictator.

Sixth, there was 'something Russian' in Elli's background. (Later, Gouzenko's wife consulted her husband's records and told me that his desk-mate had said as much.) As Gouzenko himself told me, he could not understand, particularly in view of this exceptional feature, why British security had failed to detect Elli without delay on hearing that evidence.

During the period Gouzenko had mentioned, the only member of MI5 who had regular access to the relevant files about Russian intelligence officers in the course of his duties was the officer in charge of Soviet counter-espionage, Roger Hollis, then based at Blenheim Palace. He became embroiled in the Gouzenko case in

ways that should have aroused suspicion at the time but did not
do so until a team of counter-intelligence officers began to investigate the possibility of Soviet penetration of MI5 in the 1960s and
1970s. Clearly, if the man in charge of countering Soviet agents had
been one himself, the mystery of how they had been so stunningly
successful for so long would be resolved.

The possibility was horrific because Hollis remained in MI5 for
twenty-seven years, heading it for nine. As head he would have
been privy to almost every important state secret, including details
of preparations for war. As a key member of the Joint Intelligence
Committee (JIC) he would have been crucially poised to warn the
Kremlin of any Anglo-American pre-emptive nuclear strike or
assist in any attempted Russian attack. (The JIC is not only a regular recipient of intelligence but gives advice to the government on
any action which needs to be taken.)

Wright told me that the MI5 investigators made strenuous efforts
to find 'something Russian' in Hollis's background so that they could
confront him with it. In spite of all their research and resources, the
best these professionals could do was to discover that he had visited
Moscow in 1934, when travelling to China by the Trans-Siberian
Railway. Then, in 1985, while browsing through a book called *Along
the Road to Frome*, one of several written by Hollis's elder brother
Christopher, I made a most relevant discovery. Members of the
Hollis family believed, with genealogical evidence, that they were
directly descended from the Russian Czar Peter the Great, and were
rather proud of it! In that book, published in 1958, Christopher had
stated, 'I did, indeed, I suppose, share with my distant and much
removed cousin, Annie Moberley, a claim to descent from Peter the
Great.' In another of his books, *Oxford in the Twenties*, when explaining his rather peculiar looks, Christopher stated that he was 'the
inheritor of a good deal of mixed blood, but it came from Eastern
Europe'.

Annie Moberley's father, George, had been born in St Petersburg,
where his forebears were well established as merchants before the
revolution. He became Bishop of Salisbury and firmly believed
in his descent from the heroic Czar. The Hollis brothers' mother,

formerly Margaret ('Meg') Church, was related to Richard Church, a Dean of St Paul's, in London, whose wife was a direct descendant of a woman called Sarah Cayley who, allegedly, derived from an illegitimate son of Peter the Great. The Moberleys also traced their connection with the Czar through Sarah Cayley. What better fit could there be for Gouzenko's statement – 'he has something Russian in his background'?

Christopher Hollis, who was highly intelligent, writing several books and becoming an MP, seemed to believe in the royal relationship, however distant. Whether or not it was real or taken seriously by other members of the Hollis family, they all knew about it. So, if Roger had been Elli, he could have revealed this Russian connection to some Soviet contact, who would have informed Moscow in one of the enciphered messages, which would explain how Gouzenko had heard about it while he had been based in the Soviet capital.

That information was, of course, not available when I was writing *Their Trade is Treachery* but I did include the other facts about Elli, which Wright had given me, pointing out that Hollis was the best fit for it all. Further, all the evidence concerning Hollis suggests that, if he was ever recruited by the Russians, it was by the GRU, not the KGB.

Among the mass of documents covering the Gouzenko case that MI5 has released, there are few references to Elli. There are enough to prove that MI5 made some inquiries into Gouzenko's allegation but there are none concerning Hollis's eventual interview with Gouzenko or MI5's internal efforts to discover Elli's identity. In its 1997–98 report, the Parliamentary Intelligence and Security Committee revealed that there had been massive 'weeding' of MI5's files prior to 1970 and then again after 1992, reducing the holding by 50 per cent. It also stated that the 'vast majority of the files destroyed had to do with subversion'. In 2011, in a published statement entitled 'Retention and Destruction of Files', MI5 admitted the destruction of 200,000 files since the collapse of the Soviet Union, many of them concerned with the recruitment of spies. Why these had not simply been passed to the National Archives was not explained. After more than sixty years, such documents could not conceivably threaten national security. They might, however, resurrect interest in the case against Hollis, which MI5 has conveniently dismissed as 'a myth'.

In late 2011, I renewed my efforts to wring some kind of official statement out of MI5 about Hollis's report on Gouzenko, being increasingly suspicious that it had been deliberately destroyed because it would reveal that Hollis had faked it to discredit Gouzenko as a witness. Intent on resolving the Elli riddle, I wrote to MI5 asking whether Hollis's report on Gouzenko still existed. I, and others, including some academics who had also done so, received no response.

So I wrote to the Intelligence and Security Committee's chairman, Sir Malcolm Rifkind, asking for assistance in requiring MI5 to answer the question of whether Hollis's report on Gouzenko still existed in its archives. An official of the committee spoke to MI5 on my behalf without positive response. The official, therefore, suggested that I should complain about MI5's lack of action to the Investigatory Powers Tribunal, of which I had never heard.

It transpired that this tribunal, headed by a judge, had been quietly set up in 2000 under the Human Rights Act to consider complaints against a number of public authorities, which included MI5. For example, members of the public who suspect that they are under surveillance by MI5, such as having their phones tapped, can complain to the tribunal, which may then approach MI5 to establish the facts.

At my request, the tribunal took action and required MI5 to answer my question as to whether or not Hollis's report on Gouzenko had or had not been destroyed. In May 2012, I received a letter from MI5 stating:

> We note your enquiry as to the existence of a record of an interview of Igor Gouzenko conducted by former MI5 officer Roger Hollis in 1945. I am able to tell you that, despite an extensive search of the Service's records, we have been unable to locate such a document or any reference to one. We have concluded that it is likely that no record of the interview was ever made.

This response was repeated in July 2012 in a further letter from MI5, on behalf of the director general, stating: 'Despite further research we have been unable to find evidence that Sir Roger wrote a report of any interview of Gouzenko in which he may have participated while in Ottawa.' The intended inference was that the report had not been destroyed. It had never existed.

The suggestion that Hollis, then quite junior, had been sent to question such a significant defector and had not been required to submit a written report about it on his return beggars belief. Fortunately, more positively, there are several lines of evidence proving that he did so.

In 1972, the MI5 director general, then Michael Hanley, decided that Gouzenko should be questioned again, this time concerning his recollection of his interrogation by Hollis on 21 November 1945. According to Gouzenko, in a statement to me and to several others who have recorded it in print, a British security officer, Patrick Stewart, came to see him by appointment at the Royal York Hotel in Toronto, the town in which Gouzenko was then living. Stewart needed to use a wheelchair (as a result of war wounds) but that did not stop him from travelling. Gouzenko remembered the date as being in the summer of 1972.

Gouzenko, who always feared assassination by the GRU, tried to induce the Toronto journalist Peter Worthington to be present with him but Worthington declined, being sure that the British officer would not permit it. Instead he agreed to interview Gouzenko immediately after the interview and did so, a fact which I rechecked with him in 2013. Both Gouzenko and his wife Svetlana, who was present, confirmed to me that this interview took place in a room at the Royal York Hotel. There is also contemporary witness evidence from several Canadian journalists (recorded in the book *Gouzenko – The Untold Story* by John Sawatsky, published in 1984).

The officer duly arrived and told Gouzenko that his purpose was to read to him a report about his first debriefing by MI5 in 1945 which, allegedly, Hollis had submitted, and to secure his reaction to it. Later Gouzenko told Worthington and several other journalists that he had been astonished to see that the report consisted of several closely typed pages when Hollis had spent so short a time with him. Gouzenko declared the report to be false on several counts, being worded so as to discredit his value as a witness by creating the impression that he was so unreliable that his evidence could be ignored. Gouzenko recalled that Hollis had spent only a few minutes with him and had approached him in a crouching position as though trying to shield his face.

Later, Gouzenko told me that 'I could not understand how Hollis had written so much when he had asked me so little. The report was full of nonsense and lies. As Stewart read the report to me, it became clear that it had been faked to destroy my credibility so that my information about the spy in MI5 called Elli could be ignored. I suspect that Hollis was Elli.'

This evidence was personally confirmed to me again in 2012 by Worthington, who had spoken at length to Gouzenko immediately before and after the interview in 1972. It could explain why MI5 has never released Hollis's report and now claims that it has never existed. Its official publication would undermine the MI5 stance that the whole case against Hollis is 'a myth'.

For good measure, Peter Wright told me that not only had he read Hollis's long report but he had also seen Stewart's account of his 1972 meeting with Gouzenko in Toronto – indeed, in his book *Spycatcher*, Wright recorded that he and another MI5 officer called Anne Last had seen Gouzenko's debriefing by Hollis.

If Stewart's copy of Hollis's original report of his meeting with Gouzenko no longer exists in MI5's records then it, too, has been destroyed.

An official MI5 explanation of the Elli riddle, which can only be described as fatuous, was put on record in 2009 with the publication of *The Authorized History of MI5*. The author, Christopher Andrew, claimed that Hollis could not have been the proven Soviet penetration agent codenamed Elli because that person was the proven KGB spy called Leo Long. The concept had emerged in conversations between Andrew and a KGB defector, Oleg Gordievsky, who, in scouring his memory, claimed that while serving in Moscow he had seen the KGB file on Long, who, as Andrew states, had always been a KGB sub-agent of Anthony Blunt, a proven KGB spy. Gordievsky said that the codename Elli 'appears in large letters on the cover of Long's operational file' in the KGB records.

This convenient recollection proved to be nonsense when Long's file was examined by the former KGB officer Oleg Tsarev, who told me that he found no trace of the name Elli on the cover or anywhere else, Long's true codename being Ralph. On 21 November 2008, Tsarev was questioned about Long by Dr Svetlana Chervonnaya at his Moscow home and confirmed that he had consulted Long's file several times when working on a book and that the only pseudonym in the file was Ralph.

But the theory that Long was Elli was recently finally destroyed by the papers of Alexander Vassiliev (now on the internet), which contain a copy of a personal message from the Commissar of State Security, General V. Merkulov, to Stalin on 24 November 1945. In the message, Merkulov refers to the 'GRU agent inside British intelligence codenamed Elli' and confirms that Gouzenko had betrayed the existence of Elli, who was a GRU (Military Intelligence) spy operating entirely separately from the KGB. Long was, after all, a spy for the KGB – not the GRU.

CHAPTER 30

SMOKING GUN

When discussing the Hollis case with me, by letter, former head of MI5 and MI6 Sir Dick White told me that he did not entirely dismiss the possibility that the man he had eased into MI5, Sir Roger Hollis, could have been a Soviet agent during his twenty-seven years of service. He stressed, however, that it was most unlikely because, during such a long period, he would inevitably have been seen meeting a Soviet contact. In fact, in 1990, I encountered a person who had witnessed exactly such an event at close quarters several times. Further, I was able to research his evidence to such a degree that I have no doubt about its truth, especially as part of it turned out to be a large and most unusual item of Soviet espionage equipment which eventually came into my possession.

During Christmas 1990, when the Soviet Union was in its death throes, I received a card from Michael J. Butt, of whom I had never heard, urging me to contact him. Over twelve years, I met and talked with him, when he proved to be honest and accurate. Born in a working-class family, he had left school at fourteen and later joined the Communist Party. He had contacted me because, after the demolition of the Berlin Wall, he was so disillusioned at having been duped into supporting an evil system and recruiting others to it that he wanted to 'make some amends to society'.

In 1959, he had rented the front room in a house in Belsize Park Gardens, which belonged to a pre-war German–Jewish refugee widely known as 'Comrade Bridget', then the secretary of the Adelaide ward of the Hampstead branch of the Communist Party. She and her Communist husband, Jock Nicolson, a railwayman, lived at the rear of the property so, in return for a low rent, Butt agreed to be doorman on the evenings when many leading Communists called for meetings at the house. He enjoyed the chore, feeling that he was rubbing shoulders with the great.

My inquiries have confirmed that Bridget was none other than the former Brigitte Kuczynski, a proven Soviet agent and recruiter listed as such in MI5 and CIA accounts of Russian espionage. Butt told me that in the early 1960s Brigitte paid regular visits to the London branch of Moscow's Narodny Bank, which was used for espionage purposes. She was perfectly placed for receiving and delivering copies of stolen secret documents.

Who could be delivering them to her? Butt described to me a tallish, slim, clean-shaven and very hunched man who wore dark clothes and a large black hat on his rare evening visits when there would be no other callers. Butt recalled that whenever this man was due Brigitte would warn him that 'someone will be calling tonight', which required him to stay in and admit the unnamed visitor, who walked through to her rooms. The few words uttered by the mystery man revealed that he was a cultured Englishman who was already well used to visiting the house.

Butt did not discover his identity, about which Brigitte was tight-lipped, until he found a copy of my book *Too Secret Too Long* in a public library, and saw photographs of Hollis. Butt was, then, absolutely certain that the caller had been Hollis, whom he described, in letters still in my archives, as 'very recognisable' as he had been face-to-face with him whenever the caller had removed his large black homburg hat – then a Whitehall badge of seniority – to enter the house. I could never shake Butt concerning his certainty that the mystery man had been Hollis. 'I *know* he was Hollis,' he assured me many times. 'I was this close to his face, several times,' he would say, putting his hand in front of his nose.

The allegation that the suspect MI5 chief had been in the habit of visiting a well-known Communist was intriguing but there was much more. Brigitte's elder sister, Ursula, another wartime refugee, was the notorious 'Sonia' who, when living in Oxford, had been the courier for the most damaging atomic spy, Klaus Fuchs, and other major Soviet agents before escaping to East Germany in 1950 after Fuchs's arrest.

Butt's disclosure was particularly exciting for me because a mass of evidence I had accumulated already indicated that, if Hollis was a long-term spy, he could have been serviced by Brigitte when he had been based in London before the Second World War and then have been passed to Sonia when MI5 had been evacuated to Blenheim Palace from 1941 to 1945. Sonia, who had been posted by the GRU (not the KGB) to the Oxford area (her lodgings were only three miles from Blenheim!) at just the relevant time, was necessary because she was a highly trained radio operator and could quickly encode and transmit any documents she received when making a journey to London to deliver them to the Soviet embassy might be possible because of the German bombing.

As soon as MI5 returned to London in 1945, Sonia moved away from the Oxford area and it seemed that Brigitte had then resumed her former service. If Hollis was Elli, the possibility that he had been serviced solely by these two sisters would explain why, in twenty-seven years, he had never been caught. If Brigitte had been servicing Hollis in London there could not have been a safer set-up. He had surprised his MI5 colleagues by his habit of working late in his Curzon Street office, often until 8 p.m., and, though he had a chauffeured car, usually walked home across Hyde Park. As there was no terrorist threat in those days, he did not have a bodyguard. So, whenever he may have needed to meet Brigitte to give her documents or a Minox camera film or to receive instructions, he could have telephoned her from a call-box knowing that her phone was not being tapped. He could then have taken a taxi to within easy walking distance of her house, also knowing that she was not under surveillance, as released MI5 documents have shown.

When no contact was necessary, he could have slipped an envelope containing documents or a Minox film of them through her letter-box. There was scant danger of his being recognised by anyone as there were no photographs of him and his name was unknown to the public, a fact covered by a D-notice.

Though several MI5 officers had suspected Brigitte and urged that she should be interrogated, Hollis had always found some excuse to avoid that, as MI5 records in the National Archives repeatedly show. He had even argued that it would be a waste of time because, being a committed Communist, she would never reveal anything!

Butt was willing to be questioned by MI5 but when I asked nobody there showed any interest.

I hoped that Butt could arrange for me to interview Brigitte, who in 1991 was well and active, but, though he approached her on my behalf, she declined to talk. So did Sonia, then living in East Berlin. Brigitte died, unquestioned by anybody, in 1997, aged eighty-seven.

On my last visit to Butt's house in Gloucester he went to his loft and returned with a compact case containing a Russian-made device. He told me that, early in 1961, Brigitte had given it to him in some degree of panic to get it out of the house and dispose of it at some refuse tip. It was precisely the time when newspapers were reporting the arrest of two Soviet agents, calling themselves Peter and Helen Kroger, who had been posing as antiquarian booksellers while running several important spies. Their guilt had been proved by the discovery of a Russian-made transmitter cleverly hidden in their home in Ruislip.

Butt had been so intrigued by the gadget, packed in its grey, 17" x 14" x 4" white-handled case, that he had kept it. Sadly he became gravely ill with cancer and I did not see him – or the gadget – again while he went through his tough treatment and brief remission. He died in 2002, aged sixty-five. In 2009, when I first published *Treachery*, which told Butt's story, I sent his widow a signed copy. In return she gave me the gadget, which had remained undisturbed in the loft as she had been unaware of its existence until I told her about it.

Stamped 'Made in the Soviet Union' in Russian, it is a 'portable enlarger-dark room', adapted to enlarge the tiny photographs taken by a Minox espionage camera used by spies for quickly copying secret documents without having to remove them. The Minox is so small – three and a half inches long, just over an inch wide and less than an inch thick – that it can disappear into a clenched fist. The substantial enlarger is so cleverly designed that its many parts fit neatly into the small case which can be quickly stowed away.

The gadget, which I will donate to King's College London so that researchers will be able to examine it, is solid evidence that Butt was a truthful witness and, as it stands assembled in my study in Kintbury, it gives me a frisson of excitement mixed with wonder whenever I look at it or show it to visitors. Is it a long-missing link in what is, perhaps, the most important spy case of all time? If only it could speak!

In *The Authorized History of MI5* Christopher Andrew dismissed the mass of evidence against Hollis as 'baseless allegations' concocted by 'conspiracy theorists' and pointed the finger elsewhere. Since then he has declined to discuss the issue when questioned at international conferences. Andrew was, however, very positive in his book in pointing out that, during his early career, Hollis had persistently urged the MI5 leadership to combat the intelligence assault by the Soviet Union with himself as the officer to command and control the effort, which needed to be expanded. That was intended to show Hollis's antipathy to Communism but it was, of course, precisely the argument successfully deployed inside MI6 by Kim Philby to ensure that he could wield his controlling influence in the KGB's interest, as he did with stunning success, as Andrew concedes.

In that connection, a little-known official history of the security service from 1908 to 1945, published by the Public Record Office in 1999, is highly significant. It revealed that Philby owed his position, which has been widely hailed as 'a masterstroke in the history of espionage', to the initiative of Hollis! In 1943, after Hollis had become friendly with Philby in line of duty, he suggested that MI6 should try to intercept radio transmissions between Moscow and British Communists. Hollis pointed out to his director general that MI5 would benefit because any intercepted messages would also be passed to him. The MI6 chief liked the idea and set up a new Section 9 to specialise in all aspects of international Communism and Soviet espionage. The KGB urged Philby to secure control of it, which he did, operating in the KGB's interest whenever he could.

So, whether by chance or by design, Hollis's initiative had proved highly beneficial to Soviet espionage.

Until the official history of the security service appeared, Hollis's supporters contended that he could not be held responsible for failing to detect Soviet spies such as Blunt and Philby as that had always been the exclusive responsibility of MI5's counter-espionage division ('B'). They claimed that Hollis had been responsible only for overseeing Communists and, as he had never headed a Soviet counter-espionage section, it was unlikely that he was a Soviet agent because a spy would have tried to insinuate himself into such a position. In fact, according to the official history, the main effort against Soviet espionage was switched in 1941 from B to a special new section (F2c) headed by Hollis, who remained in command of it throughout the war. With unconscious humour, that book describes Hollis as being 'in charge of Soviet espionage'.

During Hollis's time in that command, his MI5 colleague Anthony Blunt furnished the Russians with 1,771 secret documents, including plans for the D-Day landings, taking them out of the MI5 London office in a briefcase which he handed to a courier from the Soviet embassy where they were photographed in time for them all to be handed back to the traitor next morning!

The sordid deal by which Hollis, when director general, secured immunity from prosecution and publicity for (Sir) Anthony Blunt, concealing that he had been on MI5's staff when spying, is not described in *The Authorized History*. Hollis even involved the Queen, using the mystique then attached to his office to ensure that the spy not only kept his Buckingham Palace post as an art expert but also his knighthood. Perhaps the deal's worst feature was the legal consequence that the immunity automatically extended to Long and any other spies Blunt might identify, however serious their offences, because to expose them in court would inevitably expose Blunt.

In the last edition of my book *Treachery*, published in 2012, I summarised all the evidence against Hollis in the form of a 'Scroll' of fifty-six anomalies in his professional behaviour which were consistent with his having been a Soviet agent. The since-proven

Soviet agent Philby had been required to leave MI6 on the evidence of only three such anomalies.

The extent of these anomalies has so impressed an increasing number of academic historians specialising in the intelligence field, that they now consider the case against Hollis as so strong that it demands resolution. Fortunately, there are government departments, such as the Cabinet Office, over which MI5 has no control concerning its historical documents and a recent sheaf of Cabinet papers (PREM 8/1280) revealed behaviour by Hollis which, alone, should have raised deep suspicion.

The papers record that among the Canadian suspects who had been fingered by Gouzenko and his documents in 1945 was a Communist mathematician called Israel Halperin who, it was known, had befriended Klaus Fuchs when he was being held in a Canadian detention camp. The Royal Canadian Mounted Police (RCMP) had impounded Halperin's address book, which was made available to Hollis, in Ottawa, because he was being treated as a member of the investigative team into the Gouzenko affair and, especially, because it contained the names and addresses of five Britons, one of them being Fuchs, who five years later would be exposed as a major Soviet agent. (Despite MI5's lack of control, unsurprisingly, Hollis's name is deleted from the Cabinet Office file but his identity happens to be confirmed in *The Authorized History of MI5*.)

The name 'Klaus Fuchs' in the address book should have rung loud bells with Hollis because he had cleared Fuchs in 1943 for secret atomic work in the US as being 'politically inactive' and 'with no security objections' and with no mention of any Communist connections. Further, only three months earlier, he had been involved in clearing him for security after Fuchs had accepted a senior post at what would become Britain's first atomic research station at Harwell in Berkshire. Clearly, it was his urgent duty to report his find to MI5 headquarters in London so that the security section of the atomic authority could also be informed of what was an alarm bell. Instead, Hollis remained silent and MI5 HQ remained in ignorance of Halperin's address book evidence until 1949 when it was, embarrassingly, supplied by the American FBI.

The seriousness of Hollis's inaction is highlighted by the fact that the Halperin address book connection was to prove valuable in the FBI's discovery that Fuchs was a Soviet agent, as described by the FBI officer responsible, Robert Lamphere, in his book *The FBI –KGB War*. It is, therefore, difficult to believe that Hollis's breach of duty was just an understandable slip by an overworked officer, as would be argued by MI5, as PREM 8/1280 reveals.

In 1950, after the conviction of Fuchs, Hollis's breach was to cause disbelief and consternation in Canada, both in the RCMP and at the highest political levels, involving the British and Canadian Prime Ministers, when it was realised that Hollis had also failed to pass on the names of the other four Britons who, for all he knew, could have been Soviet agents.

As PREM 8/1280 discloses, Prime Minister Clement Attlee received a succession of messages from the Canadian government sent on behalf of the RCMP and the Foreign Minister, Lester Pearson, asking why the information supplied by the RCMP early in 1946 indicating that Fuchs was a Communist had been ignored by MI5. The embarrassing answer was that Hollis, who had received the information when visiting Ottawa, had failed to relay it to MI5 headquarters.

The MI5 leadership did what it could to excuse Hollis's behaviour and to suppress any inquiry into it. Nevertheless, the Canadian authorities remained angrily baffled by MI5's apparent incompetence in allowing Fuchs to impart atomic bomb secrets to Russia for a further four years when he should have been interrogated in 1946.

More revealing Cabinet Office papers may be released, including the report of the investigation into the Hollis affair by former Cabinet Secretary Lord Trend, which was completed in 1975.

This report, the existence of which was first revealed to me by Wright in 1980, has been held tightly secret and Christopher Andrew does not reveal its conclusions in his authorised history – if, indeed he ever saw them. However, two witnesses who did read it, Sir Michael Havers, when Attorney General, and Lord Chalfont, assured me that all Trend had been able to do regarding Hollis was to give him the benefit of the doubt. Andrew confirmed this in his book by revealing that after reading his personal copy of the Trend Report, Prime Minister Harold Wilson wrote on it, 'This is very disturbing stuff, even if concluding in "not proven verdicts".'

That disclosure ill accords with MI5's former website claim that 'the Trend Inquiry of 1974 cleared Hollis' and with the common belief that Hollis was cleared by Mrs Thatcher. It does, however, help to explain why, after nearly forty years, the Cabinet Office still declines to release the Trend Report as being 'not in the interest of national security'.

Its eventual release may become more likely following the death of Margaret Thatcher, who, as the next chapter will record in detail, gave an inaccurate account of the report to Parliament following publication of my book *Their Trade is Treachery*.

Everything that comes to light about Hollis's behaviour is consistent with his guilt – never with his innocence. The latest piece of my intelligence jigsaw is evidence, which I have checked with the source, that in 1984, when the Hollis case was being heavily publicised, a relative of Hollis admitted to a member of the Foreign Office that 'Roger's work for the Soviet Union was an open secret in the family'. (I have the witness's evidence in writing.)

Should the case against Hollis ever be proved beyond doubt he would rate, because of his nine-year control of MI5 and membership of the Joint Intelligence Committee, as the most important spy in all history. Though my investigations will continue, in legal terms I rest my case. The facts speak for themselves.

CHAPTER 31

MY THATCHER EXPERIENCE

In 1975, when Margaret Thatcher became leader of the Conservative Party, I made it my business to visit her. Our meeting went well and she encouraged me to deal with her directly, especially when I unearthed information that would embarrass the Labour Party, then in office.

In the following year I was lunching with the MI6 chief, Sir Maurice Oldfield, who asked me if I had access to Mrs Thatcher. When I told him that I did he gave me an important message to give to her. He had realised that she stood a good chance of winning the next general election and felt that, before she became Prime Minister, it would be good for the nation and good for her if she was regularly briefed on important secret intelligence issues. He asked me to let her know that he was prepared to brief her, regularly, himself, if she so wished.

I went to see her and her meticulous response was typical – she asked me to tell Sir Maurice that she welcomed his kind offer but only on condition that the Prime Minister, then James Callaghan, agreed to it. Callaghan, a much under-rated figure, did agree and Mrs Thatcher and Oldfield began regular meetings. (They became such good friends that in 1981 when Sir Maurice was in hospital with only a few days to live, she visited him to say farewell, as I did myself at his request.)

Eventually, I learned what had motivated Sir Maurice to make his offer. He had discovered that Mrs Thatcher was already being briefed on intelligence matters by a little group of retired MI6 officers and he did not like being usurped. Part of the deal was that she get rid of the group, which – as one of them (Nicholas Elliott) told me – she did. Nothing is ever quite what it seems in the secrets world.

The next personal connection I can recall was a sad one. Lord Beaverbrook's daughter, Janet Kidd, was a close friend of the former Prime Minister Sir Anthony Eden, as they both spent much of the year in Barbados. Early in 1977, Janet telephoned me to ask if I could approach Mrs Thatcher with a message. Lord Avon, as he was then, had told her that he had incurable cancer with little time to live and wished to talk to Margaret Thatcher, whom he had never met. For some reason, he felt that he could not make a direct approach and Janet had suggested that I could arrange it. I duly did so and Mrs Thatcher immediately responded by visiting Lord Avon's Wiltshire home. He died a few days later.

When Mrs Thatcher led the Tory Party to victory in 1979 and became Prime Minister I was delighted because I knew that one of her first actions would be to curb those power-driven trade union leaders whose excessive demands and actions had plunged the nation into a 'Winter of Discontent'.

On her entry into 10 Downing Street, one of the trade union leaders asked, on television, 'How can I have a dialogue with a woman like that?' Her answer was that the days of 'dialogues' inside No. 10, which Callaghan had encouraged, were over. Trade union leaders were told that in future they would deal with the minister responsible for their field of interest. After an eventual battle with the coal-miners led by Arthur Scargill, the power of the unions was effectively curbed by law and no Labour government has wanted to revert to the previous position.

I was to admire Mrs Thatcher's toughness in other directions and have several long and friendly letters from her. Sadly, my relationship with her was ruined for all time in 1981 – two years after she had become Prime Minister – by the publication of *Their Trade is Treachery*. The Hollis saga had been a skeleton in the reigning government's cupboard for years and Mrs Thatcher had been told the details in 1980 by the Tory MP Jonathan Aitken, who had been briefed by a retired MI5 officer. When I exposed it, she was required to deal with the consequences publicly by a most carefully worded statement to Parliament prepared for her by officials.

She had no alternative but to confirm the main newspaper headline stating that the late Sir Roger Hollis had been so deeply suspected of being a Soviet spy by his own MI5 officers that he had been recalled from retirement for tough interrogation. She then did her best to defuse the scandal by stating that, though his innocence could not be proved, neither could his guilt and that his innocence should, therefore, be assumed.

Mrs Thatcher then assured Parliament that my book was 'speculation and insinuations' when, in fact, an inquiry had been set up to discover my MI5 sources and had quickly identified Wright.

Her statement, which made no mention of the Elli evidence in my book, was worded to give the quite false impression that all the events I had described were very old and could be attributed to proven spies like Kim Philby and Anthony Blunt.

It did not reveal that, in May 1974, a government warning that Hollis may have been a Soviet agent had been given to the security chiefs of the US, Canada, Australia and New Zealand so that they could take remedial action against any damage he might have inflicted on them.

The whole statement was a deliberate concoction which has since been used, repeatedly, as the basis for claims that Mrs Thatcher 'cleared' Hollis, as MI5 has declared on its website.

After her hoped-for rubbishing of *Their Trade is Treachery*, Mrs Thatcher then announced the first independent inquiry for twenty years into the efficiency of the safeguards against further penetration of the secret services by foreign powers. Carried out by the standing Security Commission, the inquiry did not produce its thick report until May 1982 when the Prime Minister failed to fulfil her promise to publish it. Instead, a statement listed a large number of improvements, while indicating that there were others so secret that they could not be revealed to Parliament or anywhere else. I – and many others – thought it crazy that major changes affecting MI5, MI6 and GCHQ should have had to await the publication of a book by a freelance investigative writer which had been dismissed as 'speculation'.

Mrs Thatcher's attack on my reputation as an investigator could not have exerted much impact on Parliament because, in June 1982, its Defence Committee invited me to serve as a paid adviser to MPs investigating media aspects of the Falklands War. My efforts there were regarded as so effective that, later in 1982, the Defence Committee asked me to serve as an adviser on a parliamentary inquiry into positive vetting (the examination and questioning of all those with access to sector information). In each case, I received written commendation for my contribution from the committee's chairman, Sir Timothy Kitson. During the months of my service I had my own pass into the Palace of Westminster, which raised a few eyebrows among Labour MPs.

The *coup de grâce* to my relationship with Mrs Thatcher, which eliminated any chance of repairing it, was delivered, inadvertently, by our mutual friend Sir Maurice Oldfield. After Sir Maurice's death in 1981, I learned that he had, repeatedly, faked his annual positive vetting examination by denying that he was a practising homosexual, which would then have barred him from service in MI6. How this occurred is illuminating about the many ways in which secret information becomes public knowledge.

A year after Oldfield had retired as the MI6 chief in 1978 he had, at Mrs Thatcher's request, become coordinator of intelligence between the Royal Ulster Constabulary and the army in Northern Ireland. This made him a prime target for the IRA, which had previously attempted to assassinate him in 1975 with a bomb in a holdall slung on railings below his bachelor flat in Westminster. It had been spotted by an astute policeman and defused.

Soon there were rumours in Northern Ireland that he was an active homosexual and two authors mentioned it in a book they had submitted to the publishing company Sidgwick & Jackson. If true, the news was alarming because homosexuality, being a criminal offence in Scotland and Northern Ireland then, was banned for all intelligence and security staff as it made them open to blackmail by the KGB. When MI6 officers were vetted and routinely revetted, they were specifically asked if they were homosexual and Oldfield had always denied being so.

As Sidgwick & Jackson was also my publisher, I was asked to read the book and check on its accuracy. So I consulted Oldfield's successor at MI6, Sir Arthur (Dickie) Franks. Over lunch, he told me that he had investigated the rumours but had failed to prove them. I advised Sidgwick & Jackson to reject the book and it was never published.

Occasionally, Oldfield and I had lunched or dined together and sometimes met socially, so my wife Billee also knew him. As he was a confirmed bachelor, she and other women who knew him wondered about his private life and had decided that he was just a neuter. I had tended to agree.

As Oldfield was regularly in London and had retained his flat, he required protection there and the protection officers supplied by Scotland Yard became increasingly suspicious of men who visited the flat, some of whom proved to be homosexuals of the kind known as 'rough trade'. They interviewed the caretaker of the flats, whose suspicions had first been aroused when Oldfield had still been chief of MI6. He confirmed such visitors had been received and they were traced and proved to be male prostitutes. One of them looked so disreputable that he was known to the caretaker as 'the hobo'.

Eventually, the Metropolitan Police Commissioner, then Sir David McNee, felt it his duty to warn the Home Secretary, William Whitelaw, that Oldfield might be a security risk. Whitelaw informed the Attorney General, Sir Michael Havers, and Mrs Thatcher, who was deeply shocked.

After inquiries produced no evidence that he had been compromised, and as he had only three months to serve in Northern Ireland, he was confronted by Havers, when he confessed, admitting that he had lied at his vettings, and gave an undertaking not to misbehave while still in government employment. He was then allowed to finish his tour of duty there and to retire honourably, with his behaviour remaining secret.

Eventually he became seriously ill and died in 1981.

In 1984, when Sir David McNee and I were both guests of the

Forte family, he told me the whole story, which was confirmed to me by Havers. By that time, my wide reading of the literature on espionage showed that nobody had attempted a comprehensive study of the various reasons why some people are prepared to betray the land to which they owe loyalty. I had, therefore, taken on the task and when I mentioned it to Havers and McNee they both urged me to include the Oldfield story. I agreed that it would be professionally dishonest to exclude the Oldfield case just because he had been a friend. So, there was a brief mention which was taken up by the media when the book, called *Traitors: The Labyrinths of Treason*, appeared in 1987.

When the book was serialised by the *Mail on Sunday* my brief statement about Oldfield was widely disbelieved and ridiculed especially by his old colleagues, with attacks on my veracity. Sadly for them, Mrs Thatcher was required to confirm, in Parliament, that in March 1980 Oldfield had admitted that, from time to time, he had engaged in homosexual activities and that his positive vetting had been withdrawn because his behaviour had made him a security risk. The newspapers then featured the information on their front pages with lurid headlines, some of which, like 'Tinker, Tailor, Poofter, Spy', gave me cause for deep regret.

Among those of Oldfield's acquaintance then interviewed on television was Lord (David) Owen, who, as Foreign Secretary, had been responsible for MI6. He looked so shattered that I asked him to lunch at the Café Royal to find out why. Owen explained that, during his term at the Foreign Office, the resident security chief had reported that he had discovered that two male officials who had regular access to secret papers were practising homosexuals and had never declared it on their positive vetting forms. Though this meant that, under the existing rules, they should be dismissed, the security chief felt so certain of their loyalty that he recommended that they should simply be transferred to non-secret work. Owen tended to agree but felt that, for safety's sake, he should consult Sir Maurice Oldfield, who had then insisted on their dismissal for breaking the positive vetting rules!

While I continued to be in the company of Lady Thatcher, as

she became, at lunches, dinners and parties, mainly because of our mutual friendship with the wonderfully hospitable Sir Charles Forte and his family, all I ever received from her were silent, piercing looks and stony stares. It was sad, as I had always admired her and her 'Iron Lady' record, but it was understandable.

Following the massive publicity engendered by Lady Thatcher's death and magnificent funeral in 2013, Igor Gouzenko's daughter Evy told me that on the fiftieth anniversary of her father's defection – on 5 September 1995 – Lady Thatcher had kindly sent a letter to Evy's mother, Svetlana. It read:

> When you and your husband crossed over to freedom, you began the long process that led to the eventual collapse of the Soviet Union. His revelation helped the West face up to the reality of Communist subversion and tyranny. Those of us who later fought the battle for freedom to its climax in 1989 and 1991 were greatly in his debt – and in yours.

It was a splendid and most thoughtful tribute from a most admirable woman.

CHAPTER 32

A SPATE OF SPY BOOKS

For the active investigator, information spawns more information. So after my success with *Their Trade is Treachery*, which produced new sources, I was soon planning a more detailed sequel revealing the astonishing extent of the betrayals and the attempts by embarrassed officials to keep them covered from public scrutiny. I decided to call it *Too Secret Too Long*. Among many other disclosures, it would present the activities of the extraordinary GRU agent Sonia and her peculiar proximities to Hollis.

In the spring of 1983, Malcolm Wallop, a distinguished American senator who was a shooting friend of mine, suggested that I should prepare a book stressing the urgent need for independent parliamentary oversight, i.e. supervision, of the British secret services. He had spent several years on the US Senate Intelligence Committee and was convinced that oversight was essential to the efficiency of secret services which could, otherwise, conceal their failures.

I took his advice and ended each relevant chapter of *Too Secret Too Long* with 'The Potential Value of Oversight' – a note showing how the existence of parliamentary oversight could have prevented the security disasters described or, at least, have lessened their impact.

It was published in 1984 and was an immediate bestseller success, being serialised in the *Sunday Times*, reprinted and republished in the US and then marketed as an updated paperback. My cuttings book for that year shows it was well and widely reviewed over several months in both the UK and the US, being described as 'the most powerful and astonishing volume ever published about spies'. An updated paperback edition appeared later in 1984 and was reprinted.

I feel confident that *Their Trade is Treachery* and *Too Secret Too Long* contributed, eventually in 1992, to the 'Waldegrave Initiative on Open Government', resulting in the release of formerly secret files into the National Archives in 1993, and to the creation of the Parliamentary Intelligence and Security Committee (set up in 1994), now chaired by Sir Malcolm Rifkind, a former Foreign Secretary whom I have met and greatly admire.

In July 1984, Peter Wright had broken cover in Australia and appeared on a *World in Action* television programme in which he challenged Margaret Thatcher's 'clearance' of Sir Roger Hollis, claiming to be '99 per cent certain that Hollis was a spy'. Further, he had provided Whitehall officials with a 160-page document, *The Security of the United Kingdom against the Assault of the Russian Intelligence Service*, supplying first-hand evidence of the case against Hollis.

I had continued my contact with Wright through letters sent to an accommodation address, which he had given me, while his replies reached my step-daughter's house in a village near Kintbury. We had agreed to destroy each other's letters after noting the contents. I did so but the duplicitous Wright stored all mine and would eventually make them public. Some critics then accused me of 'pumping' Wright for secrets but that was what an investigative author needs to do and I make no apologies.

Early in 1983, however, Wright had ended our relationship by failing to answer my last letter to him. As I was to learn later, he had decided that there was no more money coming from my direction after the £31,827 he had received from our publisher and I never heard from him again.

He had already told me that he had been approached by a British television producer, called Paul Greengrass, about his appearance in a possible documentary about the Soviet penetration of MI5. The result was an hour-long programme which contributed little new. I became friendly with Greengrass (now a successful film director) and, in September 1984, he told me that Wright was producing a book of memoirs, for which he secured an Australian publisher.

To prevent an expensive court action, the would-be publishers sent a copy of Wright's lengthy typescript to the UK Attorney

General, Sir Michael Havers, my old shooting companion, suggesting that he could remove offensive passages. After consultation with MI5, it was decided that the book needed to be totally suppressed, if only to deter other former MI5 officers from publishing further 'memoirs'.

The reaction of Wright and his backers was the orchestrated release of alleged leaks about the book – many of them totally false – to left-wing British newspapers and Labour MPs who made political capital out of them in Parliament.

In September 1985, the government launched a case in a court in Sydney aimed at preventing publication of the book by Wright. Finally, the case of HM Attorney General v. Heinemann Australia (the would-be publisher) and Another (Peter Wright) came before Mr Justice Powell in Sydney on 24 March 1986.

The government made what would prove to be a cardinal blunder by deciding that its chief witness would be the Cabinet Secretary, the outstandingly efficient Sir Robert Armstrong, whose daily workload was so enormous that he could hardly be expected to remember all the details required. Meanwhile, the Australian publisher had put its case in the hands of a bright and ebullient lawyer called Malcolm Turnbull, who seemed to delight in showing his disrespect for authority, especially British authority. He quickly decided to concentrate on the inconsistency between the government's attitude to *Their Trade is Treachery* and to Wright's book. He particularly wanted 'to nail Mrs Thatcher' for criticising my book. In the process, Sir Robert (Eton and Oxford) was the perfect 'Pom' to be subjected to ridicule by a bellicose 'Aussie' during the nine days he would spend in the witness box.

Before the case began, I was visited by David Hooper, Wright's London-based solicitor. I told him that under no circumstances would I attend the Sydney trial, which finally opened on 17 November 1986. To set the scene here, I wrote a front-page article in the *Sunday Express* predicting that the government was on a hiding to nothing and that Sir Robert would be savaged by Turnbull. He was – mercilessly. Turnbull was allowed to take liberties that would have been curtailed by a British judge. Remarks like Sir Robert's now-famous admission that it was sometimes necessary for a civil servant to be 'economical with the truth' would have been acceptable as being obvious in a British court but alienated the court in Sydney. Not being sufficiently familiar with all the facts, Sir Robert inadvertently misled the court on details and had to apologise.

The government's lawyers made another blunder by failing to cross-examine Wright. While Australianising his image by wearing a drover's hat with a chin strap, only the pendant, anti-fly corks being missing, he had created the false impression that he was too ill to be in a witness box. It was claimed that he might well die if subjected to stress. So, he was allowed to present his evidence in a sworn affidavit which contained blatant falsehoods designed to project himself as a poor, sickly man who had been corrupted by two conspirators – me and Lord Rothschild.

At the end of the trial on 17 December 1986, Wright's 68-year-old sister Elizabeth publicly branded him as a compulsive liar and a vindictive mischief-maker prepared to betray secrets for money.

On 13 March 1987, Mr Justice Powell issued his long judgment, which found in favour of the Australian publisher and Wright. It was savagely critical of the government and Sir Robert Armstrong.

The situation then ended in farce by the publication of the book, under the title *Spycatcher*, in the US. Because of the unprecedented publicity, it became an immediate bestseller, making Wright a millionaire.

In 1987, I put all the facts on public record in a book, *A Web of Deception*, published in the US as *The Spy-catcher Affair*.

As I have already described, attempts by left-wing MPs to secure the prosecution of me and Rothschild, following Wright's fallacious statements about us, also ended in farce.

I rounded off 1991 with another book, *The Truth about Dirty Tricks (from Harold Wilson to Margaret Thatcher)*. It opened with an example told to me by my MI6 friend Nicholas Elliott, who had conceived it. Immediately following the death of Kim Philby in Moscow in 1988, Elliott, who had retired, urged his old colleagues to secure for the arch-traitor the posthumous award of the CMG (Companion of the Order of St Michael and St George), which was commonly bestowed on loyal intelligence officers. That, he suggested, should be followed by an obituary in *The Times* extolling Philby's bravery. Elliott felt sure that this would cause consternation in the KGB where there had always been some suspicion that Philby might have been a British secret service plant. The KGB would be driven to backtrack on the operations involving Philby and would never be free of doubt about him.

The plot foundered because of the danger of bringing the honours system into disrepute but remains a simple example of the deceptive 'dirty tricks' practised in the secrets world.

I was able to reveal many genuine deception operations, some of them involving assassinations, practised by various governments. The deception operation of the greatest historical importance which I was able to highlight was the brilliant American project commonly called 'Star Wars' and officially known as the Strategic Defence Initiative.

The concept was conceived towards the end of 1982 when President Reagan and his advisers realised that the Soviet Union's lead in long-range nuclear missiles could not be matched. In addition, the Russians had secured a major advantage which the Americans could never match for social reasons. They had mounted missiles on railcars and lorries so that they could be continually moved to different parts of the country. Never knowing where they were, the Americans could not knock them out in any pre-emptive nuclear strike. So, the Russians could always be certain of having enough missiles to destroy New York, Washington and other cities in any nuclear exchange. The US had been unable to follow suit because the American public would never accept the random movement of weapons of mass destruction on roads and railroads as the Soviet people had been forced to do.

The only potentially feasible solution was to try to build some kind of defence based on computer-controlled weapons, some based in space, others on the ground, that could destroy most of the Soviet warheads from wherever they might be launched – the 'Star Wars' concept. While this was seriously being considered, reliable intelligence revealed that the Soviets were so backward in the areas of technology on which Star Wars would depend that they could not possibly compete. Further, the Soviet economy was in such straits that it could not bear the enormous costs of such a protective system.

So, a major effort to convince the Russians that the US was developing a 'Star Wars' system was launched by President Reagan in March 1983 when, in an address to the nation, he called on American scientists to turn their talents in that direction. As part of the campaign to convince the Russians that the 'Star Wars' project was real, he earmarked $26 billion for it.

In December 1984, when the Soviet leader, Mikhail Gorbachev, met Mrs Thatcher in London, he revealed his concern about 'Star Wars', declaring that there could be no effective degree of disarmament unless the Americans dropped it. Aware that Mrs Thatcher was soon to visit Reagan, he asked her to argue the case on his behalf. It was no coincidence that, while Gorbachev and Mrs Thatcher were talking, the US announced big 'Star Wars' contracts for several major defence contractors. During her talks with Reagan, Mrs Thatcher was indoctrinated into the political purpose of 'Star Wars' and agreed to assist.

In 1985, the Kremlin's scientists and economic advisers had agreed that there was no way that the Soviet Union could compete. After a Soviet propaganda assault against the dangers of 'Star Wars' had failed, Gorbachev and Reagan met for talks on neutral ground – in Iceland's capital, Reykjavik, in October 1986. There, Gorbachev played his last propaganda card against 'Star Wars' by insisting that Reagan must ban all further development of the system before any peace progress could be made. Reagan refused but invited the Soviet leader to Washington for further talks.

Soon, Gorbachev was forced into meaningful negotiations in which he seized the opportunity to ask for economic and tech-nological assistance in support of his concept of *perestroika* – the restructuring of the Soviet economy. The results eventually led to the collapse of the Soviet Union and the end of the Cold War.

To make the 'Star Wars' gambit credible, a great deal of money had been spent on genuine research but it had been, essentially, a deception operation – a 'dirty trick'– that had been cheap at the price and for which historians will credit President Reagan and his advisers.

I expected *The Truth about Dirty Tricks* to be my last book about the intelligence world. Unforeseeable events would decree otherwise.

CHAPTER 33

COUNTRY MAN

In my eightieth year, I decided to concentrate my writing on country pursuits mainly through magazine articles about shooting, fishing and dogs, along with publishing and promoting *One Dog and Her Man* and the subsequent books about Dido, as already recorded. Around the same time, in 1993, I was able to present my love of the British countryside in a book called *Pastoral Symphony*, which still gives me pleasure with its record of the wonderful surroundings and rural privileges which I have enjoyed.

In 1996, I began writing profiles of the famous for *The Field* magazine, my subjects being mainly men and women with whom I was already acquainted, my first being Sir Rocco Forte, quickly followed by the Duke of Wellington. I based the profiles on specific interviews, which usually meant visiting their homes, with my wife Billee doing the driving and, of course, sharing the lunch to which I was often invited. My profiles were each embellished with portraits by Guglielmo Galvin, the finest portrait photographer of the many I have ever encountered.

It was a delight to feature some old friends like Sir Donald Gosling, Alan Bristow, Andrew Parker Bowles, Air Vice Marshal Johnnie Johnson, the Spitfire ace, and the Earl of Carnarvon, but I also took the opportunity to make a few new ones, such as Sir Paul Getty.

Another was Britain's richest man, the Duke of Westminster, who was full of surprises. Then forty-five, tall and with outstanding looks, he reminisced, nostalgically, about the boyhood he had enjoyed in Northern Ireland before his father succeeded to the dukedom and the fortune. He had spent much of his time on an island in Lough Erne which he described as being like *Swallows and*

Amazons, the classic stories by Arthur Ransome about young people set in the Lake District. 'I used to net the lough for pike and bream which I flogged to a fishmonger for pocket money,' he confessed. All that had ended when reached fifteen and his father inherited huge estates as well as 300 acres of London.

I had long admired Malcolm Rifkind, who was then Foreign Secretary, for his sharp intellect and manner of speech and, since interviewing him for *The Field*, we have remained in occasional touch through the Parliamentary Intelligence and Security Committee, responsible for oversight of the secret services, which he now chairs. I also featured William Hague, when he was Leader of the Opposition, our mutual interest being my beloved Richmond, which is now his Yorkshire constituency. Paddy Ashdown (now Lord) was another keen subject and my wife and I much enjoyed the visit to his country home.

Perhaps my oddest *Field* experience was interviewing Admiral Sir Jock Slater, the First Sea Lord, literally in the field, while he was shooting at Broadlands. Perhaps the most memorable, for my wife and me, was staying the night with the Duke of Northumberland at his shooting lodge on his Lammermuir grouse moor on our way to fish in Scotland. Ralph Percy, as he was formerly known, proved to be a delightful subject, which did not surprise me as I had been so impressed by his late father, with whom I had spent much of a day when receiving an honorary doctorate of letters (along with the late Cardinal Hume) at Newcastle University, of which he was then chancellor. To have been entertained by two most senior members of the ancient family, going back to 'Hotspur' and beyond, is a special memory.

Needing a few female subjects, I renewed my friendship with the lovely Henrietta Tavistock, interviewed Princess Anne and met Kate Hoey, the irrepressible Labour MP, then the Minister for Sport. I also featured Fiona Reynolds, the first female director general of the vast National Trust, whose determination deeply impressed me.

In West Berkshire, we were only a few miles from the home of Andrew Lloyd Webber (now Lord) and regularly attended his parties there. So, I induced his wife, Madeleine, who ran a racing stud as well as overseeing the large Sydmonton and Watership Down estate, to be one of my *Field* personalities. We spent a pleasant afternoon sitting by a big log fire, with a tiny kitten playing with two ping-pong balls betraying Andrew's life-long interest in pets which, Madeleine told me, was not unrelated to his enormously successful musical *Cats*. There was one brief call from him in his study. Presumably, he was working on his next blockbuster project.

My cuttings books show that among the mass of articles on country sports and rural life that I churned out in 1994–99, I was still in demand from newspapers for features and comment about spies and other aspects of the 'intelligence game'. So, I still kept and consulted my intelligence contacts and developed some new ones.

In March 2001, I was reminded of my atomic past by being the guest speaker at the lunch reunion of the surviving RAF men who had attended Operation Grapple, the British H-bomb tests staged off Christmas Island. More rewarding was an out-of-the-blue invitation from the directors of the most secret Atomic Weapons Establishment at nearby Aldermaston to attend a reunion of those scientists and other witnesses who were still alive to commemorate the fiftieth anniversary of Operation Hurricane, the first test of a British atomic bomb.

I enjoyed the proceedings, especially when the official sketch of the Hiroshima bomb shown during a lecture was almost identical with my sketch which had appeared in my newspaper half a century previously. But infinitely more exciting satisfaction was to come. I was invited to see the museum and there, mounted on four long walls, was a full-size replica of every British atomic weapon starting with the primitive four-tonner to the unbelievably small H-bomb warhead for the current Trident submarine missile. Further, each weapon was cut away so that the whole internal mechanism could be seen. For an old weapons buff like me – sheer ecstasy!

I also cherish the remark made by one of the old scientists to whom I was introduced. Recalling my sometimes embarrassing revelations of Aldermaston's secret operations, he exclaimed, 'Good God! I never expected to see you in here! We used to read your reports to learn what we were going to do next!'

In 2002, I was publicly dragged back into the intelligence world when a retired KGB officer, Colonel Michael Lyubimov, came all the way from Moscow to Kintbury to discuss espionage with me on British television, the programme being staged at the village Bistro Roque restaurant. Lyubimov, who spoke excellent English, having served in London, confirmed on the programme that I had been the British journalist most hated by the KGB. They had detested me because of my persistent reporting of the fact that the Soviet embassy in London was being ever-increasingly stuffed with highly trained Russian intelligence officers posing as diplomats, press officers, chauffeurs and doormen.

These men were really running agents in all manner of places such as defence factories, Parliament (where several former Labour MPs have since been exposed as paid agents) and trade unions.

As far back as 1960, I had reported that the number of Russian intelligence officers in or attached to the Soviet embassy had become so great that they were saturating the defences capable of being mounted by MI5 and Scotland Yard's Special Branch. My efforts had produced no result mainly because Harold Wilson's Labour government opposed any action as it was determined to appease the Kremlin in the interests of 'better relations' which, hopefully, would increase trade and reduce the risk of nuclear war. Those of us pressing for action were branded as anti-Communist hysterics.

I had continued my campaign with the backing of my editor and, in 1970, with Labour gone, the Tory Prime Minister, Edward Heath, was keen to secure a reduction in Russian intelligence officers because the Russians were, clearly, treating the nation with contempt, which he resented. Nevertheless, the Foreign Office held out against it for fear of reprisals against the much smaller number of British diplomats in Moscow, some of whom were officers of MI6, our espionage agency. At long last, on 24 September 1971, the Russians were given two weeks in which to remove 105 named 'diplomats' and were told of a second strike-list if they tried to retaliate against British officials living in Moscow.

There were howls from the Kremlin but that was all and Lyubimov told me, on television, that the KGB never recovered from the cull which had forced it to abandon so many of its traitorous informants.

In March 2004, my wife and my children surprised me by, surreptitiously, organising a splendid celebration of my ninetieth birthday – most appropriately a lunch – at the Bistro Roque on the edge of Kintbury. I was astonished how many old friends had journeyed far to wish me well. The Bistro's owner had concocted a 'Spy' cocktail and, appropriately, my birthday cake had a huge fish on it – perhaps prophetic of the twenty-pound rainbow trout I would catch in the Kennet three months later.

As I prophesied in my speech, there are four ages of man – youth, middle age, old age and 'God you look marvellous'.

In 2005, Nigel Bance, an independent researcher into Russian affairs who regularly visited Moscow, where he had several high-level sources, was elected to the Academy for Defence, Security and Law and Order, which had been set up, five years previously, by President Vladimir Putin to advise him and his staff on such issues. With 5,000 Russian members, the academy had decided to elect a few foreign academicians so Bance suggested me and I received official notice of the honour. More satisfyingly, for my services in the Second World War, I was also awarded the Order of the Great Victory, which had been created in 1945 to commemorate the defeat of Germany, its first recipients having been Stalin and Marshal Zhukov, the Red Army commander. It had also been awarded to a few Allied generals including Field Marshal Montgomery.

The red, leather-bound certificate made out to me in Russian and showing Zhukov wearing the star on his heavily decorated chest duly arrived, along with the large, five-pointed silver, red and blue enamelled star, accompanied by a black and gold sash. My much-esteemed Russian friend Count Nikolai Tolstoy translated the documentation for me and, seeing me wearing the award, sash and all, pronounced it all as being 'most impressive'.

Having heard of these events, my old paper, the *Daily Express*, sent a senior feature writer to see me and an adulatory, double-page spread duly appeared. It was swiftly followed by an invitation from the editor, Peter Hill, to begin writing regularly for the paper again.

Unable to resist such a challenge, I accepted and, with my usual luck, some newly released papers about the disappearance of the former Labour minister John Stonehouse provided a peg for me to present the evidence that he had been a Soviet Bloc agent. As I have already recorded, this resulted in the discovery of official Czech documents in Prague giving details of his treachery. So, I was off to a good restart and thoroughly enjoying it.

Having developed some new sources in Moscow, I was able to present some new information about the extraordinary GRU agent Sonia and followed this up with revelatory features about John Profumo and Harold Wilson. But then I made a stupid blunder. In March 2006, I allowed a *Daily Express* photographer to take a picture of me wearing my Russian Order of the Great Victory, which appeared along with a story by a woman reporter. Looking all of my ninety-two years, it was a dreadful image to appear in any paper needing to recruit young readers and, though no official explanation was ever forthcoming, no idea of mine for a feature or news story was considered again.

At someone's command, my *Daily Express* resurgence was extinguished. I had, I suppose, been my own executioner.

CHAPTER 34

MY GIANT JIGSAW

When I passed ninety I did not expect to be writing any more books about espionage. My regular publisher had pre-deceased me and I did not have an agent, which had become essential because, with so many people submitting scripts, publishers were insisting on using agents to filter out the obvious non-starters. Nevertheless, such was my fascination with the intelligence world that I continued to collect new information and update my records. I also knew that if I did not use my brain constructively every day it would rapidly decline and, for me, doing nothing has never been an option.

The whole experience was like trying to construct a giant jigsaw puzzle with all the missing pieces hidden, many concealed in officially inaccessible places or even deliberately destroyed by the security authorities 'in the national interest', meaning 'in the interest of covering up their incompetence'. Filling in the gaps with new pieces, sometimes replacing what had been probabilities by certainties, has all helped to keep my brain in trim.

So, seven days a week, I continued, glued to my computer, firing off and receiving e-mails, receiving visitors from the intelligence world and weaving new finds into the shocking exposure which I had constructed over the years. In all this, I was fortunate to acquire some productive Russian sources with remarkable access to records.

Chief among these was the Moscow-based professional researcher Dr Svetlana Chervonnaya, a historian at the Russian Academy of Sciences, to whom I was introduced in September 2007 by Dr Michael Goodman of King's College London. Dr Chervonnaya has access to revealing documents such as the papers of Molotov,

Stalin's Foreign Minister, and even the log book of Stalin's visitors at the Kremlin. More remarkably, she had been on friendship terms with former KGB agents such as Feklisov, who had controlled Klaus Fuchs while he was working at the Harwell atomic research station. She had also known the Krogers (really Cohens) and other major Soviet agents.

Being fluent in English, she can translate the many revealing books about Soviet espionage published in Moscow, especially those by a former GRU official who writes under the name of Vladimir Lota and has unique access to GRU records. His book *The GRU and the Atomic Bomb* has been especially revealing. Being a military organisation, the GRU has, generally, remained silent about its past activities, if only to encourage new informants, but was stung into action by the excessive claims by the KGB for having been responsible for securing the secrets of the first atomic bombs from Britain and America. Lota's book detailing the crucial role played by the GRU was so successful that he has been given further access to GRU records. Maybe, one day he will be permitted to reveal the full story of 'Elli'.

I have remained in regular touch with Svetlana, who visited my house in 2012, and am greatly in her debt. For a while, before he died, I was also helped by the former KGB officer Oleg Tsarev, who had access to KGB records.

In 2008, I was visited by Rear Admiral Nicholas Wilkinson, a former secretary of the D-notice Committee who had been appointed to write the official history of the committee, which appeared in 2009 under the title *Secrecy and the Media*. By chance, he lived in a village close by and became a regular visitor to my house, a cherished friendship which still continues. Nick, as I now know him, had access to the relevant Cabinet Office papers and produced a most readable reference book dealing with the D-notice affair and other intelligence events with which I had been involved. In my presentation copy he wrote, 'With many thanks for all your support in the writing of this history in which you yourself played such a dynamic part.'

Around the same time, I was consulted by Christopher Moran,

a young Warwick University academic who was completing a PhD thesis on government secrecy. I introduced him to Nick Wilkinson and the thesis (updated and published as a book called *Classified* in 2013) contained a great deal about my exploits and the government's reaction to them.

My long-suffering wife made a joke with friends about my unending connections with intelligence affairs, complaining that I was so busy that she did not see much of me. One of them, the internationally renowned sculptor Stella Shawzin, whose charming estate is just a few miles from us and whom we visited regularly, asked me when she and others were going to see the results of my labours. I explained the problem of finding a publisher at my age whereupon she announced that she had an American friend who would, surely, be interested.

I duly received a telephone call from Robert Bernstein, who, before retiring, had been the dominating figure in the big publishing company Random House. He urged me to convert my findings into a book, which took me two years to complete. I sent it to him and he placed it with Random right away, ensuring that I got the services of their most distinguished editor, Bob Loomis. (Thank you, dear Stella, for that initiative and so many other generous expressions of your friendship.)

Called *Treachery*, and published in 2009, the book was the fullest exposure to date of the appalling disloyalty of British traitors and their official cover-up by MI5 and MI6, aided by successive governments. The UK was its obvious main market but, to Random's dismay, its lawyers were so concerned about the Official Secrets Acts and other problems with British law that they declined to clear its supply to British bookshops.

British publishers took a similar view until Bill Campbell of Mainstream Publishing, based in Edinburgh, proved more courageous. An enlarged and much-upgraded UK edition of *Treachery*, incorporating new revelations greatly embarrassing to 'the authorities', was published in May 2011.

Among the 'nuggets' which I had mined and which appeared in the book was Stalin's 'Double Check Demand', which showed that the Soviet espionage assault on Britain had been far greater than ever imagined. Stalin had distrusted any intelligence report unless it could be fully confirmed from an independent source. The USSR had two main intelligence agencies, the KGB and GRU. So, Stalin ruled that they must operate independently, recruiting separate sources and being forbidden to cooperate in any way without special permission. If the KGB submitted an intelligence coup from one of its British agents, the GRU was required to verify or disprove it from its own British sources and vice versa.

The joint researches of Dr Chervonnaya and myself had also established the identity of an important wartime GRU spy known by the codename Milord. He was a British Army captain in the Intelligence Corps named James MacGibbon, a well-known figure in the post-war publishing world who died in 2000. While based in the War Office in 1942, he had access to the ultra-secret intercepts and translations of coded German messages streaming in from the codebreakers at Bletchley Park. When he learned that the Russians were not being shown the intercepts because of the essential need to avoid a leak to the Germans that their codes were being broken, he decided to supply them through a Russian woman courier and did so for the rest of the war. He continued his traitorous activities when posted to Washington in 1944, betraying everything that came his way.

Treachery's exposure of these monstrous betrayals generated much publicity in the Newbury area where MacGibbon had previously lived.

Meanwhile, Christopher Andrew's *The Defence of the Realm: The Authorized History of MI5* appeared in 2009. It contained so many statements which I believe to be inaccurate and so many serious omissions that I was able to include my detailed criticism of it in the UK edition of *Treachery*, the cover of which bore the words 'The True History of MI5'.

Inevitably, my book generated so much more new information, especially about the Hollis case, that Mainstream decided to publish a further updated paperback edition, which appeared in 2012. As I was then in my ninety-ninth year the book has given me a peculiar satisfaction.

In late 2012, MI5 released into the National Archives a large batch of the diaries which had been studiously compiled by the senior MI5 officer Guy Liddell, who had dictated them to his secretary at the end of each working day. The diaries, which cover his MI5 career after 1945, have proved to be very revealing and have confirmed the accuracy of my account of the events, such as the Gouzenko defection and the Fuchs case.

Some of the situations in the diaries are tragically hilarious with Liddell recording how he had discussed the general hunt for possible Soviet spies with Kim Philby and with Anthony Blunt! On reading the diaries, one can see why Hollis wanted nobody to have access to them. The Liddell diaries are being minutely examined and processed by Nigel West, who has been commissioned to put them on available record in two volumes. He has already expressed his view of them by declaring that 'there is a gem on every page'.

CHAPTER 35

IN RETROSPECT

Writing these memoirs has been an unusual exercise for me as I have always been so pre-occupied with the present and the immediate future. They have made me realise how fortunate I have been to have witnessed and enjoyed so many technological changes in so many areas of living.

During my youth, only a small minority had a home telephone. The now-universal mobile phone did not become available until 1983. The personal computer with its e-mails, internet access and the whole pervasive field of information technology, the cyber world, had not even entered science fiction. While the magical Internet Explorer now produces information on any subject within seconds, it used to be necessary to consult an encyclopaedia, involving, for most people, a trip to a public library.

Writers like me needed to hack out the words on a typewriter where changes to the text, such as the alteration of wording or the transposition of paragraphs, usually involved retyping. The computer has eliminated such time-consuming chores to an extent which has added much productive time to life.

In my youth, the private car was beginning to be common but air travel was limited and slow. Artificial light was mainly provided, both on roads and in homes, by coal gas, with lamplighters touring the streets each evening, usually by bicycle. Installation of the water-closet was becoming common but, in millions of homes, the sewage from outdoor 'privies' still had to be collected by 'night-soil men' using spades and a horse-drawn container.

Evening entertainment was restricted to local theatres, few of which now exist, and to the many cinemas which, until the advent of the 'talking picture' in 1927, showed silent movies with written dialogue and an accompanying pianist. I vividly recall sitting in a cinema when I was a schoolboy, perhaps fourteen, and watching the American entertainer Al Jolson in *The Jazz Singer*. The film (which we then called a 'picture') began in the old silent fashion until, suddenly, we could hear Jolson speaking and singing. It was a magical moment and, soon, silent movies were finished and 'talkies' were all the rage.

Many people had a radio set in my early days but there was no home television, which did not become available until 1936 when the BBC began the first public TV service. It resumed after the Second World War in 1946 and I have watched the various TV services become an almost universal window on the world, with the latest news now available at any time of day or night. Both young and old can be informed and entertained round the clock if they wish whereas in my youth families tended to pass the evening reading or chatting by the fireside. Being, by nature, still a newshound, I watch TV to keep up to date on the world events and wonder how our less privileged oldsters managed without it.

I have also witnessed the steady emancipation of the housewife, who in my youth tended to be housebound by her duties, with one day set aside for washing clothes in a coal-heated 'copper' and another for baking bread. The development of washing machines, tumble-driers, washing-up machines and other household gadgetry has steadily taken the drudgery out of housework.

The refrigerator, which was uncommon in a house when I was young, and the deep freeze, which was unknown then, have made food storage so much easier and safer. With the self-service supermarkets offering so much variety, shopping has become so simple that many now shop 'online' with the goods being delivered.

Ready-made meals, which can be cooked in a few minutes by microwave oven, have greatly reduced the effort and time for those content to use them. (The microwave oven contains a device called a cavity magnetron, a British invention in 1940 which greatly improved the power of radar in detecting enemy aircraft. I recall being told about it in great secrecy during the Second World War.)

The whole vast field of medicine has been revolutionised in my lifetime with astonishing results not only in life-span, which had not changed much since Victorian times when I was born, but in the relief of pain and suffering. Until the establishment of the National Health Service after the Second World War, 'going to the doctor' or having him call (expensively) at one's home usually ended in the provision of a bottle of dark-coloured medicine providing mental satisfaction but little else. Now, with antibiotics and so many other medical advances, general practitioners can treat patients far more positively.

Like every other Briton, I celebrated the defeat of Germany and then of Japan in 1945 with great satisfaction. Forty-five years later, witnessing the collapse of the Soviet Union gave me particular 'I knew that I was right' pleasure, as I had striven to expose its remorseless efforts to undermine our democracy throughout the Cold War. As a biologist, Communism had always seemed to me to be based on a fundamental genetic flaw – the cloud-cuckoo-land concept that people would be prepared to work whole-heartedly for the common good, the slogan being 'each unto his needs' rather than 'each according to his effort'. *Homo sapiens* is not made that way. He or she expects to reap the reward for extra sustained effort. However, I did not think I would live to see capitalism picking the bones of the Soviet Union.

Shortly after the Second World War, the British Interplanetary Society, which I had joined, pondered on the prospect of space travel, with little real hope of achievement except for a few stalwarts like my King's College friend Arthur C. Clarke, but I doubt whether even he really believed we would live to see a man walking on the moon. Happily, we both did so though, sadly, Arthur, who made a great name and fortune as a science fiction writer, was wheelchair bound after contracting polio in 1962. Robots have since been landed on Mars and, while nobody has yet visited a planet, that further step for mankind seems likely within the next ten years.

I am particularly grateful for having met so many interesting people, to have had so many exciting experiences on so many fronts and to have visited so many places.

I have certainly warmed my hands before the fire of life and, though it may be sinking, I am far from ready to depart. Each new day still presents challenges and the menace of the years intensifies the satisfaction of notching up even a little victory against the mounting odds. When I awoke on 29 March to begin my 100th year, I enjoyed a special surge of the gratitude I feel each morning for being alive with all my mental faculties, including my memory, intact. I was also thankful to remain blessed with a strong speaking voice, which is unusual for such an old codger. I also have no need of a hearing aid and wear spectacles only for reading. Those gifts make it particularly satisfying still to be capable of earning my keep.

Always aware that I have enjoyed far more than a fair share of lucky breaks, I am reasonably satisfied with my performance, having been 'good in a tight corner' and, when the horse was in the ditch, as countrymen say, I have, so far, always managed to dig it out. Being now largely restricted to my home, I am happy in the smallness of my personal needs.

Clearly, to cope with old age and especially to enjoy it one needs a positive purpose for living. In that respect, I recall a brief conversation I had with Robin Day, the aggressive political TV journalist, when I happened to visit London's Garrick Club, which he frequented to fill in his time after his retirement. Knowing that I had retired from Fleet Street, he remarked that we were both 'in the departure lounge waiting for the call'. I told him that such a recipe for death was not my attitude. He died aged seventy-six. I don't think I will die of boredom.

It may sound eccentric but I cannot spare the time to do nothing and am determined to die in harness. Strictly obeying the principle of KISS (Keep it Simple, Stupid!), I resist the time-wasting temptation to fiddle with Facebook, Twitter and such like. There is always something new to learn – and who knows wins in one way or another. It used to be said that it is not what you know that matters but who you know. The truth is that both matter and the more you know the more likely you are to meet distinguished people.

Now that I have passed ninety-nine, people often ask me for my 'secret', to which the answer is 'use it or lose it'. The keystone to a happy life is not freedom from care, as Cicero said, but a sense of purpose. Retire out of active mental and physical life and it will quickly retire out of you.

I was fortunate enough to inherit genes which have always kept me slim and so healthy that I can recall only one night in hospital – and that just for a nose-bleed. For as long as I could, I kept myself physically fit, mainly through my regular spells of fly-fishing on the River Kennet close to where I live. Nevertheless, the ravages of time have taken their toll on my muscles and, two years ago, I had to concede that I was too wobbly to be by a fast river.

Happily, old friends, journalists, authors and new intelligence sources with information to exchange visit me regularly. For example, the former MI6 officer Stephen de Mowbray, who was deeply involved in the inquiries concerning Sir Roger Hollis and had evaded me for years, paid me several visits which resulted in my receiving five thick files of his dealings with the KGB defector Golitsyn. My distinguished Washington friend from the CIA, Hayden Peake, makes a much-appreciated effort to visit me for a mutual update session at least once a year. In 2012 I received a visit from my Moscow-based friend and source, Dr Svetlana Chervonnya, with whom I have been in regular e-mail contact for many years.

Another regular visitor has been Dr Christopher Moran, a young don at Warwick University who, in 2013, published his book *Classified*, a meticulous study of the ingrained habit of British government officials to keep information from the public on various grounds. As I had been a prominent figure in the struggle against unnecessary official secrecy over many years, the book contained so many references to my secrets-busting activities that it further inflated my ego, especially as released documents which he had discovered revealed the extent to which I had confounded and infuriated officialdom and the extraordinary government actions to curb me.

Though I have read it thoroughly, I confess to occasionally dipping into it to recall more active days.

Enmity, particularly in the political world, is a delightful luxury

I can no longer afford. In that connection I am reminded of the advice of Hannen Swaffer, a notorious newspaper columnist who made a national name for himself by insulting celebrities – 'Never prolong a quarrel. Clear the decks for the next one.'

Regarding old friends in general, it is sad how geography is such an enemy of friendship. With increasing age, just a few miles intensifies the effort of personal visits to the point where they cease, by tacit mutual agreement. Happily, the e-mail system makes written contact immediate and simple. One of my greatest joys is consulting the inbox round about 7 a.m.

On the general issue of extreme old age, which, as statistics show, more and more people must face, what can I say from my experience that might be helpful? First, I would agree with the observation that extreme old age is not for the faint hearted. It does need determination and a positive 'I won't be beaten' attitude. For instance, a poor night's sleep or comparable set-back needs to be ignored as quickly as possible. Treat it as what I call 'water over the dam' – being no longer of significance and, therefore, to be discarded from the memory.

On days when I do not feel so well I find that 'working it off' is the best solution. When I experience pain I think of so many of my contemporaries who cannot feel anything.

Before closing my eyes in bed (around 10.30 p.m.) I muse on the day's accomplishments, however small, and ponder on tomorrow's programme so that I have something positive to anticipate. Oddly, at that time, I often conjure up an idea for some action which had eluded me during the day and I have a writing pad and pen close by.

Having no religious beliefs, I have no fear or hopes of death on that score. Whereas the religious believe that RIP on a tombstone means that someone there is resting in peace until Judgement Day, to me it simply means 'recycling in progress'. I am fortunate in having no need of religion to feel fulfilled, nor do I fear the flames of Hell.

While writing a book on religion, which I have never published, it became increasingly obvious that, as his brain developed, primitive man invented God, not vice versa. As this happened so many times in different parts of the world there have been many different concepts of God, each with its dedicated adherents. Some of them remain, with some adherents willing to die for them, as exemplified by the religious suicide bomber, a phenomenon unimaginable in my youth when fanatics might be prepared to die for their faith if forced to do so but had no murderous wish to take others with them.

I have often thought that for Christianity to become the accepted religion of the world all that would be necessary would be for the Virgin Mary to appear in glory at some event being widely watched on television. Millions believe that the Virgin Mary has occasionally appeared to small groups, mainly children, as evidence of her existence and, therefore, of God's. So why has a worldwide appearance never occurred? A similar question can be applied to other faiths.

The brain needs beliefs of some kind to function properly and I fully appreciate why so many people derive pleasure and satisfaction from religious belief and communal worship. I consider myself fortunate in having had no need of either.

Being well into my 100th year on this planet, I have experienced many of the problems of senility and, having, so far, negotiated them, I offer to others what I call My Ten Commandments:

1. The most crucial awareness that the ageing need at most times of the day, and sometimes during the night, is of the mounting danger of a fall. To understand why that is so – and, in the process, reduce the risk – it is helpful to know about a vital sense we all possess but of which most are unaware. It is called the kinaesthetic sense and is an intricate complex of nerve cells and muscle-controllers which enable the limbs and trunk to sense the position and movements of the other limbs so that, automatically, the whole body is kept in balance. It is all so wonderfully accomplished that, for most of our lives, we need to give it no conscious thought. Sadly, the kinaesthetic sense deteriorates with age and the sense of balance suffers accordingly, making us wobbly and much more susceptible to a fall. In preventing this, the eyes are all-important to the sense of balance so it is essential to avoid darkness, which, in the very old, can quickly generate

a dangerous degree of disorientation. We all need to be aware that the likeliest place for a fall is in the home, not only because of the time we spend there but because of the hazards presented to the old by stairs, furniture, carpets, dogs and other normally prosaic objects. In the event of a fall it is essential for old people to have quick access to someone strong enough to pick them up, especially at night. This means having a live-in helper, a task which, for us, is superbly served by Tibor Zimmermann, a former soldier in his native Hungary, to whom we have developed a warm mutual attachment. It is also consoling for us and our children to know that at most times of the day and for the whole of the night we have a tough bodyguard.

2.   The most effective precaution for preventing a fall is to use a walking stick at all times. The stick needs to have a rubber ferrule at the bottom so that it will not slide forwards. For me, this has been no problem because, when walking outside, I have used a thumbstick for many years. Some men and many women seem to be ashamed of using a stick and put off the day when they are forced to do so. They put themselves in unnecessary danger. Using a stick can also reduce pain. Sticks have a habit of hiding themselves so it is wise to have several in different places so that a temporary substitute can easily be found. Many people have fallen while looking for their sticks.

3.   An extension of the stick is the Zimmer frame, which I strongly recommend for use in large rooms, especially large bedrooms where trips to the bathroom involve quite a walk. The frame provides that extra confidence which can prevent much apprehension.

4.   When walking in the home without a stick or frame, as is sometimes unavoidable, the golden rule is 'always keep one hand free'. To carry something in both hands, even for a short distance, is courting danger. A free hand can so often restore balance or grab some stable object.

5.   In the last respect, I strongly recommend the installation, in selected places, of thick ceramic handles, available in stores, which can be screwed into walls at convenient places such as lavatories, bathrooms and corridors.

6. Because of the steady decay of the kinaesthetic sense, the left hand (or for those who are left-handed, the right hand), instead of remaining still, seems to have a life of its own with a determination to hit other objects, knocking them to the ground whence they have to be retrieved, sometimes painfully. The sometimes unpleasant consequences can be greatly reduced by ensuring that the handles of knives, pans, kettles and other utensils do not protrude from the bench, table or desk on which they are placed. I find that cursing also helps, my main recipient being poor old Isaac Newton and his gravitation.

7. Slippers, which most elderly people wear in the house, are well named. So it is wise to examine the soles regularly and replace them at the first sign of slipperiness. (My only fall to date, which shook me up but did no further damage, was due to failure to take that precaution.)

8. The most hazardous area in any house is the stairs because of the obvious extra danger of a fall there. So, a few years ago, my wife and I swallowed our pride and installed a stair-lift, which has contributed vastly to our safety and comfort.

9. For wobbly oldies the bath is a special hazard. As I have always regarded my bath as a 'think-tank' in which to wallow while considering problems, my kind daughter equipped me with a deflatable, and then inflatable, device which lowers then raises me in the water. An alternative is to use a shower.

10. My final commendment to the ageing is to have the eyes tested for cataracts as early as practicable and, if they are there, to have them dealt with by a specialist surgeon. Both my wife and I are deeply indebted to the outstanding NHS surgeon Peter Constable and his team for that service. Several years after undergoing a cataract operation, some people experience a steady clouding of the vision which, in my case, made one eye almost useless. This, however, was recently rectified by the nearest thing to a miracle I have ever experienced. While attending as an out-patient at the West Berks Hospital near Newbury, the offending cloudiness was subjected to a few seconds of controlled bombardment by a

laser beam. The lasting result was vision with almost the clarity
I enjoyed when young.

Surveying my experiences, it is immensely satisfying to know that,
given the chance, I would elect to repeat a career in investigative
reporting, specialising in intelligence affairs, in preference to any
other profession. I am particularly proud of my contribution to the
breaching of the barriers of unnecessary official secrecy. (The more
'mandarins' I met the more it became apparent that they enjoyed
keeping matters secret for secrecy's sake and delayed releasing them
for as long as possible because they derived pleasure out of being
exclusively 'in the know'. Several who I re-encountered after they
had retired confessed that what they missed most was the privilege
of being among the few in the know.)

I feel confident that my newspaper exposures and books made
some contribution to the now-regular release of formerly secret files
into the National Archives at Kew, where anyone can consult them,
and to the creation of the parliamentary Intelligence and Security
Committee, set up in 1994 with powers to oversee the activities of
the secret services. The files tend to be thirty years old but they
regularly reveal how they were withheld to cover up blunders and
even the discovery of Russian spies in MI5 and other secret departments. There is, however, more to do, as the hushed-up revelations
about the Hillsborough football disaster recently just demonstrated.
At ninety-nine, I am still on my anti-secrecy prowl.

My survey of my life has, also, fortified my belief that I helped to
pioneer investigative journalism as it is now generally practised by
all forms of the British media. Before my post-war start in defence
journalism, senior Whitehall 'mandarins' and their departments and
senior politicians seem to have enjoyed near-immunity to outside
investigation. Now, nobody does. Of course, other journalists were
also involved but the bound copies of the newspapers show that I
often led the way, as Christopher Moran's recent survey *Classified*
has confirmed. I can also claim a pioneering role in extending the
coverage of medical matters, which now occupy so much space
in newspapers.

I am fortunate in that I can relive my achievements at any time as my record is before my eyes in my study, for myself or anyone else to see, in the thirty-seven thick cuttings books packed with newspaper and magazine records of my investigative journalism and in the rows of my published books on my shelves. There is no other profession where one's past activities are open to such easy scrutiny.

The cuttings books, which offer a quick and easy way to see what was happening in the defence and intelligence world over the last sixty-seven years, will be donated to the Department of War Studies at King's College London, which has already received all the files of my researches.

THE FAMILY FACTOR

As promised in my introduction, this book is intended as a record of my professional life, not my personal private life. However, it would be incomplete and misleading not to make some mention of the contributions made by my wife, Billee, and by my children, Pat and Michael. I am also grateful for the support and help of my three step-children, Nikky, Wendy and John.

The demands of daily journalism can be tough on the wives of specialist reporters, who can never be sure of the time when they will reach home in the evening. A sudden incident or an unexpected dispatch from Washington, or some other source, may require immediate and lengthy action. On most nights, when I reached home from Fleet Street, I would find that there was a telephone query awaiting me. Often, there were disturbing calls at midnight or later which wives had to accept as being part of normal life. If the result was a good display in the morning's paper then a late-night call became a matter for rejoicing.

Such, for example, was the case following a most unusual telephone call at midnight on 12 May 1965 when my wife and I were asleep in bed in our London flat in St James's Place. Billee reached for the telephone but, sleepily, picked up a glass of water which she raised to her ear, showering me in the process. The call summoned me to the front door of the block of flats in my dressing gown where a Major Geoffrey Blundell-Brown awaited me with a sheaf of Cabinet papers in his hand.

The major, a company director and staunch Tory-supporter, explained that he had been enjoying a late supper with his wife at the famed French restaurant Pruniers, just a few yards away in St James's

Street, and had noticed Richard Crossman, the Housing Minister of the ruling Labour government, eating alone at a nearby table.

Crossman had been reading a thick wad of papers which were strewn about his plates and, having finished his meal, he gathered them up, put them in his briefcase and left about 11.30. When Blundell-Brown prepared to leave a little later, he noticed a lot of papers lying under Crossman's table and retrieved them. There were eighteen pages dealing with Cabinet discussions about sensitive amendments to housing aspects of the government's Race Relations Bill and included a summary of a Cabinet meeting about them.

The major told me that he was incensed by Crossman's scant concern for security, especially as Harold Wilson, the Prime Minister, had criticised the previous Tory government for security lapses only a couple of days before. In the recent past, when Wilson had been in opposition, he had accused the whole Tory administration of leaking so much that it was 'incontinent'. As he handed me the papers, I was already seeing the headline.

When I read them I realised that, politically, they were highly embarrassing for the government as they contained details of a disagreement between Crossman and the Home Secretary over the housing of immigrants. In the morning, my first move was to telephone George Wigg, Wilson's security overlord, to alert him. He telephoned Crossman, who had not yet missed the papers, and then rang me back to warn me that if we published any of the papers' contents we could be prosecuted under the Official Secrets Acts. Then, changing his tone, he urged me not to mention Crossman's gaffe, chanting, 'Charity, Harry! Charity!'

I remembered the charity Wigg and Wilson had meted out to my friend Jack Profumo, accusing him of endangering security through his affair with Christine Keeler because they had not dared to criticise him on moral grounds as so many on Labour's front bench, including Wigg, had mistresses themselves. So I told him that we would be returning the papers to the finder, who would be handing them in to the police.

The following morning my story led the front page, opening with 'Confidential Cabinet papers left in a London restaurant by

Mr Richard Crossman, the Housing Minister, were handed to the police yesterday'. There was a picture of Blundell-Brown doing so at Chelsea police station. A noisy row in Parliament ensued, with Labour turning all its anger on Blundell-Brown for failing to do the gentlemanly thing – handing the papers back to Crossman without a whisper. My wife agreed that the wet ear had been worthwhile.

Inevitably, many of the telephone calls which disturbed our sleep were fruitless and sometimes pointless. I recall being awakened after midnight by the night news editor to be told, 'A reader has just called to report that a bit has fallen out of the moon. Could you write a few paragraphs about it?' I got out of bed, looked out of the window and found the moon intact.

During another night, the same man woke us up with the news that several readers had telephoned to say that the moon had turned blue. Cursing him, I looked out and the moon was, indeed, bright blue. I dictated a few words explaining that it had to be an illusion, the colour being due to something in our atmosphere. It transpired that an enormous forest fire in Canada had sent a cloud of smoke across Britain. (Perhaps similar events in the past had generated the expression 'once in a blue moon'.)

Billee was a great professional asset through her skill and charm as hostess when we were entertaining contacts at Lowerhouse Farm, as we did so regularly, especially when we acquired Kim, a Chinese servant from Malaysia. There were three other Chinese girls serving houses close by and, occasionally, they would join forces to stage a Chinese food party with as many as eleven small but delicious courses. My distinguished friends from Whitehall and elsewhere were always keen to attend the unusual feast.

I was often able to take Billee with me on my trips to foreign conferences, at the paper's expense, when she invariably earned her keep through helping me to entertain productive delegates.

We are especially proud of my daughter Pat's remarkable career in the complex information technology world where she has distinguished herself by serving on the boards of several companies. In 2011, the all-male board of the prestigious British Standards Institution, founded more than a century ago, decided that they needed some female representation. When they chose two women as new members, Pat was one of them.

Pat and I have always been very close and I have always been impressed, not only by her professional efficiency in whatever she has attempted, but by her judgement of character. When her late mother took off with someone she found to be more compatible and with a more exciting mode of life for her, I soon met Billee and introduced her to Pat, then still in her teens. As soon as we were alone Pat's response was, 'Oh I *do* like her!' They have continued to enjoy a loving relationship.

We were both delighted when, in September 2012, Pat remarried to Jeremy Barrow, an Oxford man we both admire on many counts. It has done much for our peace of mind not only to see her so happy but to know that she will not be alone in life.

Pat inherited the genes that have made me a workaholic. As with me, her favourite stone is the grindstone. So, she intends to continue to use her many talents in the business world, also being determined to 'die in harness'. Most happily for us, Pat's base in Oxford is only half an hour's drive from our home, so we see her and Jeremy regularly. We are both deeply grateful for all that they do for us, in the process providing extra time for me to work.

My son, Michael, also distinguished himself in the computer world but having seemingly inherited my love of the countryside, lives in the delightful small town of Pershore, in the fruit-growing Vale of Evesham, where he is involved, full time, in country pursuits of many kinds, including mole-trapping and bee-keeping. For many years, he has also headed a band which played with panache at Pat's recent wedding. We are in almost daily touch by e-mail or phone and he manages to visit us regularly and make our life easier through his many skills. Thanks, Mick, for your support and infectious enthusiasm.

Between us, my wife and I have thirteen grandchildren but, for geographical reasons and because they and I are so busy, we see them only rarely but with pleasure if they care to call. In retrospect, especially observing the behaviour of our elderly friends, I have clearly been a poor grandparent except at Christmas and, until recently, on birthdays.

My attitude to my three step-children by Billee's previous marriage has been even more reprehensible by most standards. They have always been welcome at our homes but their father took custody after he divorced Billee and, because of time restrictions, our arrangement has always been that she would look after her children while I would look after mine. It has worked well to our satisfaction.

We were all surprised and delighted when, in 1987, Billee decided to obtain and publish a collection of true fishing stories from friends and others to whom she wrote requesting them to trawl their memories for unusual experiences in the sport where, as Sir Thomas Sopwith often observed, 'anything can happen because there are no rules'. The result was the publication, in 1989, of *Fish Tales: A Collection of True Angling Stories*, in which sources including the Dukes of Atholl, Fife and Wellington, Lords Home of the Hirsel, Brabourne, Forte, Kimberley, Mason, Pembroke, Dalhousie, Bruce-Gardyne and Thurso, and many others including bankside friends like Sir Michael Hordern, Roger de Vere, Professor RV Jones, George Melly, Sir Denis Mountain and Dermot Wilson told their tales.

In 1995, Billee repeated her success with *Tails and the Unexpected* – a further collection of unusual angling stories from many more sources who had escaped her first trawl. The books boosted Billee's morale and, now that I can no longer stand safely on a river bank, I dip into them, nostalgically.

In general, because of the demands on my time by my profession and my pursuits, I have had to be selfish regarding my family relationships. It is a character defect about which I see little point in having regrets. I do, however, feel deeply regretful about having failed to do more for my parents. I looked after them financially and when my mother died, aged sixty-six, my father came to live with me at Lowerhouse Farm. He was happy there and forged a close relationship with Pat when she was a schoolgirl, but I should have spent more time with him.

Time has always been my problem and still is but, in retrospect, I think I can console myself that I have made the most of it. In the process, I hope that, at least, my family have found me stimulating to know.

INDEX

Thatcher, Denis 171
Thatcher, Margaret 122, 171, 209,
    305, 309, 310, 331–4, 336–7, 343
Their Trade is Treachery (Pincher)
    221, 250, 304–312, 327–8, 332–3
Thompson, E. P. 37
Thompson, Lord (Roy) 199
Thomson, George 37–9, 65
Thorneycroft, Peter 283–4
Throsk, The 295–6
Tickell, Sir Crispin 55
Tizard, Sir Henry 33
Tommy (gun dog) 165–7
Tomu 76
Too Secret Too Long (Pincher) 323,
    338
Tortelier, Paul 143–4
Traitors: The Anatomy of Treason
    (Pincher) 336
Treachery (Pincher) 353–4
Trend, Lord 307, 329
Trinder, Tommy 5
Truman, Harry 29
Truth about Dirty Tricks, The
    (Pincher) 341–2
Tsarev, Oleg 321, 352
Turnbull, Malcolm 340
Tuttle, Sir Geoffrey 35

Uganda
    and Entebbe hijack 103–106
United States of America
    CP's visits to 278–9

Vassall, John 226–8
Vassiliev, Alexander 314, 321
Venables, Bernard 48
de Vere, Roger 77

Vigfússon, Orri 119–20
Volkova, Zina 250

Waldegrave, William 208
Wallis, Barnes 266–8
Walter, Grey 77
Ward, Amanda 168
Ward, Connie 115–16, 117
Ward, Gerald 168, 171
Ward, Reggie 115–16
Ward, Stephen 236–7, 239, 241–2
Warren, John 147
Warth, Douglas
    friends with CP in Darlington 4
    during Second World War 19
    works for *Daily Express* 20
    member of Players' Theatre
        Club 22
    ruins telepathy experiment 50
Watkinson, Harold 40, 271–2
Way, Sir Richard 'Sam' 240
Web of Deception, A (Pincher) 341
Weidenfeld, George 215, 234, 293
Weinstock, Sir Arnold 36–7
Weir, 'Ginger' 89
Wesley 202, 203
West, Nigel 355
Westminster, Duke of 345–6
White, Dick 322
Whitelaw, Gavin 106
Whitelaw, William 154, 335
Wicksteed, Bernard 47–8
Wigg, George 71
    and Profumo affair 237–8, 240,
        241, 242–4
    lunches with CP 286–8
    and Richard Crossman 368
Wilkie, Sandy 117